YALE HISTORICAL PUBLICATIONS, MISCELLANY, 123

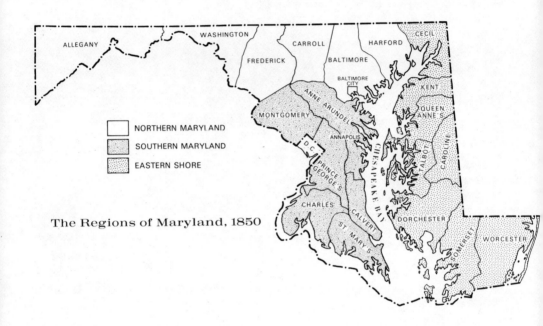

The Regions of Maryland, 1850

NORTHERN MARYLAND
SOUTHERN MARYLAND
EASTERN SHORE

Slavery and Freedom on the Middle Ground

Maryland during the Nineteenth Century

BARBARA JEANNE FIELDS

Yale University Press
New Haven and London

Published under the direction of the Department of
History of Yale University with assistance from the income
of the Frederick John Kingsbury Memorial Fund.

Designed by James J. Johnson and set in Monticello Roman.
Printed in the United States of America by
Vail-Ballou Press, Binghamton, New York.

Library of Congress Cataloging in Publication Data

Fields, Barbara Jeanne.
    Slavery and freedom on the middle ground.

    (Yale historical publications. Miscellany: 123)
    Bibliography: p.
    Includes index.
    1. Slavery—Maryland—History—19th century.
2. Afro-Americans—Maryland—Economic conditions.
3. Maryland—Race relations.   I. Title.   II. Series.
E445.M3F54 1985   975.2'00496023   84–20949
ISBN 0–300–02340–5 (cloth)
ISBN 0–300–04032–6 (pbk.)

*The paper in this book meets the guidelines for perma-
nence and durability of the Committee on Production
Guidelines for Book Longevity of the Council on
Library Resources.*

10   9   8   7   6   5   4   3   2

To My Parents and Grandparents

Contents

List of Tables   ix

Introduction   xi

1   Two Marylands: 1850
1

2   Slave and Free on the Middle Ground
23

3   Baltimore and the Problem of Slavery in Cities
40

4   Conscript Slaves: The Problem of Free Blacks in a Dual System
63

5   "The Devlish Nigger Difficulty": Slavery and the Civil War
90

6   In Lieu of Reconstruction
131

7   The New Order in the Countryside
167

Epilogue: From Country to City
194

Appendix: Problems in the Manuscript Agricultural Census   207

Notes   209

Index   259

List of Tables

Table 1.1   Ratio of Free Blacks to Slaves in Maryland, 1790–1860   2

Table 1.2   Slaves as Percentage of Black Population, 1850   2

Table 1.3   Population of Maryland by Regions, 1790 and 1850   9

Table 1.4   Percentage of State White, Free Black, and Slave Populations by Regions, 1790 and 1850   10

Table 1.5   Black Percentage of Total Population, Counties and Regions, 1790 and 1850   11

Table 1.6   Free Black Percentage of Total Population, Counties and Regions, 1790 and 1850   12

Table 1.7   Population of Maryland, All Groups, 1790–1850   13

Table 1.8   Percentage Change in Slave Population in Five Southern States   15

Table 2.1   Percentage of Males in Adult Black Population, 1850   30

Table 2.2   Percentages under Fifteen and over Forty in Slave, Free Black, and White Populations, 1850   32

Table 2.3   Free Black Percentage of Population of Ten Largest Maryland Cities and Towns, 1850   34

Table 3.1   Blacks in Baltimore Population, 1790–1860   62

Table 4.1   Free Black, Slave, and White Population by Regions, 1850 and 1860   70

Table 4.2   Members of the Committee on Colored Population   77

Table 7.1   Growth of Maryland Population, 1860–1880   176

Table 7.2   Black Farms by Tenure Classes: Charles, Frederick, and Kent Counties   179

Introduction

Slavery and freedom had a long joint history in Maryland. It is probably true that, until emancipation, slavery in some sense defined freedom all over the United States. But in Maryland the intermingling of the two was so immediate and concrete as to give a unique flavor to slavery, to freedom, and to the dramatic historical moment when the one finally yielded to the other. The rise of two free populations in Maryland, one white and one black, challenged the political, moral, and ideological coherence of slave society. The growth of a white and largely free labor society, sectionally based and far outdistancing slave society in most conventional measures of social progress, signaled a political threat of which large slaveholders never lost sight. The simultaneous growth of a free black population hopelessly entangled with the slaves lodged a conspicuous anomaly in the heart of the slave order. Either development on its own would have warranted anxiety on the part of those dedicated to the preservation of slavery. Together, they kept slaveholders in a state of constant unease that swelled to a muted uproar and finally a panic-stricken crescendo with each successive failure of efforts to exorcize their dangerous potential. When the Civil War afforded slaves a chance to intervene in the situation openly and decisively, the potential became reality. The pages that follow tell the story of how slave and free, black and white in Maryland studied their parts for the final confrontation between slavery and freedom; of how they rehearsed them in a series of tense encounters; and of how they acted those parts when the great moment came.

The story goes beyond the death of slavery as an institution. Once slavery ceased to provide the reference point for defining freedom, a struggle ensued to determine what, precisely, freedom would mean. That struggle most immediately concerned former slaves and their former owners. But redefining the relation of ex-master or ex-mistress to ex-slave also meant redefining other social relationships for which that one had provided the basis. The relationships between former free black and former slave, between former nonslaveholder and former slaveholder, between city and country, between one section of the state and another, between government and citizen: all these underwent upheaval in the revolution that overthrew the sovereignty of master over slave. Freedom had to be defined anew, not just for ex-slaves, but for the state at large.

This is a book, therefore, about slavery and freedom. But it is equally a book about the middle ground, that misty and elusive terrain that occupies such a place of honor in the geography of Americans' political ideology. The border states occupied both the geographic and the political middle ground, a circumstance about which some of their statesmen were inclined to feel smug. *Moderate* is nearly always a term of approval, regardless of the issue under discussion, and border-state moderates in the growing sectional discord of the mid-nineteenth century enjoyed a prestige wholly at variance with their effectiveness. Judging, however, by the immoderate events of their history, Americans have tended to regard the middle ground much as some uncharitable outlanders do New York City: a nice place to visit, but you would not want to live there. While their fellow Americans of the increasingly hostile sections often complimented the citizens (which is to say the white people) of Maryland upon their moderation, they sometimes did so with a rather condescending indulgence of which the recipients of the compliment, through obtuseness or intent, took no notice.

But once the Civil War had gotten under way, white Marylanders could not help taking notice. And in time, attempting to defend a middle ground that no longer existed, they revealed how insubstantial that ground had been all along. Moderation evaporated once loyal slaveholders discovered that they were playing for the same stakes as rebel slaveholders in the Confederacy—the preservation of slavery—and were losing regardless of their loyalty. Black residents knew the middle ground inch by inch from a perspective that white people could not share, for the peculiarities of border-state slavery added bitter occasions for suffering to those that accompanied slavery everywhere. Slave and free, black Marylanders expressed in action their contempt for the so-called moderate standpoint even before it could be fully defined; and they paid a heavy price, both during and after the war, for the privilege of doing so.

This is also a book about Maryland—not a "case study," with one state posing as a representative of the others, but the recounting of a profound human experience important in its own right because it was profound and because it was human. I have admired some of the characters who appear in these pages, disliked some, been moved by others to triumph, disappointment, sadness, hilarity, and most of the other emotions with which human beings may confront the at once familiar and unfamiliar lives of their fellow creatures. I have tried to discipline my reactions to respect the historian's primary task of understanding historical figures in the context of their own circumstances and their own view of these. But I doubt that anyone could remain unmoved in some sort by the events I have sought to chronicle, and I doubt even more that many readers would care to waste their time over any historian who could. At the same time, these events inevitably raise a number of broad theoretical questions: concerning the nature of slave society, for example, and the social premises underlying the contest over the meaning of freedom. I have addressed these questions freely—usually by implication in the text and by explication in the notes— in the same way that they arise, as part of the story of slavery and freedom in Maryland. Readers will therefore find my analysis woven as carefully as I could contrive into the texture of a narrative intended to do justice to the human flavor, as well as the theoretical implications, of the material at hand.

In an effort to communicate the human flavor of the material, I have quoted from sources as faithfully as was consistent with full clarity. Errors of grammar and syntax, as well as highly fanciful spelling, capitalization, and punctuation, abound in the documents—from newspaper editorials and governors' correspondence to the letters and petitions of uneducated freedmen. I have made no effort either to eliminate these or to advertise them with the label [*sic*]. Appropriate editorial symbols mark the addition or deletion of material. Otherwise, readers may assume that quotations follow the original.

Sharp-eyed readers of the notes will notice inconsistencies in the information given in citations of certain Freedmen's Bureau documents. I have ironed these out as far as possible, but some unavoidably remain. In my days as a green and naïve researcher, my citations included much less information than I now realize is necessary. It was impossible for me to retrace my steps over each document at the National Archives. For those Freedmen's Bureau documents that I used from the files of the Freedmen and Southern Society Project, or that I was able to match with documents in those files, I have adopted the Project's form of citation and included its file number in brackets. Where I could not do this, I have reconstructed as much information as possible from my notes and vowed to go and sin no more.

It is pleasant to be at last able to acknowledge those who have helped me see this book through to completion.

First I must thank the staffs of libraries, archives, and other repositories at which I have carried out research. These include the Library of Congress and the libraries of Howard University, Morgan State University, the University of Maryland, the University of Michigan, and Yale University; and the Archives of the Mill Hill Fathers in Baltimore, the Baltimore City Archives, the Maryland Historical Society, the National Archives, and the Maryland Hall of Records. I especially wish to thank Phebe Jacobsen of the Hall of Records.

For support by way of a postdoctoral fellowship, I would like to express gratitude to the Ford Foundation and the National Research Council. The Woodrow Wilson International Center for Scholars and the history department at the University of Maryland, College Park, each in turn provided me with an institutional roost during my fellowship tenure. I have also benefited by support from the College of Literature, Science, and the Arts at the University of Michigan. Susan Bailey typed the bulk of the manuscript and, in her uncanny way, foresaw and dealt with a number of potential problems before they could arise. Paul Van den Bosch of the University of Michigan's Technical Illustration Department prepared the map.

I have received a generous helping of the kind of support from individuals which is difficult to acknowledge properly in written form. Still, let me try.

Herbert G. Gutman, in a chance observation which I came across as a beginning graduate student, first turned my attention to Maryland.

A number of people read this study in dissertation form. Anyone who has ever sweated out the interval between submitting a dissertation and receiving the readers' reports will appreciate the special gratitude I feel toward my colleague at the University of Michigan, William Rosenberg, whose enthusiastic comments were by accident the first response I received. David Brion Davis produced an especially detailed reader's report that provided welcome encouragement as well as valuable suggestions, and Professor Davis has continued over the years since to urge the project forward. The anonymous reader for Yale University Press (whose identity I have since discovered) also made detailed and astute comments, as well as providing warm encouragement. Eric Foner, John W. Blassingame, and F. V. Carstensen also read and commented upon the dissertation version.

Historians who have been privileged to use the files of the Freedmen and Southern Society Project at the University of Maryland will recognize the enormity of the statement I am about to make: that I owe an even greater debt to friendship and collegial exchange with the editors than I owe to the extraordinary files they have assembled. The year I spent as a visiting editor at the Project was among the richest of my professional life. I had already learned (though never from him) that Ira Berlin was Yale's anonymous reader, and my year at the Project brought me more occasions to profit from his talent as a historian and generosity as a friend and colleague. Joseph P. Reidy not only bore patiently the brunt of responsibility for my initiation into the art and science of historical editing, but also shared his vast knowledge in Southern and many other areas of history. His suggestions have improved not just this book, but my work as a whole. Leslie S. Rowland, whose chair I occupied during my stint as editor, deserves special thanks. She waded in during the hectic final stages in the preparation of the manuscript and provided both substantive suggestions and life-saving editorial help. I owe a debt as well to those who succeeded me as gypsy editors at the Project: Thavolia Glymph and Steven Hahn. By sharing her unique knowledge of agricultural labor following emancipation, Professor Glymph has given me a great deal to think about in this and in other work. Professor Hahn read the manuscript and offered judicious and opportune suggestions.

Several colleagues at the University of Michigan read the manuscript and made helpful suggestions. For this I would like to thank Thomas C. Holt, Louise Tilly, and Michael Geyer.

A number of good friends who cheered me on over the years did not actually read the manuscript but might as well have done so, considering the dividends I have reaped through discussions of their work and my own. Many more people fall into this class than I can mention by name, but I wish to call attention to three of them: Julie E. Saville, John Higginson, and Armstead L. Robinson. Equally entitled to acknowledgement in this respect is my sister, Karen E. Fields. Through sisterly encouragement and admonitions—stern ones, upon occasion—she helped push this project over obstacles in its becoming first a dissertation and then a book.

I have saved for last the debt that is hardest to characterize properly: the one I owe to my adviser, C. Vann Woodward. How should I convey the gift of history and of humanity that always came wrapped in the same package in that corner office of the Hall of Graduate Studies? Those who have spent time there know for themselves how much greater is the debt than any conceivable thanks; for the others, I can wish nothing finer than that they may one day have the chance to find out for themselves.

CHAPTER ONE

Two Marylands: 1850

Maryland officially became a free state in November 1864. But the transition to free labor had been under way for decades. Slaves accounted for nearly one-third of Maryland's population in 1790. By 1850 their proportion had fallen to less than one-sixth. In 1790 Maryland already had the second largest free black population in the country (following Virginia) and by 1810 had achieved first rank, which it retained until the final abolition of slavery throughout the country. Between 1790 and 1810, while Maryland's slave population increased by less than one-tenth, its free black population more than quadrupled. Throughout the nineteenth century, the ratio of free to slave among black people rose steadily. By the eve of the Civil War, free black people were nearly as numerous as slaves.[1]

Maryland's closest competitor in this respect was Virginia, which in the first two federal censuses, 1790 and 1800, had the largest free black population. Even in those years, Maryland's free blacks came to a larger proportion of its total black population than Virginia's: the proportion for Maryland advanced from 7 percent to 16 percent between the two years, while that for Virginia rose from 4 to 5 percent. By 1810 Maryland had overtaken Virginia in absolute numbers, and by 1840 Virginia had fallen to a very distant second. In that year Virginia's free black population stood at 49,832 compared to Maryland's 62,136. The difference between the two in proportion of free people in their total black populations had become even more dramatic: Virginia's free black people constituted only 10 percent of its black population, while Maryland's amounted to nearly 41 percent.[2]

By 1850 Maryland occupied a class alone among slave states. Only Delaware, the small size of whose slave population made it incomparable to the others, had a higher proportion of free men and women in its black

1

TABLE 1.1
Ratio of Free Blacks to Slaves in Maryland, 1790–1860

Year	Ratio
1790	.08
1800	.18
1810	.30
1820	.37
1830	.51
1840	.69
1850	.83
1860	.96

Source: U.S. 9th Census, 1870, *Population* (Washington, D.C., 1872), pp. 6–7.

population.[3] No other slave state approached Maryland in either the absolute or the relative size of its free black population. In this respect the border states of Missouri and Kentucky resembled the slave states of the lower South more than they resembled Maryland (see table 1.2). In fact, to find free black populations similar to Maryland's in relative size, it is necessary to leave North America and turn to the slave societies of Latin America and the Caribbean. For sheer numbers, Brazil is the most dramatic example.

TABLE 1.2
Slaves as Percentage of Black Population, 1850

	Slave Total	Free Black Total	Slave Percentage of Black Population
Delaware	2,290	18,073	11.2
Maryland	90,368	74,723	54.7
Virginia	472,528	54,333	89.7
North Carolina	288,548	27,463	91.3
Louisiana	244,809	17,462	93.3
Kentucky	210,981	10,011	95.5
Missouri	87,422	2,618	97.1
Tennessee	239,459	6,422	97.4
South Carolina	384,984	8,960	97.7
Florida	39,310	932	97.7
Arkansas	47,100	608	98.7
Georgia	381,682	2,931	99.2
Alabama	342,844	2,265	99.3
Texas	58,161	397	99.3
Mississippi	309,878	930	99.7

Source: Calculated from U.S. 7th Census, 1850, *Population* (Washington, D.C., 1853), p. ix.

Estimates place Brazil's free colored population by the mid-nineteenth century at anywhere from 40 to 60 percent of the total black and colored population. It reached some 74 percent by 1872, at which time it numbered over four million. Though no rival to Brazil in absolute numbers, Puerto Rico was even more striking in percentages: by 1860 its black and colored population was 85 percent free. Closer to Maryland was Curaçao, whose free colored population came to 40 percent of its total black population in 1816, compared to 27 percent for Maryland in 1820. Even closer was Cuba, whose figure of 38 percent in 1860 approximates Maryland's 41 percent in 1840, at a comparable distance from emancipation.[4] In the British and French Caribbean—which differed from Brazil, the Spanish Caribbean, and much of the Dutch Caribbean in that slaves greatly outnumbered all other elements of the population—the free colored element still formed from 60 to 90 percent of the total free population.[5]

An important distinction, however, set Maryland apart from all these societies: the relative size of the white population. In the slave societies of the Caribbean and in Brazil, white people's share of the total population ranged from a small minority to only a slight majority: for example, 4 percent (Jamaica, 1844); 22 percent (Curaçao, 1816); 40 percent (Brazil, 1872); 57 percent (Cuba, 1860).[6] In such societies the free colored people could occupy a space that white people filled in Maryland. Free colored people formed a petite bourgeoisie—of artisans, shopkeepers, clerks, and small-holding farmers—of which slave society could make use for minor but necessary economic, administrative, and even peacekeeping functions that the white population could not have carried out unassisted.[7] As a result, free colored people came to have their own unique and more or less legitimate place in society.

In Maryland white people constituted a substantial majority at all times. They represented 72 percent of the state's total population in 1850. In 1810, at their lowest proportion within the period of the federal census, white people still accounted for 62 percent of the population. Only in the counties of southern Maryland did black people constitute a majority—and only just: 54 percent in 1850. That figure had remained the same since the peak of 1810, when blacks accounted for 57 percent of the population of the southern counties.[8] Maryland had ample whites to carry out necessary petit-bourgeois tasks. Consequently, free blacks did not occupy a unique or legitimate place within Maryland society, but instead formed an anomalous adjunct to the slave population. Though they constituted an essential element of the work force, their position in society was always problematic.

So far from using them to keep peace among the slaves, as happened frequently in other New World slave societies (or, for that matter, in the great Louisiana revolt of 1811), slaveholders in Maryland considered free blacks a standing incitement to servile disorder and placed elimination of them on the order of the day from the post-Revolutionary period right up to the eve of emancipation.[9]

Why did the free black population grow to such proportions when Maryland society had no comfortable place for it? The atmosphere of the American Revolution, with its equalitarian rhetoric and its emphasis upon natural rights philosophy, undoubtedly contributed to the surge of manumissions in the years following the war.[10] Religious scruples, intensified by revivalism and given concrete form by the outspoken policy of Quakers and Methodists, entered in as well, though strong antislavery stands adopted early on were later considerably diluted in practice.[11] The importance of religious ideas lay not only in the direct spur they provided to manumission, but also in a certain residual respectability they lent to antislavery opinions in later years, when the expectation of a gradual withering away of slavery—popular in the first flush of Revolutionary enthusiasm—had retreated into the mythology of the past. Geography reinforced religious and Revolutionary ideas, especially in the northernmost counties. A slaveholder in northern Maryland in 1854, for example, believed that proper etiquette required a degree of reserve in broaching touchy questions with a neighbor known to be "exceedingly opposed to slavery."[12] Maryland sat, after all, on the border of the movement that ended slavery in the Northern states in the years after American independence, and thereafter sat on the border of free soil itself. On their own, however, the ideological legacy of the Revolution and the force of religious discipline do not suffice to explain the growth of Maryland's free black population. Revolutionary ideology, revivalism, and evangelical religion all touched other parts of the South without producing as dramatic a result. Nor does geography provide a sufficient answer. Proximity to free territory did not lead the border states of later settlement, Missouri and Kentucky, in the same direction as Maryland.

Far more decisive were the fortunes of tobacco, the first staple crop of Maryland slavery. The cycle of boom and recession in the Chesapeake tobacco economy had swung around to prosperity again by the beginning of the eighteenth century. But soon thereafter, long-term changes began that would eventually supplant tobacco production in the tobacco-growing portions of northern Maryland (parts of Harford, Frederick, and Baltimore counties) and on the Eastern Shore. Heavy, if highly variable, demand in

New England, the West Indies, and southern Europe—and, in the later decades of the century, in Britain and France as well—encouraged the spread of wheat cultivation. By the 1740s tobacco production on the Eastern Shore had dwindled to the point that residents objected to paying public fees in tobacco. The Revolutionary War hastened things along, disrupting tobacco production and marketing. The abolition of the French tobacco monopoly in 1791 removed from the market a strategically important buyer of the inferior tobacco of the lower Eastern Shore, giving further impetus to a switch to cereal agriculture that had occurred more swiftly in the upper Eastern Shore counties. As the center of tobacco production moved south and then west, tobacco surrendered its dominant position in Maryland's economy. From 90 percent of Maryland's aggregate agricultural production in 1747, tobacco had fallen to 14 percent in 1859. Though prices experienced periodic upsurges and had even reached a new peak by the late 1850s, tobacco culture had become virtually confined to the southern counties of the western shore, the most backward region of the state, as the Civil War approached.[13]

The replacement of tobacco by cereal—in particular, wheat—cultivation brought about an important change in requirements for agricultural labor. Production of tobacco could keep a slave labor force more or less constantly busy throughout the year, with crop years actually overlapping each other. Wheat, on the other hand, required a maximum work force at harvest, but could not usefully employ a full harvest crew at other times. No extensive adjustments appear to have been necessary so long as wheat remained a supplementary crop alongside tobacco and corn: its labor demands could be reasonably well harmonized with theirs, albeit with some tense moments at harvest.[14] But once wheat became the predominant or sole cash crop, it made little sense to maintain a large slave force that could not be productively employed much of the time. Better to hire harvest hands, who could be dismissed when no longer required.[15] The retreat of tobacco and the advance of cereal agriculture in the longer-settled regions of the state thus diminished the need for a fixed labor force and created a need for a variable labor force at the very historical moment when Revolutionary and religious enthusiasm provided a spur to manumission. Moreover, the settlers who moved into Maryland's wheat-producing western interior, many of them Germans and many others migrants from Pennsylvania, had little or no slaveholding tradition: from the beginnings of settlement there, slavery played no more than a minor role.[16] Thus, the direction of Maryland's economic development lent an air of commonsense practicality to antislavery ideas, while supplying sound reasons even for owners impervious to argument from moral, political, or religious principles to get rid of their slaves.[17] Slave society in Maryland might have ideological difficulties making room for a class of free black people; but, as long as agricultural renewal undermined the old tobacco-slave economy and new settlement favored the free labor economy, the free black population was bound to grow in prominence.[18]

Whatever may have been the special contribution of the Revolutionary atmosphere, the burst of antislavery feeling and activity that accompanied it ended abruptly. The most intense period was over by 1800, and the growth of the free black population settled down to a more routine pace.[19] From that point on, the extraordinary conditions of the Revolutionary era cease to be the key to the story; otherwise, why should Virginia, which partook of these same conditions, have lagged so far behind Maryland by 1850 in respect of its free black population? After 1800, internal development, not external circumstances impinging equally upon the other states of the upper South, account for Maryland's remarkable situation.

Like the United States as a whole, Maryland was a society divided against itself. There were, in effect, two Marylands by 1850: one founded upon slavery and the other upon free labor. Northern Maryland, embracing Allegany, Baltimore, Carroll, Frederick, Harford, and Washington counties, was an overwhelmingly white and free labor society, the only region of the state in which industrial activity had grown to significant proportions. Black people contributed only 16 percent of its population, and slaves less than 5 percent. Southern Maryland (Anne Arundel, Calvert, Charles, Prince George's, Montgomery, and St. Mary's counties) was a backward agricultural region devoted primarily to tobacco, though wheat production made inroads during the 1850s, particularly in areas of large and concentrated landholdings. The population of the southern counties was 54 percent black and 44 percent slave. Occupying an intermediate position, much like that of Maryland within the Union, was the Eastern Shore, comprising Caroline, Cecil, Dorchester, Kent, Queen Anne's, Somerset, Talbot, and Worcester counties. Like the southern counties, the Eastern Shore devoted itself to agriculture to the virtual exclusion of industry. Like the northern counties, it produced mainly cereals. It was neither as slave and black as southern Maryland nor as free and white as northern Maryland. Just over 20 percent of its people were slaves and just under 40 percent were black.[20]

In southern Maryland and on the Eastern Shore, slavery shambled along in the lengthening shadow of isolation. Its gradual eclipse showed up, not in the emergence of a vigorous nonslave society, but in relative stagnation. White population either declined or barely maintained itself, many people leaving the state for more expansive prospects, while the growing free black population had to fit itself into the crevices of the slave system. Isolated on its chosen terrain, slavery turned in upon itself, dissolving slowly under influences more efficient to undermine the old basis than to create a new one. The dissolution occurred more slowly in southern Maryland, a reflection of the dominance of the tobacco economy. But neither in southern Maryland nor on the Eastern Shore was the dissolution of the old accompanied by the rise of a vital alternative.

Northern Maryland followed a different course, developing a way of life to which slavery was at most tangential. Its metropolis, Baltimore, presided over a hinterland that, in contrast to the pattern that stunted the growth of so many Southern cities, was not confined to slave territory. Not that Baltimore carried on independently of the slave economy. Varied services of marketing, processing, exchange of information, purchase and sale of slaves, and provision of food, supplies, and legal advice linked Baltimore with slave society in Maryland and with the rest of the slave South. To give only a pair of examples: 120 establishments in Baltimore in 1850 converted tobacco into cigars; and seven steam-powered factories in the city of Baltimore, another fifteen in Baltimore County, plus one in the Maryland State Penitentiary turned out an annual production of cotton worth $1,366,412. Nevertheless, Baltimore was never subservient to the slave system—at least, not economically. It rose to the status of a major city at a time when the tobacco economy was losing importance, and drew its initial impetus from the special though temporary advantages that war, especially the Revolutionary and Napoleonic wars, provided in the area of foreign trade. Large sales of grain to Europe and a brisk reexport trade in West Indian goods did not long survive the return of peace; in fact, Thomas Jefferson's embargo and then the British blockade of the Chesapeake Bay from 1813 to 1814 ended the wartime boom before the war was over. But by then Baltimore could draw upon a vast hinterland to the north and west, bringing within its orbit the Susquehanna region and the Ohio Valley. Baltimore even contrived to garner for itself a hefty share of the Ohio and Kentucky tobacco trade, even as Maryland's tobacco-growing counties were feeling the hot breath of Western competition: by 1860 Baltimore was receiving an annual average of 20,000 hogsheads of tobacco from the Ohio River region (compared to only 4,478 hogsheads as recently as 1840). Never would Baltimore become the mere kept woman of Maryland's slave counties.[21]

The influence of Baltimore quickened the social and economic life of northern Maryland, starting with the most basic element: population. From near parity in 1790—southern Maryland and the Eastern Shore each having slightly better than a third of the total and northern Maryland slightly less—the regions had so far diverged by 1850 that nearly 60 percent of the state's residents lived in the northern counties. The Eastern Shore claimed only 22 percent and southern Maryland fewer than 19 percent. During the 60 preceding years, while the population of the northern counties was expanding by 228 percent, that of the Eastern Shore grew only 19 percent and that of southern Maryland a paltry 2 percent (see table 1.3). A critic of slavery, one Dr. R. S. Steuart, commented ruefully in 1845 upon the most recent census figures and contrasted Maryland's progress unfavorably with that of Pennsylvania and Ohio: "While these states have rapidly progressed in population and domestic improvements, Maryland, by much the elder member of the union . . . has remained comparatively stationary." Had it not been for the great increase in the population of the city of Baltimore and modest increases in a handful of counties, Steuart lamented, the state's population would have stagnated altogether between 1830 and 1840.[22]

Dr. Steuart did not remark upon how much that compensating increase owed to the growth of the free black population, since he took no satisfaction from that circumstance. (Had he investigated, he would have discovered that free blacks contributed 40 percent of the overall increase between 1830 and 1840.)[23] But he obviously grasped the overwhelming importance of Baltimore, which by 1850 held nearly half the population of the northern counties and over a quarter of the population of the entire state.[24] In fact, the expansion of city and town life was yet another characteristic setting northern Maryland apart from the rest of the state. More than 56 percent of the people of northern Maryland lived in cities and towns. Baltimore accounted for most of these, of course. But even setting Baltimore aside, 14 percent of northern residents were town dwellers, a far larger proportion than either southern Maryland or the Eastern Shore could claim.[25]

The years between 1790 and 1850 had witnessed a considerable redistribution of Maryland's population, with each of its parts more unevenly distributed at the end of the period than it had been at the beginning. Though northern Maryland already in 1790 claimed a larger share of the state's white population than the other regions, by 1850 its preponderance had become overwhelming. Forty-two percent of the white people of Mary-

TABLE 1.3

Population of Maryland by Regions, 1790 and 1850

	Population in 1790	Population in 1850	Percentage of State Total		Percentage Growth 1790–1850
			1790	*1850*	
Caroline	9,506	9,692			
Cecil	13,625	18,939			
Dorchester	15,875	18,877			
Kent	12,836	11,386			
Queen Anne's	15,463	14,484			
Somerset	15,610	22,456			
Talbot	13,084	13,811			
Worcester	11,640	18,859			
Eastern Shore	107,639	128,504	33.6	22.0	19
Anne Arundel	22,598	32,393			
Calvert	8,652	9,646			
Charles	20,613	16,162			
Prince George's	21,344	21,549			
Montgomery	18,003	15,860			
St. Mary's	15,544	13,698			
Southern Md.	106,754	109,308	33.4	18.8	2
Allegany	4,809	22,769			
Baltimore City	13,503	169,054			
Baltimore County	25,434	41,592			
Carroll	*	20,616			
Frederick	30,791	40,987			
Harford	14,976	19,356			
Washington	15,822	30,848			
Northern Md.	105,335	345,222	33.0	59.2	228

Source: Calculated from U.S. 7th Census, 1850, *Population* (Washington, D.C., 1853), pp. 220–21, and from J. D. B. DeBow, *Industrial Resources, Etc. of the Southern and Western States* (New Orleans, La., 1852), 1:102.
*Not yet in existence.

land in 1790 lived in the northern counties; by 1850 almost 70 percent did. Northern Maryland had the smallest share of the total free black population in 1790, but by 1850 it held an absolute majority. The slave population, already concentrated in southern Maryland in 1790, had become even more heavily concentrated there by 1850 (see table 1.4).

Between 1790 and 1850 Maryland's population became somewhat whiter: black people accounted for 35 percent in 1790 and 28 percent in 1850. This was a reflection of the increasingly free labor character of the

TABLE 1.4

Percentage of State White, Free Black, and Slave Populations by Regions, 1790 and 1850

	Percentage of Total, 1790	*Percentage of Total, 1850*
White		
Eastern Shore	31.2	18.6
Southern Maryland	26.8	12.1
Northern Maryland	42.0	69.3
Free Black		
Eastern Shore	48.6	33.1
Southern Maryland	26.7	14.9
Northern Maryland	24.7	52.0
Slave		
Eastern Shore	37.4	28.8
Southern Maryland	47.3	52.9
Northern Maryland	15.3	18.3

Source: Calculated from U.S. 7th Census, 1850, *Population* (Washington, D.C., 1853), p. 220, and from U.S. 9th Census, 1870, *Population* (Washington, D.C., 1872), pp. 36–37.

northern counties and a tribute to their weight within Maryland's population. For, although the black percentage fell slightly in northern Maryland, it held steadily on the Eastern Shore and markedly increased in southern Maryland. Taken regionally, the facts were not such as to offer much comfort to those whose passionate wish was to see the state rid of black people altogether (see table 1.5).

Still less ould people of that mind take comfort from the changing relative position of the free black population. A century of legislative and judicial activity attempted to restrict manumission and force manumitted slaves to leave the state. Colonization in Africa occupied the attention and resources of the state to a remarkable degree, considering how abjectly it failed. (In 1852, there were in Liberia and the colony of Maryland in Africa fewer than 500 Maryland emigrants to show for more than thirty years of trying.)[26] Despite all efforts to the contrary, the free black population increased faster than any other element of the population. For the state at large, the free black share of the total population increased from 2.5 percent in 1790 to nearly 13 percent in 1850. In each region and in every single county in the state, the free black proportion of the total population increased, and in most substantially so (see table 1.6). The largest increase

TABLE 1.5
Black Percentage of Total Population, Counties and Regions,
1790 and 1850

	Percentage Black, 1790	*Percentage Black, 1850*
Caroline	26.0	37.1
Cecil	26.2	18.3
Dorchester	36.9	43.1
Kent	47.4	50.7
Queen Anne's	47.1	52.1
Somerset	47.0	40.4
Talbot	44.7	48.7
Worcester	34.5	34.2
Eastern Shore	39.5	39.5
Anne Arundel	48.4	48.9
Calvert	51.3	62.4
Charles	50.9	64.9
Prince George's	53.1	58.7
Montgomery	35.1	40.5
St. Mary's	47.1	54.6
Southern Maryland	47.6	53.9
Allegany	5.6	5.0
Baltimore	20.7	17.0
Carroll	*	9.4
Frederick	12.5	18.7
Harford	28.0	25.5
Washington	8.5	12.7
Northern Maryland	16.8	16.0
Maryland, aggregate	34.7	28.3

Source: Calculated from U.S. 7th Census, 1850, *Population* (Washington, D.C., 1853), pp. 220–21, and from U.S. 9th Census, 1870, *Population* (Washington, D.C., 1872), pp. 36–37.
*Not yet in existence.

in absolute and percentage terms occurred in northern Maryland, whose gain of 36,835 free black men and women between 1790 and 1850 amounted to 1,850 percent (see table 1.7). But, in its way, the Eastern Shore was the most dramatic. The proportion of free black people in its total population rose from 3.6 percent to 19.3 percent, and in every county the percentage in 1850 was substantial. Of the three regions, the Eastern shore had the

TABLE 1.6

Free Black Percentage of Total Population, Counties and Regions,
1790 and 1850

	Percentage Free Black, 1790	*Percentage Free Black, 1850*
Caroline	4.4	28.8
Cecil	1.2	13.8
Dorchester	3.3	20.4
Kent	5.1	27.6
Queen Anne's	4.0	22.6
Somerset	1.7	15.5
Talbot	8.2	18.8
Worcester	1.5	16.0
Eastern Shore	3.6	19.3
Anne Arundel	3.6	14.2
Calvert	1.6	15.9
Charles	1.9	5.6
Prince George's	.77	5.3
Montgomery	1.6	8.3
St. Mary's	2.2	11.9
Southern Maryland	2.0	10.2
Allegany	.25	1.8
Baltimore	2.4	13.8
Carroll	*	4.7
Frederick	.69	9.2
Harford	5.2	14.3
Washington	.40	5.9
Northern Maryland	1.9	11.2
Maryland, aggregate	2.5	12.8

Source: Calculated from U.S. 7th Census, 1850, *Population* (Washington, D.C., 1853), pp. 220–21, and from U.S. 9th Census, 1870, *Population* (Washington, D.C., 1872), pp. 36–37.
*Not yet in existence.

widest and most consistent experience of free black people and, consequently, of free black labor.

The northern counties had the most diverse population, attracting most of the state's foreign immigrants and probably most of the out-of-state migrants as well. Foreigners entering Baltimore in 1850 numbered 7,597; in the ten-year period 1841 to 1850, they numbered 68,392. Since Baltimore was an important port city, not all the immigrants who landed there

TABLE 1.7
Population of Maryland, All Groups, 1790–1850

	White			Free Colored			Slaves		
	1790	1850	Change (Percent)	1790	1850	Change (Percent)	1790	1850	Change (Percent)
Caroline	7,028	6,096	−13.5	421	2,788	562	2,057	808	−60.7
Cecil	10,055	15,472	53.9	163	2,623	1509	3,407	844	−75.2
Dorchester	10,010	10,747	7.4	528	3,848	629	5,337	4,282	−19.8
Kent	6,748	5,616	−16.8	655	3,143	380	5,433	2,627	−51.6
Queen Anne's	8,171	6,936	−15.1	618	3,278	430	6,674	4,270	−36.0
Somerset	8,272	13,385	61.8	268	3,483	1200	7,070	5,588	−21.0
Talbot	7,231	7,084	−2.0	1,076	2,593	141	4,777	4,134	−13.5
Worcester	7,626	12,401	62.6	178	3,014	1593	3,836	3,444	−10.2
Eastern Shore	65,141	77,737	19.3	3,907	24,770	534	38,591	25,997	−32.6
Anne Arundel	11,664	16,542	41.8	804	4,602	472	10,130	11,249	11.0
Calvert	4,211	3,630	−13.8	136	1,530	1025	4,305	4,486	4.2
Charles	10,124	5,665	−44.0	404	913	126	10,085	9,584	−5.0
Prince George's	10,004	8,901	−11.0	164	1,138	594	11,176	11,510	3.0
Montgomery	11,679	9,435	−19.2	294	1,311	346	6,030	5,114	−15.2
St. Mary's	8,216	6,223	−24.3	343	1,633	376	6,985	5,842	−16.4
Southern Md.	55,898	50,396	−9.8	2,145	11,127	419	48,711	47,785	−1.9
Allegany	4,539	21,633	377.0	12	412	3333	258	724	180.6
Baltimore	30,878	174,853	466.0	927	29,075	3036	7,132	6,718	−5.8
Carroll	*	18,667		*	974		*	975	
Frederick	26,937	33,314	23.7	213	3,760	1665	3,641	3,913	7.5
Harford	10,784	14,413	33.7	775	2,777	258	3,417	2,166	−36.6
Washington	14,472	26,930	86.1	64	1,828	2756	1,286	2,090	62.5
Northern Md.	87,610	289,810	231.0	1,991	38,826	1850	15,734	16,586	5.4

Source: Calculated from U.S. 7th Census, 1850, *Population* (Washington, D.C., 1853), p. 220, and from U.S. 9th Census, 1870, *Population* (Washington, D.C., 1872), p. 36.
*Not in existence in 1790.

necessarily remained in the state (though the Census Office believed that most of those landing there before 1850 probably did). Of those who stayed, very few made their way to the Eastern Shore or southern Maryland. The bulk of the 53,750 white persons of foreign birth living in Maryland in 1850 lived in the northern counties, a large proportion of them in Baltimore. As of 1860, 94 percent of the state's foreign-born population lived in the counties of northern and northwestern Maryland. It seems fair to suppose, also, that the northern region was the main beneficiary of migration from elsewhere in the United States. Far more out-of-state migrants were natives of Pennsylvania than of any other state in the Union. Most of these Pennsylvanians probably ended up in the Maryland counties lying along Pennsylvania's southern border.[27]

Migration within the state seems to have benefited the northern counties and to have involved black people in disproportionate numbers. The sluggishness of population growth in the southern and Eastern Shore counties compared to the northern ones strongly suggests the likely direction of movement. Unfortunately, the census does not address the question; even the manuscript schedules list nativity by state, not county, of origin. Nevertheless, compelling if indirect evidence exists in the records of the Maryland State Penitentiary, which furnish each convict's county of birth as well as his (or her) county of residence at the date of sentencing. Of forty white convicts admitted to the penitentiary in the years 1849 and 1850 who were natives of Maryland, thirty-six (90 percent) resided, at the time of sentencing, in their county of birth. Of seventy-three black convicts native to Maryland and admitted during the same time, only forty-nine (67 percent) resided in their county of birth. The origins of convicts living outside their native counties are revealing. The four whites were people from the Eastern Shore and southern Maryland living in the northern counties. Twenty-two of the twenty-four blacks were also Eastern Shore and southern Maryland natives living in the northern counties, most of them in Baltimore.[28]

Migration out of the state hit the southern and Eastern Shore counties harder than the northern ones, southern Maryland hardest of all. Southern Maryland's white population actually declined between 1790 and 1850, by nearly 10 percent. Only Anne Arundel County (where Annapolis, the state capital, is located) posted an increase. During the same period, the white population of northern Maryland grew by 231 percent, with county increases ranging from 34 percent in Harford to 466 percent in Baltimore County. On the Eastern Shore, half the counties lost while half gained, resulting in a regional increase of just over 19 percent (see table 1.7).

TABLE 1.8

Percentage Change in Slave Population in Five Southern States

	1790–1850	*1810–1850*
Maryland	− 12	− 19
Virginia	61	20
North Carolina	187	71
South Carolina	259	96
Georgia	1204	263

Source: Calculated from U.S. 7th Census, 1850, *Population* (Washington, D.C., 1853), p. ix.

Slaves declined in absolute numbers over the state as a whole during the period 1790 to 1850—the only segment of the population to do so. Their number dropped by 12,668, a decline of slightly over 12 percent. When measured from 1810 the decline is even more dramatic, for up to that year the slave population continued to grow. From 1810 to 1850, the slave population decreased by 21,134, a loss of nearly 19 percent. Nothing remotely similar occurred in the other slave states of comparable age.[29]

Slave population did not decline uniformly across the state. Indeed, the situation might appear paradoxical upon superficial examination. For while the slave population of the Eastern Shore declined by almost 33 percent and that of southern Maryland by just under 2 percent, that of northern Maryland registered a 5 percent increase.[30] Adopting the mode of reasoning that not long ago persuaded some scholars that slavery showed no long-term tendency to decline in cities, an unwary individual might conclude that slavery was a more vital institution in the northern counties than elsewhere in the state.[31] In fact, the northern slave population increased from a very small base, which remained small. More important, the increase of the slave population was trifling compared to the general expansion of population occurring at the same time. Already in 1790 the white population outnumbered the slave by more than five times; by 1850 it was better than seventeen times as large. Southern Maryland and the Eastern Shore, on the other hand, were losing members of a slave population that was substantial in both absolute and relative terms in 1790 and, while diminished, remained substantial in 1850 (see table 1.7).

Exactly where the losses to the slave population went is a complex question, whose answer bears largely on any assessment of the character of society, and especially of slavery, in Maryland. It has been estimated that owners manumitted 50,000 slaves over the course of the state's history. Taking these and their expected natural increase into account, most of the loss to the slave population showed up as a gain to the free black population, despite the pressure placed upon manumitted slaves to leave the state. A small number (not enough, in the view of some white Marylanders) left the state voluntarily upon achieving their freedom, as a convenience to themselves and in deference to Maryland law and opinion. A few were successful runaways, enough to make the matter a serious irritant among slaveholders, though not so many as the depth of the slaveholders' irritation might suggest. (A number of otherwise astute commentators in Maryland actually believed during the secession crisis of 1860–61 that fugitive slaves constituted the outstanding issue, whose resolution could restore the Union.) The census reported 279 escapes from Maryland during the year ending June 30, 1850. That rather modest figure nevertheless made Maryland the reluctant leader among slave states in this unsought competition.[32]

The total number of escapes reported in the census does not, of course, take the full measure of the social problem concealed behind the figures. In the first place, enumerators apparently recorded only slaves who made good their escape, not those who disappeared for a time and then reappeared or were recaptured.[33] As escapes occurred most frequently during the busiest times of the agricultural calendar—cultivation and harvest[34]—episodes of this sort would be inconvenient and disruptive even if the slaves involved were eventually recovered. In the second place, the open readiness of some individuals both within and outside the state to assist fugitives called forth a public reaction quite disproportionate to the actual number of fugitives these individuals assisted. Slaveholders themselves quickly discerned hostile intent toward the institution as such, particularly on the part of agitators purportedly infiltrating from the free states, and demanded retaliation accordingly (see chap. 4). But nonslaveholders might easily be drawn into the fray as well. The killing in September 1851 of a citizen of Maryland who was trying to recapture three runaways in Chester County, Pennsylvania, led to a mass meeting in Monument Square in Baltimore and a public outcry that probably fed as much on a sense of loyalty to state as on direct personal interest in slave property. Moreover, slave catchers, amateur and professional, were as likely as not to be people who owned no slaves themselves.[35] In the third place, demoralization of the slave population by attempted or successful escapes depended more upon how widely slaves became acquainted with these episodes than upon how many actually succeeded.[36]

Nevertheless, runaways cannot have accounted for more than a small proportion of the losses to Maryland's slave population, smaller certainly than that made up of slaves (and their issue) leaving the state upon acquiring their freedom or joining the growing free population. A substantial proportion wound up as slaves in other states. According to a careful recent estimate, 18,500 slaves from Maryland found their way to other parts of the South between 1830 and 1860, either by being sold in the interstate trade or by being forced to relocate along with emigrant owners. That figure, less than a quarter of the prevailing earlier estimate, represents a considerable movement nonetheless, especially when augmented—as it ought to be—by the number who must have left before 1830.[37] It would mean that, on average, 6.5 percent of the slave population recorded at the beginning of each decade either migrated or was sold to other slave states by the end of the decade. The Eastern Shore contributed the largest and southern Maryland the smallest share of this traffic in proportion to their slave populations, if estimates for the 1830s provide a fair indication; southern Maryland contributed the largest actual number.[38]

As in population, so in economic activity each region had its particular character. Led by Baltimore, northern Maryland accounted for close to 90 percent of the capital invested and hands employed in industry in Maryland and over 90 percent of the value of the annual product. The $29,390,410 produced by firms in northern Maryland in 1850 represented a per capita output of $85.13—far in excess of southern Maryland's $16.02 and the Eastern Shore's $10.71. Baltimore City and County accounted for most of this activity, turning out 75 percent of the annual manufacturing product of the state and 83 percent of that of the northern counties.[39]

The quickening effect of Baltimore manifested itself in agriculture as well: Baltimore in time became both a center for the processing and export of agricultural products and a formidable market for those products in its own right. Providing the diverse needs of the city population for vegetables, fruit, meat, and dairy products became the principal livelihood of many farmers in the northern counties. The value of market-garden produce in northern Maryland for the year ending 30 June 1850 came to one and a half times the combined total for southern Maryland and the Eastern Shore. Baltimore County contributed most of that (96 percent), a clear enough indication of Baltimore City's importance as a market. Annapolis and Washington, D.C. exerted a somewhat similar influence in Anne Arundel, Prince George's, and Montgomery counties, not to the same degree, but enough to place southern Maryland far ahead of the Eastern Shore in this respect. Northern Maryland produced 105,012 tons of hay, more than twice the combined total of southern Maryland and the Eastern Shore. The northern counties had nearly as many milch cows as southern Maryland and the Eastern Shore together, and produced more than one and a half times as much butter. Value of animals slaughtered was greatest in northern Maryland, as was total investment in livestock: the $3,246,325 in reported value of livestock for 1850 amounted to $3.47 per acre of improved farmland, compared to $2.55 and $2.54, respectively, for the Eastern Shore and southern Maryland. Northern Maryland led the state as well in dollar value of orchard produce; though southern Maryland, thanks largely to farmers in Anne Arundel County, lagged only slightly in total value and actually led in value per head of rural population.[40]

Agricultural reform was, of course, a preoccupation and diversification a necessity in Maryland. In view of the long-term decline of tobacco, Maryland had no staple crop economy that could bear the weight of specialization which cotton and sugar sustained in their strongholds. No region of Maryland held a monopoly of efforts directed toward agricultural improvement. Even the tobacco counties of southern Maryland made belated and hesitant progress toward more balanced farming, a trend probably helped rather than hurt by the return of high tobacco prices during the 1850s. Successful planters could afford the cost of fertilizer, high-quality seed and livestock, and a sufficient force of adequately supervised labor; they owned enough land to rest worn-out fields and engage in scientific rotation; and they could readily raise capital, if they needed it, by the sale of redundant slaves and surplus land. Showcase farms sprang up in the southern Maryland and Eastern Shore slave counties, encouraged and well publicized by the state Agricultural Society. Francis P. Blair bought a 300-acre parcel in Montgomery County from the Carroll family, and used proceeds from sale of the timber to pay for large quantities of lime and manure. Thomas Hughlett owned some 4,000 acres in Talbot County, on which he raised prize cattle, sheep, and hogs. Charles B. Calvert, a descendant of the colonial proprietors of Maryland and founder of the Maryland Agricultural College, supplied vegetables and dairy products from his estate to a Washington hotel of which he was part owner. Horace Capron used the profits of his successful business activities in Laurel to restore a farm in Prince George's County, on which he grew wheat and kept a herd of about a hundred head of Durham, North Devon, Alderney, and Holstein cattle.[41]

Nevertheless, diversification and improvement did not produce the same result all over the state. Northern Maryland could boast in 1850 the most prosperous and up-to-date agriculture in the state. The northern counties had the highest ratio of improved to unimproved farmland, even though, as an observer later remarked, two of these counties "have the Alleghany mountains to cultivate." Farms in the northern counties were worth more than those elsewhere: their average value per acre of improved farmland was $44.21, compared to $24.35 and $24.93 respectively for the Eastern Shore and southern Maryland. The $1,218,060 invested in farm implements and machinery in the northern counties amounted to $1.30 per improved acre, compared to $.61 in the Eastern Shore counties and $.73 in those of southern Maryland. Southern Maryland remained a staple-producing region, growing 98 percent of the state's tobacco but trailing in virtually every other area of production. The Eastern Shore was more nearly a cereal than a mixed-farming region: its emergence as a specialist in production of fruit and vegetables for urban markets—though already foreshadowed in the upper counties, especially Kent—lay in the future. Even in its chosen specialty it took second place to northern Maryland, holding first rank only in production of Indian corn. Northern Maryland produced 70 percent of the rye and buckwheat and over half the oats and wheat grown in the state. Frederick and Washington counties alone produced more than a third of the state's total wheat crop.[42] The superior adaptability of free labor for the production of wheat told heavily. In the northern counties, even slaveholders depended on "harvest white men" to help gather the crop. On the Eastern Shore, farmers hoping to steal a march on their neighbors had to reserve harvest crews—as often as not free blacks—weeks in advance, holding them by methods ranging from cajolery to lubrication with "harvest whiskey." The bidding war that readily ensued threatened to call into question the racial discipline needed for the smooth functioning of the slave system.[43]

Naturally enough, social and economic differences between the two Marylands had their reflection in politics. Sectionalism had a long and distinguished history in Maryland, marked by political rituals of equal age and distinction. The oldest rivalry was that between the Eastern and Western Shores of the Chesapeake Bay. Arising in part from a dispute over colonial jurisdiction between the proprietary governor and a Virginian adventurer whose settlement on the Eastern Shore predated Lord Baltimore's charter, the rivalry matured amidst the intricacies and sudden reversals of English Revolutionary affairs. It erupted repeatedly into pitched battles while the struggle went on in England and required more than twenty years to be finally, with the Restoration in 1660, resolved in favor of Lord Baltimore. Emblems of separatism simultaneously advertised and contained the conflict between east and west: separate state treasurers, registers of the land office, and judges and examiners of the land office for each shore, alternate sittings of the General Court and the Court of Appeals on each shore, with separate offices and clerks for each, and membership on the governor's council and officers of the House of Delegates divided between the two shores. The tradition that Maryland should be represented by one senator from each shore was as old as the United States Senate itself, though not reduced to law until 1809 after being, for the first time, honored in the breach rather than in the observance.[44]

At the state constitutional convention of 1850–51 an Eastern Shore delegate, Thomas Holliday Hicks of Dorchester County, proposed an amendment asserting the Eastern Shore's right of secession. As late as April 1858 an Eastern Shore convention—at the instigation of persons in Talbot County and much to the embarrassment of Hicks, who had since become governor—revived talk of secession while demanding from the state an appropriation of $800,000 for internal improvements on the Eastern Shore.[45] But by that time the east-west cleavage was no longer the important one and had not been for some time. The rapid growth of northern Maryland, and especially of Baltimore, raised a potential political force of which the slave counties on both sides of the Bay were intensely jealous. Up until the emancipation constitution of 1864 (and, though with altered terms, thereafter), the predominant form of sectionalism in Maryland was the constant study of the slave counties to keep the upper hand over the northern counties and the equally constant study of the northern counties to release themselves from political subordination.

For, however independent of slave society Baltimore and the northern counties might be in terms of their economic pursuits, they remained subaltern where ultimate political power was concerned. The dominance of movable over landed property, which marks the historical maturity of bourgeois society, had not yet come about in Maryland. Despite the superiority of northern Maryland in population and in economic strength and vitality, the landed and slaveholding upper class of southern Maryland and the Eastern Shore retained the political advantage. Unmistakable portents of change had begun to manifest themselves, true enough. The bitterly contested constitution of 1851 increased the representation of northern Maryland to a degree altogether unsettling to the slave counties. But it also hedged this new strength about with ample protection for the privileges of the slave counties. In place of the ponderous mechanism established in 1846 to protect slavery—abolition required the unanimous vote of both houses in two different sessions of the General Assembly—the new constitution took a simpler approach: it simply forbade the legislature to abolish slavery. Another provision severed Baltimore City from Baltimore County, placing the city in the gubernatorial district of southern Maryland where, presumably, it could do the least damage. (The governor was elected in rotation from districts embracing southern Maryland, northern Maryland, and the Eastern Shore.) Even the provision increasing the representation of northern Maryland did so under a formula that preserved a grossly inequitable apportionment. Baltimore City was arbitrarily limited to four delegates more than the number allotted to the most populous county, and every county, regardless of population, was guaranteed at least two delegates. Combined with a ceiling of eighty on total membership, this formula made permanent the underrepresentation of northern Maryland in the House of Delegates. (The Maryland Senate, like the federal one, was not based on population.) Moreover, slaveholders in Maryland retained a privilege that democratic reform had swept away from most of their class: slaves were included in population for purposes of legislative apportionment and were counted at their full numbers—not at the federal ratio of three-fifths. The slaves' mute voice thus augmented the voice of their owners. As the 1860 census approached, the thirty-seven delegates from northern Maryland represented more than twice as many white citizens as the thirty-seven delegates from southern Maryland and the Eastern Shore. The editor of the Cecil *Whig* scarcely overstated matters when he charged in December 1861 that "at least 20 members in the Legislature . . . represent negroes alone."[46]

Slaveholders turned their political power to useful account in another respect as well. A law passed at the first session of the General Assembly after the new constitution took effect established a privileged tax status for slave property. Under the law, land, livestock, public and private securities, bank and other stocks, merchants' stock-in-trade, household furniture, gold and silver watches, plate, and all other taxable property was to be assessed at its true value. Slaves, however, fell under a different rule. They were to be assessed at fixed rates according to age and sex, and no slave, however valuable, could be assessed higher than $400. With justice, the Cecil *Whig* complained that, in the matter of legislative apportionment, "a negro slave, is counted equal to a white man . . . but when it comes to taxation . . . he sinks into an insignificant chattel, upon whose wooly head the tax gatherers' hand must rest very lightly."[47]

For all the differences between them, the line dividing the two Marylands was not an international frontier. Slavery unified as well as divided them. The bonds that linked Baltimore to the slave economy, for example, were not those of political thralldom alone, but also the complex ones of friendship, family connection, mutual clientship, and joint endeavor. A Baltimore lawyer who presided over the Baltimore and Reisterstown Canal and directed two banks also drew up deeds of sale for slave traders and had personal friends among the tidewater planters of Maryland and Virginia. A tobacco planter from Anne Arundel County sat on the board of trustees of the Baltimore insane asylum.[48]

Social geography is an amorphous reality, seldom if ever exactly coincident with political—still less physical—geography and often more readily visible retrospectively, in the wake of a crisis, than as an immediate reality. The Civil War marked such a crisis for Maryland, revealing the lines of stress in a particularly painful form because those lines could not, in the nature of the case, be sharp and clear. The slave counties suffered the more intense trauma. Northern Maryland at least had its integration into the Northern economy and its marginal reliance upon slavery to smooth its way. But the slave portion of Maryland could afford neither separation from the northern counties, where the state's vitality largely resided, nor separation from the slave South, which offered support to the institutional basis of its society. Two Marylands had evolved in different directions for decades. The war clarified that evolutionary development, at the same time providing the starting point for the revolutionary development that was to follow.

CHAPTER TWO

Slave and Free on the Middle Ground

"It is generally supposed," Frederick Douglass remarked in his 1855 autobiography, "that slavery, in the state of Maryland, exists in its mildest form, and that it is totally divested of those harsh and terrible peculiarities, which mark [it] in the southern and south-western states of the . . . union."[1] That has proved an enduring supposition, drawing encouragement from the inclination of Americans to regard the middle ground as the natural habitat of virtue in almost all things. Contiguity to the free states, immunity from the rigor of cotton and sugar and the insalubrity of rice cultivation, the prevalence of small-scale slaveholding, and the presumedly moderating influence of a political system founded upon compromise all constitute plausible grounds for the belief that slavery was somehow benign in Maryland and in the other border states.

In explaining why his boyhood experience departed from the generally accepted picture of slavery in Maryland, Douglass laid particular emphasis upon the isolation of the corner of Talbot County where he lived as a boy. On Edward Lloyd's home plantation, Douglass maintained, slavery could develop its unsavory potential "wrapt in its own congenial, midnight darkness," beyond the restraint of public opinion. Perhaps slavery was mild, he implied, in less self-enclosed parts of the state, where it lay exposed to the "ray of healthy public sentiment."[2] Douglass may have made this concession as a tactical maneuver, in order to retain the confidence of an audience with whose presuppositions he was well acquainted. For the safest generalization seems to be that, in matters concerning the material care and treatment of their slaves, slaveholders in the border states exhibited the same range as their fellows in the lower South.[3] On the other hand, certain routine features of slave life in Maryland, arising from Maryland's special circumstances and

23

taken for granted by public opinion, gave slavery there a flavor for which *benign* and *mild* are hardly suitable terms. During the antebellum years black people in Maryland—slave and free—experienced the agony of slavery's slow death, but not the deliverance. The middle ground imparted an extra measure of bitterness to enslavement, set close boundaries on the liberty of the ostensibly free, and played havoc with bonds of love, friendship, and family among slaves and between them and free black people.

Among the more unsavory of Maryland's special features, as much a product of the slow dissolution of slavery as the growth of the free black population, was the heavy volume of the trade in slaves. This trade took three forms: intrastate sale, interstate sale, and interstate migration. Of these the most dramatic was probably the interstate and the most common the intrastate trade. A detailed examination of sales during the decade 1830 to 1840, based as nearly as available documentation will probably permit upon direct evidence, reveals that a number equivalent to nearly 12 percent of the total slave population of 1830 ended up on the block between then and 1840. Sales in all parts of the state were brisk during the decade, judging by the eight counties for which partial records survive: estimated sales for two Eastern Shore counties (Kent and Talbot) amounted to slightly over 14 percent of their 1830 slave population, those from three southern counties (Anne Arundel, Prince George's, and Howard) to nearly 12 percent, and those from three northern counties (Baltimore, Carroll, and Harford) to just over 10 percent. Some 16 percent of individuals sold and just under 2 percent of the total slave population of the eight counties in 1830 were sold out of the state by their owners. An approximately equal number left the state involuntarily when their owners emigrated.[4] The 1830s seem to have been an especially active period of trading, though the 1850s sustained a heavy traffic as well.[5]

All forms of slave trading carried with them a disastrous potential for blasting apart the fragile web of family and friendship ties joining slaves to one another and to free black people. Contrary to a recently fashionable misconception, interstate migration of owners was no less likely than interstate sale of slaves to cause this sort of disruption.[6] The most common slaveholding in Maryland by 1860 was one slave; half the slaveholders owned fewer than three slaves, three-fourths fewer than eight, and 90 percent fewer than fifteen slaves.[7] In other words, a typical slaveholding in Maryland cannot have included both parties to a slave marriage, let alone all members of an immediate family. Even holdings technically large enough to have included all members of an immediate family (whether they are in fact likely to have done so, in view of the slaves' preference for exogamous and "broad" marriage is another question)[8] would not also have embraced the aunts, uncles, cousins, and grandparents who formed the slaves' notion of family. It is true that migrating slaveowners sometimes purchased family members to avoid separating them, though it is not clear with what frequency.[9] It would have made good sense, even for owners unmoved by sentiment, since a slave separated from close family was a potential runaway and would probably prove a troublesome and unsatisfactory worker. But even an owner willing—and, more to the point, financially able—to do this would scarcely have purchased all the collateral kin, not to mention friends, simply in order to lighten the burden of anguish borne by slaves forced to remove. Sale within the state had the same potential as sale beyond the state for disrupting or destroying family connections. Maria Richardson left two daughters behind (one of them only three years old) when her owner sold her out of Calvert County but within Maryland in 1853. It required fourteen years and general emancipation for Maria Richardson to learn her children's fate. When she tried to get the younger daughter back after emancipation, she could not even be sure what surname the girl had adopted during the years of separation.[10]

Though almost anyone would select slave trading as the villain of almost any piece, small-scale slaveholding does not seem as obviously typecast for the role of villainy. Nevertheless, much of the suffering incidental to slavery in Maryland resulted, directly or indirectly, from the small size of slaveholdings, a characteristic that had become steadily more marked over the years from the Revolution to the eve of the Civil War. Few holdings in Maryland would have rated the name "plantation" in the eyes of slaveholders from the lower South, let alone those of slaveholders elsewhere in the Americas. The largest holding in Maryland in 1860, which fell in the census category "300 and under 500," stood alone in its class. Its nearest neighbors in size, the fifteen slaveholdings between 100 and 200, amounted to only .1 percent of the total, and the median slaveholding was 3. Naturally, holdings appear larger seen from the vantage point of the slaves, who outnumbered owners six times over. But even so, half the slaves of Maryland belonged to units of fewer than 11 individuals. As might be expected, the picture varied from region to region. The median slave in northern Maryland belonged to an owner of four slaves; on the Eastern Shore, to an owner of eleven; and in southern Maryland, to an owner of fifteen.[11]

Small holdings divided family members among several owners, exacerbating the potential trauma of sale and attacking the integrity of family life even when the question of sale, either within or beyond the state, did not arise. Husbands and wives might live apart for this reason, seeing each other only when granted permission. John Diggs and his wife belonged to owners in different counties. In the course of a bounty claim in 1870, Samuel Johnson was asked whether he and his wife had lived in the same house while slaves. "We did not live together," he replied, "as our masters lived apart—but I went to see her & stayed with her when I could." What went for husbands and wives also went for parents and children, and doubly so for grandparents and grandchildren, brothers, sisters, cousins, aunts, and uncles. For this reason, slaveholders who considered religious camp meetings to be hotbeds of conspiracies to escape may have been right.[12] At camp meetings slaves of different owners, enjoying a sanctioned opportunity to spend several days together beyond direct supervision, could reflect with heightened bitterness upon the perversion of family life into episodic visitation privileges.

The desire to be reunited with family members figured prominently in escapes, as owners made clear when advertising for fugitives. Dr. Thomas G. Turton of Nottingham, Prince George's County, thought fit to advise the public that his slave Margaret ("who calls herself Margaret Pinkney") might have gone either to Brandywine, where her mother's owner lived, or to Page's Chapel, where her father's owner lived. Charles Sembley's owner thought that he might be making for Calvert County because his children's owner lived there. Benjamin Duckett, sold by one Edmund B. Duvall, left his new master and was thought to have returned to the vicinity of Buena Vista Post Office, where his father and mother remained as slaves of Marcus Du Val. Eliza Ann and George Lee had been purchased from the estate of John Townshend by different individuals. Both turned up in runaway notices, believed to have returned to Piscataway, where they had relatives. The purchaser of Barbary Williams, a fifty-year-old woman who escaped soon after being sold by her deceased owner's estate, mentioned five different neighborhoods to which the fugitive might have gone seeking relatives, including her husband.[13]

The division of family members among a number of small slaveholders multiplied by that number the danger of a family's disruption by the financial mischance or simple human mortality of an owner. Small slaveholders were more vulnerable than planters to the financial reverses that might require the liquidation of slave property.[14] Slaves with families parceled out among several such owners must have lived in permanent apprehension of disaster, especially since the evidence of that disaster's having befallen others lay constantly before them. From the death of an owner slaves had more to fear, furthermore, than the possibility of sale. For every slave sold upon the death of an owner, many others must have been simply sent elsewhere— to the residence of an heir, for example—where old attachments would be sundered as surely as if a sale had taken place.[15]

The small size of holdings in Maryland combined with the variability of labor requirements, especially on the part of urban employers and farmers engaged in mixed or cereal agriculture, to make slave hiring a ubiquitous phenomenon, much more common than sale.[16] Indeed, a plausible case has been argued that profits from slave hiring tempered owners' willingness to sell, thereby limiting Maryland's participation in the interstate trade as well as preventing slavery there from succumbing to the extinction so often predicted for it during the Revolutionary era. A much less plausible case has been urged that hiring was an equal boon to the slaves. According to this view, hiring not only afforded slaves welcome autonomy, but also— since terms were limited, usually to a year, and employers generally lived nearby—preserved the integrity of family ties.[17]

As to autonomy, much hinged on the level of skill of the slave in question and on the location of his employer. Slave artisans in urban areas frequently lived on their own and found their own work; they might well count this a privilege worth fighting to secure and retain. (Whether it ought to be called "autonomy" or not depends on whether the standpoint adopted is that of the master or that of the slave.)[18] It is highly doubtful, on the other hand, that slaves hired for unskilled agricultural labor enjoyed any greater independence while living with employers than they did while living with their owners.[19] As to preserving the integrity of family ties, there is still less room for doubt or qualification. Whatever their convenience to owners and employers, hire arrangements worked vast mischief in the personal lives of the slaves. Only the caprice of owners and hirers determined how often family members could see one another—unless they ventured to do so without permission. A limited term of hire provided no automatic guarantee that the following term would place an individual any closer to family and friends. Nor did the geographical nearness of the hirer necessarily imply unhindered access to loved ones. "Near" was a relative affair. Worcester and Allegany counties, at opposite ends of the state, were nearer to each other than either was to Louisiana, to be sure. But a slave in one with relations in the other would probably see very little more of those relations than if they had gone to Louisiana. Even short geographical distances could be enormous in human terms. Twelve miles sufficed to make Frederick

Douglass and his mother virtual strangers to one another. Her rare visits required a night journey on foot, with a stiff penalty awaiting her if she should be late or unfit for work on her return. The master of John Q. A. Dennis, a slave in Worcester County, "took me Carry me some forty mile from [my children] So I Could Not do for them." As far as his ability to be a father to them was concerned, Dennis's children might as well have been sold out of the state.[20]

Even when manageable distance and agreeable owners and employers allowed regular visits, the result was hardly what a free person would have considered a genuine family life. As for relations of love or friendship that entailed neither marital nor family connection, these did not always rate even the cold comfort of visiting privileges. Nor did the severing of preexisting ties of family and friendship exhaust the occasions for suffering to which hiring might give rise. During their terms of hire, slaves were apt to form friendships or romantic attachments that the end of the hire period would unceremoniously terminate. When, as often happened, these involved free black people, the potential for trouble became still greater, for the hazards of the difference in status placed relationships crossing that divide in constant peril of interruption.

In fact, the interconnection of the worlds of free black people and slaves was another of those special features of Maryland that made the middle ground such difficult and unpredictable terrain. Marriage between slaves and free blacks was a phenomenon common enough to be unremarkable; but it was fraught with insecurity and engendered a family life constantly threatened with upheaval. A law of 1832, designed to remove free blacks from the state, invited manumitted slaves to renounce their freedom if the requirement of removal would otherwise separate them from slave relatives.[21] Not even such a backhanded law as that one protected a free black husband or wife whose spouse had been marked for out-of-state sale. "Poor Sarah called to see me this morning," John Montgomery Gordon, a Baltimore attorney, recorded in his diary. "She is in much trouble. Her husband has been sold to a negro trader who takes him to Mississippi." Sarah, who may have been Gordon's former slave, wished him to buy her husband. Should she fail to raise enough money among her friends, she planned to save money from her wages toward his purchase price. Gordon doubted that she would accomplish her object; nor, judging by the rather smug tone of his appraisal of the situation, did he intend to help. "Poor thing," he concluded, "she will never see him again! How little the most humane feel for negroes. Yet that little is more than they feel for themselves, I believe."[22]

Not all the potential problems of marriage and family connection between slaves and free blacks arose from the owners of the slave spouse. Priscilla, a free black woman, lived and worked in a different place from her slave husband. When she went to his residence to nurse him in an illness to which he eventually succumbed, she did so at the cost of her job. Hannah Toogood, a slave, was married to Risdon Snow, a free black man. Snow persuaded James Lister, his employer, to buy Toogood, promising to repay him gradually out of his wages. Lister agreed and Snow paid a total of $250 but died before paying the full amount. Being, as he explained, opposed to holding slaves, Lister set Hannah Toogood's two children free. Apparently he did not oppose other people's holding slaves, however, for he returned Toogood herself to her former owner. Years later, when she attempted to claim the $250 her husband had given Lister, she received the reply that she would probably only waste the money. Federal authorities making inquiry on her behalf heard a different version: Lister explained to them that he had settled money upon the children when he freed them, and therefore owed Toogood nothing.[23]

Slaveholders thought they discerned an active preference among free blacks for slave husbands and wives and, needless to say, had their own ready explanation. "Knowing slavery to be more congenial to their habits and tastes," according to a petition laid before the General Assembly in 1858, "most of our free negroes prefer slaves for husbands and wives, thereby securing a home, while they bask in the fruition of their own native indolence."[24] But the real explanation was a good deal simpler. Slaves in Maryland lived, after all, alongside the largest free black population to be found in any slave state (or, for that matter, in any state, period).[25] Because of numbers alone, the two were bound to come into close and frequent contact. Based on relative proportions, slaves in the northern counties stood a greater chance than slaves on the Eastern Shore, and slaves on the Eastern Shore a greater chance than those in southern Maryland, of being thrown into the society of free blacks.[26] But throughout the state, close ties between slaves and free blacks were an inescapable fact of life.

Peculiarities in the composition of the slave and free populations added to the likelihood of fraternization across the line. Women outnumbered men in the adult free black population, constituting nearly 54 percent of the total. The imbalance was greatest in northern Maryland, where 57 percent of adult free blacks were women. In southern Maryland and on the Eastern Shore, women held only a slight edge, making up 51 percent of the whole. Though men and women approximately balanced each other in the slave

TABLE 2.1

Percentage of Males in Adult Black Population, 1850

	Male, Slave	Male, Free Black	Male, Black
Eastern Shore	52.5	49.0	50.7
Southern Maryland	52.0	48.6	51.3
Northern Maryland	44.8	42.7	43.3
Maryland	50.7	45.5	48.2

Source: Calculated from U.S. 7th Census, 1850, *Population* (Washington, D.C., 1853), pp. 219–20. I have counted as adults everyone fifteen years of age or older.

population of the state at large, they did not in any of the regions taken separately. In southern Maryland and on the Eastern Shore, men accounted for 52 percent of the adult slave population; in northern Maryland, only 45 percent (see table 2.1).

Much more than simple demography worked to keep free blacks in close relationship with slaves. The vagaries of manumission did so as well. Delayed manumission was a widespread practice, embracing just over half of manumissions before 1832 and just under half thereafter.[27] That made for awkward and anomalous family situations. It could result in a family composed indiscriminately of slaves for life, slaves for a term of years, and free people. An eighteen-year-old woman offered for sale in Cecil County in 1858 was to become free in eight years, while her four-month-old child would remain a slave until the age of twenty-eight. The same year an advertiser in Calvert County offered for sale a thirty-six-year-old woman and her five children: two boys aged fifteen and two and three girls aged twelve, ten and four. By one of those twists of sardonic humor that fate now and then reveals, the woman was due to receive her freedom on 1 January 1863. The children, on the other hand, were to serve until the age of thirty, and likewise "the issue of the said Children, and the increase of said issue, in perpetuity."[28] It requires little effort to imagine the complicated results if any of these children had married an individual either enslaved for life or unconditionally free. A most interesting legal imbroglio could well have resulted had one of the boys, for instance, married a free black woman, whose children—despite the terms of the boys' emancipation— would presumably be free. Intricate arrangements of this sort had the fortunate consequence of limiting the number of out-of-state sales, since slaves for a term could be sold outside Maryland only by those daring and unscrupulous enough to break the law.[29] For the slaves themselves, the prospect of freedom with strings—or, perhaps more accurately, guy ropes—attached no doubt represented an improvement over perpetual servitude. But the inevitable product of such arrangements was a precarious edifice of family relations involving slaves and free blacks, together with a host of contingencies that could bring that edifice down.

Manumission after a term of servitude also ensured that freed black people would continue to look to slaves for companionship and social sustenance, since many of the manumitted person's social relationships would have been formed in slavery. An occasion such as a camp meeting or a funeral could recall freed people to join the proceedings alongside the slaves. Frederic, who with his wife Easter had been freed in October 1849, returned from Baltimore during the summer of 1854 to attend a funeral in the neighborhood of his former owner's farm. Later the same year, he and Easter returned once again upon hearing word of the illness of Charles, a slave of their former owner; they attended his funeral shortly thereafter. When Frederic himself died in Baltimore just after emancipation, the "darkies were sent for to attend the funeral." But this time, with resentment at emancipation still very immediate, the former owner denied a house servant of long standing permission to go. When she defied him, he dismissed her from his employ and evicted her from the cabin she and her children had been occupying.[30]

If family connection did not bring slaves and free blacks together, the routine of getting a living was likely to. Hired free blacks, whether in the city or in rural areas, met slaves unavoidably in the course of work. During his stints as a skilled urban worker and as an unskilled agricultural one, Douglass worked beside free blacks. The General Assembly evidently took it for granted that the hiring of free blacks brought them into undesirable association with slaves: in 1836 it rejected a bill forcing free blacks to hire out by the year on just those grounds.[31] But, statutory requirement or no, free blacks in rural areas earned their living largely by hired agricultural labor, necessarily in close proximity to slaves. In any case, planters and farmers found themselves in an awkward predicament. Even those who owned slaves in large numbers occasionally needed free black help; those with few or no slaves depended upon it (see chap. 4). Slaveholders might deplore the mingling of slaves with free blacks; they might heap anathema upon it and even try periodically (and ineffectually) to prevent it. But their needs conflicted with their fears and some, probably from mixed motives of humanity and practicality, even permitted the free black spouses of their

TABLE 2.2

Percentages under Fifteen and over Forty in Slave, Free Black, and White Populations, 1850

	Percentage under Fifteen			Percentage over Forty		
	Slave	Free Black	White	Slave	Free Black	White
Eastern Shore	45.8	43.6	41.3	13.9	21.4	18.2
Southern Maryland	46.7	44.1	41.1	16.2	21.5	19.5
Northern Maryland	42.7	37.1	38.7	13.8	19.7	17.7
Maryland	45.7	40.3	39.4	15.1	20.5	18.0

Source: Calculated from U.S. 7th Census, 1850, *Population* (Washington, D.C., 1853), pp. 218–20.

slaves to live on their property. Hetty, a free woman of Carroll County, lived in the slave quarter of the farm belonging to her husband's owners, who permitted him to grow and sell a small crop to support his family.[32]

The close relationship between slave and free black populations meant that free blacks moved largely within the limits that slavery placed upon their fellows. The very composition of the free black population shows how closely its fortunes were implicated with those of slaves. The logic of manumission and interstate sale together probably explains why the free black population contained a higher proportion of men and women over forty than either the slave or the white population. Over the state as a whole in 1850, people over forty composed 21 percent of the free black population, whereas only 15 percent of slaves and 18 percent of whites fell into that category (see table 2.2). Though state law discouraged the manumission of slaves too old or infirm to take care of themselves—between 1796 and 1832 owners were forbidden to emancipate slaves over 45—manumission provided a tempting means of casting aside slaves who had become a burden to their owners.[33] The higher rate of manumission among slaveowners of modest means[34] may owe something to this fact. But owners need not have had the overt intention of evading responsibility for superannuated slaves. The practice of delayed manumission ensured that manumitted slaves would be older than the slave population as a whole. Even slaves favored with immediate emancipation—on account of faithful or meritorious service, for instance—would tend to be older, as would the relatively few acquiring their freedom by gradual self-purchase or by the gradual efforts of members of their families.[35] Furthermore, if the pattern of the 1830s, when slaves sold from the estates of deceased owners accounted for some 35 percent of out-of-state sales,[36] may be safely extrapolated, then the interstate trade drew heavily on older slaves as well. Besides having more older people, the free black population had proportionately fewer children than the slave population: 46 percent of slaves, compared to 40 percent of free blacks, were under the age of fifteen in 1850 (see table 2.2). Regional variation asserted itself in this as in most other matters. The free black population of northern Maryland had a smaller proportion of children and older people than the other regions—probably because so many of its free blacks were migrants, who tend to be adults in the prime of life.

The pattern of migration by free black people, who stubbornly resisted continual pressure upon them to leave the state, further illustrates how slavery determined the boundaries within which free black people moved. The constricted and provincial routine of the slaves' lives afforded them little notion of what lay beyond the cramped limits of their own experience, and owners shrewdly fostered this parochialism. "Every slaveholder," Douglass insisted, "seeks to impress his slave with a belief in the boundlessness of slave territory." He and his fellow conspirators in a runaway plot "had heard of Canada . . . simply as a country to which the wild goose and the swan repaired at the end of winter," and were largely ignorant of the free states.[37] Other slaves might have heard of the free states through the constantly reiterated warning of slaveowners that "Cuffee" invariably fared worse at the hands of Northerners than under the benevolent care of his natural protectors. (Slaveholders were still sounding this refrain, with rapidly diminishing success, when slaves began absconding during the war at the first approach of the Union army.) Of greater importance than any of these factors in limiting the movements of free blacks, however, were the bonds of marriage, family, and friendship that linked them to the slaves and anchored both groups in the small space they managed to carve out for themselves in a hostile world.

Thus, while migration for white Marylanders usually meant leaving the state altogether in search of better prospects to the west or south, for free blacks it usually meant crowding into Maryland's cities and towns. Baltimore claimed 17 percent of Maryland's black population in 1850 but 34 percent of its free black population. Lesser towns exerted a similar attraction, though on a smaller scale. In each of the ten largest cities and towns in Maryland, free blacks congregated more densely than in the county to which that town belonged (see table 2.3).

Cities often have an allure, usually tinged with apprehension, in the imagination of the countryman or woman whose experience is bounded by the limits of the village. As a boy, Douglass listened spellbound to his

TABLE 2.3

Free Black Percentage of Population of Ten Largest Maryland
Cities and Towns, 1850

City	County	Percentage Free Black, City	Percentage Free Black, County
Baltimore	Baltimore	15.0	13.8
Cumberland	Allegany	4.4	1.8
Frederick	Frederick	13.8	9.2
Hagerstown	Washington	11.3	5.9
Annapolis	Anne Arundel	17.7	14.2
Easton	Talbot	24.3	18.8
Havre de Grace	Harford	15.2	14.3
Elkton	Cecil	20.6	13.8
Williamsport	Washington	16.5	5.9
Port Deposit	Cecil	21.8	13.8

Source: Calculated from U.S. 7th Census, 1850, *Population* (Washington, D.C., 1853), pp. 220–21.

cousin's descriptions of the wonders of Baltimore. "I could never . . . point out anything that struck me as beautiful or powerful," Douglass recalled, "but that he had seen something in Baltimore far surpassing it. Even the great house itself, with all its pictures within, and pillars without, he had the hardihood to say 'was nothing to Baltimore.' " Until a sojourn there gave him a more sophisticated and nuanced perspective on city life, Douglass "had something of the feeling about that city which is expressed in the saying that being 'hanged in England is better than dying a natural death in Ireland.' "[38]

In addition to its perennial lure for the bumpkin, the city had very particular advantages for a free black person in a slave society. For the manumitted slave, it offered greater independence and a greater sense of responsibility for his own life than the rural community, where the round of work, leisure, and associations remained closely encircled by the regime of slavery. It also offered needed anonymity to those who had not waited upon the grace of God, the majesty of the law, or the generosity of their owners to grant them their freedom; though it is open to question how many of these last are likely to have presented themselves for enumeration by the census-taker. Some fugitives found Baltimore, whether they chose it or not, the end of the line, since it was a much easier city to disappear into than to escape from. Eight slaves who escaped by boat from Baltimore in July 1849 (probably fearing sale in consequence of the death of their owner) were exceptional both in getting out of Baltimore and in doing so in such a sizable group. Most successful escapes were of one to three individuals and occurred in rural areas, the northern portion of the Eastern Shore and the counties along the Pennsylvania border.[39]

It was characteristic of the middle ground's perverseness that free black people paid heavily both for their closeness to slavery and for their detachment from it. Maryland gradually confined them within a bewildering profusion of legal restrictions whose only virtue—if such it may be termed—was that they were not always enforced to the letter. Vagrant free blacks (that is to say, those refusing to hire their services to white employers) could be bound or sold for annually renewable terms at the direction of a magistrates' or orphans' court. The children (males under twenty-one and females under eighteen) of parents caught in the toils of this law could be bound out as apprentices by the orphans' court, whereupon they became personal property liable to sale at will within the state. Any other free black child thought not to be receiving adequate regimentation into "habits of industry" could likewise be bound as an apprentice. Free black persons could not own dogs or firearms or purchase liquor or ammunition without a special license. They could not sell bacon, pork, beef, mutton, corn, wheat, tobacco, rye, or oats without written certification from a justice of the peace or three "respectable persons" of their neighborhood that they had acquired the goods honestly. They could not operate boats except under the supervision of a white person. Some counties forbade them to enter a tavern or shop between sunrise and sunset and some denied altogether their right to hold peddlers' licenses or operate boats. Only in Baltimore and Annapolis could they attend camp meetings or other religious assemblies not conducted by a white minister; and in Baltimore and Annapolis they could do so only by written permission of a white minister and before ten o'clock at night. They were liable to punishment as slaves for participation in "tumultuous meetings" or other offenses involving slaves. After 1858 they could be sold upon being convicted of crimes for which whites would be punished by imprisonment. Between 1858 and 1860 some eighty-nine black convicts were thus sold into slavery, their terms ranging from two to sixty-five years. The sheer comprehensiveness of the regulations evokes a strong suspicion that many operated, not as literal rules, but as a sort of warrant for the free blacks' good behavior. Nevertheless, a system of rewards for informers encouraged a certain minimum of surveillance, especially in rural districts.[40]

Some of the restrictions were designed to prevent free blacks from trafficking with slaves in goods belonging to the slaves' owners. Others derived from a conviction, resting on little direct evidence, that free blacks constantly busied themselves with inciting slaves to revolt. Yet others arose from a more realistic belief that free blacks fomented escapes: realistic, in that a simple desire to be together with enslaved family members, even without overt action to bring this about illegally, would naturally appear to a slaveholder as enticing slaves to run away. Whatever the individual rationales, all such restrictions testified to the prevailing suspicion of black people who operated outside the forms of control applicable to slaves.

At the same time, however, that free blacks paid a price for being outside slavery, they lived with constant reminders of how nearly they remained slaves. Surely the most frightening of such reminders was the danger of being returned outright to slavery. Because under Maryland law manumission was hostage to the financial solvency of the owner wishing to manumit, long-awaited freedom could prove very short-lived indeed. Two slaves of Frederick County learned this to their dismay in November 1859. Though freed by their owner, they were ordered sold for a term of years by the orphans' court to satisfy the debts of the late owner's estate. They escaped to Pennsylvania, but one Emanuel Myers, especially hired for the purpose, captured them there and returned them to Maryland. Although authorities in Pennsylvania arrested Myers and put him on trial for kidnapping, that detail—if they learned of it—can have brought little comfort to the slaves thus cheated out of their freedom.[41] Periodic movements to reenslave free blacks wholesale invariably failed (see chap. 4), but the continual agitation and the knowledge that the legislature held the power to do it cannot have nourished serenity of mind. Moreover, what free blacks were spared jointly could easily befall them severally. Kidnapping for sale out of state would not have to occur very often—and probably did not—to be a source of live apprehension. Under the law in Maryland, as in all slave states except Delaware, visible evidence of African descent carried with it a presumption of slave condition. Any free black person going about his business could therefore be detained, even if only temporarily, and challenged to prove his freedom.[42]

The best form of social protection a free black person could have was the patronage of a white citizen of substance. Such a patron could shield him, not just from the danger of reenslavement for want of documentary evidence of freedom, but from the manifold forms of harassment to which he might fall victim. "Respectable testimony" could persuade the orphans' court to grant permission for manumitted slaves of "extraordinary good conduct and character" to remain in the state despite the removal law of

1832.[43] Similarly, a law forbidding free blacks of Cecil, Kent, and Queen Anne's counties to leave the state and return exempted any free black person hired to a white farmer and sent out of the state on that farmer's errand for no longer than twenty-four hours. In August 1858 four free blacks who attended a religious meeting in Delaware stood trial under this law, upon the accusation of informers. William A. Martin, a white farmer, testified that he had asked one of the defendants whether he wanted to go to the meeting and, being told yes, asked him to deliver a letter in Delaware. The defendant, it transpired, had a standing agreement to work for Martin whenever his services were needed, which probably accounts for Martin's readiness to accommodate him in this instance. The prosecutor contended in vain that the delivery of the letter was merely a ruse to get around the law. All four defendants were acquitted.[44]

Though the good will of a respectable white citizen could smooth the way for a free black person, it did so only at the cost of constantly reminding him how little independence of action he possessed. In their earliest form, work arrangements between free blacks and their employers had followed the pattern of the indentures of white servants.[45] The automatic assumption that, even in freedom, black people retained a certain quality of servility remained as the years passed and their numbers grew. Dependence upon the favor of white patrons thus provided both a form of social insurance for free blacks and a galling badge of subaltern status.

Free blacks living and working in Baltimore stood the best chance of escaping these emblems of inferiority. There they congregated in sufficient numbers to sustain a network of churches, clubs, schools, and informal gathering places outside the sponsorship of whites. The economic life of the city created need for services that, although generally of a humble, even menial, character, nevertheless ensured them a reasonably secure livelihood. The busy commercial life of the city called for stevedores, grain-measurers, coal-handlers, warehousemen, carters, draymen, and carmen. Black men virtually monopolized the ship-caulking trade until the 1850s. The growth of the city required the services of hod-carriers and other assistants to building tradesmen, as well as a large number of domestic servants.[46]

Sheltered in the relative anonymity of urban life and protected in some measure by the city's economic need for them, free blacks could enjoy a modicum of independence. For this independence, however, they paid a stiff price. Without the patronage of white citizens of standing, they had to meet from their own modest resources the hostility of those who competed with them for livelihood or resented their presence on general principle.

Nor did they have the buffer between themselves and a niggling, literal-minded enforcement of the law that rural dependence might have afforded. In disproportionate numbers blacks in Baltimore were arrested, convicted, and jailed for minor violations of city ordinances, or arrested on mere suspicion because of their proximity to the scene of trouble.[47]

When the 1850s brought an influx of competitors for jobs that blacks had formerly held untroubled, rivalry occasionally erupted in ugly violence. At such times even the self-interested sponsorship of white employers could redound disastrously to the disadvantage of black workers. The black ship-caulkers are a case in point. The long monopoly black men held in this trade was not entirely a tribute to the discipline of their own organization. It seems, rather, to have been the creation of a powerful association of shipwrights, who obliged the caulkers to withhold their services from any employer who refused to abide by the association's rules. The black caulkers derived unquestionable advantages from the arrangement, not the least being security of employment, and they entered with spirit into the enterprise, devising elaborate and strict rules within their own association. But the shipwrights gained for themselves the formidable advantage of nearly total control over the wages and conditions of those employed in shipbuilding activities. The arrangement came to grief when a refractory shipwright, having been denied the services of black caulkers for violating a rule of the employers' association, imported white caulkers into the city. At this juncture the black caulkers deployed their own time-honored arsenal of devices to protect their monopoly, throwing down their tools or sabotaging the job when required to work alongside nonmembers of their association. When faced with the efforts of the black association to freeze them out, the white caulkers organized their own association and terrorized the shipyards, holding one shipyard owner, Jeremiah P. Skinner, and his black employees at gunpoint. Skinner charged that the police did little to protect him or his personnel. Eventually capitulating to force majeure, Skinner hired twelve white caulkers; and he and the other shipbuilders had to agree that black caulkers would thenceforward work only by special permit from the white association.[48] Self-interest, in addition to the urgings of sentiment, might prompt a farmer on the Eastern Shore to champion his black favorites—*his* negroes. The self-interest of an employer in Baltimore would teach him that, whatever his personal feelings, in the final analysis he had better make terms with white labor.

Nothing could ever be simple or straightforward on Maryland's middle ground. The gradual decay of slavery, dramatically marked by the steady hemorrhage of the slave population, did not signal the end of slavery as an overriding fact of life for the people—especially the black people—of Maryland. Perhaps slavery might be likened in this to a radioactive object: constantly emitting radiation but remaining, nonetheless, radioactive. Or perhaps to a strong dye that, even as it faded, tinted freedom in somber shades. The juxtaposition of slave and free black created anguishing difficulties for both. At the same time, it conferred subtle benefits while raising thorny practical and ideological problems for slaveowners. Black people living in freedom silently gave the lie to the prevailing racial justification for slavery, undermining the system's ideological underpinnings in the minds of both slaves and their owners. As a child, Douglass quickly dismissed the assertion that God had ordained the enslavement of black people. "I knew of black people who were *not* slaves," he recalled. Slaveowners showed that the same perception struck them (to different effect, of course) when they insisted that slavery and "free-negroism" could not coexist.[49] The example of free black people kept before the slaves' view the possibility of a world and a life beyond slavery. Free blacks imparted to the slaves— often in secret and at grave risk to themselves—what learning they possessed. (According to the 1850 census, over half the free black population was to some degree literate.)[50] In diverse ways, the juxtaposition of free black and slave lent slavery a defensive strain in Maryland. That conduced to suffering on the part of black people, because slavery on the defensive could be especially overbearing, arbitrary, and vindictive. But it also placed in the hands of both free black and slave a moral, ideological, and, upon occasion, practical weapon that the most determined efforts of the slaveholders never managed to spike.

CHAPTER THREE

Baltimore and the Problem of Slavery in Cities

When Frederick Douglass saw Baltimore for the first time, his impressions were of noise, confusion, and a vague sense of threat. He was, after all, a young slave not yet ten years old and fresh from the provincial isolation of the Eastern Shore. The hot pavements, the towering buildings, the unaccustomed sounds, and the "troops of hostile boys ready to pounce upon me at every street corner" nearly overcame the magical aura in which his imagination had always enveloped the city; and he almost wished he were back in the familiar, though despised, environs of Talbot County.[1] His first sight of Baltimore would have been in the late 1820s, when the city was still raw enough to remind a visitor of how recently it had been no more than a cluster of huts standing in a wilderness.

As recently as 1752, that is all Baltimore was. It was the Revolution that sent Baltimore into the giddy burst of growth that turned it into a city. Indeed, the changes that brought this about were swift and concentrated enough to be dramatically evident within one individual's lifetime. Speaking before the Maryland Historical Society in 1844, Robert Gilmor recalled what Baltimore had been like when he moved there as a little boy in 1778. Fell's Point, where he landed, was a sparsely settled outpost separated from the town by trees and cornfields. Tides lapped at the foot of Gay Street; and Market Street was a mudhole in which he watched a Revolutionary soldier and his pony narrowly avoid swamping on a march through the town.[2]

In 1846 an omnibus line (six cents a ride, whites only) connected the rather sprawling distances of the city—sprawling, because patches of wilderness still lay interspersed among settled areas of the city and its suburbs. Green fields separated the fashionable residences around Monument Square from the falls and, beyond, the "rickety old pest house called the jail." Charles Street at Madison terminated in a grove of oaks—relics, it was said, of the forest primeval. The generally undeveloped western region of the city was interrupted, in the vicinity of Lexington and Fremont, by a cotton factory and, around it, a cluster of houses for the factory operatives. But fire destroyed the factory and its residences two or three years later, and they were never rebuilt.[3]

As the omnibus knitted the city more closely together, advances in transport connected Baltimore more predictably and conveniently than ever before to Philadelphia and New York. It appeared to happen overnight. In the ten or fifteen years before 1845, Henry Stockbridge later recalled, New York and New England "were supposed to have been brought so near to Washington as to have very little room for further improvement." To an age accustomed to a choice between the air shuttle and the Metroliner, the alternatives then available appear neither impressive nor particularly attractive. But at the time the prospect of making the journey from New York to Baltimore in a day seemed headlong mobility. True, it would be a strenuous day, beginning at seven o'clock in the morning and not ending until eleven o'clock at night. And there was the cumbersome business of connecting boats, trains, and coaches with people and luggage transshipped from one conveyance to another.[4] But by these means Baltimore was, once and for all, implicated into the bustling world of the commercial Northeast and saved from dependence on the genteel somnolence of Maryland's slave economy.

In fact, Baltimore's rise to eminence never depended on slavery. In 1790, when from the handful of dwellings of 1752 Baltimore had grown to a respectable community of thirteen thousand, slaves amounted to just over 9 percent of the population; this at a time when nearly one-third of the people of Maryland were slaves.[5] In some respects, the city's rise seems almost accidental. Four earlier Baltimores at other locations preceded the one that established itself on the Patapsco River and was destined to be the only one of importance.[6] Reflecting a common nineteenth-century view that nature establishes the laws of human society, J. D. B. DeBow wrote in a tone of something like annoyance at those early Chesapeake settlers who had not had the sense to put Baltimore in the right place from the start. He accused them of placing towns at random, of "blindly experimenting with the laws of nature" and "attempting capriciously to produce a factitious determination of wealth and population to points never designed for such a fortune by their Maker." And the result was that "the most unrivaled advantages of the location of Baltimore were long quite overlooked."[7]

But it was not nature that provided Baltimore with its advantages and decreed their independence of slavery. The natural advantages of Baltimore became social advantages only with the settlement of western Maryland and the growth of wheat culture there and with the need of farmers in the Susquehanna Valley region of Pennsylvania for a more convenient route to market than the overland one to Philadelphia. With its growing importance as a transshipment point—and as a market in its own right—for wheat, Baltimore also became a milling center, a function for which its numerous falls provided convenient power. The Revolutionary and Napoleonic wars were a bonanza for Baltimore. A brisk trade in local products—wheat and flour, but also tobacco—and West Indian goods destined for reexport both stimulated and benefited from the growth of the milling and shipbuilding industries. Baltimore's location as the southernmost of the major ports gave it an advantage in the West Indian trade as a whole. And the Bay pilot boats turned out in Baltimore's shipyards proved especially adaptable to the needs of blockade-running. But bonanzas, by definition, do not last. Jefferson's embargo, and then the coming of peace in Europe, ended Baltimore's headiest period of growth. Thenceforward its development, while still remarkable by Southern standards, became no more than routine by the standards of the North.[8]

The important point is that the tobacco—which is to say the slave—economy had very little to do with the rise of Baltimore. The starting point of the city's development was the wheat economy of northern and western Maryland and of southern Pennsylvania. Newcomers from Pennsylvania and foreign immigrants, particularly Germans, accounted for much of the settlement in northern and western Maryland.[9] Though slave ownership occurred among these people, it never formed the basis of the agricultural economy: slaves accounted for less than 15 percent of the population of the northern and western counties in 1790, compared to nearly 36 percent in the Eastern Shore counties and over 45 percent in the counties of southern Maryland.[10] Moreover, the merchant community that presided over Baltimore's early surge typically had no connection with the slaveowning elite, whose capital was Annapolis. A core of relatively recent migrants from Pennsylvania, joined by an immigrant—principally German and Irish—contingent: such was Baltimore's early commercial community.[11]

Time brought diversification to Baltimore's economic base, as the special circumstances that attended the city's infancy deserted its adolescence.

Commerce remained the dominant element in the economy, and foreign trade the principal basis of commerce: it was not until the beginning of the twentieth century that the value of domestic trade overtook that of foreign trade, and the two combined continued even then to outweigh manufactures.[12] But the business community's determination to emerge from the slump that succeeded the initial windfalls in foreign trade led to an early preoccupation with both the development of manufacturing and the improvement of facilities for domestic trade.

The cotton textile industry in Baltimore, which by 1860 was turning out a product worth over $2,000,000,[13] began in 1808 with the organization of the Union Manufacturing Company by a group of Baltimore entrepreneurs. Even here commerce and shipbuilding made their contribution, for Baltimore became the national center for the manufacture of the heavy duck cotton used in the construction of sails.[14] Eventually Baltimore developed an imposing men's clothing industry, which by 1860 had a capital investment of $1,218,500, reported an annual product of $3,124,081, and employed 5,811 men and women—in all three respects the largest industry in the city.[15]

The lines on which improvement in transportation proceeded made it clear from the beginning that Baltimore was to be no mere outpost and service center for the slave economy. Naturally, convenient access to the Chesapeake assured that Baltimore's commercial importance to Maryland's slave economy would grow along with its commercial importance in the nation as a whole; before long, it had upstaged Annapolis in this respect.[16] Tobacco figured, though never predominantly, in its trade; and the making of cigars claimed the attention of 127 establishments in Baltimore in 1860.[17] But Baltimore's business community recognized that Philadelphia and New York provided their competition. They were accordingly eager to develop links with those parts of the northern and western hinterland to which nature had not provided such a magnificent highway as the Chesapeake Bay.

The earliest efforts involved the construction of roads, most importantly the Baltimore and Cumberland Road, whose construction the legislature had extorted from the banks as a condition of receiving state charters. Though the roads were important in opening up the western interior, they were never really adequate. Indeed the National Road, of which the Cumberland Road formed a part, was already obsolete by the time it was finished. So the search for alternatives went on. In 1824 the legislature got off to a protracted and very nearly disastrous false start by sponsoring the Chesapeake and Ohio Canal project, an expensive flop that led the state to the verge of bankruptcy and for which Baltimore had never shown particular enthusiasm. The decisive achievement turned out to be the Baltimore and Ohio Railroad, begun in 1828. By 1830 a stretch from Baltimore to Ellicott's Mills was ready for horse-drawn traffic; later, on the same stretch, the B & O became the first railroad to use an American-built steam locomotive. By 1839 the railroad was serving Maryland's western interior, and by 1852 it had crossed the mountains.[18] The westward migration of the center of agricultural production steadily enhanced the importance of this achievement: in the 1870s grain continued to dominate Baltimore's trade, but by then the bulk of the product came, not from Baltimore's immediate hinterland, but from the Midwest.[19]

Traffic of people proceeded along with traffic in goods and to a notable degree followed its rhythm, slumps in the latter being generally accompanied by slumps in the former. But the traffic in this case was not of slaves but of voluntary immigrants. More than 130,000 immigrants arrived in Baltimore between 1820 and 1850.[20] Although Baltimore was not the final destination of all these people, it was for the bulk of those who remained in Maryland at all. In 1860 Baltimore City contained 68 percent of the foreign-born population of Maryland, and Baltimore City and County together accounted for 80 percent.[21] Because of the magnitude of immigration, the story of Baltimore's population growth is, by and large, the story of the growth of its white population. From a peak of 22 percent in 1810, the black population—slave and free—declined to 13 percent of the total by 1860. Even the growth of the free black population, spectacular in its own way, appears trivial when compared to the growth of the white population. From 1830 to 1860 the free black population increased by 10,890, while the white population was increasing by 132,810.[22] Nothing so clearly indicates how little slavery had to do with what was vital and growing in Baltimore's economy. Even the dissolution of slavery, as represented by the free black population, was eventually overshadowed as a major item in the fortunes of the city. Between 1850 and 1860 the free black population scarcely increased at all, and the combined black population declined (see table 3.1).

Travelers to Baltimore gave the city credit for a certain elegance, something of an achievement in a city that not fifty years before had had to scrounge for personnel qualified in the maintenance and operation of the new water works.[23] But Baltimore could lay little claim to the aristocratic pretensions of tidewater Maryland. Some might live in luxurious establishments like that of Mrs. Wilkins, a widow with "three or four daughters and a great number of black servants." But fastidious travelers still had to put up with "republican carriages" in which, though black passengers were prohibited, yet "the distinctions of first, second, and third class . . . are unknown" and "you often feel annoyed that such dirty people should get in."[24] Nor did Frederick Douglass exaggerate about the racket. More experienced travelers would have identified some of the startling sounds that frightened him as simply the noise and bustle of any busy port engaged upon its routine and would have taken no further notice. But some of the sounds were Baltimore's own special trademark. Visitors arriving at the railroad station were greeted by touts, usually black, from the local hotels, each charged with attracting newcomers to his establishment by force of superior decibels: " 'Get out, brack man,' said the representative of Barnum's, himself the blacker of the two; 'tell your massa to send a gen'leman next time, will you—its lowerin' to de profession to hab you here—get out—Barnum's gen'lemen—Barnum's!' "[25] Then there was Moses, an old black man who, until 1847, hawked oysters and ice cream through the streets, announcing his progress with a whistle that "could be heard squares away in snatches between the cry of his oysters or ice cream—a curious medley the like of which we may not hear again." Moses had a competitor, Whistling Bob, also known as "Bowers chief musician," who delivered the *Telegraph* to subscribers and, according to some, exceeded Moses in the skill and volume of his whistling.[26]

Not all of the developments that turned Baltimore into an important city with such disarming speed were such as to elicit favorable comment from travelers or provide suitable material for self-congratulation at meetings of the Maryland Historical Society. Epidemics of cholera—invariable companion of "progress" in the nineteenth century—broke out in 1832 and again in 1849. And not surprisingly. Sanitation remained a matter of individual enterprise, or the lack thereof. Garbage piled up in the streets unless householders themselves arranged for its removal; or unless it happened to be dispatched by the swine which were "as thick in all the streets as the scrapers are in our day the week or two before a municipal election."[27]

Still more alarming was the perpetual riot. Baltimore's reputation for turbulence, abundantly earned during the Revolution and the War of 1812, had grown considerably as a result of the mob violence attending the failure of the Bank of Maryland in 1835. The remains of that riot were still visible in 1836, when a visitor from South Carolina pronounced them "a sad degrading relic of human passion" from which states farther south were thankfully exempt. True, there was probably as much that was sad and degrading in the activities of the local notables whose chicanery led to the bank failure as there was in the mob outburst that followed it.[28] As to "relic," on the other hand, even Baltimore's most committed promoters would have had to admit that mob violence, rowdyism, and, in general, overexuberant public behavior were far from relics there, and showed no sign of becoming so. The Police Department knew that very well. In its statistics of arrests for the year from 1 January 1849 to 1 January 1850, the largest number (566) were for offenses grouped under the following headings: disorderly and riotous conduct, breaking down fences and doors, resisting officers in the discharge of duty, throwing bricks and stones, and inciting riots at fires. Ranking second (354 arrests) were assault and battery, assault with intent to kill, and waylaying with intent to rob. "If Baltimore contains a greater number of beauties," one visitor concluded, "it also gets credit for containing a greater number of black-guards, for its population, than any other city in the Union."[29]

Much of the routine public violence, as opposed to that which broke out periodically during election campaigns, centered around volunteer fire companies. After fires or false alarms turned in specifically for the purpose, fights would break out between members of rival companies and their supporters, with weapons ranging from sticks and missiles to pistols and muskets. "Riot reigned supreme," the *Sun* reported in December 1849, barely stifling a yawn. After a stubborn and destructive fire had been put out, someone called out the engines again on a false alarm; whereupon "persons running with the apparatus, commenced a general running fight, in more than one section of the city." Efforts to curb by law the practice of running after the engine companies were without much effect, except the boomerang one, in this case, of leading to the arrest of several of the firefighters themselves. The severity of the fire had brought out a second engine company, operating outside its district in technical violation of the law. Once the fire was under control several members of the United Fire Department, in whose district the fire had occurred, brought the violation to the attention of a police captain. The policeman believed that he had no choice but to take official cognizance of the lapse by arresting the offenders, even though they had committed no breach of good order.[30] Despite the law, violence between fire companies continued. In September 1857, at least twenty people were shot and two killed in a face-down between rival firehouses. Mayor Thomas Swann could think of nothing better to do, in response to that episode, than to close one firehouse and propose more stringent enforcement of the law against running after fire engines.[31]

The firehouse organizations and their loose bands of supporters shaded into political clubs, which in their turn shaded into more or less overt territorial gangs whose areas of jurisdiction were common knowledge. Much of the manpower appears to have been furnished by juveniles. John Hogan, a boy of thirteen detained at the scene of one disturbance, was carrying "a small double barreled pocket pistol with both barrels loaded to the muzzle." In a showdown engagement between the runners of the La-fayette and Columbia fire companies, the troops consisted of some 150 "boys from twelve years of age to manhood"; the engagement ended only after a thirteen-year-old Columbian runner was killed.[32] Ethnic and nationalist sentiment was always very close to the surface of these outbreaks. It became even more so during the 1850s, when nativism and armed intimidation formed an integral part of almost every municipal election and, because of the key role it played in the confused party system of those years, was never very energetically discouraged by politicians.[33] Racially inspired violence did not occur as frequently, although when it did, it was reported with appropriate dramatic emphasis ("A colored man made a thrust at Frentz with a knife, cutting his abdomen open nearly across the body").[34]

By contrast with the turbulent presence of the free white population, the slave population was inconspicuous. Its numbers dwindled steadily during the antebellum years, falling from a peak of 4,672 in 1810 to 2,218 in 1860 (see table 3.1). Most of the slaves resident in Baltimore throughout the antebellum years probably engaged in domestic labor, and that appears to have become more and more true as time went on.[35] Slaveholdings were notably small, well over half the slaveholders by 1860 owning only one slave; holdings of five or fewer made up over 97 percent of the total. In the early antebellum period hotels were among the largest employers of slaves. A visitor during the winter of 1830–31 remarked that "the domestics in the [Indian Queen] hotel were all slaves," a situation that no doubt changed as immigration brought in more candidates for menial jobs. Some slaves were hired out by their owners for unskilled domestic and construction work. Others—Frederick Douglass was one—were hired out in skilled capacities. These increasingly constituted a minority and, as Douglass dis-covered, were highly vulnerable to the hostility of resentful whites in the same occupations.[36]

Whatever coherence slavery as an institution appeared to possess early on was only the dying echo of a system of household paternalism in gradual dissolution as a result of Baltimore's metamorphosis from a hamlet to a city. That system included whites and blacks and rested on the incorporation of subordinates—indentured servants, apprentices, journeymen, slaves—into the households of their superiors. As market relations replaced those of household paternalism, the semblance of slavery's coherence as an institution disintegrated to match the underlying reality. Independent households of free blacks, increasing in numbers along with the decline in numbers of slaves, demonstrated the growing predominance of the market for labor power over the market for the persons of the laborers themselves.[37]

The slave system could never be the center of Baltimore's social existence. By the nature of the city's economic activity, the market for labor was highly seasonal and to a large degree casual. The various services connected with trade—those of sailors, stevedores, carters and draymen, and so on—obviously depended closely on the rhythm of trade but also on the fortuity of the weather, at least in some of its operations. Oystering and the processing of seafood, fruit, and vegetables made highly irregular demands for labor. And as for that perennial of growing cities, residential construction, its dependence on weather, season, and trade cycle needs no elaboration. The slave system did not meet those irregular demands.[38]

Hire arrangements, supposed by some to lend the slave system as much flexibility as a system based on wage labor,[39] might iron out individual fluctuations in a market whose overall requirements were reasonably regular. But in a market defined precisely by its extreme variability, individual efforts to smooth over irregularities were bound to meet their collective nemesis. Nor did the owner who placed on his slave the onus of finding work escape the problem, so long as he remained responsible for the slave's upkeep even when the slave was not working. If such an owner simply abdicated this responsibility, he abandoned slaveownership in deed if not in speech, and placed on society as a whole the responsibility he was no longer willing to accept as an individual. The internal dynamic of a city like Baltimore excluded slavery as a dominant principle of organization. Though Baltimore in 1860 had a population of over two thousand slaves, it was not then or at any time in its history a slave city.

Naturally, this does not mean that those individuals in Baltimore who bore the legal status of slaves were in fact not really slaves, that the weight of slavery rested less heavily upon them because slavery as a system no longer retained its integrity. The peasants upon whom, on the eve of the Revolution, the French nobility sought to impose long-lapsed feudal obligations, were not less oppressed because the form of their oppression was anachronistic. Anachronism added its own peculiar bitterness to the position of the slave. Frederick Douglass made this point with characteristic precision, while describing the conditions under which he received the "privilege" of hiring himself out. He was to dispose of his own time, finding work, bargaining for wages, purchasing his own tools, food, and clothing, and paying his master three dollars each week. "Master Hugh seemed to be very much pleased . . . with this arrangement," Douglass commented sardonically; "and well he might be. . . . [W]hile he derived all the benefits of slaveholding . . . without its evils, I endured all the evils of being a slave, and yet suffered all the care and anxiety of a responsible freeman."[40]

Arrangements of this kind revealed slavery as a legal status attaching to individuals, not a system for the organization of social life. Needless to say, the ideological implications no less than the immediate practical consequences of such a demotion of slavery disturbed those who cared about the future of the system. By the late antebellum period a spokesman for conservative slaveholding interests was warning that public sentiment was "rotten" in Baltimore, and the city "unsound" on the question of slavery; and he urged slaveholders to take thought of how they might protect themselves against a potentially adverse white majority. But the danger could be only contained, not eradicated. Rural slaveowners well understood the difference between their own requirements, which called for "certain and fixed labor the whole year round," and those of employers in the city where, because "labor seeks employment under the stern lash of necessity, . . . it can always be commanded at call." These slaveowners did not expect the "commercial harpies" of Baltimore to sympathize with their position. Accordingly, they took jealous care that their own representation in the legislature should remain predominant.[41]

For neither misgiving nor warning nor precaution could prevent the logic of urban social life from calling forth unorthodox adaptations of slave custom and practice that placed in question the integrity of the institution. Clear-headed contemporaries grasped this fact. Until recently, historians grasped it as well. Twenty years ago, Richard Wade reached the conclusion that slavery was fundamentally incompatible with the environment of growing cities. Still an "integral part of urban life" in 1820, slavery in cities showed a steady tendency to decline thereafter: urban slave populations dropped proportionately and sometimes absolutely, numbers of slaveholders fell, and size of slaveholdings diminished. The explanation for this decline, according to Wade, lay not in the inability of slavery to meet the social and economic demands of an urban economy, but rather in the corrosive impact urban life had on the discipline and morale of the slaves. The problem was not to find work for slaves but to control them when their work was finished. "[W]hen the Negroes gathered by themselves, beyond the eye of masters and police, in homes, churches, or grog shops, the 'peculiar institution' itself was jeopardized."[42]

Econometric historians have recently disputed this conclusion, including Baltimore in arguments designed to show, by statistical means, the viability of slavery in cities. There could hardly be a less appropriate example. The decisive characteristic of Baltimore was the extent to which its development drew it away from the orbit of the slave economy altogether. A graph showing the demand for slaves in Baltimore—if such a thing can be reliably assembled at all[43]—provides information not about an urban slave economy but about the demand for slaves in a nonslave urban economy. Nor was Baltimore a special case among Southern cities except in degree. All Southern cities occupied an anomalous place in slave society. All had features that set them apart from their rural surroundings. And all experienced, to some extent, the tension that led rural slaveowners in Maryland to regard Baltimore with suspicion and disquiet.

Nevertheless, as an aspect of the larger question of the nature of slave society, the problem of slavery in cities is of sufficient interest to warrant the renewed attention it has received. A great deal is at stake. Those who conclude that the urban environment posed no particular threat to slavery generally accept the proposition that the way of life sustained by slavery was not qualitatively different from that sustained by free labor in the Northern states but was simply a variation upon it. Those who conclude that slavery was incompatible with an urban environment generally assume that the slave system supported a qualitatively different way of life from the free labor system. But before conclusions about the fate of slavery in cities can bear this kind of interpretive weight, several components of the question that are often muddled together must be separated.

Whether or not individual units of slave property could be secured in cities, the issue of slave discipline as generally posed, is one question. Whether or not slavery as a coherent and integral system of production could prosper, or indeed survive, in cities is a different question and one of broader significance. Similarly, whether or not individuals who were slaves by legal status were capable of performing urban tasks in an adequate manner is a narrow question. The broader counterpart to this question is whether or not slavery as a system could organize the performance of such tasks and compete with free labor in during so. Anyone considering the problem of slavery in cities must take care not to confound the narrow question with the broad one and then assume that settling the one automatically settles the other.

It is unrealistic, furthermore, to abstract a city from its context. Border-state cities drawing on hinterlands in the free states are different from cities serving primarily as adjuncts to a plantation economy. And, in their turn, cities that are adjuncts to a growing plantation economy are different from cities that are adjuncts to a stagnating one. A city by itself, in short, is not a meaningful unit of analysis. The fate of slavery in a particular urban area depends, not merely on the fact of urbanization, but on the precise character of the urban area in question and on the nature of its integration into its surroundings. A statistical operation combining the experiences of New Orleans and Richmond, St. Louis and Charleston, cannot produce generalizations valid for slave-state cities as a whole. Nor, since cities are not autonomous entities, can they be treated independently of the states to which they are politically subordinate. To suppose, for example, that demonstrating the incompatibility of slavery and urban development hinges on showing a steady absolute decline in urban slave population is to suppose that slave-ownership could be wiped out in a city while continuing to exist in the adjacent countryside and the rest of the state—a most unrealistic supposition.[44]

Taking all this into consideration offers some grounds to question Wade's explanation for the incompatibility of slavery with urban development. But of the fact itself there can be no serious doubt. One scholar has attempted to dispute it, substituting absolute for proportional figures in order to prove that slave population in cities showed no long-term tendency to decline. But decline it certainly did in Baltimore. Other Southern cities tell the same story in essence, if not in degree. Despite the false impression that may arise from naïvely adduced statistics, the underlying trend is clear. In Southern cities as a whole, slave population was steadily overshadowed by free (and, in disproportionate numbers, immigrant) population. Notwithstanding all cyclical fluctuations and contrary tendencies that appear when slave population stands in isolation, the decline of urban slavery is unmistakable when the figures are considered, as they must be, in conjunction with the growth of population as a whole. Baltimore may be a particularly dramatic instance, but it was not unique.[45]

Why, then, did the decline occur? According to Wade's econometric critics, it occurred for reasons which, far from indicating the weakness of slavery in urban areas, demonstrate its essential vitality. The high prices obtainable for slaves encouraged urban owners to cash in their investment by selling off to rural buyers; urban slave populations were therefore likely to register their greatest percentage declines precisely at the time when the demand for urban slaves was greatest. According to this argument, the high elasticity of demand for slaves in cities, and the ready availability of free substitutes, explain the pattern of change in urban slave populations.[46] To the extent that this contention is true, it proves the contrary of what its proponents believe it proves. It demonstrates the erosion, not the vitality, of urban slavery—the conversion of slavery from a system of social production to a form of organization within the labor market, or an item in a portfolio of investments.[47] Where slave and free workers are volatile substitutes for one another on the market, there slavery has become an attribute of individuals, not any longer of the system that organizes their labor.

Wade attributes the decline to the problem of maintaining discipline among the slaves; and, though some have tried to minimize the problem, there is no doubt that it existed and that it was serious. Those who hold otherwise have not actually attempted to confront directly the impressive amount of firsthand testimony drawn from slaves, owners, and third parties to the effect that there was a problem. Instead, they have sought to show by logical deduction that contemporaries who thought so must have been wrong.

If discipline did represent an important and growing anxiety, according to one argument, that fact should have been reflected in exploding police costs, in high and rising taxes and license fees, and in increased commitments of slaves to jail.[48] None of this necessarily follows. The number of jailings cannot provide a reliable indicator of the seriousness of discipline problems. In depriving the master of the slave's services, jailing would be a punishment nearly as burdensome to him as to the slave and would perforce be applied sparingly. Higher police costs, taxes, and license fees would result only if people could reasonably suppose that more policing would help. In fact, it would not. Once concrete social situations replace the abstract notion of discipline, it becomes apparent that police would be totally irrelevant to a good many of the potential problems. What would a policeman do about a skilled slave who concealed part of his earnings from his master? Or about one who refused to hustle as much as he might in looking for work, as Frederick Douglass once did to spite his master? Or about one, again like Douglass, who cajoled his white playmates into teaching him to read? How would he insulate the slave from contact with fellow-workers of antislavery views? And how would he combat the psychological effect of the presence of relatively large numbers of free black people (always more heavily concentrated in Southern cities than in the countryside, and nowhere more so than in Baltimore) in a society that defined slave status in racial terms?

Southern city officials who failed to translate their anxiety about slave discipline into higher police expenditures simply had a more realistic appreciation of the limits of police power than some historians confronting the problem in retrospect. Officials in Baltimore had the best of motives to keep matters in perspective, for they knew that the most serious threat to the public peace came from free citizens. Riots, gang skirmishes, incendiarism, and election-day hostilities confronted citizens in Lexington Market, at polling places, in the courthouse, on fair grounds, at railway junctions and relay houses, and in the public streets, where they were highly visible even to those citizens who escaped their direct consequences. The number of free citizens apprehended by police during 1849 amounted to nearly half the total slave population and, in the nature of the case, most of those involved in gang belligerence and firehouse rioting would escape arrest.[49] If every slave man, woman, and child in the city had committed an act of public misbehavior, slaves would not have threatened the public at large nearly as much as did the antisocial conduct of free citizens.

According to another contention, skilled and male slaves—the most likely to cause trouble—would have been sold away from the city in disproportionate numbers if discipline had really been a problem. That, it seems, did not happen. But the contention rests on faulty reasoning.[50] If a slave's skill made him more valuable in the city than his unskilled fellows, his master would hardly get rid of him simply because he posed a greater threat of insubordination. More likely, a master would sell off precisely the marginal slaves, hoping that their departure would render more manageable the task of controlling those who remained. At all events, a master would not exile to the boondocks a slave whose expensively acquired skill was of value only or chiefly in the city: for example, a slave experienced in ship carpentry, longshore work, or waiting on fashionable hotel guests. Even on the consideration of discipline alone, it would be imprudent to assume that troublesome slaves would move in one direction only, from city to country. After fighting a master to whom he had been hired, organizing an illegal Sunday school for slaves, and getting caught in a runaway plot, Frederick Douglass was actually sent back to Baltimore from the country.[51]

His master, at least, must have thought the city an appropriate place for a slave with ideas beyond his station, who was likely to contaminate his rural surroundings with mischief and subversion.

On the basis of logical deduction and what quantitative evidence is available, there is no reason to doubt the view of well-informed contemporaries, seconded by Wade, that conditions of life in cities tended to disrupt slave discipline. But contrary to Wade, who on this point differs very little from his critics, urban slavery foundered on a structural contradiction much deeper than the problem of discipline and control. For while Wade and his critics disagree on the importance of the problem of control, they agree that the decline in urban slave populations did not occur because slavery was economically unadaptable to urban conditions. The abundance of urban tasks suited to slaves, the successful employment of slaves in industrial enterprises, and increases in rates of hiring and in prices of urban slaves all seem to confirm this view. But it is a deceptive appearance. Despite the illusion arising from superficial economic indices, there was a much more profound basis for antagonism between slavery and urban development than the problem of controlling the behavior of the slaves.

The great source of error on this point is the failure to distinguish between slaves as individuals and slavery as a system. Certainly individual slaves were successfully employed in urban factories.[52] But that does not mean that slavery provided the basis for urban industry. The most obvious indication of this is the small and diminishing importance of slave population in urban areas where manufacturing industry was of any note. Of the Southern cities that ranked highest in value of manufacturing output in 1860 (St. Louis, Baltimore, Louisville, Richmond, and New Orleans, in that order),[53] slaves constituted a significant minority only in Richmond; and in all five their proportion of the total population had been declining for the previous thirty years.

Even within the narrow limits of Southern industrial development, the employment of slaves was exceptional. A comparison of the number of available slaves with the number of factory employees in Southern cities where manufacturing industry existed puts the case plainly. In St. Louis in 1860, manufacturing enterprises employed 9,352 hands. On the assumption that half of the slave population constituted the slave work force, there were enough slaves in St. Louis to contribute no more than 8 percent of the hands employed in manufacturing. And they would have reached 8 percent only if the entire slave work force had been so engaged—which is unlikely. In Baltimore, where manufacturing enterprises employed 17,054 hands, slaves could have contributed no more than 6 percent; and in Louis-ville (6,679 hands employed) the corresponding figure would be 37 percent. In these three cities there were not enough slaves physically present to make up even half the work force employed in manufacturing enterprises, even had the entire slave work force been devoted to manufacturing occupations. In Richmond and New Orleans, with their larger slave populations, there were enough slaves present to account for all or nearly all of the manufac-turing hands.[54] But even these cases forbid a hasty assumption that slaves monopolized manufacturing employment because, among other consider-ations, of the high proportion of immigrants in their populations. Twenty-one percent of the population of Richmond and 45 percent of the population of New Oreleans in 1860 were foreigners.[55]

In fact, immigrants accounted for a disproportionate share of the white population of all major Southern cities as compared with Southern rural areas, and the discrepancy was far greater than that to be found between cities and rural areas in the North.[56] This fact alone warns against assuming that where industry developed in slave territory, it must have done so on the basis of slavery as a mode of production. The disproportionate enclaves of immigrant free labor in Southern cities testify to a gap that slavery could not fill. It will not answer the case to assume that the "non-pecuniary disadvantages" of gang labor on plantations explain the preference of free workers for urban factory employment and thus sufficiently account for the concentration of immigrant free workers in Southern cities.[57] Why should the "non-pecuniary disadvantages" of rural labor have appeared so much greater to immigrant than to native white workers, who were not nearly so concentrated in cities? The answer, of course, is that immigrants for the most part arrived as proletarians. Lacking the means, except in a minority of cases, to set themselves up as independent proprietors or artisans, they naturally had to resort to the sale of their labor power to employers—or, failing that, to poor relief.[58] And why did the presumed subjective psy-chological preference of free workers for urban employment find a coun-terpart in the willingness of urban employers to hire them? To say that they could be had more cheaply than slaves is only another way of affirming that urban employers found slavery as a system less appropriate to the task of filling their need for hands than was capitalistically organized free labor. Objective structural requirements, not subjective individual preferences, explain the prevalence of free labor in urban employments.

A far more important indication of the antagonism between slavery and both urban and industrial development is the ultimate fact that, where the one thrived, the others did not. In other words, the backwardness of the slave South in the growth of cities and towns is an even more telling circumstance than the steadily decreasing importance of slaves in the few that existed. Similarly, the overall underdevelopment of industry in the South is a more significant gauge of the relationship between slavery and industry than the limited use of slaves in such industry as there was. The obviousness of the first circumstance is such that few have ventured to deny it.[59] But a handful of dramatic examples appear to dispute the second, and to attest the capacity of the slave system to accommodate industrial activity: factories like the Tredegar Iron Works, where sometimes quite large slave forces were employed. But the large scale of such activities in itself calls attention to their exceptional status. Not only in the South, but in the American economy as a whole, large-scale industrial concerns remained exceptional until well after the Civil War.[60]

Industry remained underdeveloped in the South because of the thinness of the home market and the subaltern position of the bourgeoisie.[61] Recent attempts to press quantitative techniques into the task of minimizing that underdevelopment, or of conjuring it away altogether, serve only to give it greater emphasis. The contention that industrial development in the South suffers by comparison only with England and the Northern states[62] amounts to a claim that the South compared favorably with all countries save those with which comparison is to the point. To say that the antebellum South possessed a comparative advantage in agriculture[63] is not to dispose of the matter, but only to restate it in metaphorical terms. Comparative advantage is neither a plant, an animal, nor a geological formation. It is not a fact of nature. What matters is not natural endowments, but the manner in which a particular society puts its endowments to use—which in the antebellum South, of course, meant slavery. The United States as a whole might be said to have possessed a comparative advantage in agriculture throughout the nineteenth century; but that circumstance did not preclude the development of industry in the United States as a whole.

Nor does it dispose of the matter to suppose that the availability of economies of large-scale production made agriculture more appropriate for the South than industry. The premise is false[64] and the conclusion a non sequitur. When economies of scale appeared in Northern agriculture, they took the form of a revolution in labor-saving agricultural technology, allowing large-scale agriculture to coincide with increasing productivity and a relatively decreasing work force. In this fashion, large-scale agriculture and industry can proceed hand in hand, and not one at the expense of the other. Economies of scale in agriculture do not necessarily imply a large and constant agricultural work force or labor-intensive methods of production except in a society tied to these by the nature of its social organization. Historically, agriculture organized along capitalist lines has tended to reduce the relative number of those directly engaged in agricultural production, even as the scale of that production increases.[65] The maturing of capitalist relations of production in Southern agriculture accomplished precisely this, reaching its climax with the northern and western migration of sharecroppers, tenant farmers, and others displaced by the Depression and the policies of the New Deal. The decline in agricultural population continues to this day. With it has come an industrial revolution that was no more than a vague promise in the immediate post–Civil War years. That these developments were so long deferred results from a change, not in the natural endowments of the South, but in the manner of their exploitation.[66]

Urban growth and industry were stunted in the slave South because slavery, as the dominant principle of social organization, confined them to exceptional circumstances and to the margins of Southern society. Baltimore, the metropolis of a border state whose most vigorous region was more closely integrated with the world of free labor than with that of slaves, occupied just such a margin. The large slaveholders of Maryland never lost sight of that fact, nor of the potential it contained for subversion of their interests. Baltimore was in, but not of, slave society; and by 1860 it held better than a third of Maryland's white population.[67] Who could say but that the city's turbulent masses and ambitious politicians, feeling the strength of numbers, might soon decide to reduce the political power of the planter class to match its demographic weight in the state as a whole?

Slaveholders were not alone, of course, in harboring misgivings, nor were the slave counties the only ones anxious to keep the city under firm restraint. Suspicion of Baltimore could be found in rural northern Maryland as well, mingled with pride in a curious concoction. Conversing with a stranger on a train, Susanna Warfield of Carroll County defended Baltimore point by point against his complaints. When he said the city was dull, she countered that it was a "religious community." To his charge that Baltimoreans "live very much within themselves" she replied that they were devoted to business. His assertion that Baltimore was the worst place in the world for a stranger, showing no hospitality, met her retort that the city was proverbial for its hospitality (as indeed it was). But in the very next entry in her diary Warfield wrote: "Baltimore is a wicked city."[68]

Still, slaveholders in the 1850s had a very specific object for their apprehension: the Know-Nothing or American party, which built itself a formidable machine in Baltimore.[69] In Maryland, as in the nation, the collapse of a stable party system during that fateful decade of sectional agitation prepared the ground for the dramatic, though short-lived, vogue of a political organization combining nativism, temperance, and—in the slaveholders' view—an unwholesome indifference to slavery. The Know-Nothings' municipal victories in Hagerstown, Cumberland, Baltimore, Annapolis, and Williamsport culminated in a statewide sweep that gave them, with the cooperation of a few Whig senators, control of the General Assembly in 1856. Jubilation over that success, and over the election of their candidate as governor the following year, tempted them to ignore for a time the fatal collapse of their national organization in the debacle of the 1856 presidential election. On the eve of the gubernatorial election of 1857, even their enemies believed that they were still riding high. "Look out for reform," the *Planters' Advocate* warned; if the Know-Nothing party retained control of the legislature and elected a governor, nothing could stop them from calling a state constitutional convention. The counties' representation in the legislature would then "pass under the shears of Baltimore City," bringing "slaveholders . . . face to face with a Reform, the terms of which Baltimore City is to dictate. . . . What," the *Advocate* demanded, "will become of the rights of the slaveholder in the hands of the people [of Baltimore] who send an abolitionist to Congress, and of others, in the northern part of the State, who are but little interested in slavery?"[70] The *Advocate* harbored no weakness for democracy, and no confidence that racial comity would guarantee planters the support of nonslaveholding whites. The Know-Nothings did indeed attempt to call a constitutional convention in 1858. They failed. But the *Advocate,* taking the threat very seriously, advised planters to place amendment of the constitution beyond the reach of "mere numbers," and thus to secure their interests "even, if that shall ever be, in the face of an adverse popular majority."[71]

Large slaveholders and their spokesmen justifiably suspected the intentions of the Know-Nothings, whom they regarded as the narrow and selfish representatives of commercial Baltimore against the agricultural interests of the state, and as the stalking-horse of abolitionism and Republicanism. The last two charges were premature in the 1850s—they would be validated in due time—but the logic of the Know-Nothings' position and the sources of their support accurately marked them as potential enemies of slavery. The planters were right about that, even if they overestimated the magnitude of the threat. The disproportionate representation of the slave counties in the legislature was indeed a likely target of Know-Nothing reform, and the "commercial harpies" of Baltimore, drawing some assent from the northern counties on both sides of the Bay, did indeed believe that their views were unjustly subordinated to those of the agricultural interests of southern Maryland. Whiggish editors drawn to the Know-Nothing standard did not have to dig far into their files for editorials contrasting the progressiveness of the free counties with the backwardness of the slave ones, deploring the free ride that slaveowners enjoyed at the expense of those paying taxes on less favored forms of property, or denouncing the inclusion of slaves at their full numbers when counting population for the purpose of legislative apportionment. These themes had been making their cautious way into the columns of Maryland's Whig press for years.

But the deepest source of the slaveholders' nightmare was the fear that the Know-Nothings might succeed in mobilizing a white majority that held no stake in the future of slavery. The spectacle of street violence that regularly accompanied elections in Baltimore during the Know-Nothing ascendancy embellished the nightmare in garish and sinister colors, which were heightened by occasional reminders of the watching, listening, brooding presence of the free black population. One such reminder came in the fall of 1856, when a stone-throwing melée between blacks returning from a picnic and (probably drunken) whites culminated in the blacks' driving off their adversaries, attempting to pull down a nearby Democratic flag and liberty pole, and shouting their support for the Republican candidate for president.[72]

It would be fascinating to know the precise mechanism of the connection between the leadership of the Know-Nothing party and the strong-arm cadres who patrolled the polling places on its behalf. It would be still more fascinating to know more about the social composition of those political clubs that played such an important role in the party's electoral victories in Baltimore. The evidence is tantalizing but fragmentary. The leadership of the party in the mid-1850s included (as was not uncommon) a high percentage of business and professional men, though surprisingly few lawyers. They tended to be younger than the leading Democrats and Whigs; indeed, the desire to advance outside the shadow of their elders may have attracted some young Whigs to the new party. And they were less likely than Democratic leaders to be owners, especially large owners, of slaves.

Unfortunately, the party base is not as accessible as its leadership.

Those who terrorized the polls were usually described as hoodlums, thugs, and rowdies. But the membership of the clubs was not confined to fringe or lumpen elements. William H. Davis, a printer who served as a deputy sheriff in the first ward, testified before an investigative committee in 1860 that he had belonged to the Blood Tubs four or five years earlier but had been expelled. (He also volunteered the opinion that his ward contained "a great many Germans . . . who don't take interest enough to go out and vote unless somebody pays them for it.") And the nativist brotherhoods that helped to launch the Know-Nothing party in Baltimore were, at least in part, organizations of artisan-class workingmen. A Democratic editor from Missouri described the Plug-Uglies as "an association, with regular constitution, by-laws and officers" composed of about fifty young men, "all of them decently clad, and many of them even in honorable and lucrative employment." One or two of the members, he reported, "have interests in heavy business houses, one is a magistrate and another is a turnkey at the County Jail." The members were more than willing to vindicate their principles by direct physical means, and could call to their assistance "an army of one or two hundred *outsiders,* who are anxious to do battle in their behalf."[73]

Because the Know-Nothings never managed to turn the power of sheer numbers to profitable account, Baltimore's only bid for political independence was doomed to failure. The party's initial success in Baltimore owed something to defections of Democratic workingmen, whose loyalty had been shaken by the Democratic organizations' open partiality to the employers during the citywide ironworkers' strike of 1853.[74] But the appeal to nativism limited the Know-Nothings' potential base from the outset, and prevented them from drawing full profit from Baltimore's massive numbers. Eventually the party's loss of strength at the state level put an end to its machine in Baltimore as well. Moreover, despite the coy editorial reflections they sometimes made upon the outmodedness of slavery and its irrelevance to most of Maryland's white citizens, the Know-Nothings shied away from resting their challenge to the established political order of the state upon the only ground that would have made sense: opposition to slavery. In the tussle between the Democratic governor and the Know-Nothing legislature in 1856 over nativist secret societies, each side accused the other of fostering abolition and Black Republicanism. Editors sympathetic to Know-Nothingism, if anything, outdid the Democratic press in belittling and abusive rhetoric directed against black people.[75]

But even the attenuated threat from the Know-Nothings, in its context of time and circumstance, sufficed to put the wind up the slaveowners. Depression had hit Baltimore hard after the panic of 1857. Indeed, the slump was well under way before the announcement of the panic and the suspension of bank payments made clear that hard times would be nationwide. Construction workers were idle; with more hope than substance, the *Sun* predicted relief for them in the prospect of alterations to be undertaken on the post office and customhouse, and possible construction of a new exchange building and federal courthouse. Firewood dealers were having a hard time disposing of a diminished supply (whose price had risen) because working-class families had been forced to make drastic reductions in their use of fuel. Some 37,000 women in the clothing trades were out of work all winter and by spring were reduced to a pitiful appeal for public charity.[76] Assuming the office of governor in the midst of the crisis, Thomas Holliday Hicks noted an "increase of crime and lawlessness" which, in accordance with Know-Nothing dogma, he attributed to the influx of foreigners who brought with them "acts of riot and bloodshed to which they were accustomed at home." These, together with the free blacks, supposedly formed the vagrant, vicious, and violent element of the population.[77] By 1858 overcrowding in the state penitentiary was such that the legislature decided to relieve it by providing for the sale of free black convicts into terms of slavery. The rural counties largely escaped the effects of the depression that wracked Baltimore. But the spectacle of enforced idleness in Baltimore set alongside chronic shortages of farm labor, especially on the Eastern Shore, was undoubtedly enough to convince slaveholders—if they needed convincing—of the superiority of their system of labor.[78] Coming on top of all this, John Brown's raid threw a good scare into them. They had never in any case trusted the orthodoxy of the Know-Nothings on the subject of slavery.

So, when their moment arrived, they moved with speed and grim determination. Safely back in control of the legislature in 1860 and representing more single-mindedly than ever the outlook of rural conservatives, the Democrats set about the double task of rationalizing the state's labor system and setting limits to the political independence of Baltimore. The first task they handed over to the Committee on Colored Population (see chap. 4). The second task they accomplished, with minor assistance from a supporting cast of good-government reformers in Baltimore, by a series of bold political moves. They vacated the office of clerk of the circuit court in Baltimore, impeached the judge of the Baltimore Criminal Court, voided the election of the Know-Nothing delegates to the General Assembly from

Baltimore, and, most important of all, transferred control of the Baltimore police department from the mayor to a board selected by the legislature.[79] They had reason to feel satisfied with their work, for they seemed to have the situation well in hand. But of course it was 1860. And though they did not yet know it, they were on the brink of a more momentous challenge than that of the hapless Know-Nothings. Within a remarkably short time the city would be in tumult and the hand-picked members of the Baltimore police board, along with several state legislators, would find themselves under arrest by military authorities. When Frederick Douglass visited Baltimore again, not so many years later, neither he nor anyone else around was any longer a slave.

TABLE 3.1
Blacks in Baltimore Population, 1790–1860

	Total population	Change (Percent)	Slaves	Change (Percent)	Free Blacks	Change (Percent)
1790	13,503		1,255		323	
1800	26,514	96.4	2,843	126.5	2,771	757.9
1810	46,555	75.6	4,672	64.3	5,671	104.7
1820	62,738	34.8	4,357	−6.7	10,326	82.1
1830	70,620	12.6	4,120	−5.4	14,790	43.2
1840	102,513	45.2	3,212	−22.0	17,980	21.6
1850	169,054	64.9	2,946	−8.3	25,442	41.5
1860	212,418	25.7	2,218	−24.7	25,680	.9

Source: Calculated from U.S. 7th Census, 1850, *Population* (Washington, D.C., 1853), p. 221; U.S. 8th Census, 1860, *Population* (Washington, D.C., 1864), p. 214; and from J. D. B. DeBow, *Industrial Resources, Etc. of the Southern and Western States* (New Orleans, La., 1852), 1:102.

CHAPTER FOUR

Conscript Slaves:
The Problem of Free Blacks
in a Dual System

Very late on the evening of 23 June 1858, in a rural district of Kent County, a stranger appeared at the door of James L. Bowers. It was somewhere between ten o'clock and midnight, quite late for calling in the country. But the stranger explained that his carriage had broken down in the road and asked Bowers for help. Bowers agreed and started out for the road with the stranger. He had no sooner reached the gate than he was seized by a gang of some thirty men lying in ambush, forced into a carriage, and taken to a nearby wooded area. His wife (then seven months pregnant) heard him scream as his assailants laid hold of him at the gate, and rushed out to his assistance. Reports differ about what happened at that point. According to one, Mrs. Bowers returned to the house uninjured, mollified by the men's assurances that they would do her husband no harm and were only taking him to jail. But according to another, upon reaching the scene she "commenced in good earnest to unmask some of the party" and received serious injury in the process. There is no disagreement about what happened after the group got Bowers to the woods: they stripped him, tarred and feathered him, and made him promise to leave the state within twenty-four hours. Having left Bowers to make his way home, the posse (as they no doubt thought of themselves) proceeded to the house of a free black man named Butler and asked if they might find there a black woman known as Tillison. Butler said no, but the men pushed past him into the house and found the woman they were looking for. They gave Butler a severe flogging and took Tillison off some distance from the house. There they stripped her to the waist and tarred and feathered the portion of her body thus exposed.

Bowers's only provable offense was his well-known and outspoken antislavery position, but recurring allegations connected him with the disappearance of slaves from the vicinity. Bowers denied these allegations, for which the only evidence was the word of apprehended runaways (extorted under threat, some said, while the runaways were confined in prison). He had, in fact, been acquitted of a similar charge some five years earlier. In that, as in all similar cases, slaveholders and their champions found themselves hoist with their own petard. Because of the presumption of racial incapacity that slavery attached to all black people, free as well as slave, the word of a black person could not convict a white man in the state of Maryland—not even a white man suspected of tampering with slaves.

The free black woman Tillison fell under suspicion even vaguer and harder to substantiate. Accused of preying on the superstitions of local black people, she herself seems to have been a victim of the superstitious fears of local whites. Their physical descriptions of her revealed how her supposed power over black people had invested her with an aura of bizarreness appropriate to her sinister occupation. She was "dwarfish in appearance, scarcely weighing fifty pounds," according to reports, and showed "a strong infusion of the Anglo-Saxon." About fifty years old and a resident of Cecil County, she had "for several years . . . frequently visited almost every section of [Kent] County without any ostensible business, exerting wherever she [went] her wonderful powers of conjuration and fortune-telling" and "excit[ing] a great influence upon the more superstitious portions of blacks." She led a "migratory" existence, frequented the houses of free blacks (a damning enough circumstance by itself, that); and—the chief evidence against her—"[h]er advent in the county [had] been followed by the escape of slaves, on more than one occasion." Whether she in fact connived at these escapes is impossible to say. But, as she remained at large, local slaveholders must have had even less evidence against her than against Bowers; for against a free black woman the testimony of slaves, could any be found to denounce her, would have been fully admissible in any court in Maryland.[1]

The incident publicly dramatized most of the matters that urgently concerned slaveholders: the security of slave property, the maintenance of proper discipline and subordination among the slaves, tampering and incitement by abolitionists and Republicans, and the problem of controlling the free black population. Another issue was soon added, because the incident had not yet run its course on the evening of the tar-and-feathers episode. On the following Saturday, during a show in Chestertown, a series of fights broke out when supporters of Bowers sought to vindicate him by beating up members and sympathizers of the mob. They forced one man, Frisby Brown, to duck into the local doctor's carriage and retreat into hiding some sixteen miles down Eastern Neck Island, where he remained for two or three days. The belligerents joined combat once again on Monday, July 5, during the Independence Day celebration in Chestertown. Bowers's friends reportedly knocked down twenty-five men and drove out of town two members of the mob, Samuel Baker (the attempted escape of whose slaves provoked the initial incident) and Isaac Perkins. Local peace officers watched from the sidelines, having apparently decided to let those who wished fight it out. Slaveholders could hardly feel reassured by this spectacle of public disorder or by the inability or unwillingness of police officials to stop it promptly and firmly. Nor can they have been pleased by estimates that "at least three quarters of the people are on Bowers side; nearly all the laboring class or non-slave holders, with a part of the slave holders themselves."[2] Here was a raw nerve indeed. Once it was touched, a vigorous reaction was inevitable.

Slaveholders did not dawdle over their response. At the suggestion of the board of directors of the county Agricultural Society, which happened to be in session on the Saturday following the Independence Day commotion, a county-wide slaveholders' meeting convened on July 17. An impressive body of county notables attended, including Judge E. F. Chambers (who chaired the meeting), James B. Ricaud, a member of the United States House of Representatives, and James A. Pearce, one of Maryland's United States senators. Chambers spoke bluntly from the chair. He preferred not to "enter into the merits" of whether the conduct of the tar-and-feathers mob had been appropriate, though he personally would have "advised a different course." But he most vociferously entered into the merits of the conduct of Bowers's supporters, whom he characterized as "lawless." Slaveholders must have protection against "men who manifested their aversion to everything like illegal violence, by assaulting and beating their neighbors for no other alleged offense than a decided detestation of abolitionists and incendiaries." For his part, Senator Pearce did not hesitate to embrace the actions of the mob. Bowers was guilty beyond doubt of helping slaves escape, Pearce declared, even if the rules of evidence in Maryland courts had resulted in his acquittal when formally tried on a similar charge some five years earlier. With this in mind, a number of "respectable citizens of the county" had decided after the latest attempted escape to "take measures to expel Bowers from their midst." Those who undertook this duty were "sober men, not stimulated by liquor, but quietly resolved to abate a nuisance so dangerous to them and all others, holders of slave property in the county."

A committee of ten, including Chambers, Pearce, and Ricaud, drew up a series of resolutions, which the meeting unanimously adopted. The tenor of these resolutions had little in common with the spirit of patience, moderation, and compromise in which Maryland politicians customarily took public pride; and their excitable tone belied the confidence expressed by Pearce and echoed by other speakers that Bowers's supporters numbered "not . . . one-twentieth of the adults" of the county and that "when free from the influence of John Barley Corn, they would come to their senses," their indignation evaporating with their liquor. One of the resolutions excluded from "the ordinary hospitalities of our people, or the protection of the laws" anyone who "openly, publicly and habitually proclaims hostility to slavery, and a willingness to persuade, encourage or assist our slaves to abscond." Another, while withholding encouragement or approval from "unnecessary violence or harshness," virtually negated even this limited disclaimer by declaring: "We cannot but regard such pestilent and dangerous persons as public nuisances, whose removal is a plain measure of defense." Another pledged those in attendance to "make common cause" against anyone seeking to punish citizens who removed such a nuisance from the community. The final resolution was both manifesto and threat. Declaring that in this contest "there can be no neutrality; he that is not for us must be regarded as against us," it pledged those at the meeting "not to traffic or deal with any man in the county, who will not openly and plainly, without limitation or modification, express his detestation of everything like a tampering with our slaves, . . . nor [with] anyone who shall express a desire or willingness to see violence committed on those who assist in causing such offenders to leave the county."[3]

The resolutions were not the last word on the subject, however. In October, Bowers returned to Kent County, perhaps to tie up loose ends of business left over from his earlier abrupt departure. This time some three hundred people assembled to force him by carriage to Middletown, Delaware, where he was placed on a train to Philadelphia. Bowers suffered no injury, but once again hell broke loose in the vicinity. "[T]he whole county was in motion," according to one witness; "fights occurred between the Bowers and anti-Bowers men, culminating in knock-downs, black eyes and bloody noses, in every direction."[4]

The nerves of slaveholders, particularly Eastern Shoremen, had been sensitive for years. National agitation of the slavery question gave a menacing political edge to any untoward circumstance and created an atmosphere that charged even minor incidents with a potential for calling forth overwrought reaction. Groundless rumors of slave insurrection circulated in Dorchester County in March 1855. In the Nanjemoy district of Charles County, the arrest of two black men in December 1856 upon suspicion of plotting a slave insurrection caused "some little excitement": slaveholders organized vigilante patrols and curtailed slaves' visiting privileges during the Christmas holidays before it became clear that no one had specific evidence of a plot. In October 1857 a "stampede" of some thirty slaves escaped from Cambridge (Dorchester County), reportedly by the underground railroad, raising to forty-four the number of escapes from there in a period of three weeks. Episodes like this one no doubt lent credence to the claim of a self-described agent of the underground railroad to have moved more than two thousand runaway slaves, mainly from Maryland's Eastern Shore, into the free states. Interspersed with periodic flurries over escapes and rumored insurrection were perennial complaints of a shortage of farm labor owing to the refusal of idle and indolent free blacks to hire themselves out for regular agricultural work.[5]

Against that background, the summer disturbance in Kent County sent reverberations through the entire Eastern Shore. Slaveholders in Worcester County, meeting in September, called for a general convention of Eastern Shore slaveholders to be held in Cambridge in November. Their own resolutions indicated the direction they thought the November convention should take. First of all, Maryland's congressional delegation ought to press for tighter enforcement of the fugitive slave law or for payment by the national government of the full value of runaway slaves. The General Assembly should appoint agents—in essence bounty-hunters—to "ferret out and arrest" fugitives, in the likely event that officials in the localities to which slaves escaped should prove laggard. Furthermore, postmasters ought to be given authority to open and read mail addressed to free blacks or slaves, placing incendiary material in the hands of proper authorities for prosecution. In an obvious allusion to the summer's outbreak in Kent, the delegates declared "That the State of Maryland has the power and . . . duty of protecting slave property . . . against all adversaries of her laws and institutions come from where they may." Until the state adopted measures stringent enough to fulfill this duty, it fell upon "civil officers particularly . . . and citizens generally" to exercise vigilance against those who might tamper with slaves. The delegates proposed to sharpen that vigilance by offering a bounty of $100 for every white man and $50 for every free black convicted of tampering with slaves. In the final resolution, the delegates told more than they realized about the source of their difficulties. After all the talk of tamperers and incendiaries, they identified an enemy internal to the slave system itself: the common practice among slaveholders and slave hirers of allowing the slaves to keep corn patches, of letting them leave home without passes, and of giving them freedom to select homes for themselves. Requesting that owners and hirers of slaves "discontinue" these practices—but, significantly, suggesting no legislation on the subject—they called upon constables and magistrates to "break up woods meetings and all unlawful gatherings of slaves and free negroes, and to enforce the patrol laws." Indulging no false hope that the practices would stop, they invoked the machinery of the state to deal with the predictable consequences.[6]

Obedient to the call of their fellows from Worcester County, Eastern Shore slaveholders met in Cambridge in November. Not all Eastern Shore counties chose to be represented: Cecil sent no delegates, though residents of Cecil attended as self-appointed spokesmen. Furthermore, the purpose of the enterprise had undergone an important change by November. People who had a definite end in view had assumed control of the convention movement and were guiding it toward their own object. The meetings in Kent and Worcester had concerned themselves with means of protecting slaveholders against loss of their property through tampering and escape. At the Cambridge convention, it soon became clear, the overriding preoccupation would be the status of the free black population. The new agenda took some of the delegates by surprise. The people of Talbot county, Samuel Hambleton told the convention, "were not aware that any proposition with regard to the free blacks was contemplated," though he pledged their "entire co-operation" with whatever measures the convention might adopt.[7]

Under the circumstances, those who had already worked out their ideas on the question naturally dominated the proceedings. Passing quickly from the narrower subject of the earlier meetings, speakers on the opening day of the convention dwelt upon the evil consequences of a large and "unproducing" class of free black people. One speaker unfavorably contrasted the condition of Northern free blacks with that of Southern slaves: the slave "happy, contented, and cared for in youth and age"; the Northern free black, "a friendless outcast, . . . ek[ing] out a miserable existence in the days of youth and strength, to be finally closed in the poorhouse." Another speaker complained that free blacks corrupted and demoralized the slaves, decreasing their value to their owners. "If we send our slaves out to the field they meet at every corner a vile and lazy free negro lolling in the sun-shine," he told the delegates, deploring the misguided deathbed philanthropy that led too many masters and mistresses to manumit their slaves. Several speakers alluded to the agitation and interference of Northern fanatics, which made immediate action imperative.

The resolutions adopted on the second day confirmed the direction in which the convention had been skillfully maneuvered. Declaring that "free negroism and slavery are incompatible . . . and should not be permitted longer to exist in their present relations," the delegates proposed a statewide convention to be held in Baltimore the following June "for the purpose of devising some system to be presented to the Legislature of Maryland, at its next session, having for its object the better regulation of the negro population." The convention accepted the admonition of a delegate from Dorchester County, who thought the label "slaveholders' convention" impolitic, and addressed its call to "brethren throughout the State, not as slaveholders or as non slaveholders, but as citizens of the Commonwealth." (The nonslaveholding brethren were, nevertheless, to be carefully kept in their place by a voting formula that guaranteed the slave counties the same disproportionate voice at the convention that they held in the legislature.) A delegate from Worcester, who would in time assume statewide leadership of the campaign, found the resolutions too general. Arguing that they ought to include a recommendation "of a more effective and practical character," C. W. Jacobs insisted that "the question of restoring the free negroes to servitude if they persisted in remaining in the State should at once be avowed as the only remedy for the evils complained of." The convention did not go quite as far as he urged, but did adopt an additional resolution suggesting that the Baltimore convention "act upon" the proposal to return free blacks to slavery and that the citizens select delegates with regard to their position on the question.[8]

The shift in agenda may have taken some delegates by surprise, but it was not really surprising. The joining of the issues of protecting slave property and regulating free black people revealed the inevitable weakness of a dual labor system operating in the context of a stagnating slave economy. That weakness was often summed up under the heading "labor shortage." The trouble was that the gradual disintegration of slavery did not automatically give rise to a free labor system that functioned smoothly in tandem with what remained of the slave system. Despite noticeable growth in the free black populations of the southern and Eastern Shore counties, northern Maryland claimed half the state's free black population and over 70 percent of its white population. At the same time, stagnant or declining slave populations on the Eastern Shore and in the southern counties increased those regions' dependence on free black labor. The situation had not reached

TABLE 4.1

Free Black, Slave, and White

Population by Regions, 1850 and 1860

	1850	*1860*	*Change (%)*
Southern Maryland			
Free Black	11,127	13,764	2,637 (+24)
Slave	47,785	48,905	1,120 (+ 2)
White	50,396	58,375	7,979 (+16)
Eastern Shore			
Free Black	24,770	28,277	3,507 (+14)
Slave	25,997	24,957	− 1,040 (− 4)
White	77,737	91,894	14,157 (+18)
Northern Maryland			
Free Black	38,826	41,881	3,055 (+ 8)
Slave	16,586	13,327	− 3,259 (− 20)
White	289,810	366,649	76,839 (+27)

Source: Calculated from U.S. 7th Census, 1850, *Population* (Washington, D.C., 1853), p. 220, and from U.S. 8th Census, 1860, *Population* (Washington, D.C., 1864), p. 214.

crisis dimensions in southern Maryland in the 1850s. Moderate growth in the free black population offset a stagnating slave population. Slaves outnumbered free blacks better than four to one in 1850 and more than three and a half to one in 1860. Agriculturalists in southern Maryland could not afford to ignore the problem, but neither had they reason to panic. The Eastern Shore was a different story, however. With slave population in precipitate decline, especially in the upper counties, the region depended heavily upon the labor of free black men and women. By 1860 free blacks outnumbered slaves and accounted for over 19 percent of the total population.

This made for a very complicated situation, which "labor shortage" only approximately describes. Agricultural commentators exaggerated when they claimed that fields went uncultivated or unharvested simply for lack of hands; and the larger proportion of unimproved farmland in the southern and Eastern Shore counties probably reflected as much the maldistribution of landownership as the maldistribution of labor. What people usually meant when they complained of a shortage of labor for hire was that they found unsatisfactory the terms on which that labor was available: sometimes because the wages asked were too high; more frequently because the length of contracted service was too short; occasionally both. Numbers alone ensured free blacks a certain minimum leverage in setting the terms on which they would offer their labor. The prevalence of cereal agriculture, with its heavy seasonal demands for labor, further enhanced their bargaining position. The combination upset slaveholding society both in its economy and in its ideological view of itself. Free blacks could embarrass agriculture during its vulnerable seasons; and they affronted the established order by possessing a degree of independence altogether unsuitable in black people.

Even large slaveholders who had no need of free black labor saw reason to deplore—and to fear—the unsettling spectacle of free blacks bargaining with employers over the terms of work. In painting a grossly embellished picture of the labor problem, C. W. Jacobs, a slaveholder from Worcester County, revealed both the economic and the ideological unease of his class. Free blacks, he charged, generally refused to contract by the year, preferring shorter periods that allowed them a wider range of choice. But if a free black man should agree to a year's contract, he "selects a home where he can do as he pleases and get a large additional bounty in the shape of a corn-patch, half of every Saturday, extra fine clothes and a horse, and often a carriage at his command. The perquisites," Jacobs added, unable to resist a final flourish, "generally exceed the amount of wages, to say nothing of the amount stolen through the year."[9]

It was entirely logical that Eastern Shoremen most consistently sounded the refrain of labor shortage and the need to control the free black population. It was equally logical that Eastern Shore slaveholders took the lead in the movement to do something about it. But what to do? Slaveholders, concerned that the free blacks would demoralize their slaves, might take one view, while nonslaveholders, dependent upon free black labor, might well take another. Division on the question was bound to be most intense on the Eastern Shore, whose heavy commitment to black labor rested almost equally upon slaves and free blacks. The problem of labor shortage highlighted the ambiguous position of free black people. An anomaly within slave society, time and again declared by the legislature to constitute an evil in need of eradication, free blacks also provided a necessary source of labor. The perennial movement to colonize free black people in Africa failed for a number of reasons internal to the movement itself—the resistance of black people themselves, the absence of a serious financial commitment—but the most important reason was that, whatever white Marylanders might say or think about the danger and mischief of the free black population, the economy of the state could not dispense with them.[10]

Every attempt to settle the free black question came face to face with this irreducible difficulty. Reaction to the Eastern Shore convention thus foreshadowed the debate that would accompany all subsequent proposals to regulate the free black people, exposing to uneasy public view the contradiction that threatened to split Maryland along its seams. Mixed notices greeted the convention's work. A proslavery newspaper in southern Maryland congratulated the convention on its thoroughgoing approach and comprehensive scope. Instead of confining their attention "to the establishment of local police regulations, for the detection of abductors and the capture of fugitives," remarked the *Planters' Advocate,* Eastern Shore slaveholders had "shown their determination to sift their grievances to the bottom, and to find out a plan for the protection of slavery, even . . . at the trouble of remodelling all its present statutory guaranties." But within a week the *Advocate* found itself in open disagreement with a fellow proslavery editor "to whose opinions we have always given a value not less than the admiration which [his] uniform courtesy has always deserved." Predictably enough, the dissenter hailed from Cecil, the northernmost county on the Eastern Shore. The Cecil *Democrat* thought it "strange" that the "intelligent gentlemen" of the convention should have put forward such an unrealistic plan. "No one pretends to believe that the free blacks could be brought into slavery again," the *Democrat* argued. Therefore, the convention's plan must end in the expulsion of all free blacks from the state. "In that event, what is to become of all those farmers who depend upon free labor for the cultivation of their farms? Who is to supply the places of the free colored women who are hired by the week, month or year as cooks or house servants, in thousands of families throughout the state?" The *Democrat* expressed curiosity to know how the convention would frame an address to the people of Maryland "in support of a policy . . . which would militate against the interests of every man in the State who is not a slaveholder or a hireling laborer."[11]

The arguments of the Cecil *Democrat* fairly summarized the views of the opposition, but the Whiggish and American party press had to broach its disapproval of the convention more gingerly than dissidents within Democratic ranks. Lacking either close links to slaveholding interests or party credentials entitling them to a presumption of good intentions, its editors had to guard against unduly exposing themselves and thereby incurring the same sort of wrath that had driven James Bowers from the state and given rise to the convention movement in the first place. The *Planters' Advocate* had already branded the Baltimore *American* "obnoxious to the sanctions of those of our penal laws, which were enacted to protect the people against incendiary abolition publications"; this for publishing, in the wake of the Worcester County slaveholders' meeting, a letter mildly suggesting that Maryland might be better off without slavery. The *Advocate* declared that "whatever is the leading interest of any community is the interest of every man in it, no matter by how few men that leading interest may be *directly* represented." Anyone asserting "a contrariety of interests between the slaveholders of Maryland and those who do not hold slaves" did so only "to produce discontent and jealousy in the minds of the people."[12]

Certainly anyone making such an assertion risked producing discontent and jealousy in the minds of slaveholders, and that was something prudent people knew better than to trifle with. Opponents of the convention therefore had to advance their views cautiously. To forestall any imputation of excessive sympathy for free black people, they employed gratuitously abusive language, remarking on the idleness, viciousness, and general depravity of free blacks and sprinkling their discourse with references to "nigger" and "Cuffee." They hinted that the convention was politically motivated, designed to gratify its sponsors' ambitions for public office. And they tried to finesse the inevitable accusation of abolitionism by charging the convention itself with unnecessarily making a public issue of slavery. The Cecil *Whig* eased its way into the subject carefully, noting that the people of Cecil sent no delegates to the Eastern Shore convention because they "opposed . . . the continued agitation of the negro question." However, by turning its attention to free black people, the convention altered the situation. Cecil County had fewer slaves to be tampered with than other counties on the Shore, but its citizens depended almost entirely on the labor of free black people. Therefore, Cecil could not remain detached but must send to the convention in Baltimore and to the General Assembly men who understood the county's interests. While indicating vague support for legislation aimed at "the idle and worthless free negroes who live by plunder," the *Whig* went on, somewhat disingenuously, to suggest similar legislation "for the benefit of the white loafers and vagabonds that infest every community" and to propose closing "the multitudes of little groggeries kept by whites, licensed by the laws, and around which the negroes congregate, and where they are corrupted and debauched."[13]

The ensuing dos-si-do around the issue was not very graceful, and supporters of the convention took delight in drawing attention to every clumsy maneuver of their opponents. The *Planters' Advocate* rightly asked how critics of the convention could agree that free blacks were idle and worthless but still insist that the state needed their labor. "Being *idle,* how can they be depended on for labor; being *worthless,* of what value can their labor be, even if it were to be depended on? If such be their *conceded* character, it would not seem that their exportation would involve the loss . . . of a very valuable class of laborers." Besides, the *Advocate* continued, arguments against the expulsion of free blacks only strengthened the case for their reenslavement. Nor could the opposition escape so easily the taint of abolitionism. The American party's "shins are already sore upon all topics connected with slavery and its preservation," the *Advocate* jeered. No wonder the membership detected a political threat in the planters' efforts to protect themselves: their party was so "nervous on the question of niggers" that "after the manner of thieves in the night, [they] betray their own lurking places by hollowing before they are hurt." The *Advocate* mocked with malicious accuracy when it accused opponents of the slaveholders' convention of "copying the doleful words of one another" and of employing "half-avowed arguments" before finally daring to state their opposition openly.[14]

Proponents of the convention, however, did not have long to laugh in peace at the discomfiture of the opposition. Soon disarray among proslavery commentators themselves released opponents to state their position less covertly. "Already," the *Whig* announced late in November, "among the stronger pro-slavery portion of the people, and among the locofocos, (*who originated the movement* for what purposes the future will show,) we find remarkable animadversions . . . and insinuations . . . not at all creditable to the actors in the affair." With patent satisfaction, the *Whig* quoted the *State-Rights Advocate,* a proslavery Democratic paper published in Centreville, Queen Anne's County: "[T]he devil is in the wind for mischief to slavery in Maryland, and his horns are already visible in this convention movement." Now the shoe was on the other foot. The *Whig* ridiculed the suggestion that Whiggish elements had fomented the movement in order to raise an agitation that would drive away support for proslavery measures. A week later the *Whig* turned the argument around, describing the convention as a shallow trick of the locofocos, intended to destroy the American party, and in mid-December made so bold as to suggest that "it might be quite as reasonable to compel the slaveholders to send out their slaves" as to try to expel 100,000 free blacks from the state.[15]

The passage of time demonstrated more clearly than ever the delicateness of the free black question. Those who had taken a skeptical view of the convention movement from the beginning hardened in their opinion, while some initial supporters experienced second thoughts. In June the Cecil *Whig* called the impending Baltimore convention "a useless affair" whose "doings and sayings will most likely be forgotten even before the

election, upon which some of those most active in getting it up are hoping
to make it bear."[16] The *Planters' Advocate* had had time to reconsider and
did so in a sober vein. After noting that all the schemes so far proposed
had two sides and emphasizing the need for "wisdom, deliberation and
harmonious action to secure a satisfactory solution," the *Advocate* opposed
any scheme that would result in the departure en masse of the free black
population.[17] As county conventions met through the spring of 1859 to
select and instruct delegates to the Baltimore meeting, the sponsors of the
movement came to understand that the cost of wider participation would
probably be dilution of their original intent. Extravagant rhetoric called for
the perpetual subordination of the inferior race, condemned proposals for
emancipation whether immediate or gradual, rang the usual changes upon
the benefits black people derived from enslavement, and iterated the customary formulas about the idle and vicious portion of the free black population. But in the end it was tighter police regulation, not expulsion or
reenslavement, that the slaveholder in the street demanded. The *Whig* insisted that agitation on the free black question in Cecil County was the
work of a few "mischievous" and "totally niggerless" individuals and that
the slaveholders "wish no such uproar as these pot-valiant fighters of abolition wind-mills are continually making." The *Planters' Advocate* warned
the convention on its opening day not to "suffer itself to be controlled by
passion," because "indiscreet action . . . may . . . injure the cause which is
proposed to be served." The convention ought to issue a "wise and moderate,
though efficient, appeal to the Legislature."[18]

As it happened, the convention split. The majority asked for reaffir-
mation and strengthening of state laws discouraging emancipation and requiring the removal of anyone emancipated. Beyond that, the most they
would require was "[t]hat the free negro population should be well and
thoroughly controled by efficient laws, to the end that they may be orderly,
industrious and productive." A minority refused to content themselves with
such limited measures. With C. W. Jacobs as their spokesman, they presented a report demanding that the legislature "terminate freenegroism in
Maryland at an early day, and on the most advantageous terms to our white
population." Free black people ought to be advised "that if freedom is really
worth anything to [them] . . . they shall be required to leave the State if
they wish to retain [it]." Those unwilling to leave would either voluntarily
enslave themselves to masters or mistresses of their choice or be sold for
life, along with their progeny. Bound and apprenticed free blacks would
face the same alternatives at the end of their terms of service. A new black

police system would assume jurisdiction over "all classes of negroes, slaves as well as free till the latter becomes extinct in the State." In a rather fanciful attempt to attract support for the plan among nonslaveholders, the authors of the minority report further proposed to forbid people already owning more than an unspecified maximum to acquire any "conscript slaves," to limit the number that any one person could acquire, and to make the conscripts available at low prices payable in installments.[19]

The matter might well have rested where the Baltimore convention left it, with an address to the people of the state and a mandate to the General Assembly based on the recommendations of the majority report. If there was nothing to do, best to do nothing. A good many interested observers sighed with relief that the convention had followed that eminently conservative rule, leaving free black people to the discretion and judgment of the individual magistrates, justices of the peace, slaveholders, sheriffs, and ordinary white citizens who dealt with them on a day-to-day basis. Unfortunately for anyone reposing confidence in conservatism and moderation, 1859 was an immoderate year. Election years usually were in Maryland, and 1859 brought confusion and discord enough to overwhelm any quiet resolution of a divisive issue. With slaveholders jealous and vigilant after the American party's abortive attempt to call a state constitutional convention the previous year, and with hard times threatening the Americans' northern Maryland—and predominantly urban—base, John Brown and his associates precipitated themselves into immortality. If the American party ever had any hopes of holding on, the raid at Harper's Ferry buried them. Whatever the public reaction appeared to lack in extravagance could be quickly supplied by anyone of a resourceful turn of mind. One night, in a country district of Cecil County, a sentinel shot a cow that had refused to halt on command. "[T]he report of his gun," according to an observer, "spread alarm and consternation through all ranks, civil and military—the very effect no doubt, the sentinel wished to produce." Hysteria concerning the raid subsided in Maryland with surprising rapidity, but alarm at its frightening implications did not. Southern-rights Democrats carried the fall elections of 1859 and took control of both houses of the General Assembly; a defeat for which supporters of the American party blamed the Harper's Ferry episode.[20]

The sweep carried into the legislature some of the most vocal members of the minority at the Baltimore convention, including their mouthpiece, C. W. Jacobs. When the Democrats organized the House of Delegates, Jacobs took over as chairman of the Committee on Colored Population.

TABLE 4.2

Members of the Committee on Colored Population

	County	Slaves	Real & Personal Property (In Dollars)
F. B. F. Burgess	Charles	34	42,000
E. Pliny Bryan	Prince George's	41	38,000
Thomas Claggett	Frederick	17	23,000
James V. Dennis	Somerset	39	40,000
Joseph H. Gordon	Allegany	0	10,000
William Holland	Dorchester	9	15,000
Curtis W. Jacobs	Worcester	22	150,000

Source: Information about slave and other property holdings of the committee members comes from data supplied in the appendix to Ralph A. Wooster, "The Membership of the Maryland Legislature of 1861," *Maryland Historical Magazine* 56 (March 1961): 99–102.

Instead of composing addresses and memorials to be laid before the Assembly, he could now claim to speak on its behalf. "Many of the extremists upon [the free black question] are in the Legislature," the *Planters' Advocate* remarked, adding without much conviction a hope that "the prudent councils that controlled the Convention will not be without their weight in the Assembly."[21] But the members of the Committee on Colored Population did not set about their work in the spirit of the *Advocate*'s sober second thoughts. Instead, they shared the *Advocate*'s initial eagerness that slaveholders should "sift their grievances to the bottom, and . . . find out a plan for the protection of slavery, even . . . at the trouble of remodelling all its present statutory guaranties." The members of the committee had good reason to be personally interested. All but one owned slaves, most in large numbers by Maryland standards: their median slaveholding was twenty-two. All held substantial real and personal property. The pauper of the group, a nonslaveholding Pennsylvania-born lawyer from western Maryland, owned real and personal property worth $10,000. Residents of southern Maryland and the lower Eastern Shore occupied five of the seven seats on the committee. These, in short, were not typical specimens of the Maryland slaveholder, let alone of the Maryland citizen.

The recommendations of the committee were as drastic as its diagnosis was blunt. "Nothing short of an ultimate extinguishment of the free negro element," they told the legislature, "will cure the evils we labor under or meet the emergencies besetting the peculiar condition of Maryland." Slavery could not coexist with "free-negroism"; the state had "committed a great error in legalising the emancipation of negro slaves under any circumstances to remain amongst us." Fortunately, the error was reversible. According to the committee's reasoning, emancipated blacks did not cease to be slaves; they simply ceased to be slaves of a single owner and became slaves of the state as a whole. It was now up to the state government to take seriously its responsibility as a master by providing for all free black people to be "held in perfect subordination to the citizen population, and made to work under the direction and control of our citizens."

To that end, the committee recommended that the legislature forbid all future manumission. Black people who were already free should be compulsorily hired out for terms of ten years, any children born to them thenceforward to become the property of the owner of the mother's labor. Those already bound out or serving as apprentices, as well as slaves serving limited terms, were to be hired out on the same basis once their terms had expired. Free black people twelve years old or younger were to be bound out until the age of thirty-five, after which they were to be hired for ten-year terms like the rest. Any children they might have would become the property of the owner of the mother's service. All free blacks would have, in addition, the "privilege" of choosing masters and going into slavery at any time. Any black person previously manumitted on condition that he leave the state who had failed to leave would be restored to his former owner or his former owner's heirs, subject to the restriction that he could not be sold out of the state except for crime; his children would become slaves without restriction. The committee thought it necessary to include the provision about conditionally manumitted slaves because the Court of Appeals, by giving freedom precedence over any conditions that might be attached to it, had made conditional manumissions impossible to enforce.

The committee's report also included recommendations for the "suppression of stragglers and venders of small wares and notions"; for the exclusion of foreigners from the ranks of peddlers; and for the removal of "gipsy gangs and fortune tellers" by means of "efficient police laws." The committee intended these measures to combat abolitionism, as they did a further measure—for whose legality they invoked the authority of "eminent legal gentlemen"—forbidding postmasters to deliver mail addressed to black people. They went so far as to propose a law forbidding separate assemblages of black people, even for religious purposes, and providing for the sale at auction of black churches.[22]

After suffering defeat at the state slaveholders' convention, Jacobs must have been pleased with his work on the committee. No one could accuse him of compromising his views or searching for political expedients. When the House floor opened to debate, Jacobs exposed his animus against the free black population in even more clear and direct terms. Apparently forgetting for a moment the original rationale that free blacks were idlers and layabouts who must be compelled to work, he criticized them for owning unseemly amounts of property and demanded that they be excluded from a proposed law exempting $300 of a debtor's property from execution for debt. He understood "that the free negroes in Annapolis were building more houses, and owned as much property as any other persons." And he had heard that in Baltimore "it did not take long to raise the wind [that is, to raise money] among the colored population." Pretensions of that sort had to be discouraged. Jacobs did not intend, he declared, to "legislate for free negroes on the equality with whites" but "as an inferior race." He professed to believe that the free black people of Maryland would respect a forthright proposal to return them to slavery, preferring that to piecemeal legislation designed to control their activities in freedom.[23]

Persecution came as no stranger, of course, to the free blacks. A standing challenge to the racial ideology of slave society—which held that black people were slaves by decree of nature—they operated under tight restrictions designed to negate their anomalous independence. In addition to being excluded from rights of civil and political citizenship, they faced statutory limitations, varying from locality to locality, on their right to engage in certain economic pursuits: to hold peddlers' licenses, to sell certain classes of merchandise, to operate boats on the Bay and rivers, and so forth. County sheriffs could bind out for a year free blacks they deemed vagrants. Free black children could be bound as apprentices upon determination by the orphans' court that their parents were unable or unwilling to support them and train them in habits of industry. After 1858, free blacks could be sold as slaves for crimes for which whites would be punished by imprisonment. And they labored under a presumption of slave status: they could be challenged at any time to prove their freedom.[24] Periodically, those most strongly dedicated to the institution of slavery found these routine restrictions insufficient, and movements sprang up to enact yet harsher and more punitive legislation. A slaveholders' convention in 1841 persuaded the House of Delegates to pass a series of oppressive measures. The Senate rejected the House bill, as well as similar ones proposed by the House over the next four years. A committee at the constitutional convention of 1850–51 (headed by C. W. Jacobs) recommended that language be included in the new constitution requiring registration of free blacks, obliging manumitted slaves to leave the state within thirty days, and forbidding blacks to acquire real estate or even lease it on terms longer than a year. The convention postponed the matter indefinitely without consideration, contenting itself with a provision specifically excluding free blacks from the protection of the bill of rights; and efforts to enact legislation similar to the committee's suggestions failed during the following two sessions.[25]

Typically, these onslaughts had resulted in incremental losses of the already narrow freedom of action that free black people enjoyed. But free blacks usually managed to outwait their enemies on the worst proposals, which generally failed for lack of public support. In 1860, however, in a political atmosphere heavy with menace, many dared not count on the passage of time to mellow the threat, as had happened so often before. Jacobs and his ultras were fooling themselves if they thought that free black people, respecting the forthrightness of the proposal, would stand by quietly and submit to reenslavement. Instead, they quickly mobilized to deal with the emergency. The first rumors that stringent measures lay in the offing started undeterminable numbers on a flight to asylum outside the state. They gathered such of their property as could be moved and made their way north, much to the consternation of the nonslaveholding farmers, tradesmen, and householders who depended upon their labor.[26]

Flight must have been a heartbreaking last resort for most of those who left. A small cabin with its furnishings, improvements on land that probably belonged to someone else—these did not constitute a princely estate. But they did represent a lifetime of labor and, like any family home, a world of emotional associations that nothing could replace. Free blacks attested to the effort they expended accumulating this property, and the value it held for them, by the detail with which they could list it, down to the amount of fabric and yarn and the number of sheets, pillowcases, baskets, bowls, and tumblers.[27] Some of the refugees would have to leave behind more than the material symbols of a lost world of family and friends: some would have to bid farewell to the families and friends themselves. A free black father had no recognized claim upon his slave wife and children. A free black woman sharing a domicile with her slave husband at his master's sufferance would have to abandon her husband and perhaps their jointly accumulated property as well. Free black people with slave relatives would be forced to choose between preserving their freedom and preserving their families. Friendships between free blacks and slaves, even more fragile than ties of family, would have to be put aside. Flight rudely sundered the bonds that joined the lives of free blacks to those of slaves. Husbands, wives, children, and other relatives and friends still held in slavery might be lost forever to free black refugees.

Fortunately for free black people, few white citizens could afford Jacobs's brand of stargazing. The same considerations that had tempered the action of the state slaveholders' convention therefore came into play again when the Committee on Colored Population made its plans known. Public reaction was immediate, intense, and hostile. A number of people in the legislature and among the press and public feared that the severity of the measures might furnish ammunition for the abolitionists. Even pro-slavery Democratic newspapers that favored stern measures condemned the Jacobs committee's proposals. The Easton (Talbot County) *Star* pronounced them "extraordinary," insisted that "the general feeling in this county is against . . . passage," and expressed confidence that the "humanity and prudence" of the majority would not permit the legislature to "pass any obnoxious laws on the subject." In Cumberland (Allegany County), the *Democratic Alleganian* denounced the proposals as "an experiment . . . in severe and oppressive legislation . . . , dangerous alike to our political condition and industrial prosperity." The American party press—chastened by electoral defeat—once again chose a pragmatic and oblique approach rather than a principled frontal attack. But the message was unmistakable. Under the heading "The Nigger in the Legislature," the Cecil *Whig* reminded the Democrats that the legislative session afforded less than two months to do the work of two years and upbraided them for wasting time on a "useless, not to say dangerous question." Rather than comment in its own name, the Annapolis *Gazette* printed an excerpt from the message in which the governor of Missouri had vetoed his legislature's free black bill. Using language such as opponents of free black legislation in Maryland often found convenient and politic, the governor warned against legislation that might "revive . . . misdirected sympathies in behalf of the colored race, or strengthen the too popular error in regard to the moral statu[r]e of slaveholding communities."[28]

Even the legislature could not swallow the committee's plan whole and eventually passed two bills that fell far short of the committee's proposal. Of the recommendations touching emancipation, all that the General Assembly let stand was the prohibition of future manumission, to which it added a provision authorizing free blacks over eighteen years of age to renounce their freedom and return to slavery. Specifically excluded from the terms of the assembly's prohibition were "such negroes as may have been heretofore manumitted by deed or by the last will and testament of a deceased person to become free at a period which has not arrived and who are now in service as slaves for a term of years." The assembly made no mention of black people who, having been freed upon condition of removal from the state, had failed to remove themselves.

A separate bill, containing all that remained of the reenslavement recommendation, required free black people to appear before a board of commissioners appointed for the purpose and to produce evidence of having hired their services for the coming year. Those failing to do so would be exposed to public auction for a term of one year. Minors from four to twelve years of age were to be indentured to individuals selected with the approval of the mother, the period of indenture to run to the age of twenty-one for men and thirty for women. The assembly limited application of this measure to eleven counties, and even there made it subject to the approval of the voters in a referendum to be conducted during the November general election.[29] The voters did not approve. When they had their chance to speak, they rejected even the diluted version of Jacobs's proposal that the General Assembly put before them.[30]

Controversy over the free black question brought to the surface something large slaveholders in Maryland spent much of their time denying: the conflict between themselves and nonslaveholders. Jacobs and his henchmen might merchandise their proposals as especially beneficial to nonslaveholders—the "bone and sinew of the state"[31]—but they had little hope of attracting support among people who could not afford to maintain slaves in any event. Looking back on the episode a few years later, Judge Hugh Lennox Bond of Baltimore attributed the defeat of the free black legislation to that conflict. The nonslaveholders of Maryland, he explained, "knew that the free people of color would forsake the State rather than return again to bondage." Regarding the law as "an attempt to deprive them of the services of the free population, and compel them . . . to hire the surplus slave population," they "indignantly rejected" it.[32]

The "leading interest" of Maryland was plainly not, as the *Planter's Advocate* had confidently asserted, "the interest of every man in it." Nowhere in the South was the interest of slaveholders ever the interest of the whole community, and particularly not in Maryland. In states where a sharp line demarcated Black Belt and white counties, separating the lives of most nonslaveholders from those of most planters, the conflict of interest rarely took the form of direct political contest over issues pertaining to slavery and its future. But in Maryland the growth, not just in the northern counties but within the slave counties themselves, of economic pursuits dependent upon free labor made it very difficult to sustain the appearance of harmony of interest within the white community. Planters in Maryland knew that even while they vociferously—and sincerely—professed to believe the opposite. That is why slaveholders who treated the Fugitive Slave Act as an issue between themselves and Northerners also asked the state of Maryland to pay its own citizens for apprehending fugitive slaves, charging those citizens with intentionally keeping fugitives on the run until owners posted large rewards.[33] That is why an editorial insisting that everyone shared an interest in slavery could at the same time demand that amendment of the state constitution be placed beyond the competence of a simple majority vote.[34] And that is why a comprehensive effort to deal with the free black question led to comprehensive disagreement.

Were that the whole story, however, the outcome might well have been different. It certainly would have been different in the legislature. When the General Assembly convened in 1860, the counties of the Eastern Shore and southern Maryland held over half the seats, even though northern Maryland had more than twice their combined white population. Among the legislators themselves, large slaveholders predominated out of all proportion to their numerical weight in the white population as a whole.[35] If the legislature could not speak with a single voice on the question of free black people, the reason was that slaveholders themselves could not.

On demographic grounds alone it was bound to be so. The typical slaveholding in the state, and in each of the regions taken separately, was one slave. The median slaveholding in northern Maryland fell between one and two; for the Eastern Shore, between two and three; and for southern Maryland, between five and six. Only 10 percent of slaveholders in the state owned as many as eight slaves (in southern Maryland as many as ten). C. W. Jacobs himself owned twenty-two slaves, but in his home county, Worcester, the median slaveholding lay between one and two.[36] These diminutive holdings might have sufficed for purely domestic employment, but they fell short of the needs of either tobacco, cereal, or mixed agriculture. The great bulk of slaveholders could not expect to meet all their labor needs from their slaveholdings alone. Even large holders could not: a farmer in Charles County whose inventory listed twenty-two slaves in 1850 put himself to the expense of hiring twenty-one other black hands in the same year. A correspondent from Horse Head Post Office in Prince George's County explained that, in his neighborhood, free black carpenters "saw at the whipsaw, and hew out timber for tobacco houses—work that white carpenters dont care about doing."[37] What went for large owners went doubly for those of more modest means. Thus it was not only nonslaveholders but also slaveholders who stood to lose from ham-fisted solutions to the free black question.

Marylanders, slaveholding and nonslaveholding, wanted to have it both ways. They wanted labor readily available when they needed it and prepared to serve on terms they found acceptable—something that slavery could guarantee. But they did not want the charge upon their operating capital of maintaining that labor when they did not need its services—something that slavery required. The free black bills passed by the legislature promised the former only by exacting the latter. Those employing indentured blacks had to give a bond to the state for the care and treatment of the servants throughout their terms of indenture, as well as for the support of offspring too young to be bound out on their own account.[38] In effect these provisions would have imposed upon nonslaveholders burdens that they could not assume, and upon slaveholders burdens that many were already, through various devices, attempting to avoid. After all, despite talk of labor shortage, owners themselves were disposing of slaves at a brisk rate, both by manumission and by sale. Indeed, the interval between the passage of the law forbidding manumissions and its taking effect witnessed a surge in the number of slaves manumitted: observers noted increased activity, and the census reported manumissions in 1860 more than twice those recorded in 1850.[39] Moreover, slaveholders constantly experimented with ways of shifting to others, through the clever manipulation of hire arrangements, the obligation of their slaves' upkeep. Negotiations between Susanna Warfield and a neighbor over the hire of Warfield's slave, Amos, broke down because the neighbor refused to commit himself to keeping Amos for a full year and because the two could not agree on a sum of money that would release one or the other from the responsibility of providing Amos's clothing.[40]

The Jacobs committee's proposals, as well as the more modest measures approved by the General Assembly, threatened to disrupt this precariously balanced edifice of makeshift. It is not surprising that no more was heard of Jacobs's plan to reenslave blacks who failed to emigrate after manumission; nor that one of the chief objections to the free black legislation was precisely that it might lead to an exodus of free blacks from the state.[41] In spite of the fact that every legislature since 1831 had made its obligatory bow to the goal of colonization,[42] only a small minority of slaveholders had an interest in the "ultimate extinguishment of the free negro element."

Material interest at once fed and drew nourishment from moral scruples that predisposed slaveholders against the free black legislation. Many were genuinely outraged at the cold-blooded tone of the measures, particularly those portions that seemed to call for the separation of free black families and the suppression of black people's religious privileges. There was more at work than individual conscience. Maryland's proximity to free territory, combined with the steady decline of slavery and the steady growth of the free black population within its borders, put slavery on the defensive ideologically as well as materially. It was not as easy in Maryland as in the lower South (or even in a border state like Kentucky, where the slave economy thrived and the free black population was negligible) to take slavery for granted without further ado as the natural order of things. The view of slaveholding as a duty imposed by God and a burden reluctantly accepted found a comfortable home under these circumstances, as did the peculiar notion of one person's stewardship over another's soul. Congressman John Crisfield of the Eastern Shore spoke from self-interest and perhaps self-deception, but not hypocrisy, when he told Congress in 1862: "I am the owner of slaves. . . . I have been my whole life engaged in their protection. I have . . . a duty to perform for them."[43] Concern for the slaves' religious life became, not an act of individual piety or altruism, but an essential ideological support of the slave system.

"I am unhappy about poor Charles," Susanna Warfield confided to her diary several days after the death of one of her slaves. In the last days of Charles's illness she had spoken to him of religion and had tried to effect a reconciliation between him and Sam, a slave with whom he had had a fight some time before. But Charles, stubborn unto death, set his face against her entreaties, refusing to pray aloud or show signs of penitence. "Oh!," his mistress lamented, ". . . I so deeply feel my neglect of the soul of poor Charles. . . . The Lord forgive me! How deep the responsibility of those who own Slaves."[44] Such a view of morality might appear self-serving, even hypocritical, to a detached observer. Be that as it may, slaveowners who could experience torment over matters of this kind might well feel their sense of themselves affronted by a plan to take away black people's rights of religious observance.

A slaveowner need not, moreover, have Susanna Warfield's sensitivity to religious duty—or her peculiar construction of its requirements—to feel his or her sense of self and of the world affronted by the free black proposals. Most free blacks in rural areas lived under the patronage of white citizens, often no doubt their own former owners or the former or present owners of members of their families. That was inevitable, since they would have to look to such whites for work. Futhermore, the terms of the law of 1832, which required manumitted slaves to leave the state, exempted those blacks who could get "respectable" white people to testify each year that they deserved to remain because of their "extraordinary good conduct and character." (Only once, apparently, was a sheriff ever called upon to remove a manumitted slave forcibly.)[45] These circumstances ensured continuing ties between whites and black people who had become free. In doing so, they guaranteed that a measure directed broadside against the free black population would strike many whites as oppressive of the "deserving" and "responsible" element among free black people. "[A]ny laws calculated to annoy or oppress the moral and industrious free people of color, or deprive them of religious priviliges," declared the Easton *Star,* "will be in contravention of the wishes of a very large majority of the citizens of Talbot."[46]

No one could have devised a satisfactory solution to the free black question. As long as neither of the contradictory elements—slaves or free blacks—could be eliminated, all efforts to banish the contradiction succeeded only in revealing another of its faces. Free blacks might be considered an evil in a society founded on black slavery, but undue harshness in suppressing them could undermine the very moral basis of slavery itself. And to the extent that free blacks inhabited the widening crevices of the slave system, hostility toward them in general was bound to have as its antithesis protection of them in particular. There was clearly no prospect for the wholesale return of free black people to slavery: the same causes that promoted the gradual erosion of slavery would militate against its reimposition by legislative fiat. Thus the paradoxes that slaveholders collectively deplored the increase of the free black population but individually got rid of their slaves, and that slaveholders and nonslaveholders alike condemned the free black population as a vice and an incubus, while resisting measures to remove it from the scene.

Free black people represented a contradiction nesting at the heart of Maryland's slave system that was incapable of resolution short of the overthrow of the system. This was not true everywhere. Where free blacks formed an intermediate group between white masters and black slaves, taking the place of an absent or inadequate white petite bourgeoisie—as in Jamaica for example—there was no contradiction in their presence alongside the slaves. On the contrary, they constituted a necessary prop of the slave system and could be used to advantage in maintaining control over the slaves. But Maryland's free black people were not a buffer group standing in for a white petite bourgeoisie. Instead they occupied the same social space as the slaves while eluding control by the methods employed with the slaves. In small enough numbers they posed a manageable, if ideologically troublesome, problem. But in large numbers, and under conditions that required slaveholding society to depend as much upon them as upon the slaves, they posed an unanswerable challenge both to the material and to the ideological basis of slave society.

Viewed in the light of hindsight, the ideological challenge had the more lasting ramifications. Marylanders were trying to reconcile two systems of labor discipline whose ideological preconditions stood in diametrical opposition. When Jacobs complained of the "perquisites" that black farmhands supposedly received, his point was not primarily that the extras were financially excessive, but that they were socially intolerable. What exercised him, at bottom, was not that free blacks might be in a position to demand horses and carriages and Saturdays off, but that they should be in a position to demand anything at all. Instinctively, he grasped the subversive implications of the wage relationship for a slave society. In purely formal terms, both parties to a wage contract enjoy equal standing. No sensible observer, needless to say, ought to confuse freedom of contract with equality in the context of a capitalist society. But in the context of a racially defined slave system, someone like Jacobs might well detect a family resemblance, especially when it came to free blacks' making bargains on their own behalf.

Governor Thomas Holliday Hicks must have detected the same resemblance, and felt a similar unease, judging by the way he presented the free black problem to the legislature in 1858. He asserted that the free blacks occasioned little trouble in Baltimore and in the more populous regions of the state, where they could find employment as domestics and laborers. It was in the lower counties on both sides of the Bay—that is, the slave counties—that they posed a special problem of vagrancy and crime.[47] In fact, the records of the state penitentiary up to 1858 (when the state began selling rather than imprisoning free black convicts) show that the bulk of black offenders were convicted in Baltimore and northern Maryland.[48] Hicks probably knew that. He pinpointed the source of his apprehensions when he referred to the "pernicious effects upon the worthier portion of their class, and upon the servile population" of the "notorious" vagrancy and crime of the free blacks. He probably did not mean to imply that free blacks in the slave counties were more vicious or criminal than their counterparts in northern Maryland, but rather that the social consequences of their vice and crime were likely to be more serious in the slave counties. Words like *vagrancy* and *idleness* should not be taken literally, of course. More serious than actual vagrancy would be the spectacle of a black worker holding out for a better deal or (more likely) refusing to commit himself on a regular basis at all, preferring to "eke out a capricious living by short jobs . . . with the pay in hand at once."

Was it purely a matter of race? Was it only when the free laborer was also black that he posed an ideological problem for slave society? On a superficial first glance, the answer might appear to be yes: surely even slaveholders must have come to terms with the concept of free labor when it involved white workers, since so many of the skilled or specialized jobs on the farm or plantation—those of the well-digger, the carpenter, the pump-maker, even the seamstress, for example—were done by whites.[49] Upon closer scrutiny, however, it was not in substance a question of race. Slaveholders had indeed grown accustomed to dealing with white artisans. But they were by no means reconciled to the prospect of a white agricultural proletariat. Indeed, the fear of just such a thing provided the most widely shared grounds for opposition to Jacobs's proposals. Better free blacks, the *Planter's Advocate* warned, than "a class of free white labor that would be hostile to slavery, would be entitled to vote, and might finally dictate terms to slavery itself." Jacobs disagreed with his critics, not about the undesirability of that result, but only about its likelihood.[50] Even after emancipation, when the acuteness of the labor shortage forced the state to active recruitment of immigrants, those charged with the task talked of recruiting immigrant farmers rather than immigrant laborers.[51]

The idea of a class of white laborers having neither land nor master, roving about and beyond anyone's control, held no more appeal than the specter of a ballooning free black population. The legislature was not indulging in whimsy when it attached its measures against peddlers, traveling showpeople, and fortune-tellers to the free black bills, supposedly as measures against abolitionism. It seems hardly likely that gypsies and vagrants played a major role in the abolition movement. The legislature associated the presence of these people with abolitionism, not because there was a demonstrable connection between the two, but because the mere presence of such a footloose, unattached population threatened slave society's sense of order almost as much as did abolitionism itself.

Free labor necessarily entailed a shifting population of "idlers"—at least, so they would appear to anyone confronting them from the ideological vantage point of slave society and its sense of order. If the availability and the terms of farm labor could not be secured by measures to rejuvenate slavery, they could be secured only by maintaining a population of free workers that would be surplus in all but peak periods of demand. The telltale signs of such a surplus population had already appeared in northern Maryland even before the crisis of 1857. An example is Uncle Ned, a free black man who earned his living by dipping water at a mineral spa. Other examples are the men who worked as hotel touts at the railroad station and the women who sold cakes by the roadside. The penitentiary lists include a number of city residents who gave their occupation as "farm laborer." Almost certainly such people found farm employment only at intervals, sustaining themselves by other means in between.[52] Slaveholders had no interest in inviting such a population to make its home in their rural strongholds.

Slaveholders faced a choice between equally pernicious alternatives. They must rest content with a class of free black workers whose "scarcity" enhanced their bargaining position to a socially, if not economically, unacceptable degree. Or they must open the door to an unattached population of redundant labor. The abundance of such a class would curb the pretensions of individual members, but only at the cost of recreating on a greatly expanded scale the social situation that already set slaveholders biting their nails when it appeared in the diminutive guise of a few scattered bands of gypsies and itinerant peddlers.

Most slaveholders had no heart for such a choice. They rejected the course of turning back toward slavery. And in doing so they were only being realistic, since that possibility had been long since foreclosed. But they dared not go forward, either, to the frightening world of free labor. Instead they tried to stall for time, going neither backward nor forward. Unfortunately for them, events would soon remove the alternative of staying in the same place.

CHAPTER FIVE

"The Devlish Nigger Difficulty": Slavery and the Civil War

Border-state politics have benefited from the same presumption of benignity that has given border-state slavery a better reputation than it deserves. Politicians and publicists in Maryland, Delaware, Kentucky, and Missouri did all they could to promote this flattering picture of themselves, and not a few historians and others have been taken in by it. A persistent quirk of American political writing—which equates "center" with "moderate" and attaches to both labels connotations of the reasonable, virtuous, and pacific—has beguiled a good many people into accepting the border states at their own valuation.[1] The border slave states were the ones that deplored sectional agitation and threats of disunion. They were the ones that struggled to the eleventh hour and beyond to avert war. And they were the ones that strove, once war had broken out, to define the issue in such a way as to leave room for restoration of "the Union as it was" once the fanatics of North and South had come to their senses. They were the tragic heroes of the war, the virtuous and innocent bystanders doomed to be swept up by the folly of those around them.

Some contemporaries saw the border states in a different light. Surveying the situation from abroad, Karl Marx referred to them as "ambiguous allies" of the Union. A number of Americans agreed. Frederick Douglass condemned the border states as a "mill-stone about the neck of the Government" and Wendell Phillips feared that *"in the vain effort to save Kentucky,* we [have] lost the Union."[2] Generals who had to deal with the border states, like Benjamin F. Butler and John C. Frémont, sometimes felt tempted to lay on heavier hands than their commander-in-chief was prepared to countenance. The commander-in-chief eventually came to the end of his own celebrated patience where the border states were concerned.

90

The border states made a career of occupying the middle ground. But the center is seldom moderate and the slaveholding center was never so. The position of the so-called moderates of Maryland, Missouri, and Kentucky depended upon both the vitality and the distinctness of North and South, and it assumed a perpetual stalemate between them. The center was thus parasitic upon an unstable balance between two polities and two social systems between whom, in the end, there could be no compromise. When the balance came unstuck beyond the capacity of the most resolute border-state mediator to wish the breach away with ambiguous formulas and unctuous words, the aura of moderation disappeared. Public officials in Maryland reacted with petulance when the federal government refused to overlook the geographic accident that placed Maryland between the nation's capital and the rest of the Union. Kentucky indulged in a contradiction known as "armed neutrality." Unionists in Missouri had to stage a coup d'état to maintain the loyalty of their state.[3]

When events obliterated the middle ground, the border states appeared at their worst. Denying the obvious at the start of the war, many of their citizens continued to deny the obvious at the end, when the bitterest diehard in the Confederacy had been obliged to yield. The period in between found them, as often as not, a carping and querulous body of obstructionists, forced willy-nilly to adhere to the Union and forever thereafter resentful that life could not go on quietly as before. Some of the border states continued in that attitude long after the war was over. In the 1870s Kentuckians were still litigating over the loss of their slaves, and Delaware could not bring itself to ratify the end of slavery until the twentieth century.[4] In Missouri and Maryland, on the other hand, there eventually arose political factions determined to put an abrupt end to the old order. These factions received—not always unhappily—the epithets "radical" and "fanatic" and have never found a place in the pantheon of border-state heroes. For it fell to them to cajole or coerce their fellow citizens into departing from the tradition of border-state centrism and choosing a side on the great question of the day.[5]

That question was slavery. Respectable and responsible opinion in the border states tried for a long time to deny it, to insist that disunion, not slavery, was the enemy. Determined to hold the border states in the Union, Abraham Lincoln did so for a time as well. Even after he had privately made up his mind to issue an emancipation proclamation, Lincoln continued to insist, for public consumption, that the war was over the Union and nothing more.[6] But the war's own logic quickly forced all concerned to admit that slavery was the question. In Maryland, as in the other border states, centrist slaveholders resisted that admission as long as they could, in a manner that was neither moderate nor pacific. When they eventually had to confront it face to face, they became as extremist and fire-eating as the most impassioned Confederate.

Two groups in Maryland made no detour through the middle ground but grasped the dynamics of the war immediately: secessionist slaveholders and slaves. Neither had any doubt, from the opening of hostilities, where the central issue lay. As the first federal troops made their way through Maryland en route to Washington in April 1861, slaves begged to be taken along. One who had already purchased his freedom regretted his haste. "If I had known you gun men was acoming," he told a soldier, "I'd a saved my money." Rumors of slave insurrection made their appearance with the first federal troops.[7] A number of slaveowners took the precaution of lodging their slaves in jail for the duration of the war, before leaving to join the Confederate army. Others tried to take their slaves with them into the Confederacy.[8] They knew from the outset what their fellows would soon learn: that the arrival of the federal army would inevitably incite the slaves to disobedience and escape. Slaves and secessionist masters developed remarkably similar analyses of the situation. There was no coincidence in this, for they had learned from each other. Slaves knew that the election of a Republican president portended the abolition of slavery—long before the Republican president himself knew it—because slaveholders had been saying so for years. Slaveholders knew what the commotion of a war over slavery would do to discipline among the slaves, and that the first breach of discipline would call forth another and then another, because over the years the slaves had given them practical lessons in the principle involved. Both groups thus understood from the start where the line must eventually be drawn. They differed only in standing on opposite sides of it.

A group more numerous than either slaves or secessionist slaveholders clung to a middle position. Union or disunion: that was the only issue as far as they were concerned. Governor Thomas H. Hicks stated their position as eloquently as such a morally attenuated position could be stated: "I care nothing for the Devlish Nigger difficulty, I desire to save the union, and will cooperate with the Administration in everything tending to that important result that is proper."[9] Denizens of this broad middle ground expressed dismay upon learning that South Carolina had "slipped her cable and gone adrift." A demonstration in Baltimore supporting secession represented, to them, "the laugh of the inebriate by the bed of death." Unionist meetings deplored sectional agitation, upholding "the Union *as it is*" and opposing calls for a special session of the ultra-Southern rights legislature. The Cecil *Whig* condemned those "men who . . . are moving heaven and earth, and . . . a warmer region than either, in order to bring about, as the best means of accomplishing their traitorous purposes, an Extra Session of that *patriotic* and *unpartizan* body, yclept the Legislature of Maryland, which did the State such excellent service in Annapolis last winter." Whistling in the dark, perhaps, to give itself courage, the *Whig* joined with the Baltimore *American* in belittling the opposition as "Ex. Speakers of Ex. Legislatures, Ex. Governors and ex. politicians."[10]

Contrary to the wishful thinking of unionists, ultra-Southern slaveholders initially held the advantage, not only over the slaves, but over the unionist center as well. Secessionist "ex. politicians" included in their ranks influential citizens whose adherence gave the Confederacy hope of carrying Maryland. Former governors Thomas G. Pratt and Enoch L. Lowe both contributed their authority to the Confederate cause. Pratt sent military intelligence to the Confederate army through his son-in-law and encouraged Southern forces to move into Maryland in April 1861. When the Confederates did invade Maryland in 1862, they fully expected Lowe to join them in their proclamation to the people of the state.[11] Ultra-Southern rights Democrats controlled the state legislature and had a hand-picked police board in Baltimore. With opinion volatile all over the state and especially in Baltimore, which was prone to mob violence, they might well stampede the state into secession.

Matters came to a boil on April 19, when a regiment of Massachusetts volunteers tried to pass through Baltimore on their way to defend Washington. A mob attacked, the soldiers opened fire, and in the ensuing riot four soldiers and at least a dozen civilians died, and many more were wounded. Though later denying that he had done so with traitorous intent, the chief of police telegraphed the secessionist state's attorney (and later Confederate general) Bradley T. Johnson at Frederick: "Streets red with Maryland blood. Send expresses over the mountains of Maryland and Virginia for the riflemen to come, without delay. Fresh hordes will be down on us to-morrow. We will fight them and whip them or die."[12]

That night, in order to prevent the passage of any more federal troops through Baltimore, the mayor and police commissioners ordered the "disabling" of several bridges belonging to the Philadelphia, Wilmington and Baltimore and the Northern Central railroads, insisting afterward that they acted under direct authority from Governor Hicks. Buoys were destroyed

in the harbor, apparently by the mayor's authority. The mayor issued a call
the following day for volunteers to defend the city, ordering them to report
to Colonel Isaac R. Trimble. Some fifteen thousand enrolled, many of
them—including Trimble himself—later joining the Confederate army.[13]
The police commissioners possessed themselves of a large quantity of arms
and ammunition, some of it the property of the federal government. Their
headquarters, Major General Nathaniel P. Banks reported afterward, "resembled a concealed arsenal," with arms "secreted in such places and with
such skill as to forbid the thought of their being held for just or lawful
purposes." Private individuals freely joined in the commotion. On April
20, General-in-Chief Winfield Scott received word that citizens had burned
bridges at several towns along the line where troops might pass, and on
April 23 the president of the Pennsylvania Central Railroad informed Secretary of War Simon Cameron that all the bridges of the Northern Central
had been destroyed.[14]

The uncertain state of affairs prompted Lincoln, to the great mortifi-
cation of the secretary of war, to withdraw troops headed for Baltimore and
reroute them by steamer to Annapolis. Governor Hicks pleaded against the
landing of troops anywhere in Maryland and urged Lincoln to offer a truce
to the Confederacy: "I respectfully suggest," he wrote the president, "that
Lord Lyons be requested to act as mediator between the contending parties
of our country." Hicks opposed secession, but he was a typical border-state
compromiser and he had weak nerves in an emergency. His public statements tried to embrace both Southern rights and Union, and he cringed
and swayed in response to the turmoil of the moment. Influential citizens
urged him to convene the legislature or call a state convention to consider
Maryland's position in the Union. John F. Dent of St. Mary's County
insisted that Maryland must "abandon her dumb, passive neutrality" and
begged Hicks "no longer to give aid and comfort (unintentional I must
believe) to the enemies of Southern rights and Institutions." Some zealots
made personal threats. B. Everett Smith warned Hicks that Teagle Townsend, state senator from Worcester County, had declared his intention "to
offer you personal violence upon first opportunity after his arrival in Annapolis." A less patrician version of the same promise came from a correspondent who signed himself Southern Rights: "Your destiny is fixed it is
resolved that if it takes 20 years if you life that long to be shot privately
for your being a damed black republican. . . . beneath the notice of a wolfe."
In the violent atmosphere following the riot, Hicks thought he had no
choice but to convene the legislature, a move he had been resisting for

months. Many people assumed that, once convened, the legislature would forthwith enact an ordinance of secession.[15]

Lincoln had no intention of permitting such a thing to happen. He conveyed blunt instructions to General Scott: "[W]atch and await [the legislature's] action, which, if it shall be to arm their people against the United States, [you are] to adopt the most prompt and efficient means to counteract, even if necessary to the bombardment of their cities." Scott passed the orders along to Brigadier General Benjamin F. Butler, who had been ordered to take possession of Annapolis with his brigade of Massachusetts volunteers.[16] Butler may have been an amateur general, but he was a professional politician who understood the use of power. He had no immediate interest in the question of slavery; but neither had he any truck with secessionism or any qualms about suppressing it with force. Hicks would soon have his backbone stiffened by a master.

In fact, Butler and Hicks had already made each other's acquaintance by the time Butler received formal orders to occupy Annapolis. Having politely turned aside Hicks's April 21 request that he take his men elsewhere, Butler improved the occasion to give Hicks a brief lecture on the principles of Union and national sovereignty. "I beg leave to call your excellency's attention," Butler wrote in his best schoolmasterly fashion, "to what I hope I may be pardoned for deeming an ill-advised designation of the men under my command. *They are not Northern troops; they are a part of the whole militia of the United States, obeying the call of the President.*"[17] Then, having established his brigade headquarters at the Naval Academy in Annapolis, Butler proceeded—perhaps with ironic intent—to offer his services to the nervous governor. "I have understood," he told Hicks, "that some apprehensions were entertained of an insurrection of the negro population of this neighborhood." Declaring that he wished to "convince all classes of persons that the forces under my command are not here in any way to interfere with, or countenance any interference with, the laws of the State," he requested the governor to announce publicly that his forces would "act immediately for the preservation and quietness of the peace of this community." The governor quickly declined the offer.[18]

Butler and the governor were not ready to quit for the day. Hicks next protested Butler's seizure of the Annapolis and Elk Ridge Railroad, declaring that he had summoned the General Assembly to meet on the 26th and that Butler's occupation of the railroad would prevent the members of the legislature from reaching Annapolis. Butler reminded Hicks that, at a meeting both attended, Butler had been advised not to land his troops because the railroad company had taken up the rails, which were private property. "It is difficult to see," Butler remarked, "how it could be that if my troops could not pass over the railroad one way, the members of the legislature could pass the other way." The railroad remained under military control and Scott ordered troops to secure the line between Annapolis and Washington. Hicks reconsidered his intention to convene the legislature in Annapolis. Instead he called the legislators to Frederick, in northern Maryland, explaining later that he had settled upon Frederick because of stronger unionist sentiment there.[19]

By then unionists had begun to stir in alarm. The riot in Baltimore so incensed a group of miners in Lonaconing (Allegany County) that they had formed a Union company within two days of hearing the news. A Union League appeared in Baltimore, followed by chapters around the state. Edwin E. Ewing's advent as editor of the Cecil *Whig* brought a new adamancy to the paper's unionism and made it a chief spokesman for the Union cause. Evoking "scenes of fire and blood . . . burning farm-houses, insulted women and butchered citizens" and warning Marylanders of "the manacles of the tyrant . . . clanking in your ears," the *Whig* called upon citizens to "fly to arms and repel the black and serried legions of South Carolina." It condemned Hicks's proposal that Maryland remain neutral and arraigned the governor himself as a "weak, vacillating old man, whose indecision and want of courage amount almost to criminality." Disunion, according to the *Whig,* ought to be called not secession but treason; and those within Maryland sympathetic to treason should be left to "dangle between heaven and earth, at the rope's end."[20]

The legislature met and adjourned without attempting or proposing the secession of the state, but it did nothing to calm the tempestuous atmosphere. Roundly criticizing the actions of the federal government, the legislators expressed sympathy for the South, opposition to war, and a desire that the federal government recognize the Confederacy. Unionists who had urged Hicks to call a special session regretted their advice. Alexander Randall of Annapolis had joined with several friends, including William Price, Morrison Harrison, and the author and elder statesman John Pendleton Kennedy in recommending a special session when he saw "Baltimore in the hands of an armed Mob—anarchy raging rampant." But his motive, he insisted, "had no connexion whatever with any idea that the Legislature itself could be so unwise as to attempt secession of the State." Randall excoriated the legislators for "publish[ing] for exterior circulation reports calculated to inflame the public mind against the Govt. of the U. States, and to encourage secession doctrines."[21]

The inflammatory resolutions of the legislature did not call forth immediate retribution. Of more pressing concern was continued sabotage along the rail and telegraph lines to Washington. Secretary of War Cameron lost patience with "our Maryland friends," and decided that the administration should not "temporize" with them any longer. General Scott watched the situation closely. He ordered General Butler, with one of his regiments, to establish a post at the Relay House, nine miles from Baltimore on the Patapsco River. Though he hoped it would prove unnecessary to open communication through Baltimore by force, he nonetheless laid plans for a movement on the city.[22]

Butler found enough to keep himself occupied in the meantime. Men, supplies, and munitions intended for the rebels passed freely in the vicinity, on their way to rendezvous at Point of Rocks and Harper's Ferry. Even ordinary passengers' luggage might contain caps or other items in short supply behind rebel lines. A squad of men from Baltimore seized a freight train and plundered the surrounding countryside before making their way to the Confederate army. Companies of volunteer troops headed for the Confederacy passed nearby in such numbers that Butler was not sure whether or not he ought to stop them. The question, he told General Scott, was "not of our ability so to do, but what we should do with them after we have detained them." Scott advised against attempting to stop the volunteers but encouraged Butler to detain all suspicious shipments and authorized him to arrest anyone committing an act of hostility to the government. Where the latter were concerned, Scott's adjutant informed Butler, "you are clothed with the same authority which has been conferred upon [the general-in-chief], and he has confidence in your discreet exercise of it."[23]

Scott had his confidence shaken a few days later. While he and the administration were still pondering what to do about Maryland, Butler rudely snatched the question from their hands. Acting upon what he supposed were orders from the War Department, Butler marched on Baltimore with some thousand men of his command. Under cover of rain and darkness, he ensconced his force on Federal Hill and on May 14 issued a proclamation that apparently surprised Scott and the Lincoln administration as much as it did the citizens of Baltimore. Announcing that "rebellious acts must cease," Butler forbade assemblages of armed bodies of men other than the police and the state militia and ordered an end to the manufacture and transportation of goods intended to support the rebellion. He instructed officers of the state militia to report to him so that he might "be able to know and distinguish the regularly commissioned and loyal troops of Maryland from armed bodies who may claim to be such." He banned all display of Confederate flags and emblems. His proclamation ended with a statement of confidence in the local citizenry that might easily be taken for a threat: "[T]he commanding general has brought to the city with him, of the many thousand troops in the immediate neighborhood, which might be at once concentrated here, scarcely more than an ordinary guard, and until it fails him, he will continue to rely upon that loyalty and patriotism of the citizens of Maryland which have never yet been found wanting to the Government in time of need."[24]

General Scott, who had no warning of the move, demanded to know what Butler thought he was doing. "Your hazardous occupation of Baltimore was made without my knowledge, and of course without my approbation. It is a God-send that it was without conflict of arms," Scott wrote Butler. Receiving no immediate reply, he telegraphed Butler in the middle of the night, ordering him to "answer my letter of last evening" and "issue no more proclamations."[25]

Butler's reply, when it arrived, must have caused a mixture of relief and consternation. He reported the rail connection between Annapolis and Washington complete and secure. He had, furthermore, accomplished a great deal in his brief occupation of Baltimore. He told of breaking up several factories producing supplies and munitions for the rebels, and of seizing caches of powder and arms apparently intended for "improper purposes." His report provided abundant evidence that an armed federal presence in Baltimore might be in order. Reporting that the mayor did not consider it his duty to try to prevent shipments to the Confederates, Butler recounted the theft by secessionists of "some four or five hundred stand of arms." This, he said, was "accomplished by the police under the direction of the board of police" after a false report of a riot decoyed the occupying troops. General Scott and the president might well count it a blessing, since the operation had gone without a hitch, that someone had at last done the dirty work. But Butler went on to explode a bombshell before his astonished superiors, revealing in matter-of-fact fashion that he had placed a member of the Maryland legislature, Ross Winans, under arrest on a charge of treason.[26]

Butler's actions infuriated a good many people in Maryland and irritated his superiors. Lincoln immediately ordered that Winans be released on parole. Butler found himself unceremoniously relieved as commander of the Department of Annapolis and demoted—as it seemed to him—to commander of a mere fort, Fortress Monroe, Virginia. Still, communications with the nation's capital had been secured and Baltimore had been, in his words, brought "to subjection and quiet" (or, as a correspondent of Governor Hicks put it, *"gagged by Lynn shoemakers"*). Butler's superiors enjoyed the singular luxury of benefiting by his action while clucking their tongues in disapproval. They did not cluck very hard. Butler's new command at Fortress Monroe promptly became the Department of Virginia, and Butler himself, promoted to major general, was soon establishing important precedents for the federal government's future handling of disloyal slaveholders.[27]

Butler's precedent endured in Maryland as well. Neither the occupation nor the proclamation was rescinded. General Scott directed Butler's successor in command of the Department of Annapolis, Major General George Cadwalader, to retain part of his force in Baltimore. Scott also gave Cadwalader written authority "to arrest persons under certain circumstances, and to hold them prisoners though they should be demanded by writs of habeas corpus." While enjoining delicacy in the use of the power thus conferred, Scott warned that "in times of civil strife, errors, if any, should be on the side of safety to the country." In June the War Department directed Cadwalader's successor, Major General Nathaniel P. Banks, to arrest the chief of police and the board of police commissioners of Baltimore.[28]

Still greater severity followed. The rout of the federal army at Bull Run, which enhanced the plausibility of the Confederacy, gave matters a new and sinister edge. "The *Union* is gon—there is no power in man to restore it," a lumber dealer in Charles County averred with some smugness in August. He soon discovered that the federal government retained a trump or two. "They have become very exacting—indeed oppressive on the river," he told his business associate; "day before yesterday they destroyed all my boats. . . . They assigned no reasons—other than general orders." Since the gentleman in question expected to conduct his business as a party outside the "quarrel," his boats may have been destroyed because they sometimes went the wrong way on the river. Later on, he himself was arrested several times on suspicion of disloyalty. In the fall the administration decided to round up secessionist members of the state legislature. Though all but a handful managed to elude the military dragnet, unionists expressed relief that the government had, as one put it, "manifest[ed] its strong arm in giving the quietus to our so-called Legislature." Governor Hicks, his unionist enthusiasm fully quickened, remarked with satisfaction that certain members of the legislature would soon "depart for healthy quarters." For the duration of the war the Lincoln administration kept a tight lid on Confederate sympathizers in Maryland. Private citizens, the press, even the pulpit felt the weight of federal authority.[29]

Through the determined (and, in the view of many people, heavy-handed) measures of the Lincoln administration, secessionists lost the upper hand in Maryland. In June the voters sent unionist representatives to Congress. In November, by an impressive majority to which the admonitory presence of the federal army no doubt contributed, the newly organized Union party elected a governor and swept most of the Southern sympathizers from the House of Delegates. In the state senate, only half of whose members came up for reelection, the Union party gained a slight plurality. Unionists who a few months earlier had doubted their ability to restrain the state from secession took heart. "I labored to have M^d roll up a majority, that would smother secessionism. We have given them a heavy dose," Hicks assured the secretary of war. Some unionists even felt confident enough to propose the release of arrested members of the legislature whose seats had been won by Union party candidates.[30]

The question of secession was effectively disposed of, but that of slavery was not. The slaves themselves placed it foremost, infuriating their owners and embarrassing the Lincoln administration's hopes of evading the subject. They subscribed to the philosophy later built into a defiant manifesto by an anonymous black soldier in Louisiana: "liberty is what we want and nothing Shorter. . . . we care nothing about the union. we heave been in it Slaves over two hundred And fifty years."[31] Consciously or unconsciously, the slaves acted on sound political instinct. With secession dead in Maryland, slaveowners could maneuver only on the middle ground, demanding respect for their property rights in recognition of their loyalty to the Union. That shifted the advantage to the slaves. With their owners dug in on the middle ground, the slaves quietly occupied high ground. From the outset they were engaged in a war with only one object: to secure their freedom. The property rights of loyal masters, the delicate balance of the border states, the union as it was: these abstractions meant nothing to them. From their position on the heights, they could wage a war of attrition, taking advantage of reinforcements where available and permitting the enemy to wear himself out in futile assaults from below.

As soon as federal troops appeared in the vicinity the slaves took the first step, absconding from their owners and seeking refuge with the army

they assumed had come to free them.[32] Sometimes they offered useful information about the activities and movements of the enemy. Sometimes they
pleaded that their owners were secessionists who meant to drive them into
rebel territory and force them to labor on behalf of the Confederacy. Usually,
without need or pretense of further justification, they simply indicated their
wish to be free. Soldiers took them in, found odd jobs for them to do, and
carried them along when the time came to move on. Charles B. Calvert, a
member of the United States House of Representatives, claimed that soldiers
made "tempting offers" to entice the slaves away and reported losing one
of his own in this manner. Troop movements during the Bull Run engagement in July covered the flight of a number of slaves. Slaveowners
complained, complaints made their way to Washington, and by the summer
of 1861—with Maryland not yet entirely pacified—the Lincoln administration found itself already face to face with the slavery question. Indeed,
the perversity of events placed the need to pacify the state at odds with the
effort to pacify slaveowners: the posting of garrisons at county seats around
the state to watch over the November election provided would-be fugitives
a wide choice of destinations.[33]

Lincoln wanted no trouble. Hoping that the whole matter could be
handled quietly, he recommended that owners be permitted to retrieve
slaves who had managed to slip away with the troops. His top commanders
in Maryland fully shared his concern and passed the word to their men that
fugitives must not be given refuge within federal lines. "Unless we abstain
from the reception or the capture of fugitive slaves," Major General John A.
Dix declared in August, "we shall expose ourselves to the imputation of
intermeddling with a matter entirely foreign to the great questions of political right and duty involved in the civil strife, which [has] been brought
upon us by disloyal and unscrupulous men. Our cause is a holy one, and
should be kept free from all taint." Dix cooperated assiduously with slaveholders and directed his subordinates to return fugitives to their owners.[34]

Giving orders was one thing, compelling soldiers to obey them another.
Many routinely ignored orders forbidding them to harbor fugitives. Sometimes they even instigated escapes. "[I]n Several instances," the commander
at Poolesville lamented, "Soldiers of this Corps have so far forgotten their
duty as to excite and encourage insubordination among the colored Servants
in the neighbourhood." Worse, the soldiers physically discouraged owners
who tried to reclaim their runaway property. Jeers and abusive epithets
frequently escalated to stone-throwing and the drawing of weapons. Passes
endorsed at the highest levels of the army could not protect slaveowners

from the hostility of soldiers determined not to surrender fugitives. Superior orders yielded to superior numbers when the two came into conflict.[35]

Slaveholders accustomed to respect and obedience found themselves stymied by an alliance of slaves with soldiers whose "master" repeatedly professed respect for slaveholders' property. The self-esteem of haughty owners suffered blow upon blow. Servants whose loyalty and devotion had been an article of faith deserted them, forcing upon them the distasteful chore of slave-catching. Having lowered themselves to the work, they confronted enlisted men who turned a knife in the wound. "Negro stealer, negro catcher!" the men of a Massachusetts regiment shouted at one Mr. Tucker of Anne Arundel County. Surrounding him menacingly, they taunted him that his slave was better than he was. Tucker left the camp disgusted and humiliated, without even looking for the runaway. Soldiers of a Pennsylvania regiment encamped in Charles County exhorted each other to "bayonet him, drum him out" when a constable, Richard F. Nelson, came to arrest a fugitive on behalf of a local slaveowner. Their colonel then told Nelson that "the best thing he could do would be to get on his horse & leave the Camp which this deponent did & did not get the negro." A. J. Smoot, another Charles County slaveholder, ignored a colonel's warning that some of his men were abolitionists. He soon learned the depth of the men's convictions. A large crowd followed him as soon as his errand became known, shouting "shoot him, bayonet him, kill him, pitch him out, the nigger Stealer the nigger driver." The soldiers emphasized their threats with "a few stones thrown at me which very soon became an allmost continued shower of stones a number of which struck me." The men hooted an officer who tried to defend the slaveholder, keeping up the barrage until Smoot left without his slave. When threats failed to discourage owners, or when scrupulous officers provided an armed escort, the men concealed the runaways, passing them from place to place until the search was called off.[36]

Officers could be even more provoking than enlisted men. They stood on their dignity and manifestly did not regard even the richest slaveholders as their social superiors. Instead, they treated slaveowners like any civilian Tom, Dick, or Harry, subjecting them to what for proud slaveholders must have been a mortifying routine. Adjutants—who might be quite junior officers but wielded the authority of their commanders—required owners to prove that they were who they said they were and owned the property they said they owned. The commander himself sometimes chose to be inconveniently officious in adhering to the letter of orders from above. If an order said "admit the following individuals" and the party seeking admittance included more than those named, he might direct the supernumeraries to remain outside the camp. A slaveholder reporting that witnesses had seen his servant with such-and-such a company might be given permission to search that company's quarters only. In obedience to an order from headquarters that he investigate to ascertain whether or not a given fugitive was with his regiment, a colonel might simply ask his officers and men if they had seen a fugitive answering to thus-and-such a name or this-or-that description, knowing full well that fugitives often changed their names and clothing in order to foil their masters. "Whatever name you say you was," an ex-fugitive recalled, "that was your name." When all else failed, the colonel could stall the owners indefinitely by perpetually writing to headquarters for further instructions.[37]

Some of the soldiers may have had no more in mind than to keep willing servants at hand. But for others it was a matter of principle. Colonel Henry S. Briggs, commander of a Massachusetts regiment, took direct issue with his brigade commander over an order that he "turn out from my camp any colored servant that may be claimed as a slave." After pointing out that his personal servant, brought with him from home, might well be claimed by a "pretended master," Briggs bluntly stated the limits of his willingness to abide by orders to hand over fugitives. "I shall neither give nor permit those in my command to give *aid* in the rendition of slaves beyond that required under due process of law. When such a requisition comes I shall then determine whether I will comply with the requirements of such a process or choose the penalty of a passive disobedience." Briggs had evidently left home with an abhorrence of slavery, and the regiment he commanded, as well as other Massachusetts regiments that served in Maryland, contained many who shared his views. Perhaps they agreed with Wendell Phillips that the blood of the Massachusetts volunteers who died in Baltimore consecrated the ground, making it "too sacred to be trodden by slaves."[38]

Even if they did not, they must still have been mindful of the press and public of Massachusetts and of abolitionist Governor John A. Andrew, watching from the sidelines to remind them of their duty. In December 1861 Governor Andrew made his position clear in a dispute that eventually brought him toe-to-toe with the new general-in-chief, Major General George B. McClellan. Governor Andrew received a letter from the field complaining that men of a Massachusetts volunteer regiment had been required to expel from camp, into the waiting hands of local slaveholders, some blacks who habitually came in selling cakes and other dainties. Andrew promptly protested to the secretary of war, declaring that "Massachusetts does not send her citizens forth to become the hunters of men." The secretary of war wrote to General Banks, suggesting that he "issue such directions . . . as may prevent similar complaints for the future, of injustice and oppression to negroes visiting the camps in the exercise of lawful occupations."

In the meantime, without waiting for a reply from the secretary, Andrew indirectly conveyed his displeasure to the officer who had given orders for the expulsion of the black people, one Captain Macy. That action annoyed Brigadier General Charles P. Stone, whose command included the regiment in question. Stone protested to McClellan this interference in the "interior discipline" of a regiment under his control, and McClellan told Andrew, in effect, to mind his own business. Andrew replied at characteristic length, and with his habitual eloquence, but McClellan had the last word. "I regret that you adhere to the opinion expressed [in your last letter]," he wrote Andrew. "I cannot yield mine in a matter of such consequence to the discipline of the army." Nevertheless, Andrew held the power, as he pointedly warned Macy, of commissioning and promoting officers in the Massachusetts volunteer regiments. His intermeddling, therefore, could not fail to accomplish exactly what he intended and what Stone and McClellan feared: to teach Massachusetts officers that they must answer to higher authority than their military superiors.[39]

Massachusetts soldiers were not the only troublemakers. Frequent allegations by slaveholders indicated that troops from Pennsylvania, New York, and Ohio resisted with equal obstinacy orders to exclude or surrender fugutives. Most of the men had no prior knowledge of slavery and little interest in it. They formed their impressions of slavery from what they saw in Maryland. What they saw turned some of them into abolitionists. Soldiers of a New York regiment became enraged when, before their eyes, slaveowners set about flogging runaways whom they had recaptured in the regimental camp. The soldiers forcibly released the slaves, thrashed the owners, and thenceforward refused entry to owners pursuing fugitive slaves. Men from the same regiment watched as a party of slaveholders near their camp fired a pistol at a fleeing slave. The slaveholders then entered the camp and showed the commanding officer an order from division headquarters authorizing them to search for fugitives. The soldiers grumbled and muttered "to so great an extent," their commanding officer reported, "that I almost feared for the safety of the slave owners." Only the opportune appearance of the brigade commander, who ordered the slaveowners out of camp, prevented a violent outburst.[40]

Slaveholders themselves often turned the soldiers against them by their arrogant airs and by their readiness to invoke connections in high places. In July 1861 a slaveholding family secured the special intervention of General Scott's chief of staff, charging that the soldiers of an Ohio brigade were concealing their slave. They succeeded only in annoying the officers against whom they had appealed to higher authority. In the process, they managed to offend the state pride of two Ohio regiments. Nothing brought officers and men into more stubborn agreement than any appearance of an aspersion cast upon their home states. Brigadier General Robert C. Schenck, who would eventually hold great power over political affairs in Maryland as commander of the Middle Department, did battle with both the slaveholders and the Headquarters of the Army on just that point. "The officers and men from these two regiments from Ohio are naturally somewhat excited and indignant at the imputation that they have been 'practicing on the abolition system of protecting runaway negroes,' " Schenck told his commander. One of Schenck's subordinates, Colonel Alexander McD. McCook, went so far as to say, "I do not believe Mrs. Noland has a negro in this camp and from the lying propensities of her sons I am now in doubt if she ever owned a negro." Clearly McCook's dignity and state pride, not his antislavery principles, had been offended; for later the same year, commanding a post in Kentucky, he himself proposed a policy of returning fugitives to their owners.[41]

The cumulative effect of many small defeats at the hands of fugitives and soldiers eventually showed up in the master's home. Knowing that escape was possible, slaves behaved with greater independence and—in their owners' eyes—insolence. Some slaves did not scruple to remind overbearing owners that the army was nearby to afford a haven if need be. A few got the delicious opportunity to show off after escaping. Joseph Ross escaped to a Union camp under an assumed identity. "And then his boss man arrived, and said, 'Your name isn't no Henry Washington, your name is Joseph Ross.' Papa jumped up there, 'You're a so and so liar, sir.' And they couldn't get him." One owner endured the vast indignity of reading a letter in which his slave spoke exultantly of his successful escape to federal lines. "i am now in Safety in the 14th Regiment of Brooklyn," John Boston wrote to his wife. "this day i can Adress you thank god as a free man. I had a little truble in giting away But as the lord led the Children of Isrel to the land of Canon So he led me to a land Whare fredom Will rain in spite of earth and hell." Boston gave his wife—who apparently remained a slave but of a different owner—precise instructions about how to write to him: "Direct your letter to the 14th Reigment New york State malitia Uptons Hill Virginea In Care of Mr Cranford Comary." He must have realized that these directions would become available to his owner in the likely event that the letter should fall into the wrong hands, as it evidently did. But John Boston took the occasion, while reassuring his wife, to display both his pride and his fearlessness by broadcasting his precise whereabouts and his intention to be free "in spite of earth and hell."[42]

Slaveholders who had the ear of state officials poured out their humiliation and anger and demanded relief. Governor Hicks recounted the slaveholder Tucker's tale of woe at great length to the secretary of war. While admitting that some people might find "amusement" in these episodes, Hicks expressed apprehension that the anger of loyal owners might undo all that unionists had managed to accomplish in the election of November 1861. The Devlish Nigger difficulty, which had no rightful place in the conflict, might overwhelm the real issue—Union—and drive slaveholders away from the federal government.[43] Hicks's equally verbose successor, Augustus W. Bradford, took up in turn the task of pleading the loyal slaveholders' case before the Lincoln administration.

Slaveholders had good reason for concern. The middle ground on which unionism and slavery fought as allies had begun to heave and shift. Rumblings in Congress and across the North heightened the slaveholders' anxiety to extract guarantees of their property rights from government officials. At first news of the fall of Fort Sumter, abolitionists had begun saying "I told you so" and demanding an end to slavery. In a speech at the Music Hall in Boston on April 21, Wendell Phillips quoted Jeremiah to a thunderously cheering audience: "Therefore thus saith the Lord: Ye have not hearkened unto me in proclaiming liberty every one to his brother, and every man to his neighbor: behold, I proclaim a liberty for you, saith the Lord, to the sword, to the pestilence, and to the famine." Phillips enjoined the Union to "Teach the world once for all, that North America belongs to the Stars and Stripes, and under them no man shall wear a chain."[44]

Less apocalyptic, and for that very reason more disturbing to slaveholders, were Congress's first tentative steps toward emancipation. Though restrained in wording and ambiguous in intent, they presaged trouble ahead. Early in July the House of Representatives declared it "no part of the duty

of the soldiers of the United States to capture and return fugitive slaves."
In August Congress passed the first confiscation act, declaring forfeited the
claims of owners who knowingly required or permitted their slaves to labor
on behalf of the rebellion. Slaveholders took comfort in the circumspect
language of the act, which stopped short of declaring confiscated slaves
free. Legal technicalities of this kind became a favorite refuge of border-
state slaveholders. But the ferment that produced the confiscation act could
not be contained by legalisms. Slaveholders had scarcely finished reassuring
themselves about the conservative intent of the act when Major General
John C. Frémont, in a proclamation to the people of Missouri at the end
of August, exceeded its provisions by declaring free (not just confiscated)
slaves whose *owners* took part in the rebellion (not just slaves who had
themselves been actively employed in aid of the rebellion).

Fervent unionists thought Frémont's action perfectly just. Former
Senator James H. Lane of Kansas, now "jayhawking" in western Missouri,
declared that "[c]onfiscation of slaves . . . should follow treason as the thunder peal follows the lightning flash." A unionist in Baltimore took occasion,
while complimenting Secretary of State William H. Seward upon the administration's strong measures against Maryland secessionists, to express
the hope that "the President will not have cause to break with General
Frémont." But border-state slaveholders naturally saw Frémont's action in
a different light. To their immense relief, Lincoln modified Frémont's order
and, after a decorous interval, removed him from command.[45] It was another
year before Congress was prepared to go as far as Frémont had, and longer
yet before the president felt comfortable doing so. But it was Frémont's
action, not Lincoln's repudiation, that foreshadowed the future.

Even before Lincoln's difficulty with Frémont, his administration had
started to rethink its position on slavery in the seceded states. Any such
reconsideration would necessarily have repercussions in the loyal slave
states. General Dix had reasoned out his policy of respect for slave property
in Maryland by the argument that the Union army occupying Confederate
Virginia "would not meddle with the slaves even of secessionists." Indeed,
Lincoln himself at first encouraged the army to let owners retrieve fugitives
from the occupied portion of Virginia near the District of Columbia. But,
in August, Secretary of War Cameron explicitly changed the rules. In a
letter instructing General Butler about the implications of the confiscation
act, Cameron extended the measure's laconic terms. The army, he decided,
should not return fugitives of either loyal or disloyal masters in seceded

states. That ruling ended Lincoln's policy of conciliating slaveowners in the Confederate states and brought closer the day when the status of fugitives in loyal states would in turn come up for reconsideration.[46]

The change in policy immediately complicated the lives of slaveowners in Maryland. Virginia fugitives, learning of the decision in their favor, made their way to any federal jurisdiction they could reach. Some headed for the District of Columbia, where the army, much in need of laborers, made arrangements to receive them. Some escaped to Union lines in occupied Virginia; and some sought refuge in posts and encampments in Maryland and on naval vessels in Maryland waters. The reception of Virginia slaves in Maryland gave Maryland slaves fresh encouragement to make their own getaways. Even with the best intentions, soldiers could not distinguish Maryland from Virginia slaves by appearance; and many soldiers had far from the best intentions where the fugitives' owners were concerned. By representing themselves as runaways from Virginia, Maryland fugitives could turn the government's policy to their advantage.[47]

Worse was yet to come for Maryland slaveowners, who, ironically enough, suffered a major defeat as a consequence of one of their more notable successes. Slaves living near the District of Columbia very early made it their destination once they had determined upon escape. Was it not, after all, the capital city of the liberating army? Cameron's ruling encouraged still more Virginia fugitives to run to the District. Maryland fugitives, who had less reason to expect a favorable reception, ran to the District as well. Local slaveholders achieved a temporary advantage over the runaways. In contrast to their tense relations with soldiers, slaveholders established a rapport with local officials of the District of Columbia, who willingly cooperted in the interception and arrest of runaway slaves. Jails in Washington and in neighboring Alexandria, Virginia, soon overflowed with fugitives who had been arrested by official and unofficial slave-catchers.

The slaveholders had succeeded too well. Baleful eyes watched them and powerful hands intervened. Secretary of State Seward declared that fugitives from Confederate service in Virginia were not to be molested. Their seizure as runaway slaves, he told General McClellan, "should be immediately followed by the military arrest of the parties making the seizure." Congress, too, watched the proceedings with displeasure. In December the House directed its standing committee on the District of Columbia to investigate a report that fifty-five people were being held in the government jail in Washington, not for crime, but on suspicion of being slaves. The House instructed the committee to ascertain the reputed owners of the detainees, to determine by what authority they were held, and to report "what legislation if any is necessary to relieve said persons from imprisonment and to prevent others from being similarly imprisoned." Meanwhile, the foul conditions prevailing in the jails attracted adverse publicity around the country and called forth petitions of protest. Some of the petitioners demanded that Congress do away with slavery in the one jurisdiction in which its constitutional authority to do so was unquestionable. The mood of Congress appeared favorable.[48]

The closing days of 1861 brought other signs of trouble for slaveholders. The House of Representatives planted two time bombs set to explode during the coming year. A resolution adopted on December 20 directed the Judiciary Committee to report a bill "so amending the fugitive slave law enacted in 1850 as to forbid the recapture or return of any fugitive from labor without satisfactory proof . . . that the claimant . . . is loyal to the Government." A second resolution, adopted on December 23, directed the Committee on Military Affairs to devise an additional article of war "whereby the officers in the military service of the United States shall be prohibited from using . . . the forces under their respective commands for the purpose of returning fugitives." As one of his last acts as secretary of war, Simon Cameron set a bomb with a longer fuse but an even greater destructive potential. After scandalizing official Washington and outraging polite opinion in the border states by publicly endorsing a Union officer's call for the arming of slaves, Cameron appended such a proposal to his annual report. Lincoln immediately forced him to withdraw the proposal and in January replaced him as secretary of war. But the idea, once publicly broached, could not be buried. A unionist in Washington County wrote to Senator Reverdy Johnson of his dismay: "I shudder at the thought that in an evil hour fanaticism may usurp the place of patriotism and compromise."[49]

The General Assembly looked on in an ill humor. On December 23 it adopted a joint resolution decrying "certain indications, at the seat of the General Government, of an interference with the institution of slavery." Condemning any such policy as "unwise and mischievous," the legislators insisted that the war must have no other object than "a restoration of the Union, just as it was when the rebellion broke out." In a resolution adopted on January 4, they warned that the state's loyalty was "untouched by any shade of servility" and declared that the people of Maryland would "ever regard with extreme jealousy all attempts, from whatever quarter, to make the present war . . . the means of interfering with the domestic institutions of the States." "[A]ll schemes, the object or tendency of which is, to excite insurrection among the slaves" they branded "illegal, and calculated . . . to produce results too horrible to contemplate." The panic-stricken tone of the legislators reflected the slaveholders' fear that action inimical to their interests lay in the offing.[50]

The apprehensions of slaveholders came to fruition in the new year. The first ill omen appeared when the president broached the question of voluntary compensated emancipation. Lincoln had been musing along those lines for some time. He made a feint in that direction in his annual message of December 1861, but obscured the proposal in roundabout language. In March, Lincoln decided to be direct, asking Congress to adopt a resolution supporting federal compensation for "any state which may adopt gradual abolishment of slavery." Although Lincoln intended his proposal as a conciliatory gesture, the border-state congressional delegations and their slaveholding constituents reacted as though he had struck them. They rejected the offer with righteous indignation, accusing the administration of betrayal for even opening the subject. Congress, however, was fast breaking itself of the habit of deferring to the border states. Within a month both houses had adopted the president's proposed resolution by generous margins.[51]

Hard on the heels of Lincoln's proposal for voluntary emancipation Congress delivered another blow. On March 13, it adopted the new article of war that the House had called for in December forbidding military personnel to return fugitive slaves. Word quickly spread through the ranks, with or without the assistance of official army channels.[52] Uniformed accomplices of runaway slaves could now call to their support the authority of the United States Congress. Brigadier General Abner Doubleday, in command of Defenses North of the Potomac, demonstrated what the new law might mean. "[A]ll negroes coming into the lines of any of the camps or forts under [this] command," Doubleday announced, "are to be treated as persons, and not as chattels. Under no circumstances has the commander of a Fort or camp the power of surrendering persons claimed as fugitive slaves. . . . The additional article of war recently passed by Congress positively prohibits this." He refused, furthermore, to embrace the alternative of preventing fugitives from entering the lines. "[T]hey bring much valuable information, which cannot be obtained from any other source. They are acquainted with all the roads, paths fords, and other natural features of the country, and they make excellent guides. They also Know and frequently, have exposed the haunts of secession spies and traitors, and the existance of reble organizations. They will not, therefore, be excluded." The provost marshal in Alexandria, Virginia, called upon the authority of the article of war to justify seizure of a Maryland fugitive whom civil authorities had restored to his owner. To countenance such a policy, a Maryland state senator indignantly told Lincoln, was "tantamount to issuing an Immancipation Proclamation in the Counties bordering on the Potomac River." He had a point. In the right hands, the March article of war could indeed be fashioned into an instrument of emancipation.[53]

Slaveowners had no time to rest after that setback. On April 16, Congress took the step they most feared, abolishing slavery in the District of Columbia. Owners were to receive compensation; but that did not make the measure palatable to Maryland masters. Compensation might mollify some slaveholders in the District, particularly those who devised fraudulent means of collecting more money than they were entitled to. But their counterparts in Maryland foresaw nothing but trouble. Mere agitation of the question, the legislature had unanimously declared in February, would "disturb the relation of master and slave" within Maryland. The actual carrying into effect of such a plan would "strike a serious blow at the interest of the people of Maryland and impress them with the belief that the Government of the United States have not a due regard for their rights, institutions and feelings."[54]

Maryland slaveowners and their representatives were correct to expect the worst. The abolition of slavery in the District of Columbia gave new allure to an escape route with which many slaves were already familiar. Many an ex-fugitive later reported having left Maryland for the District during or after the spring of 1862. Families packed up such of their possessions as could be compactly assembled and departed, sometimes appropriating means of transportation from their owners. Large groups banded together and headed for the District in force. On a Saturday night in June, thirty-seven slaves took abrupt and unceremonious leave of one W. H. Mitchell in Nanjemoy District, Charles County: "old and young, hale and infirm, packed off bag and baggage." As important as providing an escape route for slaves was the fact that the abolition of slavery in the District gave free blacks new leverage to extricate themselves from bondage to the slave system. Many blacks who already had their freedom remained dependent upon slaveowners, sometimes because their relatives remained in slavery and sometimes because slaveowners provided them employment and a place to live. With both freedom and government labor available in the District, they packed up their enslaved relatives and their movable property and declared independence.[55]

Slaveholders mobilized every resource to keep their slaves at home, and their resources were considerable. A Union army infiltrator learned of a meeting of some fifty slaveowners at Annie's Bridge, near Annapolis. The participants discussed ways of preventing their slaves from escaping, "avowing at the same time that no aid should be given to prevent the escape of negroes belonging to persons professing Union Sentiments." Local constables and private patrols kept an eye on the roads leading to the District. They stopped any black persons they saw, whether slave or free, seized items of property that caught their fancy, and returned the slaves to bondage. Some masters secured the assistance of professional slave-catchers and local police in the District to kidnap fugitives who had reached the city. A number of resourceful owners, deciding apparently that an ounce of prevention was worth a pound of cure, put their slaves in jail upon suspicion that they might try to escape. Public jails and private slave pens did a brisk business, what with District of Columbia masters driving their slaves to Maryland to evade the emancipation act, Maryland secessionists interning their slaves for safekeeping, and loyal Maryland owners deciding that it was only prudent to keep their property under wraps until the commotion died down.[56]

Nevertheless, for all their resources, slaveholders were engaged in a losing game. Even before the District bill had become law, the Baltimore *American* warned owners to cut losses and accept compensated emancipation. "Our slaves are walking off . . . every day. . . . The slightest coercion to compel moderate labor, and they are seized with a desire to walk to a free State." The government, which needed laborers, promptly set up makeshift facilities to receive fugitives. "Contraband" camps, into which fugitives might disappear forever from the purview of their owners, sprang up all around the District. Fugitives who could not make good an escape to Washington could still seek refuge at posts within Maryland, where Union soldiers now felt they had virtual permission to shelter runaways. Some commanders, it is true, interpreted the new article of war to mean that they might let slaveholders take their property, so long as they did not help them do so. But slaveholders availing themselves of invitations to take their slaves if they could find them increasingly gave up the attempt after sampling the temper of the soldiers. State legislator John H. Bayne, while indicating to Lincoln his "hearty concurrence" with the plan for compensated emancipation, complained that "before the adoption of that scheme . . . the slaves will all have escaped from the limits of Maryland."[57]

Delegations of angry slaveholders flattened a path to Washington, seeking an audience with anyone who would listen to their complaints. At first officials received them politely. General McClellan was gracious and conciliatory, passing their grievances along to the new secretary of war, his good friend Edwin M. Stanton. At least two such delegations spoke with Lincoln and obtained his assurance that the administration took their concerns seriously. But Lincoln could do no more than alert the War Department. The War Department, in turn, could do nothing but endorse correspondence back and forth and respectfully forward this and that complaint for the report of the brigadier or major general commanding. Eventually the War Department tired of the game. Congressman Calvert and a delegation from the Maryland legislature received blunt reminders that the secretary of war had more important duties than protecting the property of Maryland slaveowners. In May, Governor Bradford inquired about rumors that marshals in the District of Columbia had instructions not to issue warrants for the arrest of Maryland fugitives. He received a heavily ironic reply from Attorney General Edward Bates. "In these distempered times," Bates told the governor, "I am not at all surprised to hear that slaves in the border States are using all available means to escape into free territory." But he supposed it "very probable" that he would know if his own office had given any such instructions, and he had no knowledge of it. He concluded that the rumor must be a "fiction started by some evil-disposed person to stir up bad feeling and to frighten the timid and credulous." The days of conducting the war to the specifications of border-state slaveowners were fast playing out.[58]

As the cost of indecisive war, in human lives and physical resources, grew without apparent limits, the inexorable logic of events drew the army, the administration, and Congress into positions ever more unfavorable to slavery. In May 1862 Lincoln once again suffered embarrassment at the hands of one of his generals. Ironically, the new offender was the man with whom he had replaced General Frémont in Missouri. Now commanding the Department of the South, which included Georgia, South Carolina, and Florida, Major General David Hunter took an even stronger position than Frémont had. He did not stop with the slaves of rebels. Asserting that "[s]lavery and martial law in a free country are altogether incompatible," Hunter issued a proclamation abolishing slavery in his department. With his eye still, as ever, on the border states, Lincoln unceremoniously overruled Hunter. But this was no simple replay of the Frémont episode. Playing upon events as a musician plays upon an instrument, Lincoln turned Hunter's *démarche* into a subtle weapon for coercing the border states. In his proclamation revoking Hunter's proclamation, he took occasion to recall his March proposal for compensated emancipation and to plead for its acceptance. "This proposal makes common cause for a common object, casting no reproaches upon any," he insisted. "It acts not the Pharisee. The change it contemplates would come gently as the dews of heaven, not rending or wrecking anything. Will you not embrace it?"

Maryland would not. But the unionist press spoke of emancipation with more and more open approval, and a convention of Baltimore unionists late in May warned their fellow citizens that the time had come to act. Lincoln adverted to Hunter's action again at a meeting in July with the border-state congressional delegations. Though he had repudiated Hunter's proclamation, he told them, "[t]he pressure in this direction is still upon me, and is increasing." He gave them at that meeting a warning they would have done well to heed: "If the war continues long . . . [slavery] in your States will be extinguished by mere friction and abrasion. . . . It will be gone, and you will have nothing valuable in lieu of it." Lincoln knew, if slaveholders did not, that time was running out for them.[59]

Every day brought evidence of the "friction and abrasion" of which Lincoln spoke. In Union-held territory within the Confederate states, former Secretary of War Cameron's suggestion about arming slaves began to yield practical consequences. Acting broadly under guidelines that Cameron had given his predecessor, Hunter organized a regiment of slaves in his department. Word of this action caused a stir in Washington. Upon the motion of Charles A. Wickliffe of Kentucky, the House of Representatives demanded to know who had given Hunter authority to enlist fugitive slaves. Secretary of War Stanton, who had a talent Cameron lacked for keeping his mouth shut at strategic moments, let Hunter speak for himself. In an elaborately sardonic letter that Stanton passed on to the House, Hunter denied that he was enlisting fugitive slaves; rather, he was trying to bring to heel their masters, who were "fugitive rebels." "So far," he wrote, "are the loyal persons composing this regiment from seeking to avoid the presence of their late owners that they are now one and all working with remarkable industry to place themselves in a position to go in full and effective pursuit of their fugacious and traitorous proprietors." Rather than either directly sustain or directly repudiate Hunter, the War Department let his black regiment disintegrate for lack of pay or equipment. But within a short time a new regiment of slaves was under training in South Carolina with the department's full sanction. An effort similar to Hunter's by Brigadier General John W. Phelps in Louisiana also came to grief; but there, too, events quickly overwhelmed the cautious policy of Phelps's superiors.[60]

By midsummer Congress had decided upon important new steps. The militia act, adopted on July 17, specifically authorized the enlistment of "persons of African descent" for "any military or naval service for which they may be found competent." It declared free any such soldiers, and their mothers, wives, and children, whose owners had given aid and comfort to the rebellion. It would be another year before the full impact of that shift in policy struck home in Maryland, though an occasional bold spirit was ready to take it up. "The Administration has been fooling with Border State politicians and traitor apologists, and they have . . . kept it . . . under cow. . . . Let the rose-water policy be at once discarded, and the common sense plan—the rebel plan— . . . adopted. . . . Fight the devil with fire and the rebels with their own negroes."[61]

Another step taken on the same day as the militia act had immediate consequences. Despite Lincoln's grave reservations, Congress passed another confiscation act, much more sweeping than the first. The new law included a cumbersome, and therefore little-used, mechanism for confiscating the property of people in the rebellious states. But its more significant provisions, adopting a position close to that Frémont had taken a year earlier, declared "forever free of their servitude" slaves of persons who supported the rebellion. The previous December's House resolution in regard to fugitive slaves was incorporated in the act. Thenceforward, none but a loyal owner could recover slaves escaping across state lines; and military personnel were forbidden to pass upon the status of slaves or the claims of owners. In addition the act authorized the president to "employ as many persons of African descent as he may deem necessary . . . for the suppression of this rebellion . . . in such manner as he may judge best for the public welfare." Lincoln signed the measure reluctantly, after Congress passed an "explanatory" joint resolution softening the provisions about confiscation of property.[62]

The second confiscation act spelled the end of any coherent policy to safeguard the slave property of loyal owners in the border states. The administration might still pay lip service to loyal slaveholders' rights and generals might still issue orders to keep fugitives outside the lines. But the slaves, taking advantage of every favorable circumstance, had their owners on the defensive by the summer of 1862. Slaves from Maryland and Virginia mingled behind federal lines in both jurisdictions and in the District of Columbia. Whatever they needed to know of the complicated rules they quickly mastered. Almost any fugitive, if subjected to skeptical questioning, knew enough to assert that he had escaped across the state line from a disloyal master. A post commander at Point Lookout in St. Mary's County threw up his hands early in September 1862. "Contrabands are continually crossing over from the Eastern shore of va., and coming in from Md., all getting within our lines, by landing on the beech, until the number is greater than we know what to do with," he wrote to his brigade commander. "Those already here claim that their masters are disloyal: but there may be some, whose masters are loyal, what shall I do with them?" Observing affairs from Havre de Grace, J. Z. Spear wrote to his wife: "It now appears to many that the only way to put down the rebellion is to completely destroy Slavery." That step, he remarked, would kill the goose that laid the golden eggs. Slaveholders groused and grumbled, but even officials who wished to help them could do very little.[63]

The sour mood prevailing in the border states encouraged the Confederates to see what advantage they might extract from the situation. Widespread disaffection with the government's war policies was no secret. Might it touch off an uprising against the federal government if Confederate forces should launch an invasion? In late summer 1862, the Confederates gambled on that possibility in two border states. Confederate Generals Braxton Bragg and E. Kirby Smith took the war into Kentucky, tarrying long enough to give color to a secessionist state government and coming within an ace of taking Louisville before Major General Don Carlos Buell forced their withdrawal. General Robert E. Lee himself directed the invasion of Maryland. After frustrating General McClellan's peninsular campaign in Virginia and humiliating the federal army at the second Battle of Bull Run, Lee decided to take the war onto the enemy's home ground. "Stonewall (or as some say) Stonefence Jackson has not made his appearance amongst us yet," J. Z. Spear wrote to his wife on September 7. "There has been rumored for several days that an army of from 20,000 to 40,000. . . . rebbels had croosed the Potomac, and were in the upper part of this state." Spear doubted it "as we have a large army gone up the Potomac." He was right about the federal army but wrong about the rebels. On September 4 Confederate forces began crossing the Potomac and on September 7 Lee arrived in Frederick.[64]

Lee hoped that the federal government's guilty conscience would prove to be the ally of the Confederate army, keeping the Union army out of Confederate territory if not actually aiding the rebels' advance into the Union. As he later explained, "Military success might afford us an opportunity to aid the citizens of Maryland in any efforts they might . . . make to recover their liberties. . . . [W]e expected to derive more assistance . . . from the just fears of the Washington Government, than from any active demonstration on the part of the people, unless success should enable us to give them assurance of continued protection." The federals did indeed snap to attention. Lee succeeded in dragging them where he wanted them: out of Virginia, defending their capital with their backs against the wall. But he got no help from the desired fifth column. The country through which the Confederates marched was strongly pro-Union. Most residents of Frederick regarded not Lee but the Union army that ousted him as their liberator.[65]

Even rebel-sympathizing slaveholders for the most part held themselves aloof. Prospective adherents from the southern counties, where secessionist sympathy was strongest, would have had to pass through McClellan's army in order to join Lee's. In any event they stood to lose more than they would gain should the Confederates carry the day. To join the rebellion would be to sacrifice their remaining leverage with the federal government; and their property, which would become subject to confiscation, lay within easy reach of federal authority. Thus, few Marylanders heeded the call of Confederate Colonel Bradley T. Johnson to "rise at once in arms, and strike for liberty and right." Sympathizers who had not already fled to the Confederacy kept their heads well down and the rebels failed to recruit the additional division for which some had hoped. The Maryland campaign ended in stalemate. After the sanguinary battle near Antietam Creek on September 17, the Confederates withdrew in disappointment. "The Maryland pear," an interested observer in Georgia told his son, "is not ripe yet."[66]

As they were simultaneously doing in Kentucky, the Confederates had overbid their hand. Neither state's inhabitants rose to welcome the "liberators." Those who might have been expected to do so suffered in consequence of the abortive invasions. By placing federal lines within reach of still more runaways, the maneuvering of armies exacerbated the fugitive problem. Worse, the Confederates' withdrawal from Maryland after Antietam gave Lincoln the occasion he had been looking for to change the political terms of the conflict. On September 22 he issued a preliminary Emancipation Proclamation, placing his official imprimatur upon the conclusion the slaves had reached at the beginning: that slavery lay at the root of the rebellion. The president's proclamation enjoined the armed forces to "observe, obey, and enforce" the additional article of war and the emancipation provisions of the second confiscation act. It announced his intention to issue a final proclamation on 1 January 1863 freeing all slaves in areas still in rebellion. And in Maryland it prepared the ground for the appearance of a political movement dedicated to the abolition of slavery.[67]

Neither the preliminary proclamation nor the final one on January 1 embraced Maryland. But to the slaves, who cared nothing for the reasons of state that exempted their owners from the edict of freedom, that hardly mattered. Wendell Phillips dismissed the exemptions with the remark: "[Lincoln] is only stopping on the edge of Niagara, to pick up and save a few chips. He and they will go over together." Slaves in Maryland proved his point. They paid no more attention to the special status their owners continued to enjoy than they had paid to orders forbidding them within federal lines. Soldiers already inclined to lend them assistance saw little reason, now that the Union army was officially an army of liberation in the Confederacy, to stand on technicalities in Maryland. The Cecil *Whig* even dared—though with the usual racist camouflage—to ridicule its fellow citizens' fear of openly confronting the question of emancipation. Insisting that slavery had not much longer to live in the border states, the *Whig* observed: "There is nothing the American people seem to fear so much as a nigger. They would . . . as leave have the devil quartered upon them as to give a minion of Jeff Davis an opportunity of reporting them an abolitionist."[68]

With the moral, if not the legal, authority of the president now behind them, the slaves carried on with their own version of gradual emancipation. Theirs, unlike the one Lincoln had commended to their owners, did not "come gently as the dews of heaven, not rending or wrecking anything." It came at heavy cost, dispersing families, interrupting friendships, scattering belongings, and throwing vulnerable fugitives upon the uncertain mercy and inscrutable intentions of a busy army. The slow, inexorable loosening of the bonds of servitude did not soften the painful choices runaways had to make or temper the rigors of the attempt to flee; nor did it abolish the risks attendant upon failure. Successful escape carried its own sadness, an overtone clearly audible through the triumphant words of those who made it to freedom. Delivered from bondage, fugitives might spend months, years, even a lifetime in ignorance of the fate of those left behind. "I am With a very nice man and have All that hart Can Wish," John Boston told his wife. "But My Dear I Cant expreas my grate desire that i Have to See you. i trust the time Will Come When We Shal meet again. And if We dont met on earth We Will Meet in heven Whare Jesas ranes. . . . Kiss Daniel For me. Give my love to Father and Mother."[69]

Risks in harrowing abundance dogged every stage of an escape to freedom: flight was not something for everyone to attempt. Vigorous young men and women might freely take their chances with patrols, exposure, and the sheer physical punishment of what might be a very long trip on foot; old people and young children generally could not. Fugitives therefore had to weigh the risk of trying to take along dependent family members against the danger of leaving them behind to bear the brunt of reprisals. That somber calculation discouraged a good many. Owners well knew how to turn to their own advantage the slaves' concern for their families. A favored tactic was to place children beyond the control of wayward parents. In later years, many freedmen sought help from the government in reclaiming children they had been obliged to leave behind when they escaped. "If their families could be cared for or taken with them," an army officer told his superiors, "the whole slave population of Maryland would make its exodus to Washington." Sometimes the most mobile members of the family went ahead to prepare the way, then returned to escort the rest to freedom. That could be a hazardous affair and frequently ended in the jailing of all concerned. Two fugitives working for the government in Washington landed not only themselves in jail, but also two white coworkers whom they had hired to fetch their families from Piscataway, in Prince George's County. All four ended up in a Charles County jail, handcuffed together and chained to the floor. One free black man got caught attempting to take his slave wife to Delaware during the spring of 1863. He spent the next five years in the penitentiary.[70]

The middle ground held little moderation when masters caught up with absconding slaves. A mother and daughter who had fled to Washington were arrested as fugitives and returned to their owners in Piscataway. The owners tied them up in a barn and whipped them, first taking the precaution of tying their clothes over their heads "to keep their screams from disturbing the neighborhood." Then they lodged the women, the younger of whom was pregnant, in jail at Upper Marlboro. The younger woman's nine-month-old child was taken from her and died soon after, and the jailors refused to make any provision for the birth of her baby. Eight men confined in a stinking back room of the Upper Marlboro jail had been "chained to one large staple in the centre of the room, by both legs . . . each manacle had been put on hot and rivetted down with a hammer and anvil." Most had been jailed for trying to escape or helping others do so, but one man had been imprisoned for two years "because his master thought he would run away if he had a chance." A fugitive at whom a group of slaveholders "discharged two pistol shots . . . with an evident intention of taking his life" probably escaped through the interposition of soldiers who witnessed the episode. Jack Scroggins was less fortunate: his master overtook him trying to reach federal lines and beat him to death.[71]

Despite all obstacles thrown in their way, slaves contrived ways to chip away at their bondage, with free blacks often assisting them in their righteous whittling. "Borrowing" horses and carts from their owners, paddling their way to naval vessels patroling the rivers, playing Maryland against Virginia and both against the District of Columbia, they let everyone know that there would be no relief from the fugitive problem. Governor Bradford, who generally exerted himself on behalf of wealthy slaveowners, announced the limits of his power in the matter in January 1863. In response to a slaveowner's request that he use the state militia to recover slaves escaping to the military hospital at Point Lookout, Bradford gave a characteristically verbose but uncharacteristically pointed response. He was not, he said, "inclined to a course that to many might appear not less ridiculous than impracticable, of calling upon the militia of the State to compel the army of the nation, engaged in this war for national salvation, to disregard the laws established for its government, and abide by those prescribed by our Code." For their part, commanders seeking to hold the army to the laws established for its government foundered on a hopeless tangle of rules, any one of which might be confounded by the next fugitive to appear.[72]

Brigadier General Henry H. Lockwood, commanding a brigade near Point Lookout, attempted to sort the situation out in the spring of 1863. Governor Bradford had asked Lockwood to surrender as fugitives from justice some slaves who escaped before the local sheriff could sell them to discharge their owners' indebtedness. Though Lockwood's definition of fugitives from justice was broad—apparently embracing a runaway who "stole" his owner's cart in order to escape—he refused the governor's request in this instance. The slaves in question, he argued, were fugitives not from justice but from service or labor, and thus protected from surrender by the 1862 article of war. He proposed to place them outside his lines, where they would once again fall within civil jurisdiction.[73]

In April, Lockwood composed a circular embracing his understanding of the army's fugitive policy, then submitted the circular for approval to Major General Robert C. Schenck, who had assumed command of the Middle Department. Each positive statement in the circular had a matching contradiction and each instruction, an exception broad enough to invalidate the rule. Soldiers were not to interfere with the slave population "except for certain specific purposes hereinafter named." Runaways should not be admitted into military camps unless they offered information, in which case they must be rewarded and protected. Slaves entering the camp clandestinely must be put out "but in no case *delivered*—either *directly* or *indirectly*— to their Masters, Nor should they be placed without the lines, when their masters or others seeking them are in the Neighborhood of the Camps." All fugitives from the western shore of the Potomac (that is, from Virginia) must be received and protected. Quartermasters and other officers were "cautioned not to employ negroes in the Public Service unless they be free or refugees from the Western Shore"; but any black person so employed must be thereafter considered free. Intended to clarify matters for officers and men of the brigade, Lockwood's circular only demonstrated that rules and regulations could not contain the movement that the fugitives had set in train. In June the sheriff of Prince George's County informed Governor Bradford helplessly that slaves were leaving the county in large crowds and resisting recapture with armed force, while authorities in the District of Columbia arrested and imprisoned members of the posses he called out to stop them. Whether or not slaveholders were yet ready to admit it, Wendell Phillips's chip had indeed gone over the falls.[74]

Whatever may have been the view of most slaveholders, a growing number of politicians—styling themselves Unconditional Unionists—could see where events were tending. So convinced were they of the inevitability of emancipation that they staked their political careers and the future of the Union party upon it. Early in 1863 two members of Maryland's congressional delegation broke ranks with their colleagues on the question of compensated emancipation: former Governor Francis Thomas, representing the northwestern counties, and Cornelius L. L. Leary, representing part of Baltimore City and County. A Union League rally in Baltimore observing the second anniversary of the riot of April 1861 called upon the state to avail itself of the government's offer of compensation, asked Congress to write the Emancipation Proclamation into law, and advocated the enlistment of black soldiers.[75]

That proved to be only the curtain raiser. The emergence of an emancipation party would give Lincoln a political handle by which to hold onto Maryland, both for his own reelection and for the successful conduct of the war. Having laid the foundation by issuing the Emancipation Proclamation, his administration had every reason to encourage and nurture the movement, using both federal patronage and the long arm of the military. He used both. In fact the enrollment act of March 1863, which replaced the state-controlled draft with a presidentially appointed board of enrollment for each congressional district, enabled him to use both simultaneously. Under the March law the president appointed a provost marshal for each district. Each provost marshal appointed deputies, who in turn appointed assistants. The new arrangement readily became a system of patronage allowing the administration—through the Provost Marshal General—to penetrate deeply into the state electoral system. It proved a boon to the Unconditional Unionist faction in Maryland.[76]

f   General Schenck, commanding the Middle Department, did not need to be told to exert his authority on behalf of the Unconditional faction of the Union party. Taking over in December 1862, he declared that there could be "no middle-ground" for true patriots and, in a speech at the Union league rally in April 1863, suggested that those pretending to strike a middle position would do better to join the rebellion openly rather than "sneak about and crawl upon the ground, leaving a slimy path wherever [they] go, and biting the heels of patriotic men." Before relinquishing command in December 1863 to take a seat in Congress, Schenck had thrown conservatives into a frenzy. If he recalled the episode during the first summer of the war when a Maryland slaveholder went over his head to the Headquarters of the Army, he must have felt a smug satisfaction at the reversal that had since taken place.[77]

The emancipationist faction of the Union party took courage. With Henry Winter Davis as leader, men like Judge Hugh Lennox Bond, Archibald Stirling, and Henry Stockbridge at the points, and the Cecil *Whig* providing spirited editorial support, they set out to take control of the Union party. Compensation gradually dropped out of their plans as they agitated for a state constitutional convention to abolish slavery. Like the slaves, they now commanded the heights. Within a short time, those below would have to either join them or surrender the ground.

Anyone who had not already grasped the alternatives had the lesson drilled into him during the summer of 1863. By then the Lincoln administration was well embarked upon the enlistment of black men within the Confederacy and in the Northern states. The border states still enjoyed a privileged status, but it could not last much longer. Some 21,000 free black and 77,000 slave men of military age lived in the border states. Maryland alone had over 31,000, many of whom, as fugitives inside Union lines, had disposed themselves within easy reach of federal recruiters. Commanders seeking to turn the flood of runaways to military advantage and Unconditional Unionists frankly hoping to speed slavery to its death joined forces to urge that the War Department begin recruiting black men in Maryland. Following the time-honored practice of camouflaging a bold stand with a protective covering of abusive racial rhetoric, the Cecil *Whig* declared: "[A] negro, or any other animal that can handle a gun, is plenty good enough to shoot the fiends" engaged in the rebellion.[78]

In the case of General Schenck, military and political aims coincided in a single individual. An outspoken partisan of the Unconditional Unionists, Schenck also knew from direct experience how many eligible and willing black hands waited in readiness to join the military struggle. He had assembled four thousand of them to work on fortifications in Baltimore as the Confederates began the invasion that ended at Gettysburg, and he was loath to discharge these men when their work was complete. By dint of much nagging, Schenck secured the War Department's permission to raise a black regiment. Colonel William Birney, son of a prominent abolitionist, was assigned to Schenck to take charge of recruiting. Both Schenck and Birney knew, and others were soon to find, that recruitment of black men meant the end of slavery in Maryland.[79]

The War Department sought to postpone the inevitable by restricting enlistment to free black men. However well-intentioned, the effort backfired immediately. It was bound to fail, for it left out of account the intricate and precarious balance upon which slavery in Maryland depended: that between slaveholders and nonslaveholders, between large slaveholders and small slaveholders, between free blacks and slaves. By disturbing one element, the enlistment of free blacks upset the others, leaving no one satisfied.

Latent tension between slaveholders and nonslaveholders, which had risen to the surface over the Jacobs committee's proposals in 1860, boiled up again over the enlistment of free blacks. To those who did not own slaves but depended upon free black labor, the exemption of slaves looked like a scheme to rescue slaveholders at their expense. With free black men removed, slaves would dramatically appreciate in value. Nonslaveholders would be obliged to hire them at exorbitant rates and the most disloyal element of the population would reap a bonanza. Using the proceeds of their slaves' hire, a recruiter in Queen Anne's County argued, disloyal owners could easily afford to buy their way out of the draft and turn a handy profit besides. In a letter to the secretary of war that quickly reached public print, Judge Bond explicitly drew a comparison with the Jacobs committee's ill-fated proposals. By enlisting free blacks while exempting slaves, he told Stanton, the government would be, in effect, "putting in force a Statute which the people of Maryland in the heyday of slavery in this State refused a place on the Statute book."[80]

Nonslaveholders were not the only ones up in arms. Slaveholders were no better disposed than nonslaveholders toward the enlistment of free black men. The same fear that had given rise to the Jacobs plan—that independent free blacks threatened control over the slaves—arose at the prospect of free black men in uniform. And the same circumstance that contributed to the defeat of the Jacobs plan—the slaveholders' need for free black labor—weighed against voluntary assent to the departure of free black men to the army. Slaveholders joined nonslaveholders in complaints that free black hands were being enticed or forced from their employers by army recruiters.

Opposition did not stop with complaints. Owners and employers tried to intimidate black men with stories that the recruiters planned to sell them for breastworks or ship them off to slavery overseas. If that failed, they threatened the families of free black volunteers. The threats were not idly uttered. Landlords and employers evicted the families of men who refused to be intimidated; vandals pulled down their fences, trampled their fields, and rustled their livestock. Apparently prompted by politicians in Annapolis, local officials on the Eastern Shore contrived an elaborate legal stratagem allowing them to arrest both free black volunteers and those sent to recruit them. A free black, they reasoned, "is a slave for the length of time he hires himself" and has no right to volunteer for military service. On that basis they arrested John Singer, a free black man who had left his employer and was on his way to Baltimore in company with a civilian recruiter.[81]

Despite opposition, recruitment proceeded apace. Within less than two months, a regiment had been recruited. Nor need anyone have worried that enlistment would be confined for long to free blacks. General Schenck promptly exceeded his brief by authorizing Colonel Birney to "proceed to Camlin's slave pen in Pratt Street and enlist the slaves of Gen'l Stuart and other Rebels and Rebel sympathizers there incarcerated . . . and liberate all those confined there." Birney carried out his orders enthusiastically and so did his agents in the countryside, much to the disgust of local officials. Slaves had means of learning quickly that recruiters were in the vicinity and of making known their desire to enlist. A group in jail in Frederick learned that a civilian recruiter was being held in the same jail. One of their number wrote a note indicating that "they a lot of Boys in hear that wants to enlist." Someone then enclosed the note with a stone in a handkerchief and threw it into the recruiter's cell.[82]

In the ultimate provocation, Birney and his deputies formed recruiting parties of newly enlisted black troops. This was no mere grandstand play. Mobile squads of black men in uniform served both to reassure potential recruits of the army's intentions and to protect volunteers on their way to recruiting stations. That protection was needed had been amply demonstrated when John H. Sothoron, a slaveholder in St. Mary's County, murdered a recruiting officer. Naturally enough, the black soldiers who composed the recruiting squads could not resist the opportunity to parade their authority before indignant white citizens, driving many to hysteria. In the lurid accounts that spread abroad, three black soldiers guarding a boat against sabotage by local slaveholders became a steamboat full of Negroes; black troops were supposedly without discipline and bent on wholesale harassment, plunder, and abduction. Rumors that a black regiment was to be quartered on the Eastern Shore sent up squeals of horror from slaveowners and set Bradford's voluble pen once again in motion. "Must [the black regiment] be sent across the Bay only further to inflame, terrify and disgust our Citizens?" Bradford demanded of postmaster general and fellow Marylander Montgomery Blair. "Truly this would seem to be adding insult to injury." Lincoln placed enough credit in the sensational reports earnestly retailed to him by people like Bradford and Maryland's Senator Reverdy Johnson that he temporarily halted recruiting in September and later proposed confining recruiting parties to white men.[83]

Neither concession made the slightest difference in the end. The army's need for manpower dictated full-scale recruitment of black men in the border states. In October the War Department promulgated General Order 329, which provided for enlistment of free blacks, slaves of disloyal owners, and slaves of consenting loyal owners in the border states. Only obdurate Kentucky remained exempt. Consenting owners were to receive compensation and the slaves were to become free. If that arrangement failed to yield enough recruits after a month's trial, slaves could be enlisted without their owners' consent, with compensation to be paid in cases where the owners were loyal.[84]

The new policy did not immediately quiet dissension. In his next annual message, Governor Bradford denied the government's right to discriminate between loyal and disloyal owners. If slaves could be conscripted under the law, he argued, it could be only as property seized to meet an emergency, not as persons subject to military service. In that case seizure should be "governed by some such fixed rule as would make all alike subject to the burden." Still, practical-minded slaveowners might well see the wisdom of accepting the government's deal, for otherwise they stood to lose both their slaves and all hope of compensation. Less practical owners refused to fold the hand until the last card had been played.[85]

In the months after the promulgation of General Order 329, they watched the cards fall in Maryland. Though the order explicitly forbade further enlistments in Maryland except in accordance with the new regulations, complaints of forcible impressment of both slaves and free blacks increased in volume, and the War Department, in need of recruits, made little effort to curb excesses. According to repeated allegations, black recruiting squads sometimes took by force fellow blacks who showed reluctance to go along. They defied opposition and threatened physical retaliation against local citizens who interfered with them. When a slaveowner in Anne Arundel County asked one party by whose authority they were taking his slaves, "they replied by putting their hands on their swords, and saying 'by this and by our muscle.' " New missions to open jails and slave pens did not always distinguish between potential recruits and other slaves. A functionary in Upper Marlboro resigned himself to the release of able-bodied slave men upon grounds of military necessity but considered it an outrage that women and children should have been released from imprisonment as well. Governor Bradford apparently seconded his view. Slaveowners made a last desperate stand by abusing men who, having left home to enlist, had been rejected by army examiners. "Masters have refused to feed and clothe their slaves, and have beaten and illtreated them," an officer in Salisbury reported. In June 1864 the War Department removed this last lever of control. All slave volunteers, even if physically unfit, were to be mustered in, the department decreed. Those unsuitable for active duty were to be assigned to the quartermaster's department.[86]

Full-scale recruitment put an end to slavery in Maryland. Before the war was over some ten thousand black men served in the Union army and navy. If only half of them were slaves, they would represent well over a third of slave men aged eighteen to forty-five. Their numbers were augmented by family members who fled or were driven away after the enlistment of the men and by fugitives who took up residence in the District of Columbia and environs. The Cecil *Whig* estimated in March 1864 that thirty thousand slaves had escaped from Maryland since the beginning of the war. The drain in active hands alone would probably have been enough to finish slavery. "[A]ble bodied negroes between 20 & 45 have become exceedingly scarce," the superintendent of black recruitment in Maryland told his superiors in the spring of 1864. "[W]henever the U.S. gets a soldier, sombody's plow stands still." With the available work force depleted, owners found themselves bidding for the labor of the slaves and free blacks who remained. Slaves established wage or sharecropping agreements with their owners or with other employers, and could move freely between government and private employment depending on how the terms suited them.[87]

Observers marveled at the arbitrariness with which loyal and disloyal, benevolent and malevolent owners alike lost their slaves. It was a rare moment of poetic justice. Slaveowners experienced briefly, in milder form, the anguish with which slaves had been forced to live all their lives, knowing that their personal virtue bore no ultimate relation to their worldly fate. Some witnesses even insisted that the righteous suffered more than the wicked from slave defections. "[T]he slaves of the most strict and severe masters have refused to leave home," Dr. Samuel A. Harrison reported; "while the more lenient & kind have lost largely, if not all their slaves. . . ." After reporting that Colonel W. H. Garner "has had the misfortune to lose five of his negroes," J. H. Berry wondered "why servants should leave so good a house as I know Col. Gs to be."[88]

The destruction of slavery arose from more than the sheer number of defectors, devastating though the defections were. At its foundation, the collapse was a moral and political phenomenon, arising from the slaves' daily more vivid perception that their owners were no longer sovereign. Slaves and their owners together learned the relationship between power and authority. Having lost the first, owners could no longer lay claim to the second. The army, the federal government, private employers, free blacks, other slaves, even other owners stood between slaves and the authority of masters and mistresses. What to do next became a matter of unprecedented choice rather than ingrained habit. The hundred and one fragments that made up the daily routine of slavery shifted and scattered. Owners learned to their pained surprise how crucial the stable order of the wider world had been to what they assumed were purely personal ties of devotion and loyalty between themselves and favorite slaves. Martha E. Harris, wife of Congressman Benjamin G. Harris, plaintively described what happened when "Cousin Benny" tried to recover some of his favorite slaves from the post at Point Lookout: "some pretended not to know their Master, ungreatful wretches, to wish to disown one who had been like a Father. . . ." So thorough was the collapse of the slaveholders' authority that many slaves took for granted that the law itself sanctioned their new independence. After a difference of opinion with her mistress, who denied her permission to visit relatives on the Eastern Shore, a slave woman in northern Maryland asked President Lincoln to resolve the matter. "[Y]ou will please let me know if we are free. and what i can do," she wrote him. "I write to you for advice." The bond that tied the slave to the master had indeed become what Wendell Phillips once called it, a cobweb.[89]

The visible disintegration of slavery strengthened the position of those favoring immediate, uncompensated emancipation. Recruitment of slaves had accomplished the result that advocates like General Schenck and Judge Bond had hoped. Destroying slaveowners' power over the slaves, it also eroded their influence over the nonslaveholding white community. Some poor whites indulged in an open display of *schadenfreude*, witnessing the discomfiture of their haughty neighbors. "I hear that Mr. Edward Lloyd of Miles River neck, our largest slave holder, lost at one time as many as 84 able bodied hands," Harrison recorded in his journal, "and that enough have not been left to him 'to black his boots,' as a low fellow remarked to me yesterday . . . in an exulting manner. . . . It seems to give great satisfaction to the laboring whites that the non laboring slave owners are losing their slaves and that they too will be reduced to the necessity of going into the field."[90]

Small-holders whose one or two slaves had been lost to them had little heart and less motive to fight on. Accustomed anyway to free black labor, they would do better to cut the best deal possible for their immediate needs and hope for an end to the commotion. The steady exodus of slaves weakened the stamina even of more substantial owners. "[T]he loss of my negroes, one by one is making me personally indifferent upon this subject of emancipation," Harrison commented early in October 1863. That fall's "election by sword and ballot," whatever the distorting influence of the federal army, showed that many another voter shared Harrison's weariness and resignation. Unconditional Unionists and candidates committed to emancipation achieved control of the legislature and Henry Winter Davis went to Congress, where he was to plague Lincoln.[91]

Patrician conservatives who had but recently vowed hostility to emancipation began to peel off and lend support to the erstwhile heterodoxy. The most unlikely individuals began turning up among those in favor of a new constitution abolishing slavery. With the political weight of the Lincoln administration tilting the scale in favor of the emancipationists, the workaday practicality of politics instructed slow learners in the new reality. Those emancipationists with the longest pedigrees and the most determined voices saw hypocrisy and venal intent among the recent converts, the "very respectable and *very weak* 'lean and slippered Pantaloons.' " "If they are honest in their conversion," the Cecil *Whig* suggested, "let them with proper decency acknowledge their errors, but let them not again assume to take a lead in politics, where they have so lately showed their utter incompetency."[92]

Nevertheless, the process that took Reverdy Johnson, Thomas H. Hicks, Thomas Swann, and John Pendleton Kennedy to public advocacy of emancipation by the winter of 1863 was the same process that earlier had taken those who became Unconditional Unionists from reluctant collaboration with the Republicans to openly avowed support, from sarcastic denials of abolitionism to self-righteous insistence that nothing else would suit the circumstances. As recently as 1858 the Baltimore *American* had declared the question of slavery "best treated by the 'masterly inactivity' that commits its solution to time." Already by 1862 it was urging the wisdom of emancipation. In December 1861 the editor of the Cecil *Whig* had proclaimed that "not one in a thousand" Marylanders would countenance unconditional emancipation. By February 1864 he thought that nothing less could be entertained by sane people: "You can make no patch work of emancipation. . . . If a partial act of emancipation be fastened on Maryland . . . she . . . will occupy the position, and meet with the reception, a man would with a dead body strapped to him, repelling all whom he approaches. . . . Freedom will not pause to make terms with the prostrate foe who attempted its life."[93]

Black people themselves, so recently at the mercy of a legislature bent on returning the free to slavery, were on the march with unprecedented militance. As the constitutional convention deliberated during the summer of 1864, they held a series of meetings in Baltimore demanding that the convention do more than just end slavery. Black people had been "kept in the dark long enough," they declared. They would accept nothing less than full rights as citizens. The proslavery Chestertown *Transcript* looked with astonishment and dismay upon the revolution of affairs. Its editor accurately predicted that many would soon endorse civil and political equality for black people who at the moment rejected it, even as they had only recently rejected emancipation. "People of Maryland be not deceived," the *Transcript* warned, "the fanatic who clamors to-day for the freedom of the negro, will, that secured, leave no stone unturned, till the negro with his ballot swells the ranks of his party and secures him the control of the State and General Government."[94]

Enlightened Marylanders had taken comfort for decades in the dream that slavery would die peacefully of old age—at some time in the unforeseeable future. It required the alarms and commotion of civil war to demonstrate that slavery must inevitably die and to fashion black and white Marylanders themselves into its killers. A border state to the end, Maryland yielded with bad grace. In Anne Arundel County, a churchgoer regretted that the pastor had mentioned emancipation in his Thanksgiving sermon: many in the congregation, he remarked, did not consider the end of slavery an occasion for giving thanks. Harford and Carroll counties, with their small black and smaller slave populations, voted against the new consti-tution. Indeed, had it not been for ballots cast by soldiers in the field—in a procedure that many considered irregular—the inevitable would have failed to muster a majority in Maryland. Nevertheless, on 1 November 1864 the Devlish Nigger difficulty officially ended. It was not the end of the struggle. Even before the new constitution took effect, plans were brewing in various quarters to lock the former slaves into a new form of subjection. Ugly violence continued for years. Black people did not cease to be scorned, rebuked, and persecuted. But they did cease to be slaves.[95]

CHAPTER SIX

In Lieu of Reconstruction

For the brief life span of the constitution of 1864 the people of Maryland held these truths to be self-evident: "that all men are created equally free; that they are endowed by their Creator with certain unalienable rights, among which are life, liberty, the enjoyment of the proceeds of their own labor, and the pursuit of happiness."[1] They had not done so in the constitutions of 1776 or 1851, nor would they do so in that of 1867, which quickly supplanted the 1864 constitution (and which, with amendments, remains in force today). A good many white Marylanders, though resigned after a fashion to the departure of slavery, would as soon have bidden it farewell with less unseemly eagerness than was suggested by that indiscreet and sweeping affirmation. Others who made the affirmation willingly and in good faith lost heart in the face of the unpleasant and unexpected consequences it seemed to entail. Ex-slave and ex-free black Marylanders discovered to their profound disappointment (though probably not much to their surprise) that it meant a good deal less than they wished. But for all Marylanders that statement standing at the head of the new constitution's Declaration of Rights set down in digest form the unavoidable lesson of decades of gradual development capped by three and a half years of revolutionary upheaval. During the years between the Revolution and the Civil War, free labor, though irreversibly on the advance in Maryland, had been obliged to come to terms with slavery. Now slavery must come to terms with free labor.

But how? A good many people whom the war had hectored into accepting the end of slavery were by no means prepared to watch with equanimity the collapse of the entire social edifice that slavery had supported. For the abolition of slavery touched more than just former slaves

131

and their former owners. The sovereignty of master over slave determined other lines of social power: that of slaveholder over nonslaveholder, large slaveholder over small slaveholder, country over city, white over black. Once abrogation of the slave relationship upset the foundation of these other social relationships, what would fill their place? How long would the demolition be allowed to proceed? Until black people claimed social and political equality? Until Baltimore dominated the General Assembly and the power of "mere numbers," so long feared by slaveholders, ruled the state?

The new constitution tendered a mixed reply to these questions. Where black people were concerned it stayed within strict limits. By studied silence, it preserved the incompetence of black witnesses in cases involving white people. By explicit statement, it proclaimed suffrage the prerogative of white men. Few people advocated—fewer still in public—the granting of full civil and political rights to black people. Henry Winter Davis, leader of the Radical faction of Maryland's Union party and Abraham Lincoln's nemesis, concluded that black people must be accorded the vote in all the former slave states. But he died just months after Lincoln, without seeing the task accomplished. The Cecil *Whig,* the Radicals' most uncompromising advocate, placed itself in a small and despised minority when it asked rhetorically who was worthier to testify in court or cast a ballot: "the white man who has violated all his oaths for purposes of Treason; or the black man whose simple word alone, in behalf of the . . . Union has never been broken? . . . the white man who has fought four years to destroy the Government, or the black man who has fought ever since we would permit him, to preserve it?" And even the *Whig,* in a moment of embarrassing naïveté, predicted that a generation must pass before black men would vote.[2]

Had the matter been left to either the Union (Republican) or the Democratic party, more than a generation would probably have been required. The *Whig* insisted that it was "too late . . . to frighten the Union men of Maryland by shouting 'negro suffrage' at them" and predicted that those attempting to do so would "find that game is very much like themselves—about played out." But it was not. In their fear of being caught on the wrong side of this dangerous question, members of the Union party unintentionally helped to fashion it into an even more potent weapon against them. Union party meetings took to passing gratuitous resolutions abusing black people and disclaiming all intention of enfranchising them. Such conduct naturally did nothing to enhance black people's confidence in the party, nor did it attract much support from the opposition. After all, anyone favoring thoroughgoing proscription of blacks could vote for the genuine article: he would hardly tarry over the party identified with emancipation, however assiduously its members labored to spruce up their Negrophobic credentials. Republicans found at last that they had been too clever by half. They took a sound trouncing in the 1866 elections for the state legislature, in the vote on calling a constitutional convention in 1867, and on the new constitution itself. When, in time, they came to open advocacy of suffrage for black men (with the ulterior motive, their opponents jeered, of saving themselves from the electoral oblivion to which they were otherwise doomed), they could make no convincing rejoinder to the charges of mendaciousness and hypocrisy.[3]

Black people themselves were not disposed to let the matter rest before they had acquired full and equal citizenship. Even as the convention of 1864 met, mass meetings demanded that the new constitution accord them the rights of citizens. As the Republicans quietly skirted the question, black people kept thrusting it embarrassingly to the fore. Black people in Baltimore included the right to vote in a comprehensive list of demands in December 1865. They appeared—provocatively, in the view of a white citizen looking on—at the radical border state convention in Baltimore, toward the end of the campaign over the 1867 constitution. At a meeting in Cecil County in April 1867 called for the purpose of planning a school, the Reverend John Brice, a black minister from Baltimore, took occasion to predict (optimistically) that black men would vote in Maryland within six months. In September 1868 black citizens from all over Cecil held a convention and planned to march fifteen hundred strong through the town of Port Deposit. On 1 June 1869 a statewide convention in Baltimore started a hare by demanding for black people, not just the eventual right to vote, but the immediate right to participate in the counsels of the Republican party. That brought into the open a simmering dispute among the Republicans themselves, some of whom charged others with instigating the convention for their own factious purposes. Indeed, a black convention in Frederick on June 18 condemned the demands of its Baltimore counterpart. The minuet that ensued within the Republican party continued for years, with black Republicans seeking in vain a voice within the party commensurate with their importance to its existence.[4]

Maryland escaped the ignominy of Kentucky and Delaware, which held onto slavery until the thirteenth amendment snatched it from them. But there Maryland's initiative ended. The legislature of 1867 rejected the fourteenth amendment. The state did, through the constitution of 1867, affirm black people's competence as witnesses in court, but with the proviso that the legislature might countermand the decision if it saw fit. And even this mean and backhanded concession came only after the federal civil rights bill of 1866, which Maryland resisted as long as possible, deprived the state of all choice in the premises. As to suffrage, only the compulsion of the fifteenth amendment, ratified in 1870 without Maryland's concurrence, accorded the vote to black men in Maryland.[5]

Having safely restricted the sphere of black people, the constitution of 1864 took steps toward democratization where white people were concerned. It adopted white population as the basis of legislative apportionment and reshuffled seats in the House of Delegates so that Baltimore and the rest of northern Maryland briefly enjoyed representation proportionate to their population. Predictably, opposition was strong. "[R]epresentation according to population," Unionists in Anne Arundel County warned their constituents, "is unsuited to the peculiar conditions of our State." Comprising one-third of the state's population, Baltimore would assume a measure of power "unsafe to the best interests of other portions of the State" and probably even to its own.[6] The slave counties lost the fight in 1864 but got their way with a vengeance at the constitutional convention of 1867. Having taken control of the legislature by the necessary two-thirds margin, the Democrats illegally allotted the former slave counties greater weight at the convention than they had in the legislature. The resulting constitution once more placed Baltimore and the northern counties under restraints and once more decreed that the voteless black people should swell the representation of their enemies. "This they call a white man's Government," an opposition pamphlet scornfully remarked. "That is the right of a few white men, by counting the disfranchised blacks, to govern a great many white men. This is progress backward toward oligarchy."[7]

The uniform public school system inaugurated by the constitution of 1864 also fell under the axe. The constitution of 1867 left it to the next legislature to decide how (or whether) to replace it. The legislature answered with a new school law in 1868. Under that law the counties gained wide discretion in school matters and centralized direction was abolished. A statewide tax was to be distributed on the basis of total population, but for the nearly exclusive benefit of white schools: only money received in taxes on such trifling property as black people owned could be used to educate black children. Thus, complained the *Whig,* "the large colored population[s] of some of the southern counties are to serve the purpose of drawing tax from the State Treasury for their respective counties [although] none but white children are to be educated out of that fund."[8]

Reconstruction, or what served Maryland in that capacity, had a much shorter life than in the former Confederate states. From the beginning, the constitution of 1864 rested on a weak base. The war had brought into existence the Radical Republican faction that sponsored it and then ensured that faction the crucial support of the federal army; wholesale proscription and disfranchisement of rebel adherents and sympathizers and the votes of soldiers in the field gave the new constitution what narrow margin of victory it could claim (opponents insisted that by rights it was defeated); and only federal patronage, the federal army, the continued suppression of secessionists, and the electoral assistance of black voters—which the Radicals hesitated to admit publicly that they required—could sustain Republicanism in Maryland. The end of the war removed Washington's most pressing motive for lending aid, and Andrew Johnson, pursuing political ends of his own, encouraged the opposition. Just as the winds from Washington had blown unlikely supporters onto the side of emancipation, so the shift in those winds blew many of them back again once the bare act of emancipation had been accomplished. Radicals in Maryland hoped that Congress would intervene under its constitutional obligation to guarantee every state a republican form of government, and they took comfort in a House resolution calling for the removal of the Naval Academy from Annapolis. But Congress, evidently deciding that those seeking its help had in mind Republican rather than republican government, showed no inclination to enter the quagmire of Maryland politics.[9]

Without Washington's sanction for proscription of returning rebels and local sympathizers, the dynamics of state politics brought about a quickening competition for their support. Practical men of politics discovered that principle forbade the denial of the franchise to white citizens of Maryland. The Union party split on the question and suffered a number of harmful, high-level defections, including Governor Thomas Swann, former Postmaster General Montgomery Blair, and United States Senator Reverdy Johnson. Meanwhile, the Democratic party campaigned actively for restoration of the rights of the disfranchised, while setting its face like a flint against further rights for black people. Against this appeal, Republicans had only the feckless weapon of racially abusive resolutions. It is not surprising that a number of politicians, especially those but lately and reluctantly converted to emancipation, began seeking deals with the Democrats. The crude political maneuvers on both sides that accompanied this retreat made for hot tempers, extravagant personal abuse, and a most unedifying spectacle all around.

Easily the most audacious example was Governor Thomas Swann. Leader of the Baltimore Plug-Uglies and other nativist clubs during his Know-Nothing days, Swann had taken a cautious approach to emancipation, offering his endorsement only when the result was a foregone conclusion. (The Cecil *Whig* stated matters somewhat less charitably: Swann, it said, "hung back when the great battle for emancipation was being fought . . . and when won . . . was one of those to huzza the loudest . . ."). Affirming his support for a registration law to deny secessionists the franchise, he won the governorship under the auspices of the Unconditional Unionists in November 1864. But by the spring of 1866 he had decided to cast his lot with the opposition. In return for his official pronouncements against "negro equality" and for his help in getting disfranchised citizens past the barrier of the registration law, Swann expected the Democrats, once victorious, to send him to the United States Senate. And indeed, after restoring the voting rights of former Confederates, the legislature that convened in January 1867 under Democratic control set about paying off the debt to Swann. That was more than a notion. It necessitated temporary repeal of the law requiring that one senator be appointed from the Eastern Shore, which in turn meant ousting a state senator who could not be counted upon to vote correctly. Eventually the legislature passed a measure repealing the Eastern Shore law just long enough for Swann's election and restoring it thereafter.[10]

After all the fast shuffling, however, Swann did not take his seat in the Senate. His own explanation was that he feared a Radical coup d'état the minute he resigned the governorship to go to the Senate. His detractors insisted that he declined the seat rather than face the humiliation of having his bona fides challenged by the Senate itself. Commenting upon rumors that Swann's friends secretly hoped that the man elected in his stead, former Governor Philip F. Thomas, would be turned back on grounds of disloyalty, the *Whig* remarked, "The same charge might be urged against Swann, with the addition of rascality." In the end, the Senate did refuse Thomas, eventually accepting George Vickers for the long-contested seat.

Those who prided themselves on being principled Republicans watched the maneuvering with rage and contempt. The *Whig* beseeched Congress to "lay a stern hand on the head of [Andrew Johnson]," whereupon his "minions and followers" in Maryland would "vanish from our midst like Mamalukes before the pashaw's sword." Wishfully, it predicted a bad end for the "political trimmers and thimblerigs" of the "Copperjohnson" or "demi-John-Swann" faction. To a degree, the prediction proved accurate. As Reverdy Johnson's term in the Senate neared its end, Swann continued to cherish hopes of a senatorial career, this time in a seat to which the western shore was legitimately entitled. But the Democratic legislature passed him over and, finding a mediocrity with sounder party credentials, pensioned Johnson himself off with two votes. The *Whig* paused in its gloating to pay Johnson a grudging compliment. "[T]he rebels stood in their own light" in "exchanging the giant for a pigmy," its editor declared, for they could place no abler or more influential spokesman in the Senate. But that gratifying blunder on the part of the Democrats only added to the *Whig*'s satisfaction that "Mr. Reverdy Johnson and Mr. Thomas Swann, for all their falsehood and treachery to the party which elevated them to power, have been quietly retired by the men they sold out to." In the meantime, however, the "men they sold out to," having cleared questionable allies from the field, consolidated their hold on the state and, by 1869, were ready to inaugurate their own governor.[11]

Maryland permitted itself the luxury of more equivocal answers to questions of political democracy, as concerned both white and black, than Congress permitted the former Confederate states while it retained jurisdiction over their internal affairs. On the question of property in human beings, however, no such equivocation was possible. Even the constitution of 1867, reactionary in so many ways, recognized that slavery was dead beyond resurrection.[12] Emancipation answered at last the question with which slaveholders' conventions, committees on colored population, and the state at large had wrestled indecisively for years, the question that Marylanders had tried to push aside at the time—centuries before, it must have seemed—of the Jacobs committee. The abolition of slavery finally resolved the contradiction so long ensconced in the heart of Maryland's social being between slavery and free labor.

It resolved the contradiction but did not—could not—solve the problem. The years immediately following emancipation represented a comma, so to speak, in Maryland's development. The act of emancipation provided essential legal confirmation that the move toward free labor was irreversible. That established no new trend, and neither, beneath the purely formal level, could it force the pace of the one long under way. For in and of itself, emancipation carried no guarantee of a smooth transition from a hybrid slave to a consistent free labor system. Rather, it ensured that the malaise which had been growing and extending itself gradually would suddenly acquire catastrophic force. The abolition of slavery did not supply Maryland with a new basis upon which to build; it only eliminated what had been necessary to sustain the old basis, even though in stagnant and disintegrating fashion. Thereafter, the maturing of a system of social relations founded upon free labor proved to be both gradual and uneven: less problematic in areas where slavery had never been important, more problematic in areas where the opposite had been true; but, withal, a problem everywhere. Slavery had held together the parts of the old society, assigning slaves, free blacks, and nonslaveholding whites their proper spheres. With slavery gone, some new principle of cohesion had to be established.

Former slaveholders did not grasp at once that the principle must be new, but looked for ways to salvage the essence of the old one. Some few soothed themselves momentarily with the unction that the freed slave would remain loyal to old master and old mistress, though wartime defections left few in untroubled possession of that illusion. "I am told that the slaves are *generally* staying in their old homes," Dr. Samuel A. Harrison, an Eastern Shore owner who had already lost many of his slaves, noted three days after emancipation took effect. He had to revise that view two days later: "I hear that the servants of many masters leave them *en masse* and they are not those who have received ill treatment exclusively." Five days later all illusion had vanished: "I hear that the servants are leaving their homes generally— Some gentlemen are left without a single servant to perform the most necessary duties." Even those who remained with former owners did not necessarily do so out of loyalty or reluctance to embrace freedom. A unionist in Prince George's County reported that, with most of the men away in the army, the freedwomen "say they are afraid to look for a new home for fear while doing so their children will be thrown out."[13] Still, the slaveholders' belief in the salvageability of the old order rested on ground more solid than faith in their slaves' devotion. Free blacks, after all, were not new to their experience. They were a nuisance, perhaps, but not a novelty, and Maryland law had long dealt with them. Why should it not continue to do so?

The legislature encouraged former owners in their refusal to distinguish between "free negro" and "freedman." While repealing a large chunk of the black code during the legislative session following adoption of the emancipation constitution, the legislators let stand a provision punishing "free negroes" (but not free whites) for leaving employers to whom they had hired themselves. The Cecil *Whig* poked fun at this relic. "[S]ince there are no longer any slaves in Maryland," its editor remarked, " 'free negro' is about as tautological . . . as male man and female woman"; and he invited the legislators to feel ashamed of themselves for "tearing such a dirty rag from the foul garment of slavery, and fastening it as a breech-clout to the statue of Freedom."[14] A dirty rag from a foul garment it was indeed, and no laughing matter. For it typified the prevalent view that the presuppositions of slavery still governed the position of the freed men and women.

Former owners proved at once how strongly that view still compelled them. For on the very day of emancipation, all over the state, they began seizing freedmen's children and whisking them off to the county seats, sometimes in wagonloads, to be bound as apprentices by the county orphans' courts. Slaveholders who had opposed emancipation with the prediction that ex-slave children would be thrown into destitution hastened to make liars of themselves by apprenticing even infants—though they generally preferred children old enough to work. The old apprenticeship laws allowed binding to suitable masters or mistresses with the parents' consent, while giving the orphans' courts discretion to act without the consent of parents adjudged vagrant or thought not to be inculcating proper "habits of industry." Whatever scant protection black parents and children might have expected from such an open-ended law, conceived in the first instance as a means of subordinating free black people in a slave society, went by the board in the scramble that followed emancipation. Judges did not even bother to hear testimony concerning the parents' ability to care for the children; and the fact that masters and mistresses frequently hired the apprentices out and appropriated their wages sufficiently contradicted the argument that the children were without means of support. In fact, some of the children at the time of their seizure had already entered agreements, approved by their parents, to work for wages. Parents attempting to reclaim from apprenticeship children from whom they had been separated in slavery were apt to be confronted with the contention that, as they had not cared for the children before, they had no just claim to them now.

As for the consent of the parents, some judges deemed the parents' mere presence in court—even though secured by intimidation or outright force—a token of acquiescence. The parent who attempted to disabuse the court undertook a heavy risk. One mother who protested received for her effort a blow in the face administered by a constable in the presence of the judges. The constable was reprimanded, but that probably detracted little from the point he set out to make. A former owner in Kent County, one Charles Tilden, did not leave it to a constable, but personally threatened a protesting mother in open court that " 'if she did not cease talking *he* would break her d—d head' or words to that effect." The law forced upon parents its own perverse categories, as when the mother of five apprentices, three of whom had run away from their master, insisted that she was innocent of "improper interference" with her own children. No wonder a black doctor from Washington, in a petition to the United States House of Representatives, denounced apprenticeship as "class Legislation" and a "bruital system of Slavery and misanthrophy."[15]

Apprenticeship served a complex social purpose for former slaveholders. One of its tasks—arguably the most important—was to provide a temporary landmark for people as yet unable to orient themselves in the new landscape of emancipation. The speed with which former masters and mistresses landed on the idea strongly suggests this, as does their peremptory, almost disbelieving manner when challenged. Irving Spence, a former master in Worcester County, told the father of his apprentices that he "considered the children the children of his negro woman, and . . . meant to keep them and do by them as he has done by his slaves in the past, and no better than he done by them, and teach them what he intend for them to know, and no more than he intend them to know." A master in Kent County placed a newspaper advertisement for a runaway apprentice in January 1865 exactly as he might have for a runaway slave a year earlier—and offered approximately the same reward (five dollars) that a slave might have warranted at that time. (A white apprentice who absconded during the summer of 1865 was apparently worth only six cents to his master.) Samuel Harrison thought the rush to the orphans' courts not such a bad thing. He also placed credence in the argument that the children could not otherwise be provided for in the coming winter and subscribed to the view that liberty had been "forced" on the slaves, most of whom were content in slavery. But for all his blindness where the former slaves were concerned, Harrison had a certain insight into the motives of the former owners. "There seems to be," he reflected, "an ill-defined belief, a vague hope that, in the revolution of affairs, slavery will . . . be resurrected." These vague hopes drew nourishment independently of the practical benefit to be extracted from the apprentices, as witness the cases in which those bound were too young to be of service as workers. Although a three-month-old apprentice in Calvert County was an extreme example—young people in their teens seem to have been the usual targets—enough instances occurred of apprentices under ten to justify a suspicion that more was at stake than the labor supply.[16]

Apprenticeship satisfied as well an impulse of revenge against former slaves for the fact of emancipation, of punishment for disloyalty. Something of the sort must explain the aggravated violence with which some masters and mistresses dealt with apprentices and their parents. Dr. William MacDaniel caught up with an absconding apprentice at the home of the child's mother, his former slave. Apparently hoping to appeal to the freed-woman's sense of duty, he asked what she expected her mistress to do for water without the children. The freedwoman replied that "if she saw her Mistress walking about Hell with a tub of water on her head she . . . would not take it off." The good doctor beat mother and child, sent the child back to his house, and for good measure promised to serve the mother's sister, whose children he held as well, in the same way. "[T]he Dr. says that he intends just to leave life in her and that will be all," it was reported. Hester Anthony's former master, Jimmy Gailes, threatened to shoot her when she tried to collect her children from him, adding that "before I shall have my children he will blow their brains out." Ashton Garrett refused to permit Mary Hawkins and her thirteen-year-old daughter to leave after emanci-pation. The mother eventually ran away, but was unable to take her daugh-ter along. Ashton reportedly beat the girl, locked her up at night, and never allowed her off his premises. When, despite his precautions, she managed to escape, he had her arrested and charged with stealing a shawl, two dresses, and a pair of shoes—items which a witness attested that Ashton had fur-nished her himself while she remained in his service.[17]

Merging with the subtle psychological services performed by appren-ticeship was its most obvious purpose: the compulsion of labor. Some people put together considerable work forces of apprentices. John R. McQuay of Centreville, Queen Anne's County, simultaneously held eight children, five belonging to Henrietta Kelly and three others belonging to Susan Ringle. It was not uncommon for individuals to have six, eight, and ten children bound to them at once. Apprentices did not necessarily work directly for those to whom they were apprenticed. Frequently, the masters and mis-tresses hired them out, as they had done with slaves in the past, appropri-ating the wages, which could be substantial, for themselves. Parents might find their children, as a couple in Kent County did, packed off to another county in the time-honored fashion that had ravaged family life under slav-ery. And, as under slavery, physical proximity did not necessarily help. "[I]n many cases," a white unionist in Calvert County reported, ". . . the children have not the liberty to go to see there parrents, and have been treated ten times wors than they ware when they ware slaves."[18]

On the other hand, former slaveowners knew from experience the strength of family connections among the former slaves and had learned to manipulate them. Thus, apprenticing the children sometimes served as an indirect means of compelling the labor of the parents—or at least compelling their presence, which would be a necessary preliminary: parents were less likely to leave while their children remained in bondage. An instance in which this motive was especially clear was that of a couple who, with their teenage son, had traveled from North Carolina with a farmer from Anne Arundel County, intending to go to work for him. Apparently finding the situation unsatisfactory, they decided against staying, and the husband, preceding his family, returned to North Carolina. The farmer immediately seized the boy. Former owners in St. Mary's County hit upon a different method of turning family feelings to their advantage. Reportedly, they kept on freedmen too old to work, reckoning that doing so would make the apprentices more tractable. But when they realized that they could not keep the apprentices, they turned the old people out as well, telling them that "the Govt had set them free and must take care of them."[19]

Not all efforts to mend the tatters of the old order proceeded through the forms of ostensible legality, and not all those making the effort were former owners of slaves. Freelance violence, shared in democratically by whites of all classes, played a key role. Some of the violence represented the overflow of anger and resentment bred by the war; and black people, though obvious and generally easy targets, were not the only ones to feel its edge. Samuel Harrison, commenting on the persecution of blacks in Talbot County during the summer of 1864, insisted that "[w]hat these men are doing to inoffensive negroes, they would do to white loyalists if they dared." The military campaign of that summer, during which Confederate invaders deliberately destroyed the property of unionists in their path and the federal army responded by holding local secessionists responsible, gave fresh cause for hard feelings. In the wake of Lincoln's reelection and adoption of the emancipation constitution in the fall, an assistant assessor of internal revenue in Prince George's County reported that secessionist slaveholders "do not hesitate to say that we robbed them of their property." A loyalist in Calvert County expressed fear that the recent killing of a local unionist presaged attacks on all in the vicinity holding similar views.

The passage of time and, with it, the defeat of the Confederacy aggravated the bitterness of secessionists. "The treatment of loyal men in this section [Prince George's, Charles, and St. Mary's counties]," a witness reported in the summer of 1865, "has been similar to that received by the freedmen." A Methodist minister in Calvert County "who never medles in politics," according to a local unionist in April 1866, "has latly been abused

& cursed and assaulted and struck on the public road only be cause he reproved some young men for loud talking while at servis." It was the minister's unionist politics, however private and discreet, that got him into trouble: "during the preaching in church he was abused most shamefully and called a damned Yanky son of a b. and threatening to brake open the church for a southern right preacher and Kill every union man who should attempt to go in." In August 1866 a group of white hooligans, many of them self-proclaimed veterans of the Confederate army, ran riot at a Methodist camp meeting near Jessup's Cut in Anne Arundel County. Black worshipers bore the brunt of the violence and in the end lost all their belongings to theft and vandalism—tents, trunks, clothing, bedding, china, utensils, and the like. But the rioters were widely understood to have premeditated an attack on the white Methodists who organized the meeting, because of the church's unionist reputation. They had made threats against the meeting a month earlier and, during the riot itself, they abused white ministers and worshipers by name and shot a young white man as he knelt in prayer.[20]

Black people were the usual victims, however, and bitterness engendered by the war only partially accounts for the extravagance of the attacks upon them. Among the services slavery had performed for the community at large—not just its slaveholding members—was to provide the basis upon which free black people were, however uneasily, accepted. Emancipation removed the point of reference that had always defined their position and left a question mark in its place. The attempt to erase that troubling question mark accounts for the physical violence with which many people sought to hang onto the familiar world. As some tried to recapture their sense of order by seizing the freedmen's children, others—indeed, sometimes the same ones—sought to accomplish the same end by overawing the freedmen with a display of brute force.

Violent attacks on black people were frequently gratuitous and arbitrary; but they were not random, nor did they represent the caprice of deranged or especially malignant individuals. They had a clear logic, which most white people understood perfectly and accepted with little question. Black soldiers were favorite targets because they symbolized, perhaps more than anything else, the revolution that had taken hold of Maryland society. When Joe Nick showed up in Ellicott City (Howard County) in June 1865—seven months after emancipation—wearing the uniform of a Union soldier, his former owner had him jailed as a fugitive slave. At that Nick got off rather lightly (a federal marshal from Baltimore released him and arrested his ex-owner) compared to many of his fellows. Essex Barbour took a severe beating at the hands of a group of white men, including at least one returned Confederate soldier, in Chaptico, St. Mary's County. Philip Brown was shot in the head while riding along a public highway in Montgomery County. One of his assailants had urged the other to "shoot the d——d son of a b——h, he is nothing but a union soldier." A recently discharged black soldier who tried to intervene when a group of white men set fire to a black church in Anne Arundel County "was knocked down with a Colt and stamped and making his escape was over taken and beaten with a fence rail unmerciful." Charles A. Watkins complained that black soldiers in the vicinity of Centreville in Queen Anne's County "darcent walk out of an evening" for fear of groups of ex-Confederate rowdies who set upon them, took their guns, beat them up, and sometimes shot at them. Families of black soldiers came in for special punishment as well. A "white-haired old colored man" walking along the street in Chestertown, Kent County, suffered only taunts and insults from a group of young white men until his tormentors learned that his son had been a Union soldier. "[T]hat was sufficient cause to punish the old man and one of the rowdies struck him over the head and kicked him, meanwhile the white spectators laughed in chorus."[21]

Black churches attracted violence as velvet attracts lint. Hostility toward churches derived in part from anger over an order of the War Department granting the Methodist Episcopal Church, North, possession of certain church buildings that had previously belonged to the Methodist Episcopal Church, South. Disputes arising from this long-standing grievance not only sparked attacks on black congregations but also disrupted the Christian fellowship of white Methodists. Such a dispute no doubt contributed to the unhappy fate of the minister in Calvert County who never meddled in politics; and Methodists near Clarksburg in Montgomery County fell to blows over possession of a church building. The most common reason for attacks on black churches, however, was that the freedmen conducted schools in them. Magothy Methodist Episcopal Church in Anne Arundel County was set ablaze in August 1865 "for no other cause only for the teaching of a Sunday School," the members insisted. Mounted incendiaries in Queen Anne's County in March 1866 "Set fier to the church that we keep School in and burnt it to the ground," according to a black veteran in the vicinity. Vandals and arsonists attacked churches in Montgomery, Kent, and Somerset counties for the same reason. The attacks did not stop with buildings. The burning of the church in Queen Anne's County followed attempts to intimidate the black teacher, who "was collard and beaten, he got loos and ran and was Shot at." His case was not isolated. Nor did considerations of delicacy or chivalry inhibit hostile citizens from dealing in like style with women teachers. A young black woman who taught near Vienna in Dorchester County was knocked unconscious on the road near the schoolhouse while an onlooker stood by. In Havre de Grace (Harford County) a jury awarded damages of one cent to a woman teacher whom one Robert Galloway had "struck, knocked down and kicked from the sidewalk" as she walked home from school during October 1867.[22]

Any black person calling attention to his new status with inappropriate emphasis, smugness, or pride—or simply at the wrong time in the wrong place—courted summary punishment. John Diggs, who had escaped from his owner during the war and served as a military laborer in Alexandria, Virginia, went to Calvert County after hearing a report that his family had been arrested. Diggs apparently enraged a constable by indicating his intention to continue working for the government. The constable struck Diggs and foiled his efforts to locate his family. Isaac Craig, a seventy-year-old freedman, removed his hat and cheered at a public meeting in Charles County when the speaker mentioned emancipation. For this he was seized by several men who beat him "until life was nearly extinct." In St. Mary's County, Milly Sewell received a brutal beating at the hands of a neighbor, Jane Wood, whom she had insulted not only by using the term "poor white trash" but also by having a "fine crop of tobacco growing" that tended to sustain the invidious comparison. Robert Carroll of Upper Marlboro, Prince George's County, got thirty-nine lashes (prescribed, according to a state's attorney, under the "unwritten law") for declaring that he would defend himself if attacked by a white man. Hilliary Powell of Rockville (Montgomery County) suffered a beating that doctors did not expect him to survive because he had the bad luck to be walking near another man who offended a white citizen, Dr. A. H. Sommers. Sommers understood the other man, John Barker, to boast that he "could have connection with every woman in this town for money." Sommers thereupon wielded his cane, not against Barker (who was a stranger to him) but against Powell, who returned a short answer to Sommers's request for information about Barker. As to Barker himself, he may or may not have said what the doctor thought he did, but he certainly could have started a fracas with much less. A black man in Ellicott's Mills, Howard County, "had the impertinence to kiss his hand to a respectable white lady of our town," according to the Ellicott's Mills *Record*. With the vocal support of the entire community, including the magistrate, "a friend of the lady embraced the first favorable opportunity of returning the salute by the application of a good sized cudgel over the darky's pate."[23]

Officials in Maryland preferred to believe, and to persuade others, that only the "lower element" engaged in acts of brutality, while people of the "respectable class" deplored such conduct. They could indeed have called to witness instances in which former owners protected freedmen from attackers. But the disposition to inflict private and summary "justice" upon black people was not the private property of the lower element, unless the lower element could be defined as doctors and magistrates and those who wrote editorials for the Ellicott's Mills *Record*.

It is true, however, that attacks upon black people proceeded from different motives for individuals of different classes. The employment of physical force in the compulsion of apprentices and their parents or in attempts by employers to reestablish slave work discipline was likely to occur precisely among the respectable class, as was the reaction of enraged astonishment when the mask of servility dropped from the face of an especially trusted former slave. For whites who had neither owned nor been in a position to hire slaves, the reaction of violence had a somewhat different origin. The departure of slavery prepared the way for the emergence into the open of class jealousy that until then had led a largely subterranean existence. The "low fellow" who gloated during the war when Edward Lloyd lost eighty-four slaves at a go exhibited his satisfaction, not at the good fortune of eighty-four fellow human beings, but at the misfortune of one. Hatred of the black man had frequently contained an unspoken component of hatred and jealousy of the black man's owner. With slavery gone, both aspects could reveal themselves—but not equally. The abolition of slavery removed such immunity as slaves had enjoyed by virtue of being the valuable property of substantial citizens. Laboring whites and those who had owned no slaves, or very few, did not gain power at the expense of former large slaveowners. In fact, upheaval among agricultural laborers threatened farmers of modest means more immediately than it threatened former large slaveowners, since these latter generally had a thicker cushion between themselves and economic disaster. Therefore the hostility of the lower class found most unhindered expression in attacks upon defenseless freedmen and other black people.[24]

Sometimes a rough division of labor occurred in violent encroachments upon black people's freedom, with members of each class carrying out those parts of the task of intimidation that fell within the social competence of their class. Thus, substantial landowners and local citizens of means might refuse to sell land to freedmen for the establishment of schools and engage in economic reprisals against renegade whites who tried to help the freedmen. "I have endevered to do the best that I could for the colord people," lamented Joseph Hall, a white carpenter of Calvert County who had indeed labored without stint on behalf of the freedmen, "and the result is that I have lost all my paternage." With "the quality" taking the high road of genteel opposition, it devolved upon those of humbler estate to take the low road of roughing up the teachers and burning down the buildings.[25]

As often as not, high road and low road met at the crossroads. Acts confidently attributed to ruffians, ne'er-do-wells, and other disreputable elements could not have gone on to the extent they did without the condonation, indeed the complicity, of people of substance and position. Samuel Harrison decribed the "low fellows" of his neighborhood who began persecuting black people in August 1864 as "tools of better men"; and he reported that "men who are recognized as gentlemen" defended the conduct of a mob that beat up a black man for "impudence." Nor was the approval of "better men" purely tacit. Recorded instances of outrages committed against freedmen are noteworthy for two characteristics: the direct or indirect participation of local notables and the connivance before, during, or after the fact of local officials. The public meeting in Charles County at which a mob attacked a freedman for cheering emancipation supplies a particularly egregious example. Not only was one member of the mob a constable; but a local magistrate who had stepped into his civilian persona long enough to join the mob resumed his official identity in order to issue a warrant for the arrest of the victim.[26]

The most determined efforts of unreconstructed Marylanders to preserve the essence of the old order ended, however, by confirming its irretrievable dissolution. For black people harbored no affection for the slave system and refused to submit tamely to its restoration. Their weapons were limited, of course. Individual resistance against overwhelming odds no doubt possessed the same efficacy it had under slavery: while exacting a heavy price from anyone making the attempt, it served notice that *this* individual at any rate would not be mistreated without a sequel.[27] Such benefits, however, were local and frequently short-lived, requiring constant renewal at rising cost. Black people placed little confidence in the good will or fairness of state and local officials; few bothered to appeal for protection from that quarter, and those who did got scant satisfaction for their trouble. Here and there a magistrate or justice of the peace attempted to do justice to the freedmen. But they were rare and were likely to be overridden. A magistrate in Annapolis, for example, was indicted by a grand jury for taking the testimony of a black woman against a white man.[28] On rare occasions help came from extraordinary individuals like R. T. Turner and his wife in Kent County and Joseph Hall in Calvert County. But such individuals faced vicious and overwhelming opposition and could accomplish little on their own. Perhaps the strongest weapon the freedmen could have wielded would have been the presence, in force and under arms, of the black military units recruited in Maryland. (The posting of black soldiers at Paducah, Kentucky, during the fall of 1865 put a stop to attacks upon freedmen in the vicinity, according to an observer.) But most of Maryland's black soliders were shipped off to Texas with the Twenty-fifth Army Corps. When they returned, demobilized and on their own, they themselves became vulnerable to individual attack.[29] Nevertheless, black people held one trump, and it was a face card: the power of the federal government through the army and, most important of all, the Bureau of Refugees, Freedmen, and Abandoned Lands, familiarly known as the Freedmen's Bureau.

Major General Lew Wallace, Commander of the Middle Department and Eighth Army Corps, anticipated the federal Freedmen's Bureau with a "Freedman's Bureau" of his own. The rush to apprentice the freedmen's children, together with the "unfriendly" disposition of courts and law officers, persuaded him early in November 1864 that the freedmen required "remedies extraordinary for all their grievances,—remedies instantaneous without money or reward,—and somebody to have care for them, to protect them, to show them the way to . . . freedom." Accordingly, he declared all freedmen under military protection, directed provost marshals to hear and record their complaints, commandeered the Maryland Club House in Baltimore as a refuge for the indigent, and established a Bureau to superintend the freedmen's affairs, with the officer in charge empowered "to institute investigations, to send for persons and papers, and to make necessary arrests." Wallace's Bureau lasted until March 1865, when the Freedmen's Bureau established by Congress within the War Department took up its work. By September 1865 all of Maryland had been placed under the jurisdiction of the federal bureau.[30]

General Wallace made a start at halting the apprenticing of black children. He even directed Brigadier General Henry H. Lockwood to move his brigade to the lower Eastern Shore and "break up" the practice there, freeing the apprentices and arresting masters if necessary. Lockwood got as far as issuing a circular publicizing the order and announcing his intention of carrying it out, and even managed to make a token arrest or two. But the army did not have the authority to stop apprenticeship, which enjoyed the sanction of Maryland law, and Lockwood received orders a few days later not to proceed under his earlier instructions. Nevertheless, the display of military resolve, albeit temporary, impressed the orphans' courts in counties that had not in any case depended heavily on slave labor. Apprenticing in the northern counties slowed dramatically and thenceforward proceeded with greater regard to such safeguards as the law afforded the freedmen. In many instances, masters and mistresses surrendered apprentices to their parents voluntarily. In the southern and Eastern Shore counties, military interference dampened enthusiasm for new apprenticeships, but did not stop them and could not restore to liberty those already indentured. When the federal Freedmen's Bureau arrived in Maryland, it took as one of its first and most important tasks mounting a legal challenge to the system of apprenticeship.[31]

In apprenticeship, as in other matters, black people looked to representatives of federal authority as their only hope. "We have no one else to help us" was a common apology for intrusions upon the time of the president, the secretary of war, military commanders, and the commissioner of the Freedmen's Bureau; and men and women walked miles to visit the offices of the local provost marshals and local agents of the Freedmen's Bureau. The freedmen showed a fine sophistication in their manner of seeking assistance. They could never be quite sure what opinion of them unfamiliar federal officials might entertain; but they could feel reasonably certain what view these same officials would take toward anything savoring of rebellion. Therefore, freedmen often buttressed their complaints of injustice with charges of disloyalty. "He is no friend to the Union," Lucy Lee took care to add at the end of her bill of particulars against the man who held her daughter in apprenticeship.[32]

Reminders of this sort were a shrewd precaution and generally made the desired impression, particularly with agents of the Freedmen's Bureau. Most agents seem to have had a genuine sympathy for the freedmen, even if they could never fully understand or appreciate the freedmen's standpoint. But even an agent whose feelings were ambivalent would be likely to have his sympathy quickened upon being informed that the author of some outrage against a freedman had lately been his own foe upon the field of battle. Most agents, after all, were officers of the Union army. Lieutenant Edward F. O'Brien, the bureau agent in charge of certain estates in St.

Mary's County confiscated from rebels, confidently attributed mistreatment of the freedmen to the "spirit which caused the men of this State to take up arms against the Govt in 61 and to aid and shelter the assassins of our late President in 65." He departed from the stiff decorum of military correspondence as he reported yet another in a series of beatings of black veterans by returned Confederate soldiers. Branding civil remedies a "farce" ("I have had all the experience I want in that line"), he confessed that these episodes were "causing belligerent feelings to spring up that I have tried to bury" and expressed the hope that he might "soon be allowed to use Justice (Irish) with(out) mercy" upon the transgressors.[33]

Representatives of Maryland's middle ground had no use for the federal interlopers. They had reluctantly accepted emancipation as the price of peace and union. But now, in their habitual fashion, they hoped to compromise the inescapable present with elements from the past totally incompatible with it. Governor Augustus W. Bradford spoke for them when he replied in October 1865 to a communication from the Commissioner of the Freedmen's Bureau, Major General Oliver O. Howard, in regard to abuses committed against the freedmen. Never one to let slip an opportunity of deploying a long-winded cliché, Bradford dusted off several classics in answering the Bureau's charges at length. First there was the old "you're another" argument: why should Maryland be arraigned for refusing the testimony of black witnesses when Indiana had done the same thing in 1831? Then there was the familiar sonnet to the long-suffering "loyal Citizens" of Maryland, bereft of their slave property "suddenly . . . and contrary to precedents in other States." There followed the customary adversion to slaves "suddenly and unexpectedly" presented with a freedom of which they held an "inflated," "exaggerated," and "erroneous" notion. The governor even resurrected that stock figure of the slaveholders' political folklore, the outside agitator. Former owners and former slaves, he insisted, would settle down to "more correct views" were it not for the superserviceable interference of a "third party actuated by some selfish, sinister or vindictive purpose" who was "by far the greatest Mischief maker of the three." Bradford did not name the Freedmen's Bureau at this juncture. He did not need to. Commissioner Howard would have had to be decidedly slow-witted to miss the intended indictment of his own subordinates.

Bradford simply could not understand what all the fuss was about. The exclusion of testimony by black people did no harm in the end, he insisted. In all the instances of assault and battery to which the Bureau had drawn his attention a remedy was available at law, since white people had been present at the scene—as indeed they had been, assaulting and battering or cheering on the perpetrators from the sidelines. (Bradford had left office, and thus could not explicate his doctrine with respect to the case of one John H. Farmer of Calvert County, who in March 1866 shot and killed Philip Forbes and seriously wounded Forbes's wife. Though Farmer himself boasted of his act and "almost every man one meets," according to a Freedmen's Bureau agent, "can recite the details," Farmer went free for lack of a witness.) The governor agreed that the legislature ought to change the law and predicted that it soon would, "yielding," he added in an ingenuous preview of how the substance of injustice might be preserved without the form, "to that public sentiment now almost universal, that all exceptions to testimony should go to its *credit* rather than its *competency*."

As for apprenticeship, the only minor problem he could see was that black apprentices were not entitled under the law to the same education as white apprentices, and he felt sure that "an early Legislature" would see to that. Where parents alleged that their children were illegally apprenticed, they possessed the "entirely adequate security" of proceedings under habeas corpus, by which any judge could inquire into the legality of the indentures. The governor's powers of imagination evidently did not extend far enough to suggest to him the difficulty that poor and usually illiterate freedmen might experience in hiring lawyers, getting copies of indentures, posting bonds, and so on. In any event, though no "early Legislature" got around to providing for the education of black apprentices, that of 1867 did find time to remove from jurisdiction in apprenticeship cases Judge Hugh Lennox Bond of the Baltimore Criminal Court, the only judge in the state likely to issue writs of habeas corpus on behalf of the freedmen. (One judge refused a petition for habeas corpus on the grounds that, under the Dred Scott decision, the parents were not citizens and thus could not demand redress at law.) Children released under Bond's orders were promptly retaken by masters and mistresses on writs of replevin. In some cases parents of replevined apprentices went to jail for the crime of "harboring" or "enticing" their own children, and could not plead in their own behalf that they had acted under the writ of Judge Bond.

Having disposed to his own satisfaction of the major issues, Bradford went on to express moral distaste for suggestions that the "humane and benevolent" duty of caring for old and infirm former slaves might now be imposed upon former owners by law, something that "has always been sedulously avoided by every Civilized people." He warned Commissioner Howard against relying unduly upon the ex parte statements of freedmen, which "ought to be received with many grains of allowance," though he betrayed no comparable reservations in passing along the ex parte complaints of planters in St. Mary's County about the conduct of the freedmen. He ended his disquisition by "forbear[ing] to recur"—and forthwith recurring—to his well-known opinion that the Freedmen's Bureau had no business operating at all "in loyal States or among Colored persons therein, freed by its own laws and not by the progress of our Armies."[34]

The governor-elect, Thomas Swann, indicated his "entire concurrence" with Bradford's views, and soon entered the lists with the Bureau on his own account. He bristled with affronted authority and jealousy of jurisdictional prerogative at a suggestion during the summer of 1866 that the interposition of the federal army might be required in Maryland. Dismissing as isolated and "trivial" an episode in which white roughs beat up a black man driving a cart through the streets of Annapolis on an errand for his employer, Swann expressed regret that "certain citizens" insisted upon bypassing the executive authority of the state by direct appeal to the Freedmen's Bureau. He and the people of Maryland, he insisted, stood ready "to do the amplest justice to the freedmen in all that relates to his person and his property."[35]

Just as Governor Bradford could not understand the uproar about apprenticeship and the exclusion of testimony by black persons against whites, Governor Swann could not understand the furor over the sale into terms of slavery of several black people convicted of petty crimes. Outsiders assumed that this vestige of the persecution of free blacks during the 1850s had died along with slavery. So its reappearance in the courtrooms of Judges W. H. Tuck and D. R. Magruder (the latter of whom also distinguished himself by effectively nullifying the civil rights bill within his circuit) created a sensation that echoed in the United States Congress, set the Freedmen's Bureau in motion, and resulted in the indictment of Judge Magruder. Black people were sentenced, without trial by jury, to terms of slavery for offenses such as the theft of a one-dollar pocketbook, a three-dollar pig, a beehive said to be worth five dollars, and a twenty-five-dollar lot of tobacco. Swann considered the law under which they were sentenced a beneficent measure that, so far from oppressing black people, actually made "an unfair discrimination . . . against the white man . . . for whom the same privilege is withheld." He offered no evidence, needless to say, that any white convict actually requested this "privilege." And, although a Freedmen's Bureau agent reported that black people who could arrange to be purchased by relatives preferred this mode of punishment to confinement in the penitentiary, the sums required were no trifle to people disposing of little, if any, cash. Isaac Skinner, charged with the theft of a dollar's-worth of property, was reportedly sold for fifty-four dollars, and William Stepney bought his half-brother, Richard Harris, for fifty dollars.[36]

Whatever Swann might claim—and perhaps genuinely believe—the practice represented a partial exhumation of the rotting corpse of slavery. No one understood this with more immediacy than the freed man or woman exposed to sale for an act that was a crime only because of the slave past. In November 1865 a woman in Annapolis was sentenced to two years' enslavement for persuading her children to leave their former owner, who had had them bound to him as apprentices. Yielding to pressure, the legislature of 1867 repealed the law allowing such sales. One state senator could not resist thumbing his nose at federal authority in the process. "Mr. Earle (Democrat) took occasion to say that this legislation was not caused by a deference to the views of Congress," the Cecil *Whig* reported. "We venture the assertion, however, that Mr. E. is mistaken."[37]

In the final analysis, apprenticeship yielded to pressure as well. It could not last. Even in societies in which apprenticeship embraced adults as well as children and had the sponsorship of the national state—in Jamaica and Cuba, for example—the system collapsed under its own weight. Apprenticeship in Maryland not only faced opposition from the national state (as represented by the Freedmen's Bureau) but, more important, quickly outlived its usefulness to the former owners who had at first seized eagerly upon it. As a means of helping them cope with the reality of emancipation, its function was transitional. As a direct device for the compulsion of labor, its scope had been limited all along. The estimated 2,519 children apprenticed between November 1864 and April 1867 provided a meager substitute for more than 87,000 slaves.[38]

Nevertheless, apprenticeship did not die as abruptly as had the practice of condemning freedmen to terms of slavery. The legal efforts of the Freedmen's Bureau bore fruit in October 1867, when a decision of the United States Circuit Court, with Chief Justice Salmon P. Chase presiding, declared illegal any distinction in rights or privileges between black and white apprentices. That undermined the legal foundation of the system, but did not automatically restore the liberty of the apprentices. Parents then had to marshal resources to challenge obdurate masters and mistresses—no easy matter. A month after the court's decision, Susan Taylor, accompanied by a white neighbor and armed with a letter from the Baltimore attorney and Union party notable Henry Stockbridge, attempted to recover her children from one Stephen Fuller in Calvert County. Fuller sent her away with the comment that "Stockbridge is a liar and never told the truth." A year later Judge Magruder was holding a woman in jail on the charge of persuading her sixteen-year-old daughter to abscond. The mother insisted that she had not prompted her daughter; rather, the girl had left on her own accord the day after a meeting sponsored by the Freedmen's Bureau "saying she was free now, the Speakers said so." Complaints of apprenticeship remained on the Bureau's books in 1870. Nor was that the end. As late as 1876, Governor James B. Groome was advising the General Assembly to amend the apprenticeship laws so as to remove distinctions between white and black apprentices. Failure to do so in the past, he reminded the legislators, "has resulted, in many instances, in the indentures of colored apprentices being set aside by the Courts."[39]

Ironically (or perhaps it is not ironic at all), black people whose freedom predated the constitution of 1864 occasionally discovered that general emancipation did not automatically rectify injustices dating from the epoch when their freedom remained hostage to slavery. Joseph Turney's mother learned that she could not have her son's apprenticeship to Joseph Childs set aside, even though she had not consented to it. The boy had been first bound as a free person prior to emancipation, upon a showing before the orphans' court that he was likely to become a public charge. Only evidence of cruel and inhuman treatment, according to a Freedmen's Bureau agent, could warrant annulment of the indentures. And, as the boy's first mistress had found him so "refractory" after six years that she petitioned the court to turn him over to Childs, a judge would probably have allowed Childs considerable latitude in the methods he employed to control his apprentice.[40]

A combination of circumstances explains why the moribund system of apprenticeship lingered on. Part of the reason is that the Freedmen's Bureau, increasingly a vestigial and figurehead presence, eventually became reluctant to intervene when simple requests and persuasion would not suffice. In May 1869, John Maynard of Sunderlandville, Calvert County, sought the return of his deceased sister's three children, held by Philip McKinney of Huntington, Calvert County. The Bureau warned Maynard that it would take no action "further than using such influence as can be given outside of legal interference." Apparently, that "influence" was not exerted until December, when Bureau officials sent a letter to McKinney's widow. In her reply, the widow insisted that the children had been hired to her before her mother's death until the expiration of their time of bondage, and that "no law will deprive me of them." The question of the validity of a hire arrangement predicated upon a bondage that had been abolished appears not to have detained Bureau officials. On 3 January 1870, they sent the entire correspondence to headquarters in Washington; and on February 3 headquarters wrote to Maynard disclaiming jurisdiction and suggesting that "unless ill-treated the children had better remain."[41]

"Had better." That well-intentioned phrase, soon to become the hallmark of experts presuming to know better what was good for families than families did themselves, frequently greeted freedmen pursuing their own sense of order amid the cross-purposes of both adversaries and advocates who thought differently. As time passed and its influence waned, the Bureau grew more inclined to advise that parents accept indentures to which they had not consented, on the grounds that staying with the master served the child's best interests. In June 1868, Araminta Hazard sought help in recovering her son and grandson, who were held by Peregrine Hendrickson of Warwick, Cecil County. Former United States Senator John A. J. Cresswell intervened on Hendrickson's behalf, satisfying the Bureau that "the children would be benefitted by remaining with Mr. H." The complaint office closed the case in August with the statement that "if Mr. H. will give pledges to treat the children like white apprentices it may be wise to suspend further action, as it is doubtful whether the decision of the Chief Justice is applicable." It did not appear "wise," evidently, to test the doubt in the arena where such doubts are ordinarily resolved: the courtroom.[42]

The waning influence and growing complaisance of the Bureau only partly explain how apprenticeship managed to hang on. Equally important was the special way in which apprenticeship intersected the family life of the freedmen. Lying athwart the manifold complications inherent in all family relations—let alone those inherited from slavery—it brought to the surface a bewildering array of conflicts that allowed cases to drag on unresolved. Sometimes these conflicts were, in effect, family disputes over custody of a child: as when Ellen Lea sought to recover her granddaughter from an apprenticeship to which the girl's father apparently raised no objection; when Henry Offutt pleaded with the Bureau not to help his estranged wife take possession of their children; or when Joanna Brown failed to recover two children whom her husband had apprenticed to a master in Virginia. Upon occasion the children themselves declared a preference to remain with the masters or mistresses to whom they had been bound—

although such cases arouse suspicion when the children were questioned about their preference in the presence of their masters and mistresses by agents only temporarily on the scene.[43]

The most usual conflict was between freedmen and outsiders who failed to understand the freedmen's notions of family connection and responsibility or to appreciate the special arrangements that slavery had obliged them to improvise. Henry Smith of Centreville, Queen Anne's County, asked the Bureau's help in June 1868 in recovering his seventeen-year-old daughter, Maria Wright. Though investigation established that the girl was indeed being held against her will and wanted Smith to assume custody of her, Bureau officials permitted themselves to be swayed by the master's contention that Smith was not really the girl's father. They neither understood nor showed any interest in the source of the feeling of responsibility that led Smith to regard the girl as his daughter. Instead, even after the master indicated his willingness to release her, the assistant commissioner decided that it would be "for the interest of the girl" to remain where she was. In a case unusual in that the two men holding the apprentices were themselves black, Elizabeth Barney in May 1868 sought the discharge of her deceased sister's five children. The masters countered that they were treating the children well and instructing them—statements that were duly verified in a letter from a local black minister. They went on to say, proving that shared skin color carried no guarantee of shared standpoint, that in any case Barney was only the half-sister of the children's mother. Though no one suggested that the masters were related to the children in any degree at all, the Bureau placed upon Elizabeth Barney the onus of submitting evidence that she was their nearest relative and of producing letters from prominent people recommending their delivery to her. The Bureau did not even think fit to inquire whether any qualified person had consented to the indentures in the first place. Annie Cornish may not have fared any better in trying to recover her niece, Sarah Ann Kennard, in August 1868. The girl's father was dead and her mother had been sold out of the state ten years earlier and not heard from since. The records do not indicate the outcome of her appeal, but the chances are good that she, too, encountered skepticism of a mere aunt's right to demand the return of an apprenticed child. Complications of this kind obstructed the resolution of apprenticeship cases, especially once parents were thrown upon their own resources and had to seek relief individually before the courts.[44]

Clearing away the debris of the old slave principle of social cohesion was only a part—the simpler part—of what Maryland had to accomplish during its version of Reconstruction. The other part was to install a social order based on a new principle. Though an outside referee, in the guise of the Freedmen's Bureau, was on hand for a time to supervise the installation, the task fell by and large to Marylanders themselves. (Few Yankee investors foresaw a rich future in cereal or mixed farming using the labor of the freedmen, as many did, for a deluded moment, in cotton planting with freed labor in the former Confederate states.)[45] Observers from the North had no doubt what the new ruling principle ought to be: the market and the cash nexus. Surely former masters and former slaves could find here the key to mutually beneficial relations. Out of self-interest, freedmen ought to go willingly to work for former owners; and out of self-interest, former owners ought to deal fairly and justly with them. A Freedmen's Bureau agent well schooled in this theory expressed naïve dismay upon discovering that "the promptings of self interest are not strong enough to induce fair treatment" of the freedmen by planters in St. Mary's County. The planters' misconduct, he remarked to his superior, tended to produce "a conflict of interest, where there should exist most perfect harmony." Another agent urged planters in Dorchester County, who must have thought him rather simple, to "be just to the Negro & thus make demand and supply mutually advantageous." (No respecter of persons, this last gentleman exhorted the freedmen in equally simple fashion, assuring them that "the *freedom* of the *world* was but a *trifle compared with the freedom 'when with Christ maketh free.'* ")[46]

What seemed obvious to outsiders, however, was alien to the experience of those brought up under the influence of slave society. Neither ex-slaves nor ex-free blacks nor ex-slaveowners automatically assumed the habits of thought and conduct appropriate to a system of labor disciplined by the marketplace. Former slaves were accustomed to a pattern of social relations in which basic subsistence—however rude and, upon occasion, stinted—was something to be taken for granted. It was not a reward for service that the owner could withhold at his whim, nor was it the accidental byproduct of the chance workings of the marketplace. Moreover, it was confined within customary limits, not subject to expansion by individual effort. Masters had always claimed the labor of the slaves by right of personal ownership, not as a commodity which, belonging to the slaves themselves, had to be purchased from them and regulated through the impersonal mediation of the market. So fundamental was this to the slaveholders' world that the presence of free black people whose working time was in fact a commodity to be

bargained for and regulated through the market posed an intolerable challenge, calling forth repeated (though futile) countermeasures. Free blacks,
for this reason, operated as an uncomfortable auxiliary of the slave population, to which both personal ties and the logic of law and politics assim-
ilated them.

With slavery removed, black people were not likely to agree with
former slaveowners about what the next step ought to be. But neither group
was likely, without prodding, to settle into the routine of market relations.
If these were to come about, they would have to be taught to all hands and
the cook. And those undertaking the job of teaching would be working
with material as resistant as in the former Confederate states. Slavery on
the middle ground was no better preparation than slavery anywhere else
for the establishment of capitalist market social relations.[47] The apparatus
of market society, superimposed on the social habits slavery had bequeathed,
produced a caricature that grossly exaggerated some traits of capitalist relations, totally elided others, and blended the rest into a concoction for
which no self-respecting exponent of political economy would have wished
to assume responsibility.

Curious makeshifts appeared, compounded of new assumptions incon-
gruously juxtaposed with old ones. Both former slaves and former owners
gave up parts of the old habits, while simultaneously trying to preserve
others that still accorded with their sense of the fitness of things. Former
owners retained the expectation of obedience and deference on the part of
former slaves but sloughed off what remained of their sense of obligation
for the old and helpless. (The vestry of Chester Parish in Kent County
even discovered that the immemorial custom of black people's burying their
dead in the Episcopal graveyard would not suit the new state of affairs.)
Dr. Washington Duvall, a former owner in Montgomery County, asked
the Freedmen's Bureau to relieve him of two aged black people for whom
he had been providing, one of whom had a spinal injury. Duvall may have
had a stronger sense of noblesse oblige than many of his fellows, who drove
the aged and disabled away without ceremony, for he kept the freedmen
on while he sought to make other arrangements for them. But he was not
alone in his objective, as public authorities in charge of almshouses, insane
asylums, juvenile homes, homes for the blind and the aged, and the like
came to appreciate. Before long they were complaining about being saddled
with problems that had not previously belonged to the public sphere. Former slaves, for their part, readily threw off rituals of deference and servility
that they considered degrading and obsolete, supplying grounds for charges

of "uppity" or "impudent" conduct and sometimes suffering violent reprisals in the process. But often, with no shadow of a desire for the return of slavery as such, they continued to expect protection and assistance from former masters and mistresses as a matter of simple human right. Susanna Warfield spoke with disgust of her former slave Clary, "who goes about like a beggar on the streets, and says she belongs to me."[48]

The legislature of 1867 cast a revealing light upon its understanding of the new order by passing a measure reminiscent of feudal corvée. The law required able-bodied men between eighteen and fifty living in rural districts to work at least two days a year on the public roads, furnishing tools when ordered. County commissioners held discretion to determine the wages to be paid road laborers. As written, the law was a blatant piece of class legislation, since rural citizens of means could escape the duty by furnishing a substitute, by supplying teams or wagons, or by paying a fine. As locally enforced, the measure could be even more discriminatory. A resident of Prince Frederick district in Calvert County reported to the Freedmen's Bureau that "Dudug [Judge] Magruder and the Rest of Princfrederic offercurs Makeing all the colord & the Poor class white men walk [work] too days on the Roads or pay Three Dollars" (the law specified $1.50) "or go to Jaile teen days." The official designated in the law as the "road supervisor" was promptly rechristened with an older name: "[T]hay have one man in Evry sich a disstence for over seer and they gave him one hundread & fifty Dollars to super intend & all the colord Men walk for nothing."[49]

Even those marked by their occupation as bearers of the new order themselves occasionally proved how persistent the old habits were. "Labor agents," self-assigned to the task of bringing together agricultural laborers and those needing their services, provide a good example. These entrepreneurs (apparently themselves not of slaveholding background) understood at once that people who had formerly owned laborers would henceforth have to hire them. But they did not as quickly take it for granted that the laborers themselves must be equal parties to the transaction. Instead, they rounded up freedmen—from the District of Columbia and Virginia as well as Maryland—by methods ranging from misrepresentation to duress, and offered them to farmers at so much (usually five dollars) per head, deducting transportation costs and other expenses from the men's wages. Some of these labor agents brazenly approached officials of the Freedmen's Bureau to keep them supplied with hands, provoking Captain William F. Spurgin to the indignant retort that "the slave trade is stopped."[50]

The farmers' desperate need for labor, especially in the first year of emancipation, made for a rich enough host to support a goodly number of parasites. But, as parasites sometimes will, these began feeding on one another, rustling each other's hands and casting public aspersions on each other's business ethics. Oliver Wood set about his competitors during the late summer and fall of 1865, charging that "a gang of thieves and loafers" would descend upon his hands as fast as he could assemble them and "persuade [them] to run off or steal them away under faults pretentions." It was not, when all was said and done, a line of work pursued by fastidious or even merely scrupulous individuals. And although Wood, who served as an assistant sergeant-at-arms in the Maryland House of Delegates, secured endorsements from various notables, he still found himself in the rather awkward predicament of a customer robbed in a panel house: before claiming public sympathy, he must explain what he was doing there in the first place. Wood had been known during the war as a substitute broker ("not a calling," Judge Bond dryly remarked, "which superinduces the cultivation of all the Christian virtues") and had attracted the unfavorable notice of the secretary of war. In his new calling he became the subject of bitter complaints by freedmen, as well as competitors and a former employee. The charges, which he denied, included taking and holding men by force, promising them higher wages than they actually received, and taking them to places where they had not agreed to go. Men leaving home on the promise of fifteen dollars a month were actually offered six dollars upon arrival at their destination. Some expecting to work in Baltimore ended up on the Eastern Shore. One group who thought they were going "some where on the bay" found themselves on a schooner bound for the guano islands.[51] In the circus of charges and countercharges that accompanied the labor procurement business, Confederate sympathizers received credit for some misdeeds that they may have had nothing to do with—or no more to do with than anyone else. Freedmen were not the only ones who knew which buttons to press in order to elicit a favorable response from federal officials. Samuel Bentz, a farmer and lumber dealer of Hood's Mills in Carroll County, protested to the Freedmen's Bureau that rebels were sowing discontent among his hands and encouraging them to leave him. But, amid the prevailing shortage of labor, a more straightforward motive than revenge for the lost cause could have explained the pirating of help.[52]

Even when normal features of capitalist social relations duly made their appearance, they often did so slightly off-center or wearing an unexpected disguise. Former slaveholders agreed promptly enough to pay wages when they were desperate for hands. (Nevertheless, some, while bitterly denouncing the fecklessness of the freedmen in declining to work for them, permitted themselves finicking restrictions upon who was suitable as a laborer: veterans of the Union army and their relatives, for example, usually were not.) But having agreed to hire freedmen, many could not carry through on a responsible basis of employer and employee. An especially stubborn or self-confident employer might just refuse to pay, defying the freedman to do something about it. But subtler methods were available as well. It was a simple matter to get the *X* of an illiterate freedman on a false receipt or on an agreement permitting various deductions that could wipe out all earnings by the end of the season. Where agreements were verbal, the freedman's word against that of a white employer was at first inadmissible at law and, once admitted, likely to carry little weight.[53]

Freedmen's Bureau agents spent much of their time trying to resolve complaints by freedmen that employers had failed to pay them as promised. Of fifty-one complaints lodged by black persons against whites at the Bureau's Bladensburg (Prince George's County) office between June 1866 and September 1867, twenty-two were recorded as "owed for labor"; and some of the fourteen recorded as "breach of contract" or "debt" may have involved the same issue.[54] Some employers simply did not have the financial resources to meet a cash payroll. When they failed to pay wages at the end of a contract period, they were in effect defaulting on loans received from the freedmen. But for many the main problem seemed to be that they could not bring themselves to bargain with and pay those whose labor they were accustomed to command by simple, personal, and unquestioned right. The freedmen knew this perfectly well and, even when people whom they otherwise trusted attempted to reassure them, refused to be impressed by legalisms that contradicted their own understanding. "They have no faith in Contracts," the assistant superintendent of the confiscated rebel farms in St. Mary's County explained to his superior in October 1865, "and though I have taken great pains to explain I have in every case failed to convince them that Such a document is as binding on the employers as on themselves." The superintendent concurred. The freedmen steadfastly refused to work for former slaveowners, he reported to headquarters, "giving as a reason, they knew them too well."[55]

Employers made complaints of their own against the freedmen, seconded (with rather more indulgence) by agents of the Freedmen's Bureau. The most common was unreliability. The former slaves seemed to be always on the move, especially at the times when employers most needed them.

Restless, apparently purposeless movement was indeed one of the first consequences of emancipation to strike observers, in Maryland as elsewhere; and it continued in evidence after the novelty of freedom had worn off. In the fall of 1866 a Freedmen's Bureau agent declared it impossible to guess very closely at the black population of Prince George's County because freedmen were entering and leaving all the time, but he supposed the number "not more than half" that recorded in the census of 1860. In 1867 the state agricultural chemist reported that the loss of black population had depressed land values over large portions of southern Maryland and the lower Eastern Shore. Emancipation gave new impetus to what the gradual erosion of decades had begun and the war had powerfully aggravated.[56]

However it may have appeared to observers, the freedmen's moving about was not random or purposeless, but in pursuit of very particular objectives. Often freedmen went in search of relatives and friends from whom they had been separated either by the routine of life in slavery or by the confusion attendant upon the war. Sometimes they were activating their only available weapon—and a crude one it was—for punishing dishonest or oppressive employers. Occasionally freedmen exhibited their own mirror-image version of the ex-slaveholders' rules of suitability that excluded veterans of the Union army and their families. Asked why the freedmen refused contracts to work for nearby landowners, the superintendent of the confiscated farms in St. Mary's County replied, "[M]y people would rather work for three dollars a month in Washington or Baltimore than to work for the traitors here for twelve."[57]

For many freedmen, frequent changes of position provided a means of asserting independence. Forced to work at much the same tasks as before and for much the same people, they preserved their sense of free agency by staying as short a time as possible with an employer and then leaving, even if only to take up a new job just a short distance away. Susanna Warfield thought that she had solved her problem of domestic servants in January 1865, when she hired "two good colored women." But in the months that followed she contemplated with chagrin a parade of domestic help into and out of her household. "Louisa left us the 8th of March—I hired her by the day until the 16th—When W. Comas' Ellen came—She remained until June . . . then came Kitty—then Betty—all good for nothing—." Perhaps because domestic service offered so little opportunity to escape a routine barely distinguishable from slavery, house servants had a special reputation for fickleness. "They wish to be constantly gadding about the streets," as one Bureau agent saw it, "and their great desire is to get to Baltimore as their 'Summum Bonum.' "[58]

The reasons freedmen moved from job to job sometimes came close enough to the ideal precepts of market-disciplined behavior to enrage employers, embarrass sympathetic outsiders, and fool subsequent historians into the bargain. The freedmen showed, in fact, as ready a knack as former slaveholders for adopting facsimiles of proper market-oriented conduct, togged up in nonregulation garments that mark them as impostors. It took the freedmen no time at all, for example, to master the concept of seeking the best terms. They would forsake an employer without notice or ceremony, blithely disregarding prior agreements, if they thought they could do better somewhere else. "It seems they cannot set a due value on their labor, and are ever dissatisfied with their wages . . . ," an exasperated Freedmen's Bureau agent reported. Another remarked that planters could not hold onto laborers during the oyster season, when larger wages beckoned from the water. Despairing of reforming the freedmen, one agent recommended shorter contract periods. However uncomfortable a truth this may have been for those it inconvenienced or nonplussed, the freedmen's behavior in this regard approximated the ideal model of a competitive capitalist economy, in which "factors of production" are supposed to gravitate instantaneously and of their own accord to wherever they will earn the greatest return. But the freedmen gave this pet fiction of political economists their own special inflection. Not habituated to that logic of ever-increasing effort to satisfy ever-expanding needs that market society had learned to call "ambition," they did not seek higher wages with a view toward earning a maximum income. Instead, they used higher wages as a means of shortening the time spent at work on other people's behalf. "As soon as the hand earns a little money, he wants to quit," farmers time and again complained.[59]

Planters and farmers in Maryland still held the same set of contradictory expectations that had driven them into fruitless experiments with methods of controlling the antebellum free black population. In the old days they had expected the responses of both the slave and the free wage laborer from people who were outside the slave relationship but not entirely within that of free wage labor. That is, they expected workers to be available (and dismissible) at will, like free laborers, but at the same time docile as to the terms of their employment and largely immobile, like slaves. They were asking, in effect, for the best of the worlds of slavery and free labor from people on the fringes of both worlds but true inhabitants of neither. Employers of black labor carried on after emancipation with the same inconsistent expectations, arraigning the freedmen both for failing to exhibit the docility of slaves and for failing to respond in approved fashion to wage incentives.

Former slaveholders and their spokesmen automatically resorted to race as an explanation of the freedmen's maddening conduct. The editor of the Chestertown (Kent County) *Transcript* gave a classic rendition of the argument shortly after emancipation. Calling to his support the precedent of the British Caribbean (he had forgotten Haiti, or he could not have asserted that "[t]he emancipation of an enslaved race has heretofore, in the history of the world, been only effected in times of peace and tranquility"), he argued that it was in black people's nature to be indolent: "The ambition of the negro as a race . . . does not rise above the meagre necessaries of life" without outside intervention "to enforce his industry." The editor might have been speaking of English workers in an earlier era or of Asian, African, or Latin American peasants in a later one. (Or, for that matter, of the white oystermen of Maryland in his own day, who would soon be the targets of similar criticism.) For the complaint has reappeared with monotonous regularity, and without respect to color, wherever on earth would-be capitalist employers have tried to fashion wage laborers out of people formed outside the world of capitalist social relations and still standing with one foot outside that world.

No one has an innate vocation to be a proletarian, any more than anyone has an innate vocation to be a slave. The compulsion of society—not inborn nature—creates proletarians, just as it does slaves. Despite the obscuring veil of racial ideology, the editor of the *Transcript* perceived as much, since in his next breath he executed a subtle shift from the inborn characteristics of a race to the social circumstances of a class. "One fruitful source of idleness with this class," he declared, "has been the ability to possess themselves of a hut and a few acres of poverty-stricken land, thereby enabling them to preserve the semblance of the means of living." A meeting of landowners in Port Tobacco, Charles County, anticipated this conclusion without stopping to adduce historical precedents, by proposing to deny freedmen independent access to the means of living. Their first resolution "earnestly recommended" that owners "not . . . rent or lease any house or land to any free negro . . . unless such house or land is kept under the control and supervision of the proprietor or owner thereof."

Returning to the theme some months later, the *Transcript*'s editor echoed (in a different key) an analysis put forward at approximately the same time by a far more profound thinker. The freedman "seems possessed," the editor contended, "with the idea that he must secure sufficient money from three days work to live the balance of the seven in idleness." Speaking (but without reproach) of eighteenth-century English workers before the advent of large-scale capitalist industry, Karl Marx commented that "[t]he fact that they could live a whole week on the wage of four days did not appear . . . a sufficient reason for working for the capitalist for the other two days."[60]

Well-meaning historians, reacting to the ugly trappings of racial ideology in which the *Transcript* and the people for whom it spoke customarily dressed their observations, have tended to dismiss the observations themselves as delusions born of racial prejudice. Only racism, they assume, could have prevented everyone from recognizing that the freedman behaved like any other rational exemplar of the species *homo economicus*.[61] It is true, of course, that racial ideology supplied the prevailing vocabulary in which people thought and spoke of these matters, and that racial malevolence was never absent or very far from the surface.[62] But it is a mistake to leave the matter there. Even former slaveholders must be granted the integrity of their experience, which it is the historian's job to understand as a whole, complete with its ideological distortions. Taking the former slaveholders seriously naturally does not mean taking them literally. The "idleness" in which they supposed the freedmen wished to spend their absences from wage work might well include cultivating garden patches, making baskets, quilts, furniture, and other items for the home, or catching oysters, crabs, and fish in the Bay and its tributaries for sale or home consumption. But cultivating their own gardens, working for wages just long enough to earn a family subsistence, and refusing to establish themselves on a permanent basis with a single employer understandably looked like indolent and even irrational conduct to those who required the freedmen to form a disciplined proletariat, not a subsistence-oriented peasantry.

It does no more justice to the ex-slaves than to the ex-slaveholders to blink away evidence that they failed to conform to the model of the economists. Well-intentioned efforts to prove that the freedmen behaved like any rational *homo economicus* rest on an unstated assumption that everyone ought to, on an unexamined belief that such behavior is an attribute of human nature rather than a product of human society, and on a needless anxiety to defend the freedmen against any implication that they were not as good as everybody else. Once it is understood that declining the role of *homo economicus* is not a sign of inferiority but of habituation to nonmarket social relations, the urge to offer this otiose defense disappears. Then it becomes possible to respect the integrity of the experience of both freedmen and former slaveholders and to make sense of their own consciousness of their experience, not by falsifying their experience, but by understanding their consciousness.

Probably no one in Maryland—not former slaves, former owners, former free blacks, or former nonslaveholders—found that the world they eventually inherited bore much resemblance to the one they desired. Forces gathering at the national and international levels became more and more imperious in setting the pace and direction of Maryland's next steps. But that first one at which Marylanders willingly or unwillingly assisted—doing away with slavery—encompassed an enormous and still unfinished drama. The period that served Maryland in lieu of Reconstruction was in every sense a large period: large in the tasks it accomplished and large in those it left to be accomplished in the future. It required a long and costly struggle for black people in Maryland to become, not free blacks, but freed men and women. It required a longer and costlier struggle to make it clear that they were not just freed men and women but also free and equal citizens. It would be a yet longer and yet costlier struggle—one, even now, scarcely begun—to establish for all time that white and black people are more than just equal citizens, but that they, along with all the other peoples of the earth, are equally dignified members of one and the same human race, sharing in the final analysis one and the same human condition.

CHAPTER SEVEN

The New Order in the Countryside

Throughout the South the abolition of slavery worked a revolution in the social relations of the countryside. But nowhere did a new order arise immediately from the ashes of the old. Instead, a period of transition set in, so protracted in certain parts of the South as to engender a mistaken doubt in the minds of some scholars that a revolution occurred at all. The survival intact, at least temporarily, of a good many antebellum landholdings, and the rapid improvisation of means of coercing labor that to incautious observation might appear a simple continuation of slavery by other means, contributed to an illusory appearance of stasis. In the cotton heartland of the South and—though perhaps to a somewhat lesser extent—in areas where tobacco production either continued unscathed or acquired a new impetus, the persistence of old faces and superficially close mimics of old social forms hid for a time the profound change that was under way beneath the surface.

A long, agonizing transition was inevitable over most of the former Confederacy. As long as plantation slavery held sway, it suspended not only slaves and their owners but also much of the nonslaveholding white majority from participation in capitalist social relations. At the same time, it stunted the growth of an indigenous bourgeoisie, leaving the South not just a primarily agricultural society (the United States as a whole remained that throughout the nineteenth century) but a subordinate adjunct to the economies of its chief customers, Great Britain and the Northern states. Fighting the war exacted a heavy toll in sheer physical destruction. Losing the war wiped out the considerable political autonomy that the planter class had enjoyed and forced the South to reorganize its internal affairs to the specifications of the Northern victors—that is, along the lines of capitalist market

167

society. At the same time, the destruction of one major form of social wealth (slaves) dragged down the value of the other (land) and obliged the South to begin the long march toward capitalist social relations under most unpromising circumstances. In their different ways, both freedmen and white yeomanry showed themselves unenthusiastic about the prospect. Planters also hesitated to accept the full implications of capitalist relations, with their presumption of formal marketplace equality. And neither planters (land-poor as they were) nor the diminutive Southern bourgeoisie had sufficient resources to carry through the transition without outside assistance. When Northern capitalists took a hand, they did so with their own ends in view and "developed" the South as their semicolonial hinterland, with the Southern upper class—stripped for a crucial interval of power within the national state—playing a subordinate role.[1]

Both remote and more recent history guaranteed Maryland a very different sort of transition. In the first place, adherence to the Union (however qualified or reluctant on some people's part) preserved Maryland's full standing in the apparatus of the national state. In the second place, though Maryland experienced its share of battles, it sustained no equivalent of the physical destruction that cost the former Confederate states half their agricultural machinery and a third of their livestock. In the third place, slaves had ceased to be the major form of social wealth in Maryland long before emancipation. Therefore their loss, while a serious blow to their owners, did not threaten to hamstring the vital processes of economic life. Finally, Maryland had long claimed a homegrown bourgeoisie, which operated with considerable independence from the slave economy. This bourgeoisie did reasonably well for itself during the war—government contracts benefited the flour-milling, iron, copper, and shipbuilding industries, as well as railroads and coal mining—and had no need to subordinate itself to outside sponsors in adjusting to postwar conditions. Baltimore manufacturers even gave birth in 1882 to their own propaganda outlet, the *Manufacturers' Record,* which appointed to itself the task of remaking the South in the New South image. In marked contrast to the former Confederate states, Maryland had a well-developed and well-endowed banking system. Planters and farmers formerly dependent upon slave labor could call upon mortgage credit, rather than the debilitating crop-lien system that seized hold of the cotton states, to see them through the transition.[2]

Maryland was an unlikely candidate, in any case, for colonization by outside capital. It produced no agricultural staple and possessed no obvious mineral wealth (other than coal, already under intensive exploitation) that would offer as potentially lucrative a target to external capital as cotton or iron in the former Confederacy. Tobacco continued to decline, and Maryland never regained its former importance as a tobacco producer. In 1860 Maryland ranked fourth among the states in pounds of tobacco produced; in 1880 it ranked seventh, producing less than one-sixth as much as first-ranking Kentucky. Maryland's iron industry, briefly resuscitated by the war, resumed a decline that had started long before. Though outsiders showed some interest in fruit-growing on the Eastern Shore, this continued for the most part to be a local enterprise. Coal mining aside, the most important extractive industries of Maryland remained within the capacity of local entrepreneurs operating with a relatively modest initial outlay, or even within the purview of petty commodity production by individuals. In 1873 a correspondent described for readers of the Baltimore *Sun* a desolate section of Somerset County known as Dames Quarter: "a vast marsh interspersed with fields of stunted pines, growing to a height of not more than eight or ten feet, the whole frequently overflowed by the tide." In this unlikely spot, inhabited mainly by fishermen, R. S. Cohn of Princess Anne had established a steam-powered sawmill in which he filled orders for lumber from as far away as Philadephia. Lumbering and related industries became locally important at several points around the state (for example, the towns of Salisbury and Elkton at opposite ends of the Eastern Shore), but they did so under local auspices. Even Maryland oystering—which supported the largest processing and packing industry of its kind in the world—remained in 1881 open to the methods of petty commodity producers. According to a census report in that year, any tongman could "at any time, take his canoe or skiff and catch from the natural rocks a few bushels of oysters, for which there is always a market." As long as the business lay open to unlimited exploitation by anyone having access to a rude boat and a few feet of Bay shore, it would hardly offer an attractive target to outside investors.[3]

The point is not that outside capital failed to make its way into Maryland. A striking instance of such penetration occurred, indeed, between 1875 and 1877, with the Standard Oil trust's takeover of the Baltimore petroleum refining industry; though, in general, activity of this kind did not become noteworthy until the 1890s.[4] Nor is the point that Maryland was able to act independently of outside events. Quite the contrary. It was precisely national and international developments that forced the transition over which, in the early years of emancipation, Marylanders were inclined to shuffle their feet. But, in responding to those developments, Maryland enjoyed decisive advantages compared to the former Confederate states. Chief among them was a versatile economy whose most active part never depended upon slavery, presided over by a local bourgeoisie following its own initiative—it was not the creature or servant of an alien economy— and participating as an equal member in the national state. In the former Confederate states, by and large, external energy applied to the wreckage of slave society served to reinforce retrograde social forms that prolonged the transition to mature capitalist social relations. In Maryland that energy, finding assistance from local elements little beholden to slavery, dissolved lingering traces of the old forms more quickly and with less residue.

Maryland's age-old problem of agricultural labor was, in the end, not so much solved as transformed. The unremitting pressure that for decades had been doing its slow and gradual work on slavery continued with added momentum after emancipation. With tobacco in full retreat even in its southern Maryland stronghold, the westward displacement of the nation's agricultural center of gravity removed Maryland from serious contention in cereal production as well. The logic of the national and international grain markets favored the large-scale cereal cultivation of the Midwestern and Western states. In the crop year 1879, the states of Illinois, Indiana, Ohio, Michigan, Minnesota, Iowa, and California accounted for nearly 60 percent of the country's wheat production. Illinois, Iowa, Missouri, and Indiana accounted for more than 52 percent of the total Indian corn production. Farmers in Maryland found to their consternation and anger that grain could be marketed in Baltimore more cheaply from Illinois than from the Eastern Shore. Marylanders of even moderate astuteness could read the situation plainly. "It is hardly possible," Governor William Pinkney Whyte told the legislature in 1874, "for our farmers to grow grain in competition with the agriculturists of the West, and it will be far more judicious to turn our hands to other and more remunerative culture." As the protracted switch from tobacco to cereals had lessened the need for slave labor, the eclipse of cereals reduced the need for agricultural labor altogether. In 1880 agriculture claimed the efforts of only 28 percent of Maryland's gainfully employed population (compared to 69 percent in the former Confederate states). Whereas the drive to restore the staple economy in the credit-starved environment of the former Confederate states held freedmen on the land under various makeshift arrangements that camouflaged their increasingly proletarian status, the movement away from staple-crop agriculture in Maryland, lubricated by mortgage credit, gradually allowed rural employers to dispense entirely with a good many laborers, while converting most of the remainder into straightforward wage hands.[5]

The process through which all this came about did not appear in the least straightforward, however, to rural Marylanders. Too many things were happening at once: emancipation, the shift in the competitive position of Maryland's agriculture, the decline of agriculture with respect to other forms of economic activity. The victims and (often reluctant) accomplices of these disruptive changes could understand them only in part—that part of which they had direct knowledge or experience—and did not necessarily grasp the dynamic underlying them. There were as many different understandings of what was going on as there were ways for people to experience it. Emancipation bore a larger share of the blame than rightly belonged to it because its consequences merged so subtly into those of competition with Western producers. Planters and farmers whose course through Maryland's long apprenticeship in the dual labor system had led them to heavy specialization in cereal production had a fresh adjustment to undergo before they had fully absorbed that imposed by emancipation. At first, therefore, they tended to attribute their difficulties entirely to the indiscipline of the black work force.[6]

Public authorities and agricultural commentators, even when they took a more realistic view of Maryland agriculture's long-term prospects, shared the preoccupation with securing an adequate rural work force. What they usually meant by that was promoting the immigration of white people. "This waiting upon the negro," the Montgomery *Sentinel* insisted in 1873, ". . . will not be borne with by the independent farmers of the State." Already in 1868 the *Maryland Farmer* had predicted a "great demand . . . for white men to occupy the place of tenants, or to purchase the small farms which will soon be in the market by the thousand." In the same year the state superintendent of labor and agriculture told the General Assembly—most of whose members hardly needed persuasion on the point—that "the almost universal voice of the Southern people and press is in favor of . . . European immigration, as the only means, not only of promoting their material interests, but of preserving civilization itself in many vast, and once prosperous districts."[7]

No one seriously expected white Americans to migrate to Maryland from the Northern states. Officials sometimes assigned as the reason continuing agitation and excitement over sectional issues. "Efforts to attract emigrants from the northern and eastern states," the General Assembly was told in 1867, "have been largely unsuccessful owing to the uncertainty of the future, engendered by the discussion of many points of national policy which it was hoped and expected would have been settled long ago." But everyone also understood another and probably more important reason: the difficulty that Maryland farmers would find in offering wages sufficient to interest Northern white laborers. White farm workers in Maryland had always commanded higher wages than hired slave or free black hands. This resulted from no whimsical "taste for discrimination" on the part of the employers but from the fact that whites stood a good chance of owning or acquiring land which they might farm on their own account. Wages therefore competed—without notable success—against the preference of whites for independent farming and their readiness, if shut out of farming in Maryland, to move to Baltimore or leave the state altogether. The discrepancy between wages for white and black farm laborers persisted in the immediate aftermath of emancipation. But even considering the advantage that white farmhands thus enjoyed in Maryland, their counterparts in the Northeast commanded higher wages, while in the West prospects were better (though fast disappearing) for dispensing with wage work altogether and farming independently.[8]

The Maryland Bureau of Labor and Immigration, created by the General Assembly in 1866, made a largely unsuccessful effort to solve the labor problem by encouraging foreign immigration. The commissioner inspired an invitation to a young German farmer to observe conditions in Maryland at first hand and then return home to report his observations to his countrymen. There is no telling how many Germans emigrated to Maryland as a direct result of the young man's reports. But the commissioner, evidently taking satisfaction in the figure, told the legislature that 178 Germans had been placed in Maryland during 1866. Needless to say, that did not represent a massive immigration. The people in question were, furthermore, "distributed throughout the counties, and some placed at labor in the city of Baltimore." It is not unlikely that this German "immigration" favored, as past ones had, the counties of northern Maryland and the city of Baltimore over the former slave counties.

In addition to the attempt to influence potential immigrants at their point of departure, the Bureau sent agents to intercept those arriving at the port of Baltimore and engage them for agricultural service. In this enterprise, however, the agents faced formidable competition from runners for the railroads, who just as busily intercepted immigrants hoping to induce them to ride the trains west. Only about two thousand of over ten thousand immigrants arriving in Baltimore in 1867 decided to stay in Maryland, and it is not clear for how long. Moreover, as with the Germans, those who did stay did not go exclusively to the former slave counties, but also to Baltimore City and County and to Harford, Carroll, Washington, and Allegany counties. The Bureau lapsed with little to show for its activities. In 1874 Governor Whyte called for the establishment of a new Board of Immigration whose task, apparently, would be to succeed where its predecessor had failed. Taking determined flight from reality, he proposed to plant "a colony of English farm hands" at the Maryland Agricultural College, hoping thereby to establish "a nucleus for such immigrants to cluster around, and then to distribute them among the farmers of the State"— rather like seeding an oyster bed.[9]

As emancipation receded into the past, the shortcomings of the work force lost plausibility as an all-purpose explanation for the ills of agriculturists in Maryland. Meanwhile, however, another scapegoat hove into view: the Western grange. "There are some people," the Port Tobacco *Times and Charles County Advertiser* pronounced in August 1877, "who are never satisfied but are ever looking for a grievance." Such were the Western grangers, who blamed the railroads for their difficulties in moving their grain to Eastern markets rather than "the location of the Western farmer or that of the Eastern buyer or the intervening space over which it was necessary to transport the grain." The grangers had not only set their face against natural law, the Montgomery *Sentinel* implied in February 1879, but had actually secured its repeal, to the detriment of the Eastern farmers to whose benefit the law had always operated. The grangers had gained the advantage by their agitation "to so reduce railroad rates, or to obtain such special rates, as would enable them to put their crops into the great wheat markets of the country so as to compete with profit with those farmers living nearer the markets." Before the advent of the grange, the *Sentinel* complained, "we enjoyed the benefits of living near the markets, but now the tables are turned."[10]

The tables had certainly been turned, but not by the Western grange. Improvements in transportation and agricultural technology, the opening of vast new areas to cultivation, and the tightening network of the world market were well embarked on a process that bred rural unrest over a large portion of the world during the late nineteenth century. In Maryland they supplied the impetus for a change in the pattern of agriculture that would in time make obsolete both the old preoccupation with maintaining a large agricultural work force and the new resentment of the activities of Western grangers. Even as the Port Tobacco *Times* and the Montgomery *Sentinel* railed against the grange, a group of some fifty farmers from a portion of Howard County near the city of Baltimore expressed an entirely different concern in a petition to the city council. They sought permission "to stand and sell our produce on Market days as heretofore in Pine Street North of Lexington Street up to Saratoga and Mulberry Streets," a privilege they believed had been withdrawn "by the influence and manipulations of the Hucksters here."[11]

The concern of the Howard County farmers, not that of the *Times* and the *Sentinel,* represented the new direction of farming in Maryland. For the future lay increasingly with agriculture specializing in the production of items essential to urban areas and not generally amenable to transportation over long distances: vegetables and fruits, meat and dairy products. Improvements in transportation had widened the radius from within which a city might be supplied but, until the advent of refrigeration, were not yet sufficient to change the essentially local, or at most regional, character of urban market areas. Truck farming played an ever growing role, especially in northern Maryland and in those parts of southern Maryland and the Eastern Shore that felt the gravitational pull of urban markets. Food-processing enterprises grew up in areas where they had been unknown before. In 1868 the *Maryland Farmer* approvingly reprinted from a Philadelphia journal a prediction that Delaware and the Eastern Shore of Maryland would one day be "the fruit garden of America."

It was perhaps an optimistic expectation, but not an utterly fanciful one. The value of orchard products reported for the state rose from $252,196 in 1860 to $1,563,188 in 1880. For the Eastern Shore, which by 1880 accounted for 54 percent of the state's total, the value had increased more than sixfold, from $132,774 to $845,244. Considering that the level of wholesale farm prices rose less than 4 percent during those years, both increases were substantial. The growth of the fruit industry was sudden and imposing enough to impress itself upon the memory of local residents. "[T]he whole county [Queen Anne's] was practically covered with peach orchards," Charles C. Hopper recalled. "Well I remember that——Trosker . . . established [a cannery] right in the center of town. . . . The ladies of the town congregated in daily attendance upon the work of paring the peaches. . . . Such music I have never heard as made by the great concourse of colored peach workers." Other areas did not match the dramatic growth of fruit production but still showed substantial progress. The value of market-garden products increased 65 percent, while butter production increased 42 percent. The total number of milch cows in the state increased 24 percent, and the total value of livestock rose by $1.2 million.[12]

A number of noteworthy changes marked the growing acceptance of the new role by farmers in Maryland. One was a decline in scale as agriculture increased in specialization. Between 1860 and 1880 the average size of farms in Maryland dropped from 190 acres to 126 acres. This trend had been under way since the 1850s, and in part simply reflected the decision of landowners to rent part of their holdings rather than cultivate them all directly. But the growth of tenancy does not tell the whole story. The trend continued between 1880 and 1910 (a period during which the census paid closer attention than before to questions of land tenure), even though the proportion of tenancies held virtually steady. Smaller size went hand in hand with greater intensity of cultivation. Earlier censuses provide no data with which to compare the $0.92 per acre of tilled land expended on fertilizer in 1880. But the increase in value of farm implements and machinery from $0.53 per acre of farmland in 1850 to $1.13 per acre in 1880 affords some indication of the process that had been under way in the interval. By 1880 farm values had substantially recovered the ground lost in the upheaval of the war and emancipation, averaging $32.33 per acre, compared to $18.18 in 1850 and $30.19 in 1860.[13]

Reshuffling of population accompanied the overhaul of Maryland's agriculture. Between 1860 and 1880 northern Maryland somewhat increased its share of the state's white population, from 71 percent to 73 percent. Meanwhile, reversing a long-established historical pattern, black population in the southern and Eastern Shore counties grew more slowly than white (see table 7.1), and the proportion of the black population living in those counties fell sharply. Though in general the counties that had claimed the highest proportion of black people in 1850 preserved their rank with respect to the other counties, their black populations had become proportionately smaller. Southern Maryland and the Eastern Shore continued to be home to a majority of the state's black people, but that majority had diminished from 69 percent in 1850 to 59 percent in 1880.[14]

Black people had to content themselves, by and large, with a menial position in the developing landscape of rural Maryland. Few obtained land of their own at all, and those few generally in very modest amounts: the garden patch of slavery times carried over into freedom. According to one study, 1,078 black people owned land in 1870 in eight counties of the Eastern Shore and southern Maryland (Anne Arundel, Charles, Dorchester, Kent, Montgomery, Prince George's, Queen Anne's, and St. Mary's). That

TABLE 7.1

Growth of Maryland Population, 1860–1880

	WHITE		BLACK		Change (Percent)	
	1860	*1880*	*1860*	*1880*	*White*	*Black*
Caroline	7,064	9,600	3,525	4,166		
Cecil	19,994	22,644	3,868	4,464		
Dorchester	11,654	14,634	8,807	8,476		
Kent	7,347	10,400	5,920	7,205		
Queen Anne's	8,415	12,067	7,456	7,189		
Somerset	15,332	12,974	9,660	8,694		
Talbot	8,106	11,736	6,689	7,329		
Wicomico	*	12,943	*	5,073		
Worcester	13,442	12,522	7,219	7,017		
Eastern Shore	91,894	119,520	53,234	59,613	30	12
Anne Arundel	11,704	14,649	12,196	13,877		
Calvert	3,997	4,842	6,450	5,696		
Charles	5,796	7,700	10,721	10,848		
Howard	9,081	11,741	4,257	4,399		
Montgomery	11,349	15,608	6,973	9,150		
Prince George's	9,650	13,965	13,677	12,486		
St. Mary's	6,798	8,244	8,415	8,690		
Southern Md.	58,375	76,949	62,689	65,146	32	4
Allegany	27,215	36,463	1,133	1,549		
Baltimore	46,722	72,766	7,413	10,565		
Baltimore City	184,520	278,584	27,898	53,716		
Carroll	22,525	28,706	2,008	2,286		
Frederick	38,391	42,962	8,200	7,520		
Garrett	*	12,063	*	112		
Harford	17,971	21,385	5,444	6,657		
Washington	28,305	55,495	3,112	3,066		
Northern Md.	365,649	528,424	55,208	85,471	45	55
Maryland, aggregate	515,918	724,693	171,131	210,230	40	23

Source: Calculated from U.S. 10th Census, 1880, *Population* (Washington, D.C., 1883), pp. 394–95.
*Not yet in existence.

amounted to 2 percent of the total black population of these counties and 8 percent of the black families—assuming that each landowner belonged to a different family and that families averaged five members. The median landholding of this group was worth between three and four hundred dollars. Most black people in these eight counties, undoubtedly including some of the landowners themselves, could ensure their subsistence and that of their families only by working for wages. And the level of prevailing wages for black farm help was such that the whole family, including children, would have to be so employed (one reason why apprenticeship came as such a blow to affected families).[15]

Considering the demanding character of the adjustment that Maryland's agriculture underwent during these years, it would be most surprising if prospects for black rural dwellers improved with time. Available indications are that they did not. In three counties selected one from each region (Charles in southern Maryland, Kent on the Eastern Shore, and Frederick in northern Maryland), black people owning their own land in 1880 formed an insignificant fraction of the total. Charles County's seventy-five black landowners fell shy of 1 percent of the county's black population and amounted to about 3 percent of black families. Thirty-four black landowners in Kent County came to less than 0.5 percent of the black population and about 2 percent of the black families. In Frederick, twenty-one black landowners accounted for a vanishingly small percentage (less than 0.3) of the black population and only 1 percent of black families. Judging by these counties, a grim situation was becoming grimmer insofar as landownership by black people was concerned.[16]

In fact, a substantial proportion of the black people identified as "farmers" in the population schedule of the census appear in the agricultural schedule as tenants of some kind rather than owners of their own land. In Charles County cash or share tenants accounted for 67 percent of black farmers; in Frederick, 32 percent; and in Kent, 33 percent. For both Charles and Frederick counties that was a higher percentage than among white farmers: 38 percent of white farmers in Charles and 25 percent of those in Frederick were listed as tenants. Tenants accounted for a higher proportion (52 percent) of white than black farmers in Kent County. It is inadvisable, however, to rest any very optimistic conclusion upon that. For the figures in all cases obscure a crucial distinction. Although the census of 1880 distinguished between cash and share tenancies, it did not distinguish share tenants from sharecroppers, who were not really tenants at all. Share tenants paid a share of the crop as rent to the landlord. Sharecroppers were in essence wage hands, receiving a portion of the crop (or the value of that portion) as a wage, but having no control themselves over the disposition of the crop.[17]

There is no firm evidence from which to determine how many black "share tenants" were in fact sharecroppers, but there is good reason to suppose that some must have been. While the Freedmen's Bureau remained on the scene, a number of its agents reported freedmen working the land on shares. The shares described in some of these arrangements (one-third to one-fourth) as well as the conditions (the landowner to supply teams and tools, fertilizer, seed, even provisions and medical care) strongly suggest that the freedmen in question were croppers rather than tenants—or, perhaps, recipients of "share wages." That freedmen sometimes asked the Bureau's help in collecting their share from landowners for all intents and purposes settles the question in those instances: in a true tenancy relation, the crop would have been under the tenant's, not the landlord's, control. The irremediable ambiguity of the evidence plays hob, of course, with any attempt to compare the extent of tenancy among black and white farmers. There is reason to suspect that the totals for black share tenants conceal more sharecroppers than those for whites; but there is no way to settle the question definitively.[18]

Comparison of the economics of farms cultivated by black owners to that of farms cultivated by black "share tenants" strengthens the suspicion that a goodly proportion—perhaps a majority—of the tenants were actually sharecroppers. For in almost every area, the share tenants appear to have disposed of superior resources belonging in all likelihood to the landowners and not to themselves. Black farmers listed as share tenants generally worked larger and more valuable farms than black owners, had a larger investment in farm implements, machinery, and livestock, produced a larger output measured in money terms, and even (in Charles and Kent counties) hired more help.[19] In Frederick County the average value of share tenancies held by black farmers was $3,511.11, compared to $979.33 for black owners. The average acreage of share tenancies was 151.7, as against 39 for owners. Share tenants' estimated output for the 1879 crop year averaged $555.56 in value, more than twice the figure for owners ($213.05). In Kent County share tenancies held by black people averaged $4,218.75 in value and 153.9 in acreage, compared to $529.71 and 16.4 acres for farms cultivated by black owners. Census enumerators in Charles County did not trouble themselves to record systematic information concerning the value or acreage of farms not cultivated by owners, but a pattern similar to that of the other two counties obtains in value of output: for black share tenants the figure was $360.11, compared to $119.68 for black owners (see table 7.2). Farms cultivated by black owners seem, in fact, to have been largely subsistence plots. Many of them undoubtedly failed even to afford subsistence. Farming their own land may have enhanced black people's sense of freedom, independence, and accomplishment. It may also—though this is

TABLE 7.2

Black Farms by Tenure Classes: Charles, Frederick,
and Kent Counties

	Avg. No. of Acres	Avg. Value Farm	Avg. Value Impl. & Mach.	Avg. Value Lvstck.	Avg. Value Product
Charles					
Owner-Cultivated	51.9	$ 492.84	$ 16.19	$136.43	$ 119.68
Share Tenancies	*	*	19.71	188.74	360.11
Cash Tenancies	*	*	13.37	203.89	284.03
All Black Farms	*	*	17.47	173.86	267.12
All Farms in County	176.1	$2,236.24	$ 57.23	$332.45	$ 556.79
Frederick					
Owner-Cultivated	39.0	$ 979.33	$ 30.76	$121.00	$ 213.05
Share Tenancies	151.7	3,511.11	108.33	273.33	555.56
Cash Tenancies	60.0+	800.00+	30.00+	50.00+	150.00+
All Black Farms	72.4	1,708.58	53.26	162.94	310.45
All Farms in County	104.6	$4,976.21	$177.00	$426.93	$ 843.72
Kent					
Owner-Cultivated	16.4	$ 529.71	$ 36.71	$133.79	$ 169.09
Share Tenancies	153.9	4,218.75	101.56	441.69	692.50
Cash Tenancies	50.0+	1,000.00+	50.00+	300.00+	300.00+
All Black Farms	60.2	1,696.27	57.31	233.65	335.86
All Farms in County	183.5	$7,240.27	$285.77	$696.19	$1,504.62

Source: Tabulated from Manuscript Census, 1880, Schedule 2, Charles, Kent, and Frederick counties, and from U.S. 10th Census, 1880, *Agriculture* (Washington, D.C., 1883), p. 119.
*Information not available.
+Only one farm in class.

much more dubious—have added to their standing in the eyes of the community at large.[20] But it certainly did not suffice to place even the tiny minority concerned upon the high road to economic security.

This is not to say, however, that the cultivator privileged to draw upon the superior resources of a well-to-do landowner necessarily found himself in an enviable position. The advantage that Maryland enjoyed over the former Confederate states, that of being able to call upon mortgage credit, stopped with those suitably provided with collateral. The sharecropper—or even the true tenant—dependent upon the resources of the landowner might not be appreciably better situated than his fellow in the cotton states. In May 1871 one John T. Norris of St. Mary's County put his mark on an agreement conditionally selling to John L. Lancaster "one yoke of oxen, one ox cart, two horses, or mares, one colt, and all my parts of the crops of oats, corn and tobacco, that I may grow or make during this year." The condition was that, if Norris should clear by 1 May 1872 a debt of $142.74 with accrued interest, together with any other debt subsequently contracted, the agreement would become void. Norris evidently did not manage to clear the debt, for in October 1873 an auctioneer, acting under the agreement, sold a yoke of oxen, a cart body, and a pair of cart wheels, for a total of $79.25. The record does not indicate whether Norris retained the rest of the enumerated property because he had already discharged part of the debt, or whether a yoke of oxen and the *disjecta membra* of an ox cart were all that he had left for anyone to sell.[21]

Putting up the wherewithal to run a farm could confer broad power upon a landowner, even in a transaction with someone who bore the formal status of a tenant. John F. Dent executed an agreement in August 1881 to rent a farm to J. F. Dines, who was to pay Dent two-thirds of the wheat, corn, and tobacco crops and all of the field crops made during the year and accord Dent first refusal of the corn blades at current market value. Dent was to supply the team and farming tools, all grass seed and two-thirds of the seed wheat and corn, and one-third of the manure. He agreed to leave on the farm such of his own cattle and provender as he thought fit, as well as chickens and turkeys at his discretion, for which he would supply half the feed. He then proceeded, at nearly three pages' length, to give detailed instructions as to how the land must be worked, livestock tended, fences maintained, and crops (carefully specified) planted. For fear that any detail had escaped mention, Dent ended by reserving to himself "the right to direct the general management & working of said farm." Dines, who signed the agreement with a mark, may have been either white or black: the rental agreement gives no indication. Whichever the case, he exercised precious little discretion in the running of the farm. Indeed, he probably differed very little in that respect from a hired hand.[22]

Black people farming under all tenure arrangements operated with fewer resources than their white counterparts. The average value of farms of all tenure classes operated by black people in Frederick County was $1,708.58, compared to a county average of $4,976.21. The $1,696.27

average value of farms run by blacks in Kent County compared to a county average of $7,240.27. Charles County would beyond doubt show a similar pattern had enumerators there taken care to record the necessary information. In all three counties, farms of all tenure classes under cultivation by black people ranked far below the county average in value of implements and machinery, value of livestock, and value of total output (see table 7.2).

The precarious position of black farmers declared itself in another striking particular: the marked elderliness of the group. The median age of black farmers in Frederick was fifty-five; 81 percent were forty or older. Black farmers in Kent had a median age of 50, and 80 percent were at least forty years old. That Charles County's black farmers, while exhibiting the same characteristic, did so to a lesser degree (median age forty-eight, 71 percent forty or above) may reflect no more than a larger proportion of wage workers among their number, disguised as share tenants; for agricultural laborers in the first election district of the county had a median age of thirty-two years, and only 31 percent of them were forty or older. The figures seem to indicate that young black people, perhaps discouraged by the odds, were not becoming farmers. Another possible reading of the situation is that blacks wishing to farm spent their younger years trying to accumulate the necessary means. There is no need to enlarge upon the somberness of that picture, both in the narrow expectations of the productive early and middle adult years, and in the modesty of the results later in life.[23]

Black people pursuing skilled trades in the countryside belonged to a minority as small as black farmers (perhaps smaller) and as elderly, if the situation in Anne Arundel County is anything to go by.[24] In 1870, only 24 black people (out of a rural black population of 9,870) held what could be called skilled employment. One of these was a schoolteacher. The others were spread out among six trades as follows:

Carpenter	7
Cooper	6
Blacksmith	4
Miller	3
Wheelwright	1
Wheelwright's apprentice	1
Shoemaker	1
Total	23

Their median age was fifty-two; seventeen of them (71 percent) were forty years of age or older. Only three (including the schoolteacher) were in their teens or twenties.

By 1880 the picture had changed a bit, but it would be hard work to construe the difference as an improvement. The number of black people declaring skilled occupations had risen to 37, in a total black population of 11,331.[25] Excluding three schoolteachers and a minister, they were distributed as follows among ten trades:

Carpenter	19
Blacksmith	5
Carpenter/farmer	2
Cooper	1
Wheelwright	1
Upholsterer	1
Boat captain	1
Shoemaker	1
Miller	1
Basketmaker	1
Total	33

Though the list of trades had grown longer, most had only one representative: carpenters and blacksmiths constituted a lopsided majority. Even more markedly than in 1870, the group comprised individuals of mature years. The median age (fifty) was somewhat lower, but men and women in their twenties (three, again including a schoolteacher) were proportionately fewer and there were no teenagers. Thirty of the 37 (81 percent) were forty or older. The evidence suggests an already thin craft tradition dying slowly by attrition.[26]

Some black people—along with a good many whites—living in the counties along the Chesapeake Bay and its tributaries managed to preserve a rough sort of independence by tonging for oysters. The market for oysters seemed inexhaustible. And such was their economic importance that in some of the lower counties, according to an 1881 census report, "oysters often pass current as money, and in one town there is a weekly paper . . . about 50 of the subscribers to which annually pay in oysters." It is impossible to say precisely how many individuals took up this activity from time to time, but an investigation during the 1870–71 season found that 1,649 canoes were licensed to tong for oysters in ten of the eleven oyster counties (one had no licensing law). No doubt numbers of people tonged without the benefit of a license, especially before laws on the subject came to be more uniform, restrictive, and seriously enforced.[27]

Tongers set out on boats from thirty feet long "down to any size that will float a man and his load." Making fast over a thickly covered portion of an oyster bed, they removed the oysters using tongs that resembled two long-handled garden rakes hinged together near their business ends. As the tonger brought oysters up from the bed, his assistant—usually a boy— culled them, throwing the shells back onto the bed together with oysters too small for the connoisseur's market that they served. During the part of the season that fell during the winter months, the work was especially harsh. Tongers must haul dripping rakefuls of oysters into small, open boats, standing in the half-frozen water until the load (ten to fifty bushels) was complete. When the weather became too severe, they could not go out at all. "Probably there are not more than two of three days out of a week on the average during the winter that they can profitably work," the com- missioner of the Fishery Force of Maryland reported in 1872. Furthermore, "much time must be thrown away in waiting for a chance to go out, and in going out to a distance and having to return disappointed." In warmer months, unless the oyster ground lay close by a railroad, there was risk of spoilage if making up a load and getting it to market took too long. Apart from the natural difficulties of the job, tongers faced the illegal competition of large oyster-dredging vessels, which had no business working the shoal- water natural beds but often did so anyway. The dredgers threw nothing back. They sold oysters by the load to the canning and packing houses, whose customers formed a less discriminating market than the raw oyster devotees served by the tongers. As the commissioner put it in the idiom of his time, "[I]t makes no difference to the heathen Chinee or the King of Dahomy in the can, so long as he gets the flavor." The dredging boats thus depleted the sheltered beds to which the tongers were of necessity confined. If a dispute arose in the matter, they could easily run down small tonging craft that got in their way. Dredgers sometimes even threatened to burn or carry off property on shore belonging to tongers. Taken all in all, tonging for oysters was a precarious, demanding, and occasionally dangerous way to make a living.[28]

Polite society looked upon the tongers—as upon virtually everyone involved in oystering, from the water to the packing houses—with distaste and disapproval. This view had long roots. In 1855 Frederick Douglass branded oystering "a course of life highly unfavorable to morals, industry, and manners." Using the excuse of exposure, he explained, oystermen developed a "drinking habit [that] fostered coarseness, vulgarity and an indolent disregard for . . . social improvement." Tongers were considered a cut above the rest, but that said very little. The Fisheries Commissioner, a generally sympathetic observer, described them in 1872 as "an uneducated class of men" given to "local notions and prejudices which are hard to eradicate." A census report nine years later—perhaps reflecting the constant, bitter disputes that had gone on in the meantime over oyster grounds and their regulation—took a much harsher view. "[T]he oystermen . . . as a class," the agent declared, "are illiterate, indolent, and improvident." The natural abundance of the Chesapeake Bay permitted them to live without engaging in any steady occupation. Instead, they would work long enough to earn a dollar or two, and then quit "until that is used up, often a large part of it being spent for strong drink." An absurdly small amount of money would satisfy them. Most lived near the water, often owning "a small house and an acre or so of land" whose value (to them and to the tax assessor) depended on the closeness of good oyster and fishing grounds. With the acquisition of that minimal property "their ambition seems to be satisfied." He singled out black tongers, about a third of the total number, for special mention, but by no means confined his indictment to them. All would be better off, he suggested, if compelled to engage in other work; and he expressed approval of recent acts of the Maryland legislature which, without explicit acknowledgment, were intended to accomplish exactly that.[29]

The real sin of the oystermen, from the standpoint of respectable opinion in Maryland, was that they stood outside acceptable forms of social responsibility. They were neither regular cultivators in their own right nor regular wage workers. Some preferred the independence of life on the water to hiring on under someone else's supervision; oystering permitted them either to avoid wage work altogether or to escape it at intervals. Others used oystering to eke out a living from submarginal holdings—the "acre or so of land" of the census investigator's description. All would in time feel pressure, from actions of the legislature and from the economic logic of the industry, driving them from their precarious haven.

The General Assembly passed a series of measures, starting in the 1870s, that increased restrictions upon citizens catching oysters (and terrapins, another local delicacy) in the waters of the state. One group of enactments restricted the waters bordering certain counties to residents of those counties, forbade commercial oystering during the summer months in some places, and set aside definite areas for catching oysters by means of scoops, scrapes, or dredges. A more inclusive law passed in 1878 confined the oystering season to the five and a half months between October 15 and April 1, forbade the catching of oysters at night or on Sunday, and declared that oysters taken from natural beds must be culled there. The same law required a license for all vessels scooping, dredging, or dragging for oysters, and for tonging vessels in counties bordering the Potomac River. Dredging licenses cost three dollars per ton of vessel capacity. Tongers paid according to the length of their boats (not really a reliable indicator of the potential size of their catch), the fees ranging from two dollars for boats up to 20 feet long to a maximum of six dollars. The law also required tongers, as a condition of the license, to "make, or assist in making, arrests of persons, and seize any boats, vessels and equipment" found violating the law. A yet more inclusive measure followed. This one extended licensing requirements to cover all state waters for all methods of oystering, with the validity of tonging licenses limited to the county of issue. The law furthermore established sweeping rights of private property in the waters of the state. Owners of land bordering navigable waters acquired the right to "locate and appropriate in any of the waters adjoining [their] lands, five acres, for the purpose of protecting, preserving, depositing, bedding or sowing oysters or other shell fish," subject only to the restriction that no one could appropriate natural beds. Other citizens of Maryland could exercise the same power only in areas not located or appropriated by the adjacent landowners, and only on condition that the landowners relinquished their prior claim to these areas.[30]

The census investigator of 1881 was probably correct in remarking that an unstated purpose of these laws was to drive the tongmen to other occupations. The additional restrictions placed upon an already limited season were in themselves enough to exert strong pressure on anyone depending on oystering for a living. The fees and bureaucratic formalities attached to taking out an annual license put further pressure upon ignorant, illiterate tongers disposing of little cash at any given moment. The right of landowners to appropriate neighboring waters for private beds directly threatened oystermen who owned little or no property, or owned property not directly bordering on the water. Naturally, it was one matter to pass such laws and another matter to enforce them. The poacher was a common figure in local literature and folklore, as in life. But the future clearly lay with planned, systematic production by those adequately provided with capital. By the early 1890s, yields for tonging and scraping (the methods accessible to individual enterprise) had fallen dramatically compared to those obtained by dredging, a technique requiring substantial capital equipment and a large force of wage laborers.[31]

People who continued to seek a living oystering on their own account with modest resources did so as much out of insistence upon being their own boss as for the sake of the material rewards they could expect. And they did so in the teeth of widespread prejudice against their way of life. Even their families might not understand or approve of their attachment to the water. "I don't know why you don't leave the river and get yourself a decent job. It ain't right just catching fish and crabs for a living," a woman nags her husband in a novel based on the lives of watermen early in the twentieth century. And, with even sharper insistence: "Don't you start mixing him [their son] up with the river. He's never going to follow the river." The man's rejoinder might have been spoken by any waterman— any, that is, who even deemed it necessary to reduce his feelings to words: "The river was good enough for my pappy and it's good enough for me. I ain't going to tie myself down like a slave for nobody. Folks have forgotten about 'life, liberty and the pursuit of happiness.' All they want is to make a pile of money." The inspectors who patroled the waters to see that no one took oysters in restricted areas were "brass buttons" to be gotten around by any convenient stratagem. "Them's the Lord's oysters and the Lord is a cheerful giver," one oysterman assures another during an illegal run. The Lord's oysters they may have been; but the state of Maryland claimed jurisdiction. "The legislature passed another food bill last spring and now we can only work a few of the bars," a waterman tells his son, predicting that "[s]omeday, that fool legislature will give the bay to the big boys."[32]

If respectable observers could have selected a more suitable occupation for oyster tongers, especially black ones, agricultural labor would have been their choice. And indeed most black people in rural Maryland did occupy themselves with agricultural labor, remaining—as in the days of slavery— unskilled and interchangeable parts of the agricultural economy. Enthusiasts of the free and competitive market—then and since—theorized that the abolition of slavery ought to place them in a strong position. President Andrew Johnson, in his 1866 message vetoing the Freedmen's Bureau bill, explained as clearly as anyone how that was to come about. Competition for labor, he declared, "will enable [the freedman] to command almost his own terms." If mistreated or ill-paid in one state, "he can move to another where . . . labor is more esteemed and better rewarded." But in fact there would be small need for that, since "each State, induced by its own wants and interests, will do what is necessary and proper" to retain a contented labor force. Majestically invoking "the laws that regulate supply and demand," he dismissed any "danger that the exceedingly great demand for labor will not operate in favor of the laborer."[33]

That optimistic mise en scène has enjoyed a revival, virtually word for word, in the fancy of one branch of neoclassical econometric history. Whatever may be said in its favor as regards the states of the former Confederacy— and its claims there have sustained grave damage—it had no validity whatever in Maryland. As cultivators moved away from tobacco and grains, their need for a large force of laborers diminished. Well-to-do landowners, particularly those heavily committed to wheat farming, might have had their moments of regarding the market as a gigantic conspiracy in restraint of trade. But to the extent that the market strengthened anyone's hand, it was the agricultural employer's, not the laborer's.[34]

The immediate aftermath of emancipation, when landowners were still feeling their way in a new situation, provided the most favorable background for Johnson's happy portrait; time, however, militated against it. And even the early years failed to bear Johnson out in Maryland. However desperate for labor planters and farmers may have been, the "laws that regulate supply and demand" brought no dramatic advance in wages for black agricultural laborers. Wage rates approximated the hire of slaves during the late 1850s and varied but little during the years that Freedmen's Bureau officials remained on the spot to record them: five to seven dollars per month for women, ten to twelve per month for men, plus board. (In 1882, Susanna Warfield could still hire a servant woman for five dollars a month, though the index of consumer prices had risen 10 percent during the intervening years.) The *Maryland Farmer* remarked with satisfaction in 1868 that wages for field hands (not only black ones) had "scarcely kept pace with the high cost of living." Unlike Andrew Johnson and his latter-day followers, the *Maryland Farmer* understood the social context within which the law of supply and demand operated. Skilled artisans and mechanics, its editor reflected, "are beginning to feel and know the power of numbers in combination. . . . If the same facilities for banding together and exacting their demands were in possession of our agricultural laborers, . . . our agriculture would have received a shock which . . . it could not have sustained." Because farm laborers "are scattered over wide districts," they "cannot easily form associations against capital."[35]

The *Maryland Farmer* neglected to mention another circumstance far more powerful than geographic dispersal in reducing the leverage of agricultural laborers: competition among themselves for employment. In the former slave regions of Maryland it was the sellers of labor power, not its buyers, who more nearly acted within a competitive market. Competition among black farm laborers had already put in scattered appearances in the early years of emancipation, even while planters and farmers remained preoccupied with the threat of labor shortage. A Freedmen's Bureau agent described an ominous example in Montgomery County in 1866. In that part of the county bordering the District of Columbia, he reported, freedmen wandered out from the city at harvest time "in such numbers as to compete with the resident laborers and reduce the price of labor." At exactly the time of year when the market might be expected to enhance the power of rural laborers, competition for work intervened to redress the balance.[36]

With the passage of time, competition of this sort grew more intense. However much former slaves may have dragged their feet over adopting the full trappings of capitalist wage laborers, at least one attribute imposed itself without the assistance of those concerned: unemployment. Insecurity of employment became a baleful companion in the lives of working people in Maryland and stayed with them through the last three decades of the nineteenth century. No picture of people's lives during those years can be complete without some attention to this problem. Unfortunately, there is little direct evidence with which to work. The rare statistics on the subject do not—could not possibly—capture the phenomenon in its full complexity. In some instances it was permanent; in others, temporary; in still others, chronically recurring. Taking at times the form of days lost during a week; at times, seasonal or bad-weather pauses in work; at times, days, weeks, or months lost during troughs in the business cycle, it would have defeated even careful and systematic record-taking, let alone such episodic attempts as were actually made. By the nature of the case, no statistical generalization can give more than a hint of the numerical extent of unemployment, or so much as a hint of the human reality concealed behind the summary figure.

As far as they go, however, the figures tell a grim story. Before very much time had elapsed after emancipation, field hands just lately arraigned for quitting work erratically found themselves, for long periods at a time, without work to quit. In 1880 the Census Office charged enumerators with the task of asking gainfully employed persons how many months they had been unemployed during 1879. Although most enumerators in Maryland failed to carry out the charge to the letter, recording only the fact of unemployment and not its duration, the results still provide a sobering glimpse into the lives of agricultural workers. In the first election district of Charles

County, for instance, every single black agricultural laborer reported having been unemployed for some period during 1879. In that portion of the district whose enumerator was conscientious enough to record the actual number of months each worker was without employment—an area around Port Tobacco taking in 52 laborers—the average period was 2.7 months. It is true, of course, that the year 1879 culminated the worst depression Maryland had ever known. But depression proved to be a not unusual experience during the years between emancipation and the end of the nineteenth century. Every decade had its own. Insecurity of employment was a common predicament throughout those years, even if it took an especially acute form in the worst of them.[37]

A particularly distressed group in 1879 were the iron miners of Anne Arundel County, most of whom were black. They represented the fag end of Maryland's iron ore industry, which had been in decline since the mid-1850s, had come to life briefly during the Civil War, and then relapsed into torpor. Iron mining was mainly a winter occupation, operating on too slim a margin to compete with agricultural wages during the summer season. Most of the miners were day laborers who paid royalties to the owners of the ore banks and mined, usually by open-cut methods, wherever they found the best showing. The increasing uncertainty of the market for Maryland ore and the seasonal restriction of its production guaranteed that anyone making a living chiefly by this means had a doubtful livelihood at best. All the miners spent time without work during 1879.[38]

Skilled black workers did not escape the corrosive effects of depression. Of the thirty-seven skilled workers in rural Anne Arundel County, thirty reported spending some time without work during 1879. As in Charles County, enumerators were not scrupulous in recording the length of these stints of unemployment. Only for the second election district do the manuscript schedules provide this information; and it is sobering enough. Six black people in the district pursued skilled occupations, if that designation may be stretched to embrace two schoolteachers and a minister, as well as two carpenters and a carpenter/farmer. Only the minister and one of the schoolteachers held steady employment during the year. The other schoolteacher was without work for three months, the carpenter/farmer for four months, and the two carpenters for six months each. It is likely that unemployed skilled workers, if they could not take up the slack by cultivating holdings of their own, entered the market to compete with laborers for unskilled work and odd jobs.[39]

The freedom of movement that, according to Andrew Johnson and the free-market econometricians, would so embellish the prospects of the freedmen in the event made very little difference. The right to move on provided a clumsy weapon of last resort against overbearing, abusive, or dishonest employers. Even before endemic rural underemployment placed the employer resolutely in the catbird seat, freedmen must have been well aware that formal freedom of contract added nothing material to their power. It was, indeed, easy enough to walk away from an offensive employer. But the practice of paying after a period of work and, sometimes, of holding out a portion of wages until the end of a contracted period limited the effectiveness of this simple expedient. Unless a freedman managed to exact more in provisions and advance wages than he produced during the time he worked, his departure could well be more gift than punishment for the abandoned employer. Refusing contracts with employers who had shaved on crop division during the previous season was an even more bootless weapon from the freedmen's point of view. In the nature of the case, there could be no division until there was a crop, and the freedman could not take back effort already expended. The embarrassment (as likely as not temporary) in which a short-handed employer might find himself scarcely compensated the laborer who, however many times shy, had been at least that once burnt.

As for out-of-state migration, the freedmen do not appear to have treated that as an "investment" decision, as so many microeconomic interpretations of their conduct take for granted. At the census of 1880, 80 percent of black people who had been born in Maryland lived in Maryland. Of those who did not, 29 percent lived in the former slave states (excluding Virginia and Delaware), where they are likelier to have gone under compulsion before emancipation than in search of "opportunity" afterward. Another 22 percent lived in the neighboring states of Virginia and Pennsylvania, where they are as likely to have gone before as after emancipation. The District of Columbia, a magnet for fugitives during the war, alone accounted for 26 percent of black Maryland natives living outside Maryland in 1880. The evidence, in short, suggests no great exodus of freedmen seeking economic opportunity outside Maryland after emancipation.[40]

Reluctance to leave relatives, friends, and homes to which they had only recently acquired a genuine right no doubt played the major role in keeping black Marylanders in Maryland, just as reluctance to surrender a much more tenuous right to these things had done during the days of slavery. The assumption, common among agrarian people, that those who work the soil thereby earn a right to it may have sustained the freedmen and their

children in the belief that their modest bit of Maryland belonged to them
by a title that no lawyer could prove and no money alienate. Perhaps a
strain of pure, dogged stubbornness entered in as well. Perhaps, recalling
the long-standing eagerness of their enemies to see the state rid of them,
black Marylanders reflected as Ned Cobb (Nate Shaw) later would: "I stays
on if it gives em satisfaction for me to leave and I stays on because it's
mine." Whatever the reason, relatively few seem to have left Maryland after
emancipation, and those who did tended not to go very far. Most black
people who abandoned Maryland's countryside went to the city—to Washington or to Baltimore.[41]

Anyone fleeing the country to search out better prospects—or just a
simple job—in the city was apt to meet on the way people headed in the
opposite direction on the same errand. For the depression of the 1870s
visited upon rural areas, particularly those along railroad lines or near cities
and towns, a frightening phenomenon: tramps. Susanna Warfield reported
her neighborhood in Carroll County beset with them well into the 1880s.
Some had ranged far from home: two superintendents of woolen factories,
one from Maine and one from Massachusetts, passed through on their way
to look for work in Harper's Ferry. Others were Marylanders who had
simply taken to the road. An amiable, ingratiating, even occasionally picturesque quality about the tramps at first captured Susanna Warfield's fancy.
A devout tramp "said grace and . . . crossed himself and . . . blessed me
because I gave him meat and bread." One "sober and honest" fellow requested (and received) $1.60 for railroad fare. An urbane and "plausible"
tramp who wangled a twenty-five-cent handout addressed her cousin as
"Gentleman Holmes." A "genteel lady" from the Eastern Shore sounded a
note with which Warfield, a former slaveholder, could sympathize, claiming
to have fallen upon hard times as a result of emancipation. Two little Italian
boys, one carrying a violin and the other a harp, ate breakfast at the Warfield
farm before setting off—in the cold of January—for Westminster. Not all
the tramps, however, were good-humored, heart-rending, or picturesque.
Some conducted night raids for the provisions they required or menaced
householders with direct violence. "Their last exploit," Warfield recored in
her diary during April 1876, "was the burning of my posts—and the shooting of Mr. Chew the Railroad Conductor for refusing to let them ride on
the cars free." An official investigation concluded that tramps generally
concentrated their attention upon smaller farmers, who were likelier than
the wealthy to feed and house them either from "feelings of charity" or "a
well grounded dread of incurring . . . resentment."[42]

State officials inquiring into the situation believed that the tramps were professional vagrants, an "aristocracy of beggary," who followed a regular beat during the summer and courted the hospitality of jails and almshouses in winter. "[A] change has taken place in the habits of our people," they lamented; "their industry has abated; their love of independence is less conspicuous and their reluctance to receive relief . . . is less marked." The Frederick County Almshouse alone housed more than eight thousand vagrants between 1 October 1876 and 1 March 1877. Farmers and rural householders expressed much the same view in local terms. During the early spring of 1877, Susanna Warfield and her neighbors shook their heads at the spectacle of "tramps going from house to house to be fed—and refusing to work, and of the negroes walking up and down the railroad" while farms in the neighborhood lay idle for want of hands. She conceded later, however, that the tramps sometimes begged for work, and that the farmers had little to offer them.[43]

Neither Susanna Warfield and her kind nor the official state investigators fully grasped the meaning of what they saw. The internal dynamic of Maryland's agriculture undermined the orderly routine of the countryside, loosening the ties that had once bound people to the rural areas and leaving many without a dependable livelihood. Meanwhile the city, so far from filling the breach and absorbing the displaced, disgorged its own surplus into the country. The meeting of these two surplus elements eventually resolved itself into a population of more or less perpetual floaters—people who followed the seasons from country to city and back, competing with one another for such work as was offered. Whatever adventitious leverage field hands might once have derived from the seasonal urgency of farmers' labor requirements vanished with other relics of the past. Fragmentary evidence suggests that, by the 1890s, the discrepancy between wages for black and white field hands had narrowed. It would not be surprising, if so; and it would indicate, not that black field hands enjoyed flattering prospects, but rather that depending on rural wage work for a living was by then no one's good fortune, white or black.[44]

Regrettably, reflections of this kind sometimes tempt historians (and even civilians) into odd and altogether inadmissible conclusions. If conditions after emancipation proved so unfavorable, the reasoning goes, were black people not, after all, better off as slaves? The only valid answer to such a question is that the question itself is improper. Slavery and freedom are incommensurable qualities, the difference between them an existential matter touching the dignity and worth of human life. People suffer, certainly, in freedom as well as in slavery (and, for that matter, in every known condition of human existence). But that unquestionable truth does not license anyone to tote up the suffering of one—in dollars of gold, calories of food, or pounds of flesh—and weigh it against the suffering of the other, in order to determine in which state people are better off. Nor should historians deceive themselves that they can tiptoe around the impropriety of the question by distinguishing the "material" from the "moral" or "psychological" dimension of slavery and freedom. If human beings were vegetables, it would be proper to conclude that they are best off materially when most amply and efficiently provided with what they require for vegetation. But human beings are not vegetables, and their material and moral needs overlap to a degree that makes nonsense of any effort to measure the one in the absence of the other. What mechanistic and unimaginative scholars would probably call the moral or psychological dimension of freedom consists in no small part of exercising discretion in the manner of satisfying material needs. Was Frederick Douglass stating a moral or a material objection to slavery when he condemned the monotonous slave diet of ash cake and fat meat and justified the slaves' unauthorized forays into their owners' pantries and smokehouses?

Black people in Maryland's countryside during the decades following emancipation confronted, beyond doubt, a bleak situation. The ending of slavery placed in their hands at best only modest resources to meet it: land in marginal amounts; some access, though progressively restricted, to the produce of the water; the right to marriage and family relationships; and formal rights of citizenship. The importance of these resources, poor as they were, was that they were attributes of free men and women and, as such, preconditions for facing those challenges that do not arise in slavery but belong uniquely to the domain of freedom. If, possessing these few resources, black people could not construct a secure future for themselves, it must at least be said that they had no hope of doing so without them. At the same time it must also be said that the situation was turning inexorably against farmers without land and workers without tools, and even against farmers who still—but only just—owned their land and workers who still—but only just—owned their tools. Black Marylanders were not alone in discovering during those years that freedom was no fixed condition but a constantly moving target.

EPILOGUE

From Country to City

Democratic Governor John Lee Carroll took an extraordinary step in July 1877: he invited federal troops to enter Maryland for the purpose of quelling a labor disturbance. Only once before had the federal military taken a side in a labor dispute in Maryland; and that precedent—the handiwork of President Andrew Jackson—was too old to be more than a curiosity. On the other hand, not much time at all had elapsed since Governors Thomas H. Hicks, Augustus W. Bradford, and Thomas Swann had mustered as much eloquence as they could command in opposing the encroachment of the federal military upon the civil affairs of their state. Times had assuredly changed. Even while drawing the stereotyped contrast between the turbulence of relations between labor and capital in the North and the relative quiescence of labor in the South, the Baltimore *Sun* tacitly admitted that the distinction had lost its force in Maryland. Carroll's invitation to federal intervention revealed the distance the state had traversed in a short time, as well as the wealth of new and contested meanings that *freedom* had taken on. Those whose actions during the troubled summer of 1877 incited Carroll to call for federal help no doubt believed that they were demanding simple justice for themselves, exercising the right of free white men and women. But in Carroll's eyes they threatened "subversion of all government" and—if not promptly and forcibly checked—"national insurrection."[1]

The immediate occasion of the trouble was the nationwide railroad strike of that summer. But four years of depression, with many out of work and many others forced to accept cuts in their wages, had prepared the ground, and several premonitory rumbles sounded beforehand. In March, miners in the coalfields of western Maryland sought to resist a reduction in their pay rate from $.65 to $.50 a ton following closely upon an earlier

194

reduction to which they had reluctantly acceded. The coal companies resorted to a lockout, and the miners eventually returned to work on the companies' terms. There was no violence. In fact, so low-keyed were the miners that the local press of Allegany County congratulated them (albeit rather patronizingly) for tailoring their actions "with a view to keep from being misrepresented in any action they may propose."[2]

For all the good it did them, the miners received a certain amount of public sympathy. Exemplifying one strain of it, a correspondent of the Frostburg *Journal* insisted in the course of a long, plaintive, and excruciatingly naïve plea that matters might be more amicably settled if only the mine owners would talk to the miners with understanding.[3] A more concrete source of sympathy was the widespread public conviction that the iniquity of the railroads lay at the bottom of everything. The railroads offered a target at which both miners and mine operators could take shots, with the assent of the press, public, and even some local and state officials. Henry Loveridge, president of the Maryland Coal Company, apportioned blame for the difficulties of the Allegany coal industry equally between the Consolidation Road and the miners: the railroad for requiring excessive freight charges and the miners for asking excessive wages. A miner from Lonaconing echoed Loveridge's claim with, naturally enough, a significant difference. His suggestion: "Let your railroad companies reduce their tolls and mining companies give up this foolish notion of reducing miner's wages every spring." The Cumberland *Alleganian and Times* blamed both the Baltimore and Ohio and the Consolidation railroads for exorbitant freight charges, agreeing with the miners' argument that these charges artificially raised the price of food. For its part, the B & O was already embroiled in a dispute with the state of Maryland over its tax-exempt status, which state officials were trying to rescind.[4]

In accepting what they could not help, the miners took due notice of the patronizing tone habitual even to those who expressed a certain sympathy with their predicament. The Lonaconing miner complained that, while the press went along "almost daily throwing out hints and giving advice gratis," the miners had "no advocate to champion our cause or no one . . . to write a line in our favor or in our behalf." He pointed out that, should the miners accept the companies' terms as purported well-wishers in the press advised, they could have no "guarantee that those mining companies will not use the shears again next spring to cut the miners' wages and put more money in their own coffers." About the annual spring shearing he was right. In the spring of 1878 the mine operators did indeed reduce rates (to $.40 per ton), in accordance with a sliding scale that was supposed to reflect the state of the industry. In August of the following year, when the state of the industry suggested that the scale ought to slide back in the other direction, the companies balked. The result was an autumn strike that lasted thirty-five days, laying idle not only miners but also the drivers, dumpmen, carpenters, and blacksmiths who served the mines.[5]

The miners' strike, as well as those called by Baltimore can and box makers in July 1877, proved to be mere curtain raisers for the railroad strike and its satellite, the strike of boatmen on the Chesapeake and Ohio Canal. Confronted with the prospect of wage reductions, the railroad and canal workers eschewed the decorum and restraint—or, differently put, the abstention from direct action—for which the miners had received public congratulation but little else. The boatmen tied up their boats along the banks of the canal and "assumed so threatening an attitude against any one who might wish to use that highway," the governor later told the General Assembly, "that trade by that route became entirely suspended." Railroad conductors, brakemen, and firemen gathered angrily in Cumberland to stop trains moving from West Virginia under the aegis of federal troops. When it became obvious to the governor that the railroad trainmen had active supporters among their fellow citizens ("unemployed and evil-disposed persons," to his way of thinking), he ordered one regiment of the state militia to Cumberland to put down the strikers and directed another to remain in readiness at its armory. Before the commotion ended, he had activated two additional infantry regiments and a battery of artillery.[6]

Carroll's action succeeded in joining to the anger of trainmen and boatmen the simmering rancor of the Baltimore citizenry. In the early evening of July 20, an alarm bell summoning the National Guardsmen to their armories attracted crowds of spectators into the streets. What started as a small group of curiosity-seekers around the railroad station swelled into a shrieking, missile-throwing mob which—abetted by women hurling objects from upper-story windows—menaced the Fifth Regiment of the Maryland National Guard as it made its way from the armory to Camden Station en route to Cumberland. No one died, but twenty-five militiamen suffered injury. Outside the armory of the Sixth Regiment, located in the factory district, an enraged crowd of unemployed and underpaid workmen and unruly boys set upon militiamen emerging under orders to support the Fifth Regiment at the railroad station. Panic-stricken, the troops fired into the crowd. Shooting and stoning continued all along the line of march to the station. Ten civilians died, some of them bystanders or citizens abroad in the street upon their normal business. Meanwhile, several thousand rioters at Camden Station prevented the troop train from leaving. The outbreak of fire near one end of the passenger platform sent the governor careering to the direst conclusions. Declaring that the forces of the state could not control the situation, Carroll called upon President Rutherford B. Hayes for military assistance. But order had substantially returned before the federal troops arrived. A detachment of the federals joined a regiment of the Maryland National Guard in reopening the C & O Canal. But the most important task of the federal troops, in the end, was to avoid grandstand maneuvers that might rekindle public antagonism.[7]

Understandably, Baltimore's first reaction was shock, despite a long-standing reputation for public disorder. The Baltimore *Sun* exclaimed in horror at the carnage—its suddenness and impetuousness more, perhaps, than its quantity. While conceding, as though in duty bound, that only "judicial investigation" could determine whether the mobilization of military force had been judicious in conception and execution, the *Sun*'s first editorial reaction flirted with justifying—or at least palliating—the conduct of the rioters. "The errand upon which the military were understood to be bound," the editor ventured, "was undoubtedly an obnoxious one to a considerable portion of the community." And whatever the result of judicial investigation, the "natural feeling and first impression" must be that the "slaughter . . . might and ought to have been avoided." A sufficient number of citizens shared this feeling, with perhaps less concern to await the final judgment of experts, that both the colonel of the Sixth Regiment and the president of the B & O dropped from sight for a time.[8]

With two more days' reflection, and with the terrifying spectacle of the subsequent explosion in Pittsburgh before it, the *Sun* found its way to a more secure editorial footing. Pronouncing the riot the work of the "idle and vicious [who] have no sympathy with honest labor," but simply seized upon the railroad strike as a pretext to "indulge their native and normal propensities for mischief," it nevertheless attached greatest blame to the railroad strikers themselves. Through their efforts to stop movement of the trains, they both "furnished the opportunity for all this riot and disorder" and "set the first example of lawlessness."[9]

After a bit more reflection, the *Sun* delivered a homily upon political economy and industrial ethics for the edification of the "intelligent workingman." It might well be difficult, the *Sun* admitted, for working people to absorb wage reductions, given that the business contraction had effected little or no reduction in the price of necessities. But workingmen must remember that "the question of wages has two sides to it and must be determined with reference to the employer's ability to pay as well as the employee's ability to live upon the wages actually offered." Workers who found their wages inadequate had a right to refuse them. If all workers in an industry did this (presumably without consulting each other, for that would be improper), then either the employer must accede to their point of view or the industry must close. But, the *Sun* pointedly warned, "the business of transportation cannot stop." By attempting to stop it through intimidation of employers and fellow workers, the strikers had overstepped permissible limits and risked forfeiting the community's sympathy for even their just complaints.[10]

The outbreak in Baltimore grew in frightening connotation as the strike sped across the country along the railroad lines, and as violence repeatedly greeted efforts to stop it. Press reports of the strike's progress read like war dispatches and appeared under headlines such as "Anarchy and Ruin at Pittsburgh" and "Communism in Richmond." (This last reported a statement by Julian Wright, former president of the Richmond Typographical Union and director-general of the Workingmen's Union of Virginia, expressing sympathy with the strikers and support for "equal distribution of property.") As if to reinforce the fear engendered by the strike, the Workingmen's party held a mass meeting in Baltimore in September, a meeting at which speakers denounced the entire regime of capital in colorful language. The Workingmen's Address to the People of Maryland laid the blame for the suffering of the working class on "consolidated capital," a "hell born power" and "insidious monster" that had "coiled its slimy folds around the political parties of the country" and now sought to degrade the American workingman to the level of his European counterpart. "Men of toil," the address concluded, "bread winners, without regard to race, nationality or political creed, it is to your interest to help us. . . . Mothers, sisters we plead for your influence. . . . Brothers, let our watchword be, 'Equal rights and equal duties.' "[11]

The press took instant note of the emphatic turns of phrase, the words *hell born, slimy,* and *monster* receiving particular attention. The meeting itself had drawn attention to them. One participant, a Dr. Wayson, suggested that milder words might be better calculated to attract friends "outside." Another man expressing a similar view lost his seat at the meeting. J. J. Ward, the secretary of the organization, lent his authority to the proposal to delete the offending words. But a round of applause greeted one Mr. Graham, who insisted that workingmen believed in telling the truth, and that "the abuse of capital to which the term was applied was hell born, for it could spring from no other source, and it was slimy." To greater applause John George Rieker declared that workingmen had always been too anxious to avoid offending "oversensitive persons" and ought now to express themselves "not as they wish it, but as we feel it." His motion to leave the address as it stood carried almost unanimously.

For all the emotional exuberance of the language, however, the address presented a straightforward reform platform, which explicitly disavowed any "communistic" tendencies. The fight, the address explained, was not against capital, but against its unjust monopoly by a monied aristocracy. The fathers of the country had been workingmen, and the "great object of the American Revolution [had been] to vindicate the rights of labor." In order to restore the country to its original purpose, American workingmen possessed a weapon unavailable to their counterparts in other countries: the ballot. To make the most effective use of this weapon, they must support only working-class candidates and the Workingmen's platform, avoiding the "dead issues" debated by the major political parties. Included in the platform were currency inflation, eight-hour legislation, equal taxation of all property, and the abolition of convict labor and the boss-contractor system of letting public work.[12]

The episode represented Maryland's rather improvisatory role in the brief, illusory upsurge of the Workingmen's party of the United States that actually marked the party's end. The occurrence of this episode so closely in the wake of the great strike planted sinister implications in the minds of some representatives of public order. But not all conservatives in Maryland panicked. Those cast in the agrarian mold, to whom the pretensions of the urban industrial order itself were as repulsive as the periodic insubordination of working people, appeared remarkably relaxed in their response. The Port Tobacco *Times* duly deplored the "wild talk" in which the workingmen's meeting had indulged and the "senseless legislation" it proposed. But the underlying tone was a rather smug and condescending indulgence. Because of the constricted view of the world dictated by their "modes of life and methods of thought," workingmen understandably lacked "deep insight into political economy." That explained their failure to penetrate to the root of their problems and look to the only genuine solution: abolition of the tariff.[13]

Perhaps rural conservatives seemed less hysterical because the events of the summer did not surprise them. As far as they were concerned, a rot had set in long before—in 1864?—and they could see no call for astonishment at the utterly predictable consequences. Susanna Warfield believed that emancipation had "crazed every body—blacks and whites." Housekeeping and rural life in general had become impossible. Darkies would not work, poor whites did not know how. Reviewing in disgust her interviews with teenage white girls for domestic work, she recalled that one dared not sleep in a room alone and was terrified of thunder and lightning. Another did not know how to cook, wash and iron, or clean mirrors, lamps, silver, or walls. "How is it," she asked the mother of one girl, "that you white people bring up your children without work?" In her eyes, the strike of 1877 offered just one more illustration of the madness that had overtaken society. "On Wednesday," she recorded in her diary during July 1877, "news came of a rebellion among the Baltimore and Ohio Railroad hands at Martinsburg [West] Vir—and Baltimore. . . . It is all about wages—The people are crazy in this country." When two canal men appeared at her house asking for food, she assumed that they were strikers and promptly relegated them to the same category as the tramps with whom she was already well acquainted.[14]

To whatever chorus of "I told you so" from rural conservatives, the strike of 1877 served notice of Maryland's arrival in the world of industrial capitalism. But Maryland arrived in that world in hesitant, sidelong fashion. In 1880, it is true, manufacturing, mechanical, and mining industry occupied 26 percent of the state's gainfully employed work force, compared to 7 percent in the former Confederate states. Only in the light of that comparison, however, did Maryland's industrial development appear impressive. By the standards of the Northeast, Maryland was an industrial mediocrity. That circumstance laid a special burden upon ordinary citizens trying to achieve some semblance of a dependable livelihood; for Maryland's rather shallow industrial resources could not provide simultaneously for those displaced from the countryside and for the growing native and immigrant population residing in the city of Baltimore.[15]

Baltimore exemplified in distilled form the problematic character of Maryland's development during the declining years of the nineteenth century. The only large city in Maryland by national standards,[16] it dominated the state's industrial activity. In 1880, there were concentrated in Baltimore over half the manufacturing establishments, 66 percent of the capital invested in manufacturing, 73 percent of the value of annual output, and 80 percent of the wages paid. Nevertheless, commerce remained Baltimore's main business. Not until 1890 did the value of manufactures overtake that of foreign trade, and even then foreign and domestic trade taken together probably still outweighed manufacturing. Economic life in the city continued to follow the old irregular rhythm, whose ill potential was compounded by increasing population and recurring depression.[17]

Even during good times, work tended to be irregular. Some of the most important industries had a pronounced seasonal cast. The packing and processing of vegetables, fruit, and oysters followed the seasonal availability of the raw material. Those who were employed in preparing vegetables and fruit during the summer months drifted toward the oyster-packing houses, the clothing trades, or domestic service during the winter. Tongers unable to work when the oyster grounds froze over would seek work as oyster shuckers, perhaps moving on to the fields as pluckers in summer, when there was no oystering. Raw oyster shucking also attracted those employed in brickmaking, whose season ran only from April to November. Oyster-dredging vessels drew their crews in part from among men driven into the city during the winter and drifting back to the country when warmer weather set in. Their migration took on a regular pattern and, according to an estimate in 1885, involved four to five thousand men every season.[18]

Even during the proper seasons of many jobs, work tended to be sporadic. In nonmechanized brickmaking establishments, work could not proceed on wet days; the digging of clay for bricks ceased as well when the ground became wet or frozen. Oyster shuckers reportedly averaged no more than half-time during the season. Fruit and vegetable packing, employing more hands by 1880 than any industry except men's clothing, yielded no more than a hundred days' work in a season. Nor is it surprising that the semiskilled or unskilled employees of brickyards and packing houses suffered frequent bouts of idleness, when even skilled workers could not escape it. Railroad trainmen never worked more than eighteen days in a month, by their own testimony, and did well to average twelve during the winter.[19]

Time and economic "progress" made insecure employments even more so. Mechanization put an end to such precarious livelihood as hand-workers had managed to eke out in the brickyards. Bulk shipping of oysters gravely reduced the availability of shucking as a recourse for workers during enforced winter idleness. Massive hiring of immigrant, female, and child labor removed whole areas of work from those who traditionally relied upon them. By 1885, two-thirds of the packing-house workers were foreign (mainly Bohemian) and half were children. "Mothers bring their whole families to the packing-house," explained Thomas Weeks, head of Maryland's Bureau of Industrial Statistics and Information, "and the baby often slumbers in the pea hulls while the older members [that is, children three years of age and up] work." Immigrant women in large numbers began to invade oyster shucking, traditionally an occupation for black men, during the late 1870s. Immigrants even made their way into domestic service. Weeks maintained that by the late 1880s they were "driving the old colored domestic servant out of the field." Although that may have been an exaggeration, it is probably true that black domestics found less and less full-time work and had to resort increasingly to casual jobs like taking in laundry.[20]

Some people ended up suspended between rural and urban life, unable to sink permanent roots in either environment. An undeterminable but probably substantial proportion of people listed in the Baltimore census schedules as "laborers" were actually farmhands who took work—when they could find it—in nearby rural areas. Less fortunate even than these were the oyster dredgers—bedraggled and ill-fed men who, driven from the country by winter cold, signed or were shanghaied onto the crews of the dredge boats. Polite society rated oyster dredgers the lowest of a low industry: "one of the most depraved bodies of workmen . . . in the country," declared a census investigator, "gathered from jails, penitentiaries, work-houses, and the lowest and vilest dens of the city." Most of them were white and, by the 1880s, a good many were foreign; although black men, who had constituted as much as a third of the total in 1871, still figured among them. A report of the Bureau of Industrial Statistics and Information men-tions three black casualties of dredging trips during the months of December 1884 and January 1885: Joseph Good, found wandering on the wharf "in a helpless condition"; Fred Peterson, admitted to jail suffering from frostbite; and John T. Folly, drowned.[21]

Depression, superimposed upon the habitual irregularity of work even in good times, laid a further weight upon a population disposing of few resources to bear the added stress. The balance of forces, never especially favorable to ordinary working people, became even less so. During the depression of the 1870s, laborers working for city contractors asked the intervention of the mayor and city council to stop abuses against which they themselves could do nothing, compelled as they were to compete with tramps who would "work for almost any kind of wages." Contractors, according to the laborers' petition, could with impunity pay men for fewer hours than they actually worked, threatening the sack for anyone voicing a complaint. Some of the contractors kept taverns and compelled the men to receive their wages there, the laborers added, shrewdly featuring a point that might well attract sympathy from the respectable representatives of the government; for which of these gentlemen would be surprised to learn that by the time the men left the tavern "their wages amounted to a few dollars and very often a few cents"?[22]

The petition did not specify what the city council ought to do beyond providing "Justice for the suffering Workingmen of Baltimore." But a mass meeting in Monument Square in April 1878 suggested that the council "put in to operation all necessary [public] work thereby releving the sufferings of the mass of people who are now un employed." It also urged the council to pursue "the motion of Mr. Moony in the City Council (*a man with a hart*) fixing wages at one Dollar and a half perday may his life be long and prosperous." The council took no action with respect to providing public work. But the Joint Standing Committee on City Property reported favorably upon a proposed ordinance fixing the wages and hours to be observed by city contractors. The report concluded that the ordinance would benefit contractors as well as laborers, since it would "put on equal grounds, all City Contractors and prevent the temptation to oppress, to which many are liable to succumb in the eager desire to increase their gains." It would also, the committee predicted, no doubt recalling the previous year's riot, "do much to produce a healthy and contented feeling among the laboring men of our community."

The process of legislation took its time, however. It was May 1879 before the city counselor and the city solicitor made their report to the Joint Standing Committee on Ways and Means on the legality of the proposed measure. Their report was not promising. They found no legal objection to the first provision of the ordinance, establishing a ten-hour workday at a fixed rate of $1.50 a day for all laborers in the city's direct employ, though they pointed out that the ordinance by implication established a maximum as well as a minimum wage and might therefore place the city at a disadvantage in attracting hands should economic conditions improve. They objected, however, to the second provision, requiring the same wages and hours for laborers employed by city contractors. First of all, the city had no authority to extend the rule to its contractors. "As well," they argued, "might the city assume to regulate the wages to be paid for different grades of skilled labor . . . or to say what the contractor shall pay his book-keeper or his foreman"—a proposition they apparently deemed self-evidently absurd. Second, the provision was discriminatory, in that it established $1.50 a day as a fixed rate for the city itself but as a minimum for city contractors. Third, the provision was legally "inoperative." Even with the requirement written into all contracts for city work, the city could not successfully maintain a suit upon the bond of a contractor who failed to comply. In order to claim damages, the city would have to show what damage it had sustained through the breach—something it could not do so long as the contracted work had been satisfactorily performed, whatever the pay of the laborers. The city, it appeared, could sustain injury only in its capacity as an owner of property, not in its capacity as a community of human beings.

The law officers' report gave unwanted publicity to the fact that the council's measure would actually set a maximum as well as a minimum wage for city laborers. But the council passed the law in that form anyway, omitting mention of employees of city contractors. When the measure arrived on the desk of Mayor Ferdinand Latrobe in February 1880, he vetoed it, quoting the law officers' report in explanation. He made much of the argument that the ordinance would place a ceiling on wages, expressing his hope that labor might soon "command . . . $1.75 or $2.00 per day— the price paid in 1874 and 1875" and his conviction that the city ought not to put an arbitrary limit on such an increase. But he had no more interest than the council in setting a minimum level of wages, for the language he proposed as a substitute would simply instruct departments of the city government to "pay . . . the highest current rates." He doubted, in any case, that even that much legislation was necessary. After failing to pass the bill over the mayor's veto, the council let the matter drop.[23]

The depression of the 1870s had given the working people of Maryland a bitter foretaste of the industrial world, and 1877 demonstrated the immensity of the force that might be quickly arrayed against them. Relief greeted the recovery that was under way by 1880; Baltimore celebrated the recovery—and its own 150th anniversary—with a flourish. Still, few workers managed to recover the level of wages they had commanded in the early 1870s. They might take some comfort from a simultaneous decline in the level of consumer prices. But probably not much, for the mid-1880s brought a new depression which, though shorter than that of the 1870s, proved "exceptionally disastrous" for working people in the view of the Bureau of Industrial Statistics and Information.

Nevertheless, something new appeared in the wake of the next recovery: a spectacular surge in trade-union activity. Membership in labor organizations quadrupled in the three months between the time the Bureau submitted its 1885 report to the governor and the time the report went to press. The city of Baltimore alone claimed eighty-nine labor organizations. Many of them, born in a moment of exuberance, collapsed soon thereafter.

Others went under in the new catastrophe that the 1890s had in store. (When the black hod carriers struck in 1897, the naked eye could scarcely perceive that a strike was on, since nine-tenths of the membership had been idle anyway.) In 1884 the General Assembly ratified labor's principal demand—the elementary one for recognition of its right to exist. But other obstacles proved less tractable. One was the vulnerability of fledgling unions to business slumps that regularly wiped out the gains of previous periods of industrial advance. Another was animosity between black and white workers, which debilitated the movement as a whole and particularly injured the weaker and more isolated efforts of black organizations.[24]

Conflict between black and white workers had long, complex roots in the past. With the disappearance of slavery, it acquired a new rationale and new forms of expression; and it occasionally received fresh encouragement from white workers' attempts to press their own definitions of freedom. The long-standing feud between white and black ship-caulkers offers a case in point. As part of their effort to gain higher wages and establish an eight-hour workday, white caulkers had set out in 1865 to drive black caulkers from the trade. It was a maneuver familiar to black caulkers, and once again they looked to white patrons for help—in this instance, to a group of merchants in Baltimore. Holding no brief for eight-hour agitation, the merchants readily subscribed $4,000 toward purchase of a shipyard to be run by black people. The resulting venture, the Chesapeake Marine Railway, provided employment for black workers driven from the other yards, but it did not survive the economic crisis of 1883.

The white caulkers, meanwhile, had only a short time to savor their victory—if that is what it was. The replacement of wooden by iron hulls relentlessly eroded their livelihood. By 1899 only 150 caulkers remained in a city that had once supported 600, and those 150 could never all find work at once. When they sought a wage increase in 1899, they dared not call a strike. Instead, they deferentially appointed a delegation to "wait upon" the employers, who had no trouble persuading them to withdraw their request.[25]

Emancipation had once and for all decreed that the struggle for freedom would no longer be a struggle against slavery. That fundamental act shifted the social terrain. The state shed for good its role as final guarantor of one human being's property in another; and, by abolishing the sovereignty of master over slave, removed all formal intermediaries between its citizens and itself. Even familiar relationships, like the one that pitted white ship-caulkers against their black counterparts, thenceforward played themselves out in a different world. Aspects of society that struck observers then (and have struck many since) as invariable changed their specific gravity through immersion in a new atmosphere. The habits and rituals of race, for example: reenacted in a world where slavery no longer established the limits of black people's actions, these became new in essence, even when they persisted in form. So much had emancipation decreed.

But emancipation alone could not set the terms of the new struggle. In the world of wage workers and their employers, of industry and trade unions, of depression and unemployment, of nationwide strikes and military strikebreakers, the old definition of freedom did not apply. The very terms *state* and *citizen* had to be redefined. Emancipation settled that the slave-owner no longer stood between state and citizen but left open to dispute what the relationship between the two would become. The Baltimore workingmen's insistence that the state (represented in this instance by the city government) should provide employment and enforce a minimum wage represented one view; Governor Carroll's call for the state (represented by the federal government) to put down the railroad strikers through military force represented quite a different view. New terms of contest remained to be worked out in the push and shove of daily life, by men and women, whether black or white, whose notions of freedom—and of citizen, state, and race—were being constantly formed and reformed in response to the unprecedented situations they constantly faced.

The circumstances of time and place were not, perhaps, the most favorable for taking on such a task. For the common people of Maryland, the closing years of the nineteenth century cannot have cast the monumental accomplishments of that century in a very inspiring light. The relentless social force that had first isolated slavery by building up free society all around it, then majestically demolished its shrunken remains, now seemed bent on creating a world that showed its worst face to everyone. Measured by the distance traveled since the Maryland legislature had deliberated making slaves out of free men and women, Maryland had taken an unqualified step forward. But, through the eyes of those Marylanders to whom the last years of the nineteenth century were years of waking nightmare made routine by repetition, Maryland must have seemed to be moving at the pace of the diamondback terrapin, and in the direction—now backward, now sideways—of the crabs that live in the Bay.

APPENDIX

Problems in the Manuscript Agricultural Census

The 1880 manuscript agriculture schedules unfortunately do not distinguish the color of farm operators. The only means, therefore, of extracting from this source information about black farmers is to identify them first in the population schedules and then carry out the tedious business of cross-matching. That is what I have done in this instance. I entered on a list every black man or woman listed as a farmer on the population schedule. I then attempted to find in the agricultural schedule each name on the list.

The circumstance that the same enumerator completed both schedules at the same time ought to have enhanced the prospect of successful matching by minimizing the risk that individuals listed in one schedule might have been overlooked in compiling the other. Perhaps it did. Nevertheless, I could not find every black farmer listed in the population schedule when I turned to the agricultural schedule. For Kent County, I succeeded in matching 85 percent of the names from the population schedule; for Frederick, I matched 84 percent; and for Charles, only 63 percent.

Some of the failures resulted from the careless and apparently semiliterate work of certain enumerators. A few scrawls remained impervious to all efforts at decipherment. In some instances, whimsical and inconsistent spelling of names was the culprit. Ellucius and Alutius (for Aloysius), Oconal and O'Connell, Camel and Campbell as successive references to the same individual create grave, though not insuperable, difficulties. Variations yet further afield, however, may well have resulted in my failing to match someone's name.

More important—because it touches on a matter of deeper substance— is the care and precision with which enumerators recorded information. Most enumerators took care to distinguish as "farmer" only the head of the

207

household working a particular farm. If family members worked on the farm, they were usually listed as "farming" or "working on farm." That procedure, if consistently followed, would adequately distinguish them from "laborers" or "farmhands." It would also spare a harried researcher from looking for two or more different farms where only one is actually in question. Unfortunately, some enumerators used the designation "farming" indiscriminately to refer to a farm owner, to family members working on a farm, and perhaps (though this was very rare) even to farm laborers. To compound the problem, enumerators who wrote illegibly and spelled erratically were also the most likely to use designations in a haphazard fashion. This was most dishearteningly the case with the fifth, sixth, and seventh election districts of Charles County. As a result, the discrepancy between the percentage of successful matches in Charles County, on the one hand, and Kent and Frederick counties, on the other, is not as large as it may appear. Many of those recorded as "farming" in the population schedules for Charles County were not heads of farming households and were therefore properly omitted from the agricultural schedule. It remains probable, nonetheless, that I missed more people in Charles County than in Kent or Frederick.

Notes

A bracketed figure following a document citation is the file number of that document at the Freedmen and Southern Society Project, University of Maryland, College Park.

CHAPTER 1

1. U.S. 9th Census, 1870, *Population* (Washington, D.C., 1872), pp. 5–7, 36.

2. Calculated from U.S. 9th Census, *Population,* pp. 6–7.

3. In a certain sense, Delaware was not a slave state at all. Its small slave population resembled those of the Northern states before the abolition of slavery during the post-Revolutionary years. Individually, the members of that population bore the status of slaves, but collectively they were simply an alternate source of labor within a system of which slavery was not the organizing principle. At an early date, Delaware became the only slave state ever to prohibit both importation and exportation of slaves. In fact, the relative size of Delaware's free black population should occasion less surprise than the failure of several attempts to abolish slavery there. See H. Clay Reed, *Delaware: A History of the First State* (New York, 1947), p. 574; Carol E. Hoffecker, *Delaware: A Bicentennial History* (New York, 1977), pp. 92–94; Arthur Zilversmit, *The First Emancipation: The Abolition of Slavery in the North* (Chicago, 1967).

4. Herbert S. Klein, "The Colored Freedmen in Brazilian Society," *Journal of Social History* 3 (Fall 1969): 34–36; Luis M. Díaz Soler, *Historia de la esclavitud negra en Puerto Rico, 1493–1890* (Madrid, 1953), p. 259; Johannes Hartog, *Curaçao: From Colonial Dependence to Autonomy* (Detroit, Mich., 1968), p. 179; Franklin W. Knight, *Slave Society in Cuba during the Nineteenth Century* (Madison, Wis., 1970), p. 86; U.S. 9th Census, *Population,* p. 36.

5. See, for example, Mavis C. Campbell, *The Dynamics of Change in a Slave Society: A Sociopolitical History of the Free Coloreds of Jamaica, 1800–1865* (Rutherford, N.J., 1976), p. 45; R. Montgomery Martin, *History of the Colonies of the British Empire* (London, 1834), pp. 248, 265, 325, 333n; Augustin Cochin, *L'Abolition de l'esclavage* (Paris, 1861), p. 242.

6. Campbell, *Change in a Slave Society*, p. 45; Hartog, *Curaçao*, p. 179; Klein, "Colored Freedmen," p. 36; Knight, *Slave Society in Cuba*, p. 86.

7. Campbell, *Change in a Slave Society*, pp. 27, 57–58, 147; Klein, "Colored Freedmen," pp. 32, 45–50; Eugene D. Genovese, *From Rebellion to Revolution: Afro-American Slave Revolts in the Making of the Modern World* (Baton Rouge, La., 1979), p. 59.

8. Calculated from U.S. 9th Census, *Population*, p. 36.

9. On the 1811 slave revolt in Louisiana, see Herbert Aptheker, *American Negro Slave Revolts* (New York, 1943), pp. 249–51; Ira Berlin, *Slaves without Masters: The Free Negro in the Antebellum South* (New York, 1974), p. 124; and Genovese, *From Rebellion to Revolution*, pp. 4, 43. The fear that free blacks would incite slaves to disorder was characteristic of slaveholders in the upper South; it was not confined to Maryland (see Berlin, *Slaves without Masters*, pp. 188–89). The relative weight of the free people of color in the total population of a slave society went far to decide which social tasks would be allotted to them. However, it is necessary to place the demographic question in its broader class and institutional context in order to understand the entire pattern of what is usually (though inadequately) referred to as "race relations." For an analysis along these broader lines, see Eugene D. Genovese, *The World the Slaveholders Made: Two Essays in Interpretation* (New York, 1971), chap. 3.

10. James Wright, *The Free Negro in Maryland, 1634–1860* (New York, 1921), pp. 36ff., and Berlin, *Slaves without Masters*, pp. 15–50, agree in laying stress on this point. Also see Zilversmit, *First Emancipation*, pp. 155, 226–29.

11. Berlin, *Slaves without Masters*, pp. 24–26; Kenneth Carroll, "Religious Influences on the Manumission of Slaves in Caroline, Dorchester, and Talbot Counties," *Maryland Historical Magazine* 56 (June 1961): 176–98; Donald G. Mathews, *Slavery and Methodism: A Chapter in American Morality, 1780–1845* (Princeton, N.J., 1965); William Calderhead, "Experiment in Freedom: The Negro in Maryland to 1860," unpub. MS, p. 124. Professor Calderhead kindly allowed me to see his work.

12. Susanna Warfield Diaries, MS 760, Maryland Historical Society, Baltimore, 21 September 1854.

13. Lewis Cecil Gray, *History of Agriculture in the Southern United States to 1860* (1933; repr. Gloucester, Mass., 1958), 1: 164–69; 2: 606–09; Jacob Price, *France and the Chesapeake: A History of the French Tobacco Monopoly, 1674–1791, and of Its Relationship to the British and American Tobacco Trades* (Ann Arbor, Mich., 1973), 2: 728–29, 841–42; Paul W. Gates, *The Farmer's Age: Agriculture 1815–1860* (1960; repr. [1977], White Plains, N.Y.), pp. 105, 107–15; Ronald Hoffman, *A Spirit of Dissension: Economics, Politics, and the Revolution in Maryland* (Baltimore, 1973), pp. 6–7; Paul G. E. Clemens, *The Atlantic Economy and Colonial Maryland's Eastern Shore: From Tobacco to Grain* (Ithaca, N.Y., 1980), pp. 19–23, 173–74, 193, 204–05, 217; Russell Menard, "Farm Prices of Maryland Tobacco, 1659–1710," *Maryland Historical Magazine* 68 (Spring 1973): 80–85; Wright, *Free Negro*, pp. 39–42.

14. Gates, *Farmer's Age*, pp. 102–03, 165, 170; Ulrich B. Phillips, *Life and*

Labor in the Old South (Boston, 1963; orig. ed. 1929), pp. 126–27, 138; Carville Earle and Ronald Hoffman, "Staple Crops and Urban Development in the Eighteenth-Century South," *Perspectives in American History* 10 (1976): 38–39; Clemens, *Atlantic Economy,* pp. 183–87.

15. Edward C. Papenfuse discusses the relation between the decline of tobacco and the growth of the free black population of Prince George's County in "Planter Behavior and Economic Opportunity in a Staple Economy," *Agricultural History* 46 (April 1972): 306. Carville V. Earle, "A Staple Interpretation of Slavery and Free Labor," *Geographical Review* 68 (January 1978): 51–65, recognizes the distinctive labor requirements of wheat as opposed to tobacco and corn cultivation. Unfortunately, Earle overwhelms a sound insight with a naïve and reductionist theoretical apparatus that seeks to explain everything, up to and including the Civil War, as the result of individual microeconomic calculation. This approach leads him to the absurd conclusion that "[s]lavery was headed for the North in the wake of a corn economy; the only way to halt the laws of economics and preserve northern free labor was to destroy the peculiar institution in a civil war." Among the arguments Earle employs to support his view is the assertion that black laws in the Midwest were pushing free blacks "toward servitude if not enslavement." Since the main object of the black laws was not to make either servants or slaves of blacks but to exclude them from the area, this evidence contradicts rather than supports Earle's conclusion.

16. Clarence P. Gould, "The Economic Causes of the Rise of Baltimore," in *Essays in Colonial History Presented to Charles McLean Andrews by His Students* (New Haven, Conn., 1931), pp. 227–30; Dieter Cunz, *The Maryland Germans: A History* (Princeton, N.J., 1948); Richard Walsh, "The Era of the Revolution," in Richard Walsh and William Lloyd Fox, eds., *Maryland: A History, 1632–1974* (Baltimore, 1974), p. 89; Gray, *History of Agriculture,* 1: 115–16.

17. Nothing is more misguided or self-defeating than the effort to divorce moral from economic reasons for the decline of slavery and to assign one primacy over the other. Morality represents the distillation of a sense of what is right from the material of quotidian experience—of which economic practicality naturally forms an integral part. Moreover, once the evolution of society has generalized a certain moral outlook, that outlook becomes as surely a part of the circumstances constraining people's actions as price levels, wage rates, and the other economic phenomena that some scholars evidently consider to be the only "real" social entities. Earle, "Staple Interpretation," provides an example—by no means isolated—of an artificial attempt to draw a strict line between economic and "ideological-moral" motives, treating the latter as though they were subject to instantaneous nullification at the behest of individual calculations of marginal economic advantage.

18. The best recent studies of the changeover to cereal agriculture give little or no attention to the consequences of this switch for the slave system. Gregory A. Stiverson's informative study, *Poverty in a Land of Plenty: Tenancy in Eighteenth-Century Maryland* (Baltimore, 1977), dealing as it does with people who seldom owned slaves, could not be expected to say much on the matter. But Clemens, *Atlantic Economy,* deals with the economy of the Eastern Shore as a whole, including

both planters and small farmers. It is unfortunate, therefore, that the author did not apply his formidable skills of rigorous analysis and lucid presentation to detailed consideration of this important aspect of the problem.

19. During the period 1755–90, the free black population increased 343 percent; from 1790–1800, 144 percent; from 1800–10, 73 percent. Thereafter it averaged 20 percent per decade, with a high figure of 33 percent for 1820–30 and a low of 12 percent for 1850–60. U.S. 7th Census, 1850, *Compendium of the Seventh Census* (Washington, D.C., 1854), p. 64; Berlin, *Slaves without Masters,* pp. 46, 136.

20. Percentages calculated from U.S. 7th Census, *Population,* p. 220. Agricultural and manufacturing statistics appear on pp. 226–28 and in U.S. 7th Census, 1850, *History and Statistics of the State of Maryland* (Washington, 1852), pp. 38–62. For the argument that the shift to wheat in the southern counties was associated with large landholdings, see Gates, *Farmer's Age,* p. 111; Phillips, *Life and Labor,* p. 127. On sectionalism within Maryland, see also Hoffman, *Spirit of Dissension,* pp. 3–11; and Charles L. Wagandt, *The Mighty Revolution: Negro Emancipation in Maryland, 1862–1864* (Baltimore, 1964), pp. 1–5.

21. U.S. 7th Census, *Maryland,* pp. 52, 54; J. D. B. DeBow, *The Industrial Resources, Etc. of the Southern and Western States* (New Orleans, La., 1853), 2: 49–50; Matthew Page Andrews, *History of Maryland: Province and State* (Garden City, N.Y., 1929), pp. 452–54; David T. Gilchrist, ed., *The Growth of the Seaport Cities, 1790–1825* (Charlottesville, Va., 1967), pp. 62–67; Hoffman, *Spirit of Dissension,* pp. 74–80; Earle and Hoffman, "Urban Development," pp. 48–51; Jacob M. Price, "Economic Function and the Growth of American Port Towns in the Eighteenth Century," *Perspectives in American History* 8 (1974): 170–72; Gould, "Rise of Baltimore"; Gary Lawson Browne, *Baltimore in the Nation, 1789–1861* (Chapel Hill, N.C., 1980); Gray, *History of Agriculture,* 2: 756.

22. *Letter to John L. Carey on the Subject of Slavery by Dr. R. S. Steuart* (Baltimore, 1845), pp. 4–5.

23. Calculated from U.S. 9th Census, *Population,* pp. 3, 6.

24. Even excluding Baltimore, the population of the northern counties grew by 165 percent between 1790 and 1850, incomparably more than the rest of the state. Calculated from U.S. 7th Census, *Population,* pp. 220–21, and from DeBow, *Industrial Resources,* 1: 102.

25. The comparable proportions for the Eastern Shore and southern Maryland were 4 percent and 3.6 percent, respectively. Calculated from U.S. 7th Census, *Population,* pp. 220–21.

26. *Laws of Maryland,* 1752, chap. 1; 1796, chap. 67; 1832, chap. 281; 1858, chap. 307; Maryland Colonization Managers, *Colonization of the Free Colored Population of Maryland* (Baltimore, 1832) and *News from Africa: A Collection of Facts Relating to the Colony in Liberia for the Information of the Free People of Colour in Maryland* (Baltimore, 1832); *Letter to John L. Carey,* pp. 10–11; U.S. 7th Census, *Compendium,* p. 63n.; Report of the Board of State Colonization Managers, *Maryland Senate Journal and Documents,* 1858, doc. F; Calderhead, "Experiment in Freedom," p. 107; Berlin, *Slaves without Masters,* chaps. 4, 6; Penelope Campbell, *Maryland in Africa* (Urbana, Ill., 1971); Jeffrey R. Brackett, *The Negro in Maryland:*

A Study of the Institution of Slavery (Baltimore, 1889), pp. 166, 176; Aaron Stopak, "The Maryland State Colonization Society: Independent State Action in the Colonization Movement," *Maryland Historical Magazine* 63 (September 1968): 275–98.

27. U.S. 7th Census, *Maryland,* p. 21; U.S. 8th Census, 1860, *Population* (Washington, D.C., 1864), p. 215. The published census of 1850 does not tabulate foreign and out-of-state migrants by county of residence. In lieu of analyzing the manuscript schedules for the state at large—much too tall an order for the purpose at hand—I have had recourse to the 1860 published schedules.

28. These figures are based on prisoner lists in the records of the Maryland State Penitentiary, Liber 5656, Maryland Hall of Records, Annapolis. Obviously, a prison population is not randomly drawn and cannot be assumed to yield a faithful reflection of the larger population of which it is a component. Nevertheless, in this instance the data can serve at least as a rough guide. Certain principles of selection are admittedly at work. More convicts—both black and white—came from Baltimore City and County than from elsewhere in the state. There were more foreign-born among the white convicts than in the general white population, though for the purpose of this computation I have excluded foreigners. Black people were disproportionately represented among convicts. However, there seems no good reason to expect white people resident in their native counties to show a systematically higher propensity to become prisoners than black people in similar circumstances, or black people living elsewhere than their native counties to show a systematically higher propensity to become prisoners than similarly situated white people.

29. Once again Delaware is the exception but, for the reason discussed in note 4, may be set aside for the purpose of these comparisons.

30. Calculated from U.S. 7th Census, *Population,* p. 220, and from U.S. 9th Census, *Population,* p. 36.

31. Claudia Dale Goldin has concluded on the basis of percentage increases in urban slave populations that there was no long-term tendency toward decline. See Goldin, *Urban Slavery in the American South, 1820–1860: A Quantitative History* (Chicago, 1976) and "A Model to Explain the Relative Decline of Urban Slavery: Empirical Results," in Stanley L. Engerman and Eugene D. Genovese, eds., *Race and Slavery in the Western Hemisphere: Quantitative Studies* (Princeton, N.J., 1975). The argument also appears in Robert W. Fogel and Stanley L. Engerman, *Time on the Cross: The Economics of American Negro Slavery* (Boston, 1974), 1: 97–102; 2: 152–55. Chapter 3, below, takes up the specifics of this question.

32. William Calderhead, "How Extensive Was the Border State Slave Trade? A New Look," *Civil War History* 18 (March 1972): 42–55; Elwood Bridner, "The Fugitive Slaves in Maryland," *Maryland Historical Magazine* 66 (Spring 1971): 33–50; U.S. 7th Census, *Maryland,* p. 35; U.S. 7th Census, *Compendium,* p. 64. The incidence of runaways appears to have been on the decrease; see U.S. 8th Census, 1860, *Statistics of the United States (Including Mortality, Property, Etc.) in 1860* (Washington, D.C., 1866), pp. 337–38. For commentary upon the fugitive slave question during the secession crisis, see Baltimore *American,* 21 November 1860.

33. U.S. 7th Census, *Compendium,* p. 65.

34. Bridner, "Fugitive Slaves," p. 38.

35. *Planters' Advocate,* 17, 24 September 1851; 22 September 1858; "Report of Attorney General Brent, to His Excellency Gov. Lowe, in Relation to the Christiana Treason Trials, in the Circuit Court of the United States, Held at Philadelphia, 22 Dec. 1851," Annapolis, 1852; Frederick Douglass, *My Bondage and My Freedom* (1855; repr. New York, 1969), pp. 170, 326.

36. Herbert G. Gutman's discussion of the ramifications of sales of slaves away from their families may be taken as exemplary; see Gutman, *Slavery and the Numbers Game: A Critique of "Time on the Cross"* (Urbana, Ill., 1975), pp. 127–28.

37. The estimate appears in Calderhead, "Slave Trade," p. 53. Following Frederic Bancroft's method of estimation, Kenneth M. Stampp gives 75,000 as the number exported by Maryland between 1830 and 1860. Stampp, *The Peculiar Institution: Slavery in the Antebellum South* (New York, 1956), p. 238; Bancroft, *Slave Trading in the Old South* (New York, 1959; orig. ed. 1931), pp. 382–406. Neither Calderhead, Bancroft, nor Stampp offers an estimate of the number exported before 1830. But, as Bancroft recognized, a substantial interstate traffic must have lain behind the rapid accessions to the slave populations of what became the states of Tennessee, Kentucky, Alabama, Mississippi, and Louisiana in the years after the Revolution. See Allan Kulikoff, "Uprooted Peoples: Black Migrants in the Age of the American Revolution, 1790–1820," in Ira Berlin and Ronald Hoffman, eds., *Slavery and Freedom in the Age of the American Revolution* (Charlottesville, Va., 1983). Kulikoff estimates that the Chesapeake region exported some 98,000 slaves between 1790 and 1810, and another 124,000 between 1810 and 1820, but provides no separate estimate for Maryland (pp. 149, 152).

38. Calculated from figures in Calderhead, "Slave Trade," pp. 51, 53; U.S. 9th Census, *Population,* p. 36. Richard Sutch has estimated the rate of exportation of slaves from Maryland between 1850 and 1860 at 19.7 percent. Unfortunately his analysis, employing the survival rate technique, does not permit a distinction between slaves leaving the state and those joining the free population. Because of the importance of manumission in Maryland, this procedure probably results in an overestimate. Sutch, "The Breeding of Slaves for Sale and the Westward Expansion of Slavery, 1850–1860," in Engerman and Genovese, eds., *Race and Slavery,* esp. appendix, pp. 173–210. Calderhead reports an average of 370 manumissions per year between 1845 and 1850, and a total of 493 in 1850 ("Experiment in Freedom," chap. 4).

39. Calculated from U.S. 7th Census, *Compendium,* p. 253, and from U.S. 7th Census, *Population,* pp. 220–21.

40. Figures calculated from U.S. 7th Census, *Population,* pp. 226–28.

41. The classic study of agricultural reform in the upper South is Avery O. Craven, *Soil Exhaustion as a Factor in the Agricultural History of Virginia and Maryland, 1606–1860* (Urbana, Ill., 1925). Acute comparative observations about Maryland can be found in Eugene D. Genovese, *The Political Economy of Slavery: Studies in the Economy and Society of the Slave South* (New York, 1965), chaps. 4, 5, 6. Also see Gray, *History of Agriculture,* 2: 908–19; Gates, *Farmer's Age,* pp. 108–11; Vivian Wiser, "Improving Maryland's Agriculture, 1840–1860,"

Maryland Historical Magazine 64 (Summer 1969): 105–32; Memoirs of Horace Capron, typescript in National Agricultural Library, Beltsville, Md., pp. 58–64; Herbert A. Kellar, ed., *Solon Robinson, Pioneer and Agriculturist: Selected Writings* (New York, 1968), 2: 245–46; Frederick Law Olmsted, *The Cotton Kingdom,* ed. Arthur M. Schlesinger (New York, 1970; orig. ed. 1861), pp. 26–28.

42. Figures calculated from U.S. 7th Census, *Population,* pp. 226–27; quotation in Cecil *Whig,* 12 April 1862.

43. Warfield Diaries, 12 July 1849; 23, 24 June 1853; 4 July 1855; Charles C. Hopper Papers, MS 461, typescript at Maryland Historical Society. The adverse social consequences of the Eastern Shore's reliance upon free black labor receive detailed consideration in chapter 4.

44. "The Eastern Shore Question—Its Historical and Legal Aspects," pamphlet reprinted from the Baltimore *Sun,* 23, 24 December 1895, in Hopper Papers; Aubrey C. Land, "Provincial Maryland," in Walsh and Fox, eds., *Maryland: A History,* pp. 5–8, 11–13. The Eastern Shore's separate bureaucracy was abolished in 1841; *Laws of Maryland,* Extra Session, 1841, chap. 200.

45. "The Eastern Shore Question"; *Planters' Advocate,* 21 April 1858; Cecil *Whig,* 27 March, 3, 17 April 1858; W. Wayne Smith, "Politics and Democracy in Maryland, 1800–1854," in Walsh and Fox, eds., *Maryland: A History,* p. 296. Eastern Shore secessionism—by that time a quaint vestige—received a curious bit of encouragement in late 1861, when Secretary of War Simon Cameron proposed redrawing state lines so as to incorporate the Eastern Shores of Maryland and Virginia into the state of Delaware. Annual Report of the Secretary of War, 1 December 1861, in U.S. War Department, *The War of the Rebellion: A Compilation of the Official Records of the Union and Confederate Armies,* ser. 3, vol. 1 (Washington, 1899), pp. 707–08. The Cecil *Whig* favored the plan but admitted that there was little support for it on either of Maryland's shores or in Delaware (14, 21 December 1861).

46. Constitution of Maryland, 1851, art. 3, secs. 3, 43; U.S. 8th Census, *Population,* p. 214; Cecil *Whig,* 28 December 1861; Smith, "Politics and Democracy in Maryland," p. 297. Smith exaggerates when he maintains that the terms of the 1851 constitution "effectively shifted the power in the General Assembly to Baltimore and the western counties." Nor can anyone realistically claim, as he does, that "democracy in its fullest political extent inundated the shores of the Chesapeake Bay"—even with the addition of the missing qualifier *white* to the word *democracy.* See Smith, "Jacksonian Democracy on the Chesapeake: The Political Institutions," *Maryland Historical Magazine* 62 (December 1967), p. 393. Slaveholders in Louisiana were the only others who retained the privilege of counting slaves at their full numbers for purposes of legislative apportionment. Ralph A. Wooster, *The People in Power: Courthouse and Statehouse in the Lower South, 1850–1860* (Knoxville, Tenn., 1969) and *Politicians, Planters, and Plain Folk: Courthouse and Statehouse in the Upper Soutth, 1850–1860* (Knoxville, Tenn., 1975).

47. *Laws of Maryland,* 1852, chap. 337, sec. 9; Cecil *Whig,* 7 June 1862.

48. John Montgomery Gordon Diary, MS 1584, Maryland Historical Society, 25 August 1835; 9 October 1835; 11 April 1836; 27 March 1836; 30 March

1841; Alexander Randall Diaries, MS 652, Maryland Historical Society, 12 June 1862.

CHAPTER 2

1. Frederick Douglass, *My Bondage and My Freedom* (1855; repr. New York, 1969), p. 61.

2. Ibid., pp. 61–62.

3. Eugene D. Genovese, *Roll, Jordan, Roll: The World the Slaves Made* (New York, 1974), pp. 7–9.

4. Calculated from figures in William Calderhead, "How Extensive Was the Border State Slave Trade? A New Look," *Civil War History* 18 (March 1972), table, p. 51. I have made certain modifications in the figures that table gives for the total slave population of the eight counties in 1830. First, I have corrected an arithmetic error in the addition of the county figures. Second, I have deducted from the base slave population of 1830 Calderhead's figure for Howard County, which he takes from the 1860 census. The Howard district of Anne Arundel County became a separate county in 1851 (Constitution of Maryland, 1851, art. 8, sec. 1). Anne Arundel's total for 1830 should therefore include the share for that year of what was to become Howard County. A similar difficulty cannot be as neatly resolved for Carroll County, which was created in 1836 out of pieces taken from Baltimore and Frederick counties (U.S. 7th Census, 1850, *History and Statistics of the State of Maryland* [Washington, D.C., 1852], p. 12). Using Calderhead's figure, taken from the 1840 census but—somewhat arbitrarily—apportioning it evenly between Baltimore and Frederick counties, I have subtracted Baltimore's half from the 1830 base population. Calderhead makes no estimate of the number of sales that may have taken place unrecorded, but neither does he provide grounds to believe that there were none of this sort. Probably even more important, he makes no mention of Maryland owners who may have taken their slaves to the District of Columbia, a notorious slave emporium, for sale. Washington dealers advertised regularly in Maryland newspapers.

5. Calderhead, "Slave Trade," pp. 49–53. Maryland's rate of sales must have been extraordinary. As Herbert G. Gutman has pointed out, projecting Calderhead's estimated rate for Maryland to the whole South would lead to the incredible conclusion that close to two million slaves were sold between 1820 and 1860—out of a total slave population that by 1860 had reached just short of four million. Even Frederick Douglass and William Lloyd Garrison, Gutman comments, "never hinted at so large a volume." Gutman, *Slavery and the Numbers Game: A Critique of "Time on the Cross"* (Urbana, Ill., 1975), p. 126.

6. See Robert W. Fogel and Stanley L. Engerman, *Time on the Cross: The Economics of American Negro Slavery* (Boston, 1974), 1: 47–49. Gutman, *Numbers Game,* pp. 104–07, convincingly refutes this contention.

7. Calculated from U.S. 8th Census, 1860, *Agriculture* (Washington, D.C., 1864), p. 231.

8. Herbert G. Gutman, *The Black Family in Slavery and Freedom, 1750–*

1925 (New York, 1976), pp. 131–43; Genovese, *Roll, Jordan, Roll,* pp. 464, 472–73.

9. Gutman, *Numbers Game,* p. 106; Kenneth M. Stampp, *The Peculiar Institution: Slavery in the Ante-Bellum South* (New York, 1956), pp. 242–43.

10. Thomas I. Durant to Bvt. Maj. W. L. VanDerlip, 17 January 1867, Letters Received, ser. 2013, Annapolis, Md. Agt., RG 105, Records of the Bureau of Refugees, Freedmen and Abandoned Lands (Freedmen's Bureau), National Archives. In their famous discussion of the consequences of the slave trade, Fogel and Engerman not only minimize family relations other than those of mother and infant (on this point see *Time on the Cross,* 1: 5, 44–52, and Gutman's eloquent rebuttal in *Numbers Game,* pp. 138–40), but they also totally ignore the question of friendships among slaves. See Douglass, *My Bondage and My Freedom,* pp. 182–83, 274, 300–01, for a moving portrayal of what such friendships could mean.

11. Lewis Cecil Gray, *History of Agriculture in the Southern United States to 1860* (1933; repr. Gloucester, Mass., 1958), 1: 529–32. The figures shown in Gray's tables are misleading, however.

12. Julian M. Spencer to Capt. E. C. Knower, 25 April 1870, Case Files for Bounty and Pay Arrearages, ser. 2000, Claim Division, Md. Asst. Comr., RG 105, Records of the Freedmen's Bureau [A-4105]; John Diggs to Lt. Col. W. E. W. Ross, 20 December 1864, D-320 1864, Letters Received, ser. 2343, Middle Dept. & 8th Army Corps, RG 393 Pt. 1, Records of the U.S. Army Continental Commands, National Archives [C-4134]; *Planters' Advocate,* 22 September 1858.

13. *Planters' Advocate,* 27 January, 10 February, 24 March, 2 June, 18 August, 8 September 1858; 30 January 1861. Also see Genovese, *Roll, Jordan, Roll,* pp. 648–57; Stampp, *Peculiar Institution,* pp. 112–13; Elwood Bridner, "The Fugitive Slaves of Maryland," *Maryland Historical Magazine* 66 (Spring 1971): 33–50.

14. Genovese, *Roll, Jordan, Roll,* pp. 9–10.

15. See Douglass, *My Bondage and My Freedom,* pp. 173–77.

16. Fogel and Engerman, *Time on the Cross,* 1: 56; 2: 54.

17. Calderhead, "Slave Trade," p. 54; Fogel and Engerman, *Time on the Cross,* 1: 55–56; Claudia Dale Goldin, *Urban Slavery in the American South, 1820–1860: A Quantitative History* (Chicago, 1976), pp. 36, 64.

18. See Douglass's acidic comment on this point in *My Bondage and My Freedom,* pp. 328–29, and p. 49 above.

19. See, for example, Douglass's descriptions of his stints as a hired agricultural laborer in ibid., pp. 203–49, 261–70.

20. Ibid., pp. 53–57; John Q. A. Dennis to Hon. [Edwin M.] Stan[ton], 26 July 1864, D-1049 1864, Letters Received, RG 107, Records of the Office of the Secretary of War, National Archives [L-51].

21. *Laws of Maryland,* 1831, chap. 281, sec. 4.

22. John Montgomery Gordon Diary, MS 1584, Maryland Historical Society, Baltimore, 20 June 1834.

23. Susanna Warfield Diaries, MS 760, Maryland Historical Society, 2, 7, 8 September 1854; Complaint of Hannah Toogood, 12 August 1867–13 July 1868,

vol. 17, p. 78, Registers of Complaints, ser. 2008, Md. Complaint Division, RG 105, Records of the Freedmen's Bureau [A-9701].

24. Excerpted in Cecil *Whig,* 27 February 1858. Also see Port Tobacco *Times,* 24 February 1859.

25. Among the free states, Pennsylvania led in 1850 with 53,626 (compared to Maryland's 74,723). New York followed with 49,069. U.S. 7th Census, *Population* (Washington, D.C., 1853), p. ix.

26. Slaves constituted 30 percent of the black population of northern Maryland in 1850, 50 percent of that of the Eastern Shore, and 81 percent of that of southern Maryland. Calculated from U.S. 7th Census, *Population,* p. 220.

27. William Calderhead, "Experiment in Freedom: The Negro in Maryland to 1860," MS, pp. 125–26.

28. Cecil *Whig,* 20 March 1858; *Planters' Advocate,* 8 September 1858.

29. Calderhead, "Slave Trade," p. 54.

30. Warfield Diaries, 24, 26 August, 27 October 1849; 10 June, 3, 5–7 September, 29 October 1854; 6 December 1864.

31. Jeffrey R. Brackett, *The Negro in Maryland: A Study of the Institution of Slavery* (Baltimore, 1889), p. 222.

32. Warfield Diaries, 22 August 1854.

33. *Laws of Maryland,* 1796, chap. 67, sec. 13; 1831, chap. 281, sec. 3; 1858, chap. 307, sec. 2; Ira Berlin, *Slaves without Masters: The Free Negro in the Antebellum South* (New York, 1974), pp. 152–53.

34. Calderhead, "Experiment in Freedom," p. 113.

35. See Berlin, *Slaves without Masters,* pp. 154–57; James M. Wright, *The Free Negro in Maryland, 1634–1860* (New York, 1921), pp. 76–77.

36. Calculated from figures in Calderhead, "Slave Trade," pp. 52–53.

37. Douglass, *My Bondage and My Freedom,* pp. 281–82.

38. Ibid., pp. 134–36.

39. Marlboro' *Gazette,* 20 July 1849; Stampp, *Peculiar Institution,* p. 111; Bridner, "Fugitive Slaves," p. 39; Berlin, *Slaves without Masters,* p. 159.

40. *Laws of Maryland,* 1831, chap. 323; 1832, chap. 40; 1839, chaps. 35, 38; 1858, chap. 324; *Maryland Code of Public General Laws,* 1860, art. 66; Report of the House Committee on Colored Population to the Legislature of Maryland, 1 February 1860, *Maryland House Documents,* 1860, doc. 0; Brackett, *Negro in Maryland,* p. 232. For a discussion of such of the local laws regarding free blacks as remained in force in 1866, see James C. Carlisle to Gen. C. H. Howard, 11 March 1866, C-124 1866, Letters Received, ser. 15, Washington Hdqrs., RG 105, Records of the Freedmen's Bureau [A-9706].

41. *Planters' Advocate,* 30 November 1859.

42. *Maryland Code,* 1860, art. 66, secs. 3–4; Berlin, *Slaves without Masters,* pp. 160–61; Calderhead, "Slave Trade," p. 48.

43. *Laws of Maryland,* 1831, chap. 281, sec. 5. The law was passed during the December 1831 session, but its actual date of passage was 12 March 1832.

44. *Laws of Maryland,* 1839, chap. 38, secs. 1–2; 1849, chap. 538; 1853, chap. 177; 1856, chap. 161; Cecil *Whig,* 14 August 1858.

45. Wright, *Free Negro,* pp. 32–33.

46. Ibid., pp. 152–55; Leonard P. Curry, *The Free Black in Urban America 1800–1850* (Chicago, 1981), chap. 2 and appendix B; Berlin, *Slaves without Masters,* pp. 228–29.

47. Curry, *Free Black,* pp. 114–15.

48. Baltimore *American,* 8, 9 July 1858. For discussion of competition between white and free black labor in Baltimore during the 1850s, including interpretations of the caulkers' episode somewhat different from mine, see M. Ray Della, "The Problems of Negro Labor in the 1850's," *Maryland Historical Magazine* 66 (Spring 1971): 14–32, and Berlin, *Slaves without Masters,* pp. 231–32; 349–50. Also see Wright, *Free Negro,* pp. 171–73.

49. Douglass, *My Bondage and My Freedom,* p. 90. On slavery and "free-negroism" in Maryland, see chap. 4.

50. Calculated from U.S. 7th Census, *Population,* pp. 219, 225.

CHAPTER 3

1. Frederick Douglass, *My Bondage and My Freedom* (1855; repr. New York, 1969), pp. 135–42.

2. Robert Gilmor, "Recollections of Baltimore, Read before the Maryland Historical Society, 9 May 1844," *Maryland Historical Magazine* 7 (September 1912): 236–37. Gilmor's father established a profitable mercantile operation in Baltimore during the Revolutionary War. See Ronald Hoffman, *A Spirit of Dissension: Economics, Politics, and the Revolution in Maryland* (Baltimore, 1973), pp. 76–78.

3. Henry Stockbridge, Sr., "Baltimore in 1846, Read before the Maryland Historical Society, 10 December 1875," *Maryland Historical Magazine* 6 (March 1911): 23–24.

4. Ibid., pp. 20–22.

5. Calculated from U.S. 9th Census, *Population* (Washington, D. C., 1872), p. 36.

6. George Armistead Leakin, "The Migrations of Baltimore Town," *Maryland Historical Magazine* 1 (March 1906): 59.

7. J. D. B. DeBow, *Industrial Resources, Etc. of the Southern and Western States* (New Orleans, La., 1852), 1:101–02.

8. David T. Gilchrist, ed., *The Growth of the Seaport Cities, 1790–1825* (Charlottesville, Va., 1967), pp. 34–36, 39, 62–64; Eleanor Bruchey, "The Development of Baltimore Business, 1800–1914," *Maryland Historical Magazine* 64 (Spring 1969): 19; Clarence P. Gould, "The Economic Causes of the Rise of Baltimore," in *Essays in Colonial History Presented to Charles McLean Andrews by His Students* (New Haven, Conn., 1931); Jacob M. Price, "Economic Function and the Growth of American Port Towns in the Eighteenth Century," *Perspectives in American History* 8 (1974): 169–72; Carville Earle and Ronald Hoffman, "Staple Crops and Urban Development in the Eighteenth-Century South," *Perspectives in American History* 10 (1976): 47–51; Gary Lawson Browne, *Baltimore in the Nation, 1789–1861* (Chapel Hill, N.C., 1980), pp. 3–13, 70–89; Hoffman, *Spirit of Dissension,* pp. 76–78.

9. Richard Walsh, "The Era of the Revolution," in Richard Walsh and William L. Fox, eds., *Maryland: A History, 1632–1974,* (Baltimore, 1974), p. 89.

10. Calculated from figures in U.S. 9th Census, *Population,* pp. 36–37.

11. Gilchrist, *Seaport Cities,* p. 64.

12. Bruchey, "Development of Baltimore Business," p. 20; Charles Hirschfeld, *Baltimore 1870–1900: Studies in Social History* (Baltimore, 1941), p. 32.

13. This figure, taken from U.S. 8th Census, *Population* (Washington, D.C., 1864), pp. 221–22, combines production for Baltimore City and County (which by then were legally separate) because most of the mills were located in unincorporated outskirts of the city.

14. Eleanor Bruchey, "The Industrialization of Maryland, 1860–1914," in Walsh and Fox, eds., *Maryland: A History,* p. 423; Richard W. Griffin, "An Origin of the Industrial Revolution in Maryland: The Textile Industry, 1789–1826," *Maryland Historical Magazine* 61 (March 1966): 27–29. A full discussion of Baltimore's industrialization may be found in Brown, *Baltimore,* chaps. 3, 8, and 9.

15. U.S. 8th Census, *Population,* p. 221.

16. Douglass C. North, *The Economic Growth of the United States, 1790–1860* (New York, 1966), p. 32; James S. Van Ness, "Economic Development, Social and Cultural Changes: 1800–1850," in Walsh and Fox, eds., *Maryland: A History,* p. 171.

17. U.S. 8th Census, *Population,* p. 221.

18. Gilchrist, *Seaport Cities,* pp. 66–67; Matthew Page Andrews, *History of Maryland: Province and State* (Garden City, N.Y., 1929), pp. 452–54; Van Ness, "Economic Development," pp. 174–75, 192–97, 204; Bruchey, "Industrialization of Maryland," p. 460. As late as 1858 a group of bondholders in the Chesapeake and Ohio Canal were still memorializing the legislature, seeking support for the doomed project. Professing to have abandoned illusions of "seeing realized, in this day and generation, the extravagant expectations of those who commenced this Canal," they nevertheless betrayed continued illusions that these expectations could be realized at some time in the future when "immense amounts of capital, and a large additional population have been located in the Alleganies" (Document G, *Maryland Senate Journal and Documents,* 1858). Still more absurdly, a meeting was announced for "friends of the extension of the Chesapeake and Ohio Canal to the Ohio River," to be held in Cumberland in September 1873 (Baltimore *Sun,* 6 September 1873). Cf. editorial in the *Planters' Advocate,* 9 February 1859, dismissing "this canal bore" as "the grossest imposition that was ever practised upon any community . . . a well-sustained insult . . . to the sober-suited character of common sense itself" and as a device to "feed and clothe more or less broken-down politicians."

19. U.S. 7th Census, *History and Statistics of the State of Maryland* (Washington, D.C., 1852), p. 21.

20. U.S. 8th Census, *Population,* p. 215.

21. Ibid.

22. Ibid., p. 214.

23. James Dixon, *Personal Narrative of a Tour through a Part of the United States and Canada* (New York, 1849), p. 70; Alexander Mackay, *The Western*

World (London, 1850), p. 161; "Autobiography of John Davis, 1770–1864" (excerpts from manuscripts in Maryland Historical Society, Baltimore), *Maryland Historical Magazine* 30 (March 1935): 23.

24. Dixon, *Personal Narrative,* p. 52; Ebenezer Davis, *American Scenes and Christian Slavery* (London, 1848), p. 187.

25. Mackay, *Western World,* pp. 159–60.

26. Stockbridge, "Baltimore in 1846," p. 31; John H. Naff, "Recollections of Baltimore, Thrown Together as they were collected, at different times, from conversations with the elders of the city," *Maryland Historical Magazine* 5 (June 1910): 115.

27. Stockbridge, "Baltimore in 1846," pp. 24–25.

28. Caroline Gilman, *The Poetry of Travelling in the United States* (New York, 1838), p. 26; William E. Bartlett to Edward Stabler, 12 August 1835 (from collection of Maryland Historical Society), *Maryland Historical Magazine* 9 (June 1914): 157–62; Van Ness, "Economic Development," pp. 200–10; Browne, *Baltimore,* pp. 122–25; Hoffman, *Spirit of Dissension,* chap. 8; W. Wayne Smith, "Politics and Democracy in Maryland, 1800–1854," in Walsh and Fox, eds., *Maryland: A History,* p. 249.

29. Baltimore *Sun,* 3 January 1850; Mackay, *Western World,* p. 161.

30. Baltimore *Sun,* 17 December 1849.

31. Ibid., 7, 9, 10 December 1857.

32. Ibid., 14 September 1857; 8 February 1858.

33. Ibid., 14, 16, 18, 22 September 1857; Cecil *Whig,* 17 January 1857; 11, 25 September 1858; Annapolis *Gazette,* 17 September 1857. In 1856 Democratic Governor Thomas Watkins Ligon charged a committee of the Know-Nothing–controlled legislature with investigating the election activities of nativist secret societies. The committee majority seemed more disturbed by the governor's syntax than by the secret societies, for whose conduct they managed to discover constitutional sanction. (In his message the governor had, in fact, misplaced a modifier.) Report of the Majority of the Committee on Secret Societies, 3 March 1856, and Report of the Minority of the Committee on Secret Societies, 4 March 1856, *Maryland House Documents,* 1856.

34. Baltimore *Sun,* 5 September 1857.

35. Richard C. Wade, *Slavery in the Cities: The South 1820–1860* (New York 1964), p. 32; Browne, *Baltimore,* p. 192; Cecil *Whig,* 27 February 1858.

36. Thomas Hamilton, *Men and Manners in America* (1843; repr. New York, 1968), p. 212; Douglass, *My Bondage and My Freedom,* pp. 309–10.

37. Browne, *Baltimore,* pp. 98–99.

38. Interestingly enough, even the C & O Canal, which was beset by labor shortages and disruptions from the beginning, never relied on slave labor. Van Ness, "Economic Development," p. 197.

39. Robert W. Fogel and Stanley L. Engerman, *Time on the Cross: The Economics of American Negro Slavery* (Boston, 1974), 1: 56–57; also Claudia Dale Goldin, *Urban Slavery in the American South, 1820–1860: A Quantitative History* (Chicago, 1976), pp. 35, 42, 127.

40. Douglass, *My Bondage and My Freedom,* pp. 328–29. Wade and Goldin

both provide examples of the unorthodox arrangements to which urban slavery gave rise.

41. *Planters' Advocate,* 4 November 1857, 29 September 1858; Report of the Committee on Colored Population to the Legislature of Maryland, January Session, 1860, *Maryland House Documents,* 1860, Doc. O.

42. Wade, *Slavery in the Cities,* p. 244.

43. It is no straightforward matter to separate urban from rural slaves. Where a slave was purchased and where he lived and worked were not necessarily the same. The large slave dealers had headquarters in the city, but their transactions by no means involved only urban slaves. And once purchased, slaves could be—and were—moved back and forth between city and country employment (Stockbridge, "Baltimore in 1846," pp. 26–27; Susanna Warfield Diaries, MS 760, Maryland Historical Society, Baltimore, 4 January 1849; Douglass, *My Bondage and My Freedom,* pp. 135, 137, 174, 179, 182, 302). The residence of owner or slave at the moment of sale, the criterion employed in Goldin, *Urban Slavery,* 69, 73, is thus uncertain ground on which to rest a distinction between urban and rural slaves.

44. This assumption lurks in the argument of Claudia Dale Goldin, *Urban Slavery,* and "A Model to Explain the Relative Decline of Urban Slavery: Empirical Results," in Stanley L. Engerman and Eugene D. Genovese, eds., *Race and Slavery in the Western Hemisphere: Quantitative Studies* (Princeton, 1975). Both studies reduce the question of the institutional integrity of slavery in cities to the microeconomic question of the demand for the services of individual slave laborers. And both treat slavery the institution and slavery the legal condition as one and the same.

45. Goldin, *Urban Slavery,* chap. 4; idem, "Model"; Harold D. Woodman, "Comment on C. Goldin," in Engerman and Genovese, eds., *Race and Slavery.* Apparently basing them on Goldin's data, Robert W. Fogel and Stanley L. Engerman have extrapolated even more extravagant conclusions; see *Time on the Cross,* 1: 94–102 and 2: 153–55.

46. Goldin, *Urban Slavery,* chap. 5 and pp. 9, 124–25; see also, idem, "Model."

47. The greater persistence of female over male slaveowners in Baltimore, and the use of slaves by female owners as sources of rental income, provide further evidence on this point. Browne, *Baltimore,* p. 193.

48. Goldin, "Model," p. 430; idem, *Urban Slavery,* pp. 4–5.

49. Calculated from U.S. 7th Census, *Population,* p. 221, and Baltimore *Sun,* 3 January 1850. Baltimore did, in fact, experience an explosion of police costs between 1845 and 1860 (Browne, *Baltimore,* p. 203); but slavery had little if anything to do with it.

50. Goldin, "Model," p. 433. The argument is also propounded in *Urban Slavery,* pp. 8–9, and is taken up in Fogel and Engerman, *Time on the Cross.* Leonard P. Curry, *The Free Black in Urban America 1800–1850: The Shadow of the Dream* (Chicago, 1981), employs similar reasoning but reaches an opposite conclusion. Because female slaves outnumbered male slaves consistently in Baltimore from 1820 to 1850, reaching a ratio of over two to one in 1850, he assumes that owners must have sold male slaves disproportionately from fear of the effects of Baltimore's perennial riot upon the "male slave psyche." He is on stronger ground

in calling attention to the preponderant employment of slaves in Baltimore as domestic servants (see pp. 8, 252).

51. Douglass, *My Bondage and My Freedom,* chaps. 14, 17, 18, 19, and 20.

52. Robert S. Starobin, *Industrial Slavery in the Old South* (New York, 1970), and Charles B. Dew, *Ironmaker to the Confederacy: Joseph R. Anderson and the Tredegar Iron Works* (New Haven, Conn., 1966), adequately establish this point.

53. U.S. 8th Census, *Statistics of the United States (Including Mortality, Property, Etc.) in 1860* (Washington, D.C., 1866), pp. xviii–xix.

54. These percentages have been calculated from figures given in U.S. 8th Census, *Statistics,* p. xviii, and Wade, *Slavery in the Cities,* appendix, pp. 325–28.

55. U.S. 8th Census, *Statistics,* p. lviii.

56. Ibid., table NN, pp. lvii–lviii.

57. Among other difficulties, this concept resorts to the self-contradictory shift of expressing in pecuniary terms individual preferences that it begins by describing as nonpecuniary. See Fogel and Engerman, *Time on the Cross,* 1: 235–39.

58. U.S. 8th Census, *Statistics,* pp. lvii–lviii; Eugene D. Genovese, *The Political Economy of Slavery: Studies in the Economy and Society of the Slave South* (New York, 1965), p. 232.

59. One scholar does appear, however, to have persuaded himself that the South's lag in the development of cities and towns is a "myth." He has accomplished this by dismissing the low absolute level of urban population in the South, proposing instead an index (the Comparative Urban Rate of Increase) that compares the percentage change in urban population to the percentage change of total population. Seen through the distorting mirror of this index, the South from 1800 to 1850 had a slightly higher rate of urbanization than the North; that is to say, urban population in the South grew slightly faster, by contrast with a sluggish rate of total population growth, than urban population in the North, by contrast with a much more robust rate of total population growth. The index thus treats overall population growth as a fortuitous given, independent of urban growth. It is also worth noting that the figures for Southern urban growth include three border-state cities—Baltimore, St. Louis, and Louisville—whose expansiveness had more to do with their economic ties to the North than with their political connection to the South. The worst feature of the index is its extreme aggregation: an index that homogenizes Massachusetts and New York with Michigan and Indiana reveals something about statistical summary but very little about actual urbanization. See Leonard P. Curry, "Urbanization and Urbanism in the Old South: A Comparative View," *Journal of Southern History* 40 (February 1974): 43–60.

60. David Montgomery, *Beyond Equality: Labor and the Radical Republicans, 1862–1872* (New York, 1967), p. 8.

61. Genovese, *Political Economy of Slavery,* part 3. Genovese's argument has provoked impassioned dissent. But the dissenters have not so far come to terms with this fundamental point, which is now receiving reinforcement from those devoting close study to the Southern white yeomanry. Recent and forthcoming work demonstrates that this, the largest part of the Southern white population, lived on the fringes of the market economy, and that it was social forces given their head by the defeat of the Confederacy and the abolition of slavery that finally

converted them, often unwillingly, into a home market. See, for example, Steven Hahn, *The Roots of Southern Populism: Yeoman Farmers and the Transformation of the Georgia Upcountry, 1850–1890* (New York, 1983), esp. chaps. 4–7; and Armstead Robinson, *Bitter Fruits of Bondage: Slavery's Demise and the Collapse of the Confederacy* (New Haven: Yale University Press, forthcoming). Fred Bateman and Thomas Weiss, *A Deplorable Scarcity: The Failure of Industrialization in the Slave Economy* (Chapel Hill, N.C., 1981) addresses—but cannot explain—the slave South's failure to industrialize.

62. Fogel and Engerman, *Time on the Cross*, 1: 255.

63. A particularly naïve argument along these lines occurs in Goldin, *Urban Slavery*, pp. 7, 126.

64. The great advantage enjoyed by large estates—feudal as well as slave— lay not in economies of scale but in their capacity to assign a larger share of their production to the market, in contrast to the mainly self-sustaining peasant or yeoman farmer's holding. That capacity, in turn, rested on the lord or slaveowner's power to command the surplus labor or appropriate the surplus product of others. Grasping this fact has never posed a problem for commonsense historical analysis (for example, see Eric J. Hobsbawm, *The Age of Capital, 1848–1875* [London, 1975], pp. 186– 87, and Witold Kula, *An Economic Theory of the Feudal System* [London, 1976; 1962 ed.], pp. 49–52). Recently, econometric historians have confirmed it as well: Gavin Wright, *The Political Economy of the Cotton South: Households, Markets, and Wealth in the Nineteenth Century* (New York, 1978), pp. 74–87, and "Prosperity, Progress, and American Slavery," in Paul A. David et al., *Reckoning with Slavery* (New York, 1976), pp. 316–20. The view that economies of scale account for the overwhelming dominance of agriculture in the antebellum South may be found in Fogel and Engerman, *Time on the Cross*, 1: 255, and Goldin, *Urban Slavery*, pp. 10, 125.

65. Karl Marx, *Capital* (Middlesex, Eng., 1976), 1: 637, 795–96, and (Middlesex, Eng., 1981), 3: 372, 775; Ernest Mandel, *Late Capitalism* (London, 1975), pp. 377–79; Eric J. Hobsbawm, "Looking Forward: History and the Future," *New Left Review* 125 (January-February 1981): 13–14; New York *Times,* 15 April 1977; U.S. Department of Agriculture, "A Time to Choose: Summary Report on the Structure of Agriculture," January 1981.

66. This process deserves further study in the light of its historical antecedents in the post–Civil War era. Pete Daniel, "The Transformation of the Rural South, 1930 to the Present," *Agricultural History* 55 (1981): 231–48, offers an indication of the rich material that awaits exploration; and the exchange between Harold D. Woodman and Jonathan Wiener in "Class Struggle and Economic Development in the American South, 1865–1955" points up the sorts of questions that need to be asked (*American Historical Review* 84 (1979): 970–1006). Work forthcoming and in progress by Pete Daniel, Harold Woodman, Thavolia Glymph, and Nan E. Woodruff will be of vast importance in revealing the link between the history of the nineteenth century and that of the twentieth.

67. In fact, Baltimore's white population was 36 percent of the state's total. Calculated from figures in U.S. 9th Census, *Population* (Washington, D.C., 1872), pp. 4, 163.

68. Warfield Diaries, 8 March, 7 April 1849.

69. Accounts of the Know-Nothing party include: Laurence F. Schmeckebier, *History of the Know Nothing Party in Maryland* (Baltimore, 1899); Benjamin Tuska, *Know Nothingism in Baltimore* (New York, 1925); Jean H. Baker, *Ambivalent Americans: The Know-Nothing Party in Maryland* (Baltimore, 1977); idem, *The Politics of Continuity: Maryland Political Parties from 1858 to 1870* (Baltimore, 1973), chap. 3; William Evitts, "A Matter of Allegiances, Maryland from 1850 to 1861" (Ph.D. diss., Johns Hopkins University, 1971); Douglas Bowers, "Ideology and Political Parties in Maryland, 1851–1856," *Maryland Historical Magazine* 64 (Fall 1969): 197–217; Richard R. Duncan, "The Era of the Civil War," in Walsh and Fox, eds., *Maryland: A History,* and Browne, *Baltimore,* chap. 10. Browne criticizes scholars who wrote before him for neglecting the administrative accomplishments of municipal Know-Nothingism. Though his case for these may be overstated, he is right to rescue them from oblivion. But earlier scholars were also right to attribute primary importance to the political aspect of Know-Nothingism.

70. *Planters' Advocate,* 4 November 1857. The charge of abolitionism was directed at Henry Winter Davis.

71. Ibid., 29 September 1858.

72. Ibid., 17 September 1856. This incident, which the *Advocate* anxiously followed in the Baltimore press, is described at greater length in Ira Berlin, *Slaves without Masters: The Free Negro in the Antebellum South* (New York, 1974), pp. 346–47. See also Annapolis *Gazette,* 1 January 1857, which charged that the overheated rhetoric of the Southern Democrats promoted conspiracy and unrest by "saluting" the "eager ears" of "ignorant negroes" with news of John C. Frémont and the Republican party.

73. Testimony Taken before a Committee of the House of Delegates of Maryland on Contested Elections, *Maryland House Documents,* 1860; Cecil *Whig,* 8 August 1857; Browne, *Baltimore,* p. 207; Duncan, "Era of the Civil War," p. 313; Baker, *Ambivalent Americans,* chap. 5.

74. Browne, *Baltimore,* pp. 184–86.

75. Report of the Majority of the Committee on Secret Societies; Report of the Minority of the Committee on Secret Societies; Cecil *Whig,* 4 July 1857; 20 February 1858; 14, 21 January 1860; Baker, *Ambivalent Americans,* chap. 2.

76. Inaugural Address of Thomas H. Hicks, *Maryland House Journal and Documents,* 1858, Doc. E; Baltimore *Sun,* 23 September, 9 October 1857; 24 March 1858; Cecil *Whig,* 3 October 1857; 2 October 1858. In the clothing industry, the factory system properly so-called had probably proceeded further than in any other industry in the city, as illustrated by the average number of hands per establishment (forty-six, compared to eleven for all other industries) and by the fact that a majority of the employees were women. Still, most of the needlewomen did not work in manufacturing establishments—fewer than 4,000 of some 40,000 in the industry as a whole. Calculated from figures in U.S. 8th Census, *Population,* pp. 220–22, and in Baltimore *Sun,* 24 March 1858.

77. Inaugural Address of Thomas H. Hicks.

78. *Laws of Maryland,* 1858, chap. 324; Report of the President and the Directors of the Maryland Penitentiary, January 1860, in Maryland Hall of Records;

Cecil *Whig*, 11 July 1857; Inaugural Address of Thomas H. Hicks; Report of the Committee on Colored Population to the Legislature of Maryland, January Session, 1860, *Maryland House Documents,* 1860, Doc. O.

79. Duncan, "Era of the Civil War," pp. 330–31; Cecil *Whig*, 21 January 1860.

CHAPTER 4

1. The account of the Bowers episode has been constructed from reports in the Cecil *Whig*, 3, 17, and 24 July 1858, and the *Planters' Advocate,* 21 July 1858. Jeffrey R. Brackett, *The Negro in Maryland* (Baltimore, 1889), pp. 190–94, summarizes the evolution of Maryland's laws on the subject of testimony by slaves and free black people.

2. Cecil *Whig*, 17 July 1858.

3. Baltimore *American*, 19 July 1858; Cecil *Whig*, 24 July 1858; *Planters' Advocate,* 21 July 1858.

4. Cecil *Whig*, 23 October 1858.

5. Annapolis *Gazette*, 16 March 1855; *Planters' Advocate,* 10, 31 December 1856; Cecil *Whig*, 31 October 1857; *Planters' Advocate,* 8 September 1858; Brackett, *Negro in Maryland,* p. 224.

6. *Planters' Advocate,* 22 September 1858.

7. Cecil *Whig*, 13, 20, 27 November 1858; *Planters' Advocate,* 10 November 1858.

8. Cecil *Whig*, 13, 20 November 1858; *Planters' Advocate,* 10 November 1858.

9. Port Tobacco *Times and Charles County Advertiser*, 24 February 1859.

10. Penelope Campbell, *Maryland in Africa* (Urbana, Ill., 1971); Aaron Stopak, "The Maryland State Colonization Society: Independent State Action in the Colonization Movement," *Maryland Historical Magazine* 63 (September 1968): 275–99. Discussion of colonization at a black convention in Maryland in 1852 led to violent disturbances outside the hall and lively discussion within it. See Brackett, *Negro in Maryland,* pp. 250–52; Proceedings of the Maryland Free Colored People's Convention, 27–28 July 1852, in Philip S. Foner and George E. Walker, eds., *Proceedings of the Black State Conventions, 1840–1865* (Philadelphia, 1980), pp. 42–49.

11. *Planters' Advocate,* 17 November 1858. Editorial from Cecil *Democrat* reprinted in *Planters' Advocate,* 24 November 1858.

12. *Planters' Advocate,* 29 September 1858.

13. Cecil *Whig*, 20 November 1858.

14. *Planters' Advocate,* 24 November 1858; 12 January 1859.

15. Cecil *Whig*, 27 November, 4 December 1858.

16. Cecil *Whig*, 4 June 1859; *Planters' Advocate,* 18 May 1859.

17. Cecil *Whig*, 30 April, 28 May 1859; *Planters' Advocate,* 13, 20 April 1859; 1 June 1859.

18. Cecil *Whig*, 30 April 1859; *Planters' Advocate,* 8 June 1859.

19. *Planters' Advocate,* 15 June 1859; Cecil *Whig*, 11 June 1859.

20. Cecil *Whig,* 19, 16 November 1859: *Planters' Advocate,* 19, 26 October 1859.

21. Richard R. Duncan, "The Era of the Civil War," in Richard Walsh and William Lloyd Fox, eds., *Maryland: A History, 1632–1974* (Baltimore, 1974), p. 330; *Planters' Advocate,* 19, 26 October 1859; 4 January 1860; Cecil *Whig,* 22 October, 5, 19, 26 November 1859.

22. Report of the Committee on Colored Population to the Legislature of Maryland, 1 February 1860, *Maryland House Documents,* 1860, doc. O.

23. *Planters' Advocate,* 22 February 1860.

24. Brackett, *Negro in Maryland,* pp. 219–20; James M. Wright, *The Free Negro in Maryland, 1634–1860* (New York, 1921), pp. 130–38, 151, 191–96; Ira Berlin, *Slaves without Masters: The Free Negro in the Antebellum South* (New York, 1974), pp. 208–09, 210–11, 226; James S. Van Ness, "Economic Development, Social and Cultural Changes: 1800–1850," in Walsh and Fox, eds., *Maryland: A History,* pp. 231–32; Grace Hill Jacobs, "The Negro in Baltimore" (Master's thesis, Howard University, 1945), p. 17; *Laws of Maryland,* 1858, chap. 324.

25. Brackett, *Negro in Maryland,* pp. 242–50; Berlin, *Slaves without Masters,* pp. 208–11.

26. Berlin, *Slaves without Masters,* p. 377; Brackett, *Negro in Maryland,* p. 259.

27. See, for example, Affidavit of Humphrey Ware and Catherine Ware, 27 September 1865, Unregistered Letters Received, ser. 457, D.C. Asst. Comr., RG 105, Records of the Bureau of Refugees, Freedmen, and Abandoned Lands (Freedmen's Bureau), National Archives [A-9881].

28. Easton *Star,* 14, 28 February 1860; *Democratic Alleganian,* 18 February 1860; Cecil *Whig,* 14 January 1860; Annapolis *Gazette,* 29 March 1860.

29. *Laws of Maryland,* 1860, chaps. 232, 322.

30. Easton *Star,* 13 November 1860; Brackett, *Negro in Maryland,* pp. 261–62; Berlin, *Slaves without Masters,* p. 380.

31. The Jacobs committee used this phrase in an effort to attract support for its plan among nonslaveholders. See Report of the Committee on Colored Population, p. 6.

32. Hugh L. Bond to Hon. E. M. Stanton, 15 August 1863, in *Freedom: A Documentary History of Emancipation, 1861–1867,* ser. 2: *The Black Military Experience* (New York, 1982), ed. Ira Berlin, Joseph P. Reidy, and Leslie S. Rowland, doc. 71.

33. *Planters' Advocate,* 22 September 1858.

34. Ibid., 29 September 1858.

35. Approximately 13 percent of white households held slaves; 53.4 percent of the legislators did. Even in southern Maryland and on the Eastern Shore, slaveholding households accounted for just under 32 percent of the total. Legislators also owned many more slaves than their slaveholding constituents: the median slaveholding was two for the state, twenty-seven for the legislature. Calculated from data in U.S. 8th Census, 1850, *Agriculture* (Washington, D.C., 1864), p. 231; U.S. 8th Census, 1850, *Population* (Washington, D.C., 1864), p. 214; and Ralph A. Wooster, "The Membership of the Maryland Legislature of 1861," *Maryland*

Historical Magazine 56 (March 1961): 99–102. I have assumed an average of five individuals per household.

36. U.S. 8th Census, *Agriculture,* p. 231, and Wooster, "Membership," pp. 99–102.

37. Lawrence Posey Account Books, 1850, MS 665, Maryland Historical Society, Baltimore; *Planters' Advocate,* 10 October 1860.

38. *Laws of Maryland,* 1860, chap. 232, secs. 6 and 7.

39. Reprint from Federick *Examiner* in Cecil *Whig,* 9 June 1860; U.S. 8th Census, 1860, *Preliminary Report on the Eighth Census* (Washington, D.C., 1862), p. 137.

40. Susanna Warfield Diaries, MS 760, Maryland Historical Society, 24, 25 January, 3 February 1849.

41. Democratic *Alleganian,* 18 February 1860.

42. Stopak, "Maryland Colonization Sociey," pp. 279–80. See also Colonization Managers Appointed by the State of Maryland, *Colonization of the Free Colored Population of Maryland* (Baltimore, 1832); Colonization Managers, *News from Africa: A Collection of Facts Relating to the Colony in Liberia for the Information of the Free People of Colour in Maryland* (Baltimore, 1832); *Laws of Maryland,* 1832, chap. 145; 1833, chap. 87, sec. 1; 1834, chap. 197, secs. 1–4; 1836, chap. 274; 1839, chap. 38; and 1849, chap. 283; Report of the Board of State Colonization Managers, *Maryland House Documents,* 1858, doc. F.

43. See Eugene D. Genovese, *Roll, Jordan, Roll: The World the Slaves Made* (New York, 1974), pp. 75–86. Crisfield quoted in Charles L. Wagandt, *The Mighty Revolution: Negro Emancipation in Maryland, 1862–1864* (Baltimore, 1964), p. 42.

44. Warfield Diaries, 1, 9 August; 2–8 September 1854.

45. *Laws of Maryland,* 1831, chap. 281, sec. 5; Narrative of Caroline Hammond, in George P. Rawick, ed., *The American Slave: A Composite Autobiography* (Westport, Conn., 1972), 16: 20; Brackett, *Negro in Maryland,* p. 166.

46. Easton *Star,* 28 February 1860.

47. Inaugural Address of Thomas H. Hicks, *Maryland House Journal and Documents,* 1858, doc. E.

48. Maryland Penitentiary, Prisoners' Records, Liber 5656 (1840–69), Maryland Hall of Records, Annapolis.

49. Warfield Diaries, 7, 25 September 1849; 15 June, 9, 26 September 1854; Posey Account Book, 1859; Charles C. Hopper Papers, MS 461, Maryland Historical Society.

50. *Planters' Advocate,* 15 June 1859; Port Tobacco *Times and Charles County Advertiser,* 24 February 1859; *Democratic Alleganian,* 18 February 1860.

51. Report of the Committee on Labor and Immigration, *Senate Journal and Documents,* 1867, doc. Y; Message of Gov. Swann to the General Assembly of Maryland, January 1867, doc. A; and Report of the Commissioner of Immigration of the State of Maryland to the General Assembly, doc. N, *Maryland House Journal and Documents,* 1867.

52. Maryland Penitentiary, Prisoners' Reports. The manuscript census schedules unfortunately distinguish only erratically among types of laborers. The adjective

"farm" was attached to "laborer" only when an individual enumerator had the whim to be specific.

CHAPTER 5

1. A recent example is Michael F. Holt, *The Political Crisis of the 1850s* (New York, 1978). Holt argues that the vitality of two-party competition proved to Marylanders that "the fundamental goal of American voters could be and was achieved within the normal political process" and sustained Kentuckians' "faith in the political process." That supposedly insulated them from the attraction of secessionism. (See chap. 8, esp. pp. 248–49.)

2. Karl Marx, "The Civil War in the United States," in *Surveys from Exile,* ed. David Fernbach (Middlesex, Eng., 1973), p. 351; Philip Foner, *Frederick Douglass: A Biography* (New York, 1964), p. 198; Wendell Phillips, "The Times: The Fraternity Lecture Series," The *Liberator,* 31 January 1862.

3. On the position of the border states at the outbreak of the Civil War, see J. G. Randall and David Donald, *The Civil War and Reconstruction,* rev. ed. (Boston, 1969), pp. 227–42. The particular *parti pris* of this account gives it both a piquant flavor and—to some palates—a slightly off aftertaste.

4. Harold B. Hancock, "Reconstruction in Delaware," in *Radicalism, Racism, and Party Realignment: The Border States during Reconstruction,* ed. Richard O. Curry (Baltimore, 1969), p. 202; Roy P. Basler, ed., *The Collected Works of Abraham Lincoln,* vol. 5 (New Brunswick, N.J., 1953), pp. 512–14.

5. See William E. Parrish, *Turbulent Partnership: Missouri and the Union, 1861–1865* (Columbia, S.C., 1963) and Charles L. Wagandt, *The Mighty Revolution: Negro Emancipation in Maryland, 1862–1864* (Baltimore, 1964). Wagandt's study and its sequel ("Redemption or Reaction? Maryland in the Post-Civil War Years," in Curry, ed., *Radicalism, Racism, and Party Realignment*) are models of their kind; written with subtle insight into Maryland politics, unfailing sensitivity to the human drama beneath political incidents, and considerable literary flair.

6. LaWanda Cox provides a careful reconsideration of Lincoln's views about slavery in *Lincoln and Black Freedom: A Study in Presidential Leadership* (Columbia, S.C., 1981).

7. Tyler Dennett, ed., *Lincoln and the Civil War in the Diaries and Letters of John Hay* (New York, 1939), p. 12; B. F. Butler to Thos. H. Hicks, 23 April 1861, U.S. War Department, *The War of the Rebellion: A Compilation of the Official Records of the Union and Confederate Armies,* ser. 1, vol. 2 (Washington, D.C., 1880), p. 593.

8. Colonel William Birney to Lt. Col. Wm. H. Chesebrough, 27 July 1863 and Lt. Col. Joseph Perkins to Col. S. M. Bowman, 28 March 1864, in *Freedom: A Documentary History of Emancipation, 1861–1867,* ser. 2: *The Black Military Experience,* ed. Ira Berlin, Joseph P. Reidy, and Leslie S. Rowland (New York, 1982), docs. 70 and 80B.

9. Tho. H. Hicks to Hon. S. Cameron, 18 November 1861, M-595 1861, Letters Received, RG 107, Records of the Office of the Secretary of War, National Archives [L-5].

10. Cecil *Whig,* 29 December 1860, 5 January, 9 February 1861.

11. Brigadier-General Philip St. Geo. Cocke to General Robert E. Lee, 25 April 1861, *Official Records,* ser. 1, vol. 2, p. 780; Richard R. Duncan, "The Era of the Civil War," in Richard Walsh and William Lloyd Fox, eds., *Maryland: A History 1632–1974* (Baltimore, 1974), p. 359.

12. Report of Col. Edward F. Jones, 22 April 1861, *Official Records,* ser. 1, vol. 2, pp. 7–9; George Whitmarsh Diary, 19 April 1861, Maryland Historical Society, Baltimore; George William Brown, *Baltimore and the Nineteenth of April, 1861* (Baltimore, 1887); Brigadier-General Bradley T. Johnson, *Maryland,* in *Confederate Military History,* ed. General Clement A. Evans (no place or date given), 2: 22; Marshal Geo. P. Kane to Charles Howard, Esq., 3 May 1861, *Official Records,* ser. 2, vol. 1 (Washington, D.C., 1894), pp. 628–30. The number of casualties resulting from the riot remains in dispute. No one knows exactly how many civilians died or were wounded. Wagandt, *The Mighty Revolution,* p. 11, says that four soldiers died, but an 1874 notation by the Adjutant General of Massachusetts on the report of Col. Jones lists three soldiers killed.

13. Extracts from the Report of the Baltimore Police Commissioners to the General Assembly of Maryland, 3 May 1861; Report of the Mayor of Baltimore to the General Assembly of Maryland, 9[?] May 1861; Statement of Geo. P. Kane, Marshal, 9 May 1861; Statement of J. Cumming Brown, 9 May 1861; E. Louis Lowe to Hon. John C. Brown, 10[?] May 1861; Extracts from the Message of the Mayor to the City Council of Baltimore [11 July 1861]; Statement of George M. Gill, 12 July 1861; *Official Records,* ser. 1, vol. 2, pp. 9–21; Attorney-General Edward Bates to William Meade Addison, Esq., 17 February 1862, *Official Records,* ser. 2, vol. 1, p. 618; Johnson, *Maryland,* pp. 23, 27; Duncan, "The Era of the Civil War," p. 344. Isaac R. Trimble eventually rose to the rank of major general in the Confederate army and was captured by Union forces at Gettysburg. Ezra J. Warner, *Generals in Gray: Lives of the Confederate Commanders* (Baton Rouge, La., 1970), pp. 310–11.

14. Major General Nath. P. Banks to Lieutenant-General Scott, 1 July 1861; D. Wilmot to [General Scott], 20 April 1861; J. Edgar Thomson to Hon. Simon Cameron, 23 April 1861; *Official Records,* ser. 1, vol. 2, pp. 139–40, 583, 596–97. The "arsenal" included six 6-pounder iron cannon; two 4-pounder iron cannon; 332 muskets, rifles, and pistols; and a "large quantity" of ammunition. Memorandum of Ordnance, &c., Captured by the Provost-Marshal at the Time of Arresting the Police Commissioners of Baltimore, 1 July 1861, *Official Records,* ser. 2, vol. 1, p. 142. The mayor insisted that the weapons had been obtained in order to arm the police force in the event of an emergency; that he had purposely not ordered their removal from city hall from fear that federal authorities might seize them, as they had seized others, "under circumstances very mortifying to the pride of the people"; and that any concealment had taken place without his knowledge. Extracts from the Message of the Mayor to the City Council of Baltimore [11 July 1861], *Official Records,* ser. 1, vol. 2, pp. 18–19.

15. Orders: Headquarters of the Army, 21 April 1861; Simon Cameron to J. Edgar Thomson, 27 April 1861; Simon Cameron to John Tucker, 3 May 1861; Thos. H. Hicks to the Commander of the Volunteer Troops on board the steamer,

21 April 1861; Thos. H. Hicks to his Excellency A. Lincoln, 22 April 1861; Brigadier-General Philip St. Geo. Cocke to General Robert E. Lee, 25 April 1861; *Official Records,* ser. 1, vol. 2, pp. 584, 603–04, 617–18, 586–87, 588–89, 780; Southern Rights to Thomas H. Hicks, 23 April 1861, John F. Dent to Thomas H. Hicks, 17 April 1861, and B. Everett Smith to Thomas H. Hicks, 24 April 1861; Thomas Holliday Hicks Papers, Maryland Historical Society. Accounts of Hicks's role include George L. Radcliffe, *Governor Thomas H. Hicks of Maryland and the Civil War* (Baltimore, 1901); Duncan, "The Era of the Civil War," pp. 334–52; Wagandt, *The Mighty Revolution,* pp. 7–13, 35; and Jean H. Baker, *The Politics of Continuity: Maryland Political Parties from 1858 to 1870* (Baltimore, 1973), pp. 47–55.

16. Winfield Scott to Brig. Gen. B. F. Butler, 25 April 1861; Winfield Scott to [Brig. Gen. B. F. Butler], 26 April 1861; *Official Records,* ser. 1, vol. 2, pp. 600, 601–02.

17. Brigadier-General Benj. F. Butler to His Excellency Thos. H. Hicks, 22 April 1861, *Official Records,* ser. 1, vol. 2, pp. 589–90.

18. Gen. B. F. Butler to his Excellency Thos. H. Hicks, 23 April 1861; Thos. H. Hicks to Brig. Gen. B. F. Butler, 23 April 1861; *Official Records,* ser. 1, vol. 2, pp. 589–90, 593.

19. Thos. H. Hicks to Brig. Gen. B. F. Butler, 23 April 1861; Brigadier-General B. F. Butler to his Excellency Thos. H. Hicks, 23 April 1861; Winfield Scott to Major-General Patterson, 25 April 1861; *Official Records,* ser. 1, vol. 2, pp. 592–93, 593–94, 600–01; Message of the Governor of Maryland to the General Assembly, 4 December 1861, *Maryland House Journal and Documents,* 1861–62, Document A; Duncan, "The Era of the Civil War," p. 351; Wagandt, *The Mighty Revolution,* p. 12.

20. Cecil *Whig,* 27 April, 4, 11 May 1861; Katherine A. Harvey, "The Civil War and the Maryland Coal Trade," *Maryland Historical Magazine* 62 (December 1967): 364; Wagandt, *The Mighty Revolution,* pp. 97–98.

21. Alexander Randall Diaries, Maryland Historical Society, 21 April, 20 May 1861; Duncan, "The Era of the Civil War," p. 351; Wagandt, *The Mighty Revolution,* p. 12.

22. Simon Cameron to John Tucker, 3 May 1861; Winfield Scott to Major-General Patterson, 4 May 1861; *Official Records,* ser. 1, vol. 2, pp. 617–18, 619–20.

23. Brigadier-General Benj. F. Butler to Lieutenant-General Scott, 6 May 1861; E. D. Townsend to Brig. Gen. B. F. Butler, 7 May 1861; Benj. F. Butler to [Secretary of War], 8 May 1861; E. D. Townsend to Brigadier-General Butler, 10 May 1861; *Official Records,* ser. 1, vol. 2, pp. 623–24, 627, 629–30, 633; Johnson, *Maryland,* p. 27.

24. Report of Brig. Gen. Benjamin F. Butler, 15 May 1861; General Butler's Proclamation, 14 May 1861; *Official Records,* ser. 1, vol. 2, pp. 29–32.

25. Winfield Scott to Brig. Gen. Benjamin F. Butler, 14 May 1861; Winfield Scott to Brigadier-General Butler, 15 May 1861; *Official Records,* ser. 1, vol. 2, p. 28.

26. Report of Brig. Gen. Benjamin F. Butler, 15 May 1861, *Official Records,*

ser. 1, vol. 2, pp. 29–30; Major W. W. Morris to Assistant Adjutant-General [E. D. Townsend], 16 May 1861, *Official Records,* ser. 2, vol. 1, p. 571.

27. Assistant Adjutant-General E. D. Townsend to Bvt. Maj. Gen. G. Cadwalader, 16 May 1861; Winfield Scott to Brevet Major-General Cadwalader or Commanding General of Baltimore, 15 May 1861; Winfield Scott to Maj. Gen. B. F. Butler, 18 May 1861; Brigadier-General Benj. F. Butler to Hon. Simon Cameron, 18 May 1861; General Orders, No. 1, Hdqrs. Department of Virginia, 22 May 1861; Major-General Benj. F. Butler to Lieutenant-General Winfield Scott, 24 May 1861, *Official Records,* ser. 1, vol. 2, pp. 639, 638–39, 640–41, 641–42, 643, 648–52; Benj. F. Butler to Lieutenant Genl. Scott, 27 May 1861, B-99 1861, Letters Received Irregular, RG 107, Records of the Office of the Secretary of War [L-77]; Johnson, Finley & Co. to Thomas H. Hicks, [June? 1861], Hicks Papers.

28. E. D. Townsend to Brevet Brigadier-General Cadwalader, 15 May 1861; Winfield Scott to Brevet Major-General Cadwalader, 15 May 1861; E. D. Townsend to Bvt. Maj. Gen. G. Cadwalader, 16 May 1861; *Official Records,* ser. 1, vol. 2, pp. 638, 638–39, 639; Winfield Scott to Maj. Gen. N. P. Banks, 24 June 1861; *Official Records,* ser. 2, vol. 1, p. 621.

29. Simon Cameron to Maj. Gen. John A. Dix, 11 September 1861; Simon Cameron to Maj. Gen. N. P. Banks, 11 September 1861; N. P. Banks to Lieutenant-Colonel Ruger, 16 September 1861; R. Morris Copeland to Major-General Banks, 18 September 1861; Major-General N. P. Banks to Col. R. B. Marcy, 20 September 1861; Allan Pinkerton to Hon. William H. Seward, 23 September 1861; Arthur Rich, M.D. to Hon. William H. Seward, 19 September 1861; Tho. H. Hicks to Maj. Gen. N. P. Banks, 20 September 1861; *Official Records,* ser. 2, vol. 1, pp. 678, 678–79, 681, 682–83, 684–85, 688, 684, 685; George W. Carpenter to J. Z. Spear, 15, 30 August 1861, Spear Papers, Maryland Historical Society; Richard R. Duncan, "Bishop Whittingham, the Maryland Diocese, and the Civil War," *Maryland Historical Magazine* 61 (December 1966): 329–47; Charles B. Clark, "Suppression and Control of Maryland, 1861–1865," *Maryland Historical Magazine* 54 (September 1959): 241–71; Sidney T. Matthews, "Control of the Baltimore Press during the Civil War," *Maryland Historical Magazine* 36 (June 1941): 150–70.

30. Wagandt, *The Mighty Revolution,* pp. 18–21, 33–34; Frederick Schley to Hon. W. H. Seward, 12 September 1861, *Official Records,* ser. 2, vol. 1, pp. 679–80; Tho. H. Hicks to Hon. S. Cameron, 18 November 1861, M-595 1861, Letters Received, RG 107, Records of the Office of the Secretary of War [L-5]; Reverdy Johnson to Hon. William H. Seward, 12 November 1861; J. W. Crisfield to Hon. William Seward, 22 November 1861; S. C. Hawley to F. W. Seward, 25 November 1861; *Official Records,* ser. 2, vol. 1, pp. 704, 708, 709–10. By no means all unionists agreed that leniency should be shown to the arrested legislators. See Thos. H. Hicks to Hon. W. H. Seward, 12 November 1861; Geo. R. Dodge to Maj. Gen. John A. Dix, 16 November 1861; *Official Records,* ser. 2, vol. 1, pp. 704–05, 707.

31. Statements of A Colored man and one of the union Colored friends, [September ? 1863] in Berlin et al., eds., *Black Military Experience,* doc. 54D (punctuation added).

32. Discussions of the problem of fugitive slaves in Maryland may be found

in Wagandt, *The Mighty Revolution,* pp. 116–21; Duncan, "The Era of the Civil War," pp. 363–64; and Ira Berlin, Barbara J. Fields, Thavolia Glymph, Joseph P. Reidy, and Leslie S. Rowland, eds., *Freedom: A Documentary History of Emancipation, 1861–1867,* ser. 1, vol. 1: *The Destruction of Slavery* (New York: Cambridge University Press, 1985).

33. Col. Alfred H. Terry to Capt. Theodore Talbot, 12 June 1861, T-28 1861, Letters Received, ser. 5263, Dept. of Washington, RG 393 Pt. 1, Records of the United States Army Continental Commands, National Archives [C-4101]; Chas. B. Calvert to Hon. Simon Cameron, 8 July 1861, C-137 1861, Letters Received, RG 107, Records of the Office of the Secretary of War [L-137]; Chas. B. Calvert to Genl. Mansfield, 17 July 1861, C-28 1861 and Chas. B. Calvert to Genl. Mansfield, 27 July 1861, C-30 1861, Letters Received, ser. 5364, Dept. of Washington, RG 393 Pt. 1, Records of the United States Army Continental Commands [C-4100]; William Richardson to Col. B. F. Larned, 6 August 1861, R-473 1861, Letters Received, ser. 12, RG 94, Records of the Adjutant General's Office, 1780s–1917, National Archives [K-20].

34. Lieutenant-Colonel Schuyler Hamilton to Brigadier-General McDowell, 16 July 1861; Major-General John A. Dix to Col. Joseph C. Pinckney, 9 August 1861; *Official Records,* ser. 2, vol. 1, pp. 760, 763; General Orders, no. 33, Headquarters Dep't of Washington, 17 July 1861, Orders & Circulars, ser. 44, RG 94, Records of the Adjutant General's Office, 1780s to 1917, National Archives [DD-18]; Maj. Genl. [John A. Dix] to S. R. Richardson Esq., 12 October 1861, vol. 27 8AC, pp. 357–58, Letters Sent, ser. 2327, Dept. of Pennsylvania, RG 393 Pt. 1 [C-4153]; Maj. Genl. John A. Dix to Col. A. Morse, 14 October 1861, Letters Received, ser. 4882, Post Naval Academy Annapolis, RG 393 Pt. 2 No. 315, Records of the United States Army Continental Commands [C-4120].

35. General Orders No. 16, Head Quarters, Corps of Observation, 23 September 1861, vol. 44/187 2AC, pp. 39–40, General Orders, ser. 3813, Corps of Observation, Army of the Potomac, RG 393 Pt. 2 No. 242, Records of the United States Army Continental Commands [C-3216]; Caroline F. Noland to Lieut. General Scott, 27 June 1861, enclosed in Brig. Genl. Robt. C. Schenck to Capt. Jas. B. Fry, 6 July 1861, Letters Received, ser. 12, RG 94, Records of the Adjutant General's Office [K-601].

36. Affidavit of Thomas Martin, 25 October 1861, M-298 1861, Letters Received, ser. 3976, Dept. of the Potomac, RG 393 Pt. 1, Records of the United States Army Continental Commands [C-4552]; Tho. H. Hicks to Hon. S. Cameron, 18 November 1861, M-595 1861 [L-5]; Affidavit of Richard F. Nelson, 25 February 1862, Affidavit of A. J. Smoot, 1 March 1862, enclosed in Jno. H. Bayne et al. to Hon. E. M. Stanton, 10 March 1862, M-387 1862 [L-136]; Letters Received, RG 107, Records of the Office of the Secretary of War.

37. Lt. Col. Ed. A. Parrott to Col. A. McD. McCook, 6 July 1861, enclosed in Brig. Genl. Robt. C. Schenck to Capt. Jas. B. Fry, 6 July 1861, S-1789 1861; Don Piatt to Brig. General Schenck, 6 July 1861, enclosed in Brig. General Robt. C. Schenck to Captain James B. Fry, 8 July 1861, filed with S-1789 1861; Letters Received, ser. 12, RG 94, Records of the Adjutant General's Office [K-601]; Col. Henry S. Briggs to Brig. Gen. D. N. Couch, 3 October 1861, Letters Received,

ser. 4464, Couch's Brigade, Army of the Potomac, RG 393 Pt. 2 No. 287, Records of the United States Army Continental Commands [C-3181]; Major John Toler to Lieut. J. L. Palmer, Jr., 27 March 1862, *Official Records,* ser. 2, vol. 1, p. 813; F. B. F. Burgess to Honrble Charles B. Calvert, 27 March 1862, enclosed in Chas. B. Calvert to Hon. E. M. Stanton, 31 March 1862, C-545 1862, Letters Received, RG 107, Records of the Office of the Secretary of War [L-10]; George W. McDaniel, *Hearth & Home: Preserving a People's Culture* (Philadelphia, 1982), p. 147.

38. Col. Henry S. Briggs to Brig. Gen. D. N. Couch, 1 October 1861, Letters Received, ser. 4464, Couch's Brigade, Army of the Potomac, RG 393 Pt. 2 No. 287, Records of the United States Army Continental Commands [C-3183]; John A. Andrew to Hon. Simon Cameron, 7 December 1861, M-1250 1861, Letters Received, ser. 12, RG 94, Records of the Adjutant General's Office [K-600]; Wendell Phillips, "Under The Flag," lecture delivered in the Music Hall, Boston, 21 April 1861, *Speeches, Lectures, and Letters By Wendell Phillips* (Boston, 1863), p. 408.

39. John A. Andrew to Hon. Simon Cameron, 7 December 1861, M-1250 1861; Thomas Drew to Lieut. Colonel Palfrey, 9 December 1861, enclosed in Chas. P. Stone to Brig. General S. Williams, 15 December 1861, S-1749 1861; [Maj. Gen. George B. McClellan] to His Excellency John A. Andrew, 20 December 1861; John A. Andrew to Major General George B. McClellan, 24 December 1861; [Maj. Gen. George B. McClellan] to His Excellency John A. Andrew, [27] December 1861; Letters Received, ser. 12, RG 94, Records of the Adjutant General's Office [K-600].

40. Major John Toler to Lieut. J. L. Palmer, Jr., 27 March 1862, *Official Records,* ser. 2, vol. 1, p. 813; *Report of the Joint Committee on the Conduct of the War,* 1863, pt. 3, 37th Cong., 3d sess., Senate Report no. 108 (serial 1154), pp. 638–39.

41. James B. Fry to Brig. Gen. Schenck, 2 July 1861, vol. 2/3, p. 100, and James B. Fry to Brig. General Schenck, 11 July 1861, vol. 2/3, pp. 116–17, Letters Sent, ser. 3684, Dept. of Northeastern Va., RG 393 Pt. 2 No. 234, Records of the United States Army Continental Commands [C-3224]; Asst. Adjt. Genl. E. D. Townsend to General [Irvin McDowell], 25 June 1861; Lt. Col. Ed. A. Parrott to Col. A. McD. McCook, 6 July 1861; Col. A. McD. McCook to Capt. Donn Piatt, 5 July 1861; enclosed in Brig. Genl. Robt. C. Schenck to Capt. Jas. B. Fry, 6 July 1861, S-1789 1861, Letters Received, ser. 12, RG 94, Records of the Adjutant General's Office [K-23]; Brig. Genl. A. McD. McCook to Genl. W. T. Sherman, 5 November 1861, Miscellaneous Records, ser. 3534, Dept. of the Ohio, RG 393 Pt. 1, Records of the United States Army Continental Commands [C-1].

42. McDaniel, *Hearth & Home,* p. 147; John Boston to Mrs. Elizabeth Boston, 12 January 1862, enclosed in Maj. Gen. Geo. B. McClellan to Hon. Edwin Stanton, 21 January 1862, A-587 1862, Letters Received, ser. 12, RG 94, Records of the Adjutant General's Office [K-23] (punctuation added).

43. Tho. H. Hicks to Hon. S. Cameron, 18 November 1861, M-595 1861, Letters Received, RG 107, Records of the Office of the Secretary of War [L-5].

44. Phillips, "Under the Flag," pp. 396, 400.

45. Resolution Adopted by the House of Representatives, Special Session, 9

July 1861, *Official Records,* ser. 2, vol. 1, p. 759; U.S., *Statutes At Large, Treaties, and Proclamations of the United States of America* (Boston, 1863), 12: 319; Proclamation of Major-General J. C. Frémont, 30 August 1861; A. Lincoln to Major-General Frémont, 2 September 1861; J. C. Frémont to the President, 8 September 1861; A. Lincoln to Maj. Gen. John C. Frémont, 11 September 1861; Arthur Rich, M. D. to Hon. William H. Seward, 19 September 1861; J. H. Lane to General S. D. Sturgis, 3 October 1861; *Official Records,* ser. 2, vol. 1, pp. 221–22; 766–67; 767–68; 768; 771–72; A. Lincoln to Brig. Gen. S. R. Curtis, 24 October 1861; General Orders No. 18, Headquarters of the Army, 24 October 1861; *Official Records,* ser. 1, vol. 3 (Washington, D.C., 1881), p. 553. For a discussion of other circumstances surrounding Lincoln's decision to remove Frémont, see William E. Parrish, *Turbulent Partnership: Missouri and the Union, 1861–1865* (Columbia, Mo., 1963), pp. 48–76; Randall and Donald, *Civil War and Reconstruction,* p. 323; and Allan Nevins, *Frémont: Pathmaker of the West* (New York, 1961), pp. 529–49, 663–67.

46. Col. Thos. A. Davies to Colonel Miles, 14 July 1861; Lieutenant-Colonel Schuyler Hamilton to Brigadier-General McDowell, 16 July 1861; Assistant Adjutant-General E. D. Townsend to General Mansfield, [16 July 1861]; *Official Records,* ser. 2, vol. 1, pp. 759–60; Major-General John A. Dix to Hon. S. Cameron, 8 August 1861; Simon Cameron to Brig. Gen. T. W. Sherman, 14 October 1861; *Official Records,* ser. 2, vol. 1, pp. 763, 773; Simon Cameron to Major General B. F. Butler, 8 August 1861, vol. 45, pp. 263–65, Letters Sent, RG 107, Records of the Secretary of War [L-309].

47. J. A. Dahlgren to Hon. G. Welles, 26 August 1861, Washington Navy Yard Papers, 1858–62, p. 120, ser. 354, RG 45, Naval Records Collection of the Office of Naval Records and Library, National Archives [T-704]; Maj. Gen. John A. Dix to Maj. Genl. G. B. McClellan, 21 August 1861, vol. 27 8AC, pp. 194–95, Letters Sent, ser. 2327, Dept. of Pennsylvania, RG 393 Pt. 1, Records of the United States Army Continental Commands [C-4152]; Simon Cameron to Maj. Gen. John E. Wool, 20 September 1861, *Official Records,* ser. 2, vol. 1, p. 771.

48. William H. Seward to Major General George B. McClellan, 4 December 1861, S-1440 1861, Letters Received, ser. 12, RG 94, Records of the Adjutant General's Office [K-123]; Resolution adopted by the House of Representatives, 4 December 1861, *Official Records,* ser. 2, vol. 1, p. 782; John Emmery et al. to the Honorable Senate and House of Representatives in Congress Assembled, 14 December 1861; Chas. H. Loomis et al. to the Senate and House of Representatives of the United States, [December 1861]; C. W. Slagle et al. to the Congress of the United States, [February 1862], 37A-G7.1, Abolition of Slavery in the District of Columbia, Petitions & Memorials, ser. 467, 37th Congress, RG 233, Records of the United States House of Representatives, National Archives [D-13]. The Senate later directed its own District Committee to investigate the management of the Washington jail. Report on the Condition and Management of the Washington Jail, 21 June 1862, U.S. *Senate Reports,* 37th Cong., 2d sess., no. 60 (serial 1125).

49. Resolution Adopted by the House of Representatives, 20 December 1861; Resolution Adopted by the House of Representatives, 23 December 1861; Thomas Maddox to Hon. Reverdy Johnson, 22 January 1862; *Official Records,* ser. 2, vol.

1, pp. 790, 791; Benjamin P. Thomas and Harold M. Hyman, *Stanton: The Life and Times of Lincoln's Secretary of War* (New York, 1962), pp. 133–34; Dudley Taylor Cornish, *The Sable Arm: Negro Troops in the Union Army, 1861–1865* (New York, 1966), pp. 20–24. On deficiencies in Cameron's administration of the War Department that contributed to his removal, see Randall and Donald, *Civil War and Reconstruction,* pp. 320–24.

50. Joint Resolution of the General Assembly of Maryland, 23 December 1861; Joint Resolution of the General Assembly of Maryland, 4 January 1862; *Maryland House Journal and Documents,* 1861–62.

51. Extract from President Lincoln's Annual Message, 3 December 1861, *Official Records,* ser. 2, vol. 1, pp. 781–82; *Statutes at Large* (Boston, 1863), 12: 617; Wagandt, *The Mighty Revolution,* pp. 56–59. As early as February 1861, Representative James B. Kean of New York introduced in the House a resolution looking to voluntary compensated emancipation in the border states. At the instance of a Kentucky representative the resolution was tabled. Edward McPherson, *The Political History of the United States of America during the Great Rebellion* (Washington, D.C., 1865), p. 209.

52. *Statutes at Large,* 12: 354. Brigadier General Daniel E. Sickles, recently relieved as commander of a brigade within the Army of the Potomac, testified before Congress on 10 April 1862 that he had learned of the new article of war only through the press; he had to that date received no general order on the subject from divisional headquarters (*Report of the Joint Committee on the Conduct of the War,* 1863, p. 640.)

53. E. P. Halsted to Lt. Col. John D. Shaul, 6 April 1862, vol. 21/240 5th Army Corps, p. 35, Letters Sent, ser. 3714, Military Defenses North of the Potomac, Army of the Potomac, RG 393 Pt. 2 No. 235, Records of the United States Army Continental Commands [C-4575]; John H. Bayne to Abraham Lincoln, 3 July 1862, John H. Bayne Papers, Maryland Historical Society; Wagandt, *The Mighty Revolution,* p. 120.

54. *Maryland House Journal and Documents,* 1861–62, pp. 460, 475–76, 615–16. In June, Congress followed up emancipation in the District of Columbia with prohibition of slavery in the territories. *Statutes at Large,* 12: 377, 432; Wagandt, *The Mighty Revolution,* pp. 63–64; Duncan, "The Era of the Civil War," p. 364.

55. Affidavit of Grandison Briskoe, 6 February 1864, B-430 1864, Letters Received, RG 107, Records of the Office of the Secretary of War [L-32]; Dola Ann Jones to Col. Jno. Eaton, Jr., 16 August 1865 [A-9858]; Affidavit of Humphrey Ware and Catherine Ware, 27 September 1865 [A-9881]; Unregistered Letters Received, ser. 457, D.C. Assistant Commissioner, RG 105, Records of the Bureau of Refugees, Freedmen, and Abandoned Lands (Freedmen's Bureau), National Archives; Harriette Carter to Col. Rogers, 14 May 1866, #1424, Letters Received, ser. 456, D.C. Assistant Commissioner, RG 105, Records of the Freedmen's Bureau [A-9757]; Statement by Mrs. Laura A. Moody, 25 May 1864, M-1590 1864, Letters Received, RG 107, Records of the Office of the Secretary of War [L-134]; Brig. Gen'l. E. B. Tyler to Lieut. Col. S. B. Lawrence, 15 June 1864, T-156 1864, Letters Received, ser. 2343, Middle Dept. & 8th Army Corps, RG 393 Pt. 1, Records of the United States Army Continental Commands [C-4145]; Cecil

Whig, 28 June 1862, reprinted from Port Tobacco *Times;* Wagandt, *The Mighty Revolution,* p. 117; Leon F. Litwack, *Been In the Storm So Long: The Aftermath of Slavery* (New York, 1979), pp. 56–57.

56. Col. John F. Staunton to Maj. Genl. John A. Dix, 24 May 1862, vol. 145/288 8AC, Letters Sent, ser. 4876, Post of Annapolis, RG 393 Pt. 2 No. 315, Records of the United States Army Continental Commands [C-4168]; Colonel William Birney to Assistant Adj. General, 13 July 1863, B-434 1863, Letters Received, ser. 2343, Middle Dept. & 8th Army Corps, RG 393 Pt. 1, Records of the United States Army Continental Commands [C-4125]; Wagandt, *The Mighty Revolution,* p. 120.

57. Baltimore *American,* 20 September 1858; Cecil *Whig,* 12 April 1862; John H. Bayne to Abraham Lincoln, 17 March 1862, Bayne Papers.

58. P. H. Watson to John H. Bayne et al., 17 March 1862, filed with Jno. H. Bayne et al. to Hon. E. M. Stanton, 10 March 1862, M-387 1862 [L-136]; P. [H. Watson] to Honorable Charles B. Calvert, 14 April 1862, filed with Chas. B. Calvert to Hon. E. M. Stanton, 31 March 1862, C-545 1862 [L-10]; Letters Received, RG 107, Records of the Office of the Secretary of War; Attorney-General Edw. Bates to Excellency A. W. Bradford, 10 May 1862, *Official Records,* ser. 2, vol. 1, p. 817.

59. Proclamation of Abraham Lincoln, 19 May 1862, *Official Records,* ser. 2, vol. 1, p. 818; McPherson, *Political History,* pp. 213–14; Cecil *Whig,* 12 April 1862; Wagandt, *The Mighty Revolution,* p. 85.

60. Berlin et al., eds., *Black Military Experience,* pp. 37–39, 41–43; doc. 3.

61. *Statutes at Large,* 12: 597–600; Cecil *Whig,* 19 July 1862.

62. *Statutes at Large,* 12: 589–92, 627.

63. Capt. H. J. Van Kirk to Capt. R. W. Dawson, 8 September 1862, P-47 1862, Letters Received, ser. 5063, Dept. of Virginia & 7th A.C., RG 393 Pt. 1, Records of the United States Army Continental Commands [C-3005]; J. Z. Spear to Sarah Spear, 7 September 1861, Spear Papers, Maryland Historical Society.

64. J. Z. Spear to Sarah Spear, 7 September 1861; E. Merton Coulter, *The Civil War and Readjustment in Kentucky* (Chapel Hill, N.C., 1926), pp. 165–69; Randall and Donald, *Civil War and Reconstruction,* pp. 219–23, 407–09; E. B. Long with Barbara Long, *The Civil War Day by Day: An Almanac, 1861–1865* (Garden City, N.Y., 1971), pp. 246–48.

65. Report by General R. E. Lee on the Capture of Harper's Ferry and Operations in Maryland, *Official Records,* ser. 1, vol. 19, pt. 1, p. 144; Wagandt, *The Mighty Revolution,* p. 72.

66. Johnson, *Maryland,* pp. 88–91; Wagandt, *The Mighty Revolution,* p. 72; Long and Long, *Civil War Day by Day,* pp. 261–68; Rev. C. C. Jones to Lt. Charles C. Jones, Jr., 2 October 1862, Robert M. Myers, ed., *The Children of Pride* (New Haven, 1972), p. 972.

67. Preliminary Emancipation Proclamation, 22 September 1862; Final Emancipation Proclamation, 1 January 1863; McPherson, *Political History,* pp. 227–29.

68. George Lowell Austin, *The Life and Times of Wendell Phillips* (Chicago, 1969), p. 221; Cecil *Whig,* 29 November 1862.

69. John Boston to Mrs. Elizabeth Boston, 12 January 1862, enclosed in Maj. Genl. Geo. B. McClellan to Hon. Edwin Stanton, 21 January 1862, A-587 1862, Letters Received, ser. 12, RG 94, Records of the Adjutant General's Office [K-23] (punctuation added).

70. Affidavit of Danl. Chase, 24 August 1865, enclosed in John Eaton Jr. to Maj. Genl. O. O. Howard, 18 September 1865, Unregistered Letters Received, ser. 16, Washington Headquarters, RG 105, Records of the Freedmen's Bureau [A-9674]; John Q. A. Dennis to Hon. [Edwin M.] Stan[ton], 26 July 1864, D-1049 1864, Letters Received, RG 107, Records of the Office of the Secretary of War [L-51]; Endorsement by Brig. General Wm. Birney, 28 January 1864 on Chs. E. Worthington to Major C. W. Foster, 15 January 1864 in Berlin et al., eds., *Black Military Experience,* doc. 79; Statement by Mrs. Laura A. Moody, 25 May 1864, M-1590 1864, Letters Received, RG 107, Records of the Office of the Secretary of War, RG 107 [L-134]; Brig. Gen'l. E. B. Tyler to Lieut. Col. S. B. Lawrence, 15 June 1864, T-156 1864, Letters Received, ser. 2343, Middle Dept. & 8th Army Corps, RG 393 Pt. 1, Records of the United States Army Continental Commands [C-4145]; Complaint of Amanda Dorsey, 9 October 1866, Registers of Complaints, ser. 2008, Md. Complaint Division, RG 105, Records of the Freedmen's Bureau.

71. Affidavit of Grandison Briskoe, 6 February 1864, B-430 1864, Letters Received, RG 107, Records of the Office of the Secretary of War [L-32]; Bvt. Brig. Gen. [Charles H. Howard] to Hon. John P. C. Shanks, [20 Nov.] 1867, Miscellaneous Reports, ser. 481, D.C. Assistant Commissioner, RG 105, Records of the Freedmen's Bureau [A-9914]; Lt. Col. Joseph Perkins to Col. S. M. Bowman, 28 March 1864 in Berlin et al., eds., *Black Military Experience,* doc. 80B; Major John Toler to Lieut. J. L. Palmer, Jr., 27 March 1862, *Official Records,* ser. 2, vol. 1, p. 813.

72. Cecil *Whig,* 31 January 1863.

73. J. Thompson Yates to A. W. Bradford, 10 March 1863, and Henry H. Lockwood to A. W. Bradford, 27 March 1863; State Papers, 1860–63, Military and Miscellaneous Correspondence, Executive Papers, Maryland Hall of Records, Annapolis.

74. Brig. Genl. Henry H. Lockwood to General [Robert C. Schenck], 1 April 1863, enclosing a clipping from the New York *Tribune* and Circular, Head Quarters First Separate Brigade, 8th Army Corps, 30 March 1863, L-93 1863, Letters Received, ser. 2343, Middle Dept. & 8th Army Corps, RG 393 Pt. 1, Records of the United States Army Continental Commands [C-4130]; Peter G. Grimes to Gov. A. W. Bradford, 20 June 1863, State Papers, 1860–63, Military and Miscellaneous Correspondence, Executive Papers.

75. Wagandt, *The Mighty Revolution,* pp. 78–79, 91–92; McPherson, *Political History,* p. 226.

76. *Statutes at Large,* 12: 731–37; McPherson, *Political History,* pp. 115–16; Wagandt, *The Mighty Revolution,* pp. 114–115.

77. Wagandt, *The Mighty Revolution,* pp. 97, 99.

78. Berlin et al., eds., *Black Military Experience,* pp. 12, 183–86; Cecil *Whig,* 7 February 1863.

79. Maj. Genl. Robt. C. Schenck to His Excellency Abraham Lincoln, 30 June 1863, 1: 134, Telegrams Received by the President; Sec. of War Edwin M. Stanton to Major General Schenck, 6 July 1863, 19: 50, Telegrams Sent; RG 107, Records of the Office of the Secretary of War [L-213]; Berlin et al., eds., *Black Military Experience,* p. 184 & doc. 69; Wagandt, *The Mighty Revolution,* pp. 122–23. Recruitment of black soldiers receives thorough treatment in Berlin et al., eds., *Black Military Experience,* esp. chap. 4 on the border states. Other treatments are Charles L. Wagandt, "The Army versus Maryland Slavery, 1862–1864," *Civil War History* 10 (June 1964): 141–48; John W. Blassingame, "The Recruitment of Negro Troops in Maryland," *Maryland Historical Magazine* 58 (March 1963): 20–29.

80. Hugh L. Bond to Hon. E. M. Stanton, 15 August 1863; William T. Chambers to Hon. Edwin M. Stanton, 22 August 1863; in Berlin et al., eds., *Black Military Experience,* docs. 71, 73; Wagandt, *The Mighty Revolution,* p. 123; Blassingame, "Recruitment," p. 21.

81. Wm. T. Chambers to Col. Wm. Birney, 24 August 1863, C-134 1863, Letters Received, ser. 360, Colored Troops Division, RG 94, Records of the Adjutant General's Office [B-616]; Colonel William Birney to Capt. C. W. Foster, 26 August 1863, in Berlin et al., eds., *Black Military Experience,* doc. 74.

82. Special Orders No. 202, Head Quarters 8th Army Corps, 27 July 1863, vol. 54/65 8AC, p. 412, Special Orders, ser. 2354, Middle Dept. & 8th Army Corps, RG 393 Pt. 1, Records of the United States Army Continental Commands [C-4127]; Colonel William Birney to Lt. Col. Wm. H. Chesebrough, 27 July 1863; J. P. Creager to Col. Wm. Birnie, 19 August 1863; in Berlin et al., eds., *The Black Military Experience,* docs. 70, 80B.

83. Thos. Clagett Jr. et al. to Hon. Reverdy Johnson, 28 October 1863; A. W. Bradford to Hon. M. Blair, 11 September 1863 in Berlin et al., eds., *Black Military Experience,* docs. 78, 75, and p. 185. Lincoln viewed the murderer of the recruiting officer rather tolerantly. See Lincoln to Sec. of War Edwin M. Stanton, 18 March 1864, in *Collected Works of Abraham Lincoln,* ed. Basler, 7: 255.

84. General Orders No. 329, War Dept., Adjt. General's Office, 3 October 1863, *Official Records,* ser. 3, vol. 3, pp. 860–61; Berlin et al., eds., *The Black Military Experience,* p. 185; Wagandt, *The Mighty Revolution,* p. 129.

85. Message of the Governor of Maryland to the General Assembly, 7 January 1864, *Maryland Senate Journal and Documents,* 1864, doc. A.; McDaniel, *Hearth & Home,* pp. 226–28. Eventually the General Assembly recognized the wisdom of yielding to the recruitment of slaves, which would help to fill the state's draft quota, and offered bounties to black as well as white recruits (Berlin et al., eds., *The Black Military Experience,* p. 186; Wagandt, *The Mighty Revolution,* p. 199). The commissions appointed to investigate loyal owners' claims for compensation from the federal government approved awards totaling $242,283 for the states of Maryland and Delaware. Apparently only $6,900 was actually paid before Congress terminated the activities of the commissions and the fourteenth amendment ended all further prospect of compensation. Assistant-Adjutant-General C. W. Foster to Adjutant General, U.S. Army, 20 October 1864, *Official Records,* ser. 3, vol. 4, p. 790; Assistant Adjutant-General C. W. Foster to General, 20 October 1865; Assistant Adjutant-General C. W. Foster to the Adjutant-General U.S. Army, 20

October 1866; Assistant Adjutant-General E. D. Townsend to General U.S. Grant, 20 October 1867; *Official Records,* ser. 3, vol. 5, pp. 139–40; 1030–31.

86. Henry Tydings to Lieut. Jno. S. Wharton, 28 May 1864; Lt. Col. Joseph Perkins to Col. S. M. Bowman, 28 March 1864; in Berlin et al., eds., *Black Military Experience,* doc. 80B; A. W. Bradford to Abraham Lincoln, 16 March 1864, M-94 1864, Letters Received, ser. 2343, Middle Dept. & 8th Army Corps, RG 393 Pt. 1 [C-4140]; Col. A. L. Brown to Captain, 4 June 1864, enclosed in Maj. Gen. Lew. Wallace to Col. E. D. Townsend, 7 June 1864; A. A. Genl. C. W. Foster to Col. S. M. Bowman, 17 June 1864, filed with Wallace to Townsend, 7 June 1864; M-436 1864, Letters Received, ser. 360, Colored Troops Division, RG 94, Records of the Adjutant General's Office [B-567]; Chestertown *Transcript,* 27 February 1864; Petition of Loyal Colard men of Baltimore City, 20 August 1864, enclosed in Maj. Gen. Lew Wallace to Asst. Sec. of War C. A. Dana, 30 August 1864, Letters Received, RG 107, Records of the Office of the Secretary of War [L-49]. Also see Wagandt, "Army versus Maryland Slavery."

87. Berlin et al., eds., *The Black Military Experience,* p. 12; doc. 82B; Cecil *Whig,* 12 March 1864.

88. Dr. Samuel A. Harrison Journal, 25 September 1863, Maryland Historical Society; J. S. Berry to Gov. A. W. Bradford, 2 March 1863, State Papers, 1860–63, Military and Miscellaneous Correspondence, Executive Papers.

89. Mrs. Benjamin Harris Diary, 21, 22 October 1864, Maryland Historical Society; Annie Davis to Mr. president, 25 August 1864, D-304 1864, Letters Received, ser. 360, Colored Troops Division, RG 94, Records of the Adjutant General's Office [B-87]; Wendell Phillips, "The War for the Union," lecture delivered in New York and Boston, December 1861, in *Speeches, Lectures, and Letters By Wendell Phillips* (Boston, 1863), p. 438.

90. Harrison Journal, 25 September 1863.

91. Ibid., 2 October 1863; Reinhard H. Luthin, "A Discordant Chapter in Lincoln's Administration: The Davis-Blair Controversy," *Maryland Historical Magazine* 39 (March 1944): 25–48. On the "election by sword and ballot," see Wagandt, *The Mighty Revolution,* chap. 11, where the phrase appears. Baker, *Politics of Continuity,* pp. 87–91, discounts the importance of military interference, arguing that the Unconditional Unionists won a genuine victory at the polls.

92. Cecil *Whig,* 26 December 1863.

93. Ibid., 7 December 1861, 6 February 1864.

94. Chestertown *Transcript,* 20 August 1864.

95. Randall Diaries, 24 November 1864; Chestertown *Transcript,* 26 November 1864; Wagandt, *The Mighty Revolution,* pp. 256–60.

CHAPTER 6

1. Constitution of Maryland, 1864, Declaration of Rights, art. 1. On the adoption of the 1864 constitution, see Charles L. Wagandt, *The Mighty Revolution: Negro Emancipation in Maryland, 1862–1864* (Baltimore, 1964), esp. chap. 14.

2. Cecil *Whig,* 29 July, 21 October 1865; Charles L. Wagandt, "Redemption or Reaction? Maryland in the Post-Civil War Years," in Richard O. Curry, ed.,

Radicalism, Racism, and Party Realignment: The Border States during Reconstruction (Baltimore, 1969), pp. 175–76; Wagandt, *The Mighty Revolution,* pp. 267–68. The *Whig*'s naïveté did not last long, and its editor further singularized himself later on by declaring that "[n]o reason worthy of the name has ever yet been given by the opponents of woman suffrage, and it is fair to infer that none can be given . . ." (19 January 1867, 21 November 1868).

3. Cecil *Whig,* 19 May, 2 June, 8 September, 17 November 1866; Wagandt, "Redemption," p. 169; Jean H. Baker, *The Politics of Continuity: Maryland Political Parties from 1858 to 1870* (Baltimore, 1973), pp. 177–79.

4. Chestertown *Transcript,* 20 August 1864; Dudley A. Randall Diary, MS 648.1, Maryland Historical Society, Baltimore, 12 September 1867; Cecil *Whig,* 20 April 1867, 4 April, 26 June, 19 September 1868, 26 June 1869; Baltimore *American,* 22 April 1868; Wagandt, "Redemption," pp. 178–79. The Republican party in Maryland did not elect its first black state chairman until 1977 (Washington *Post,* 20 September 1977). A detailed, and rather more optimistic, treatment of the role of black people in the Republican party of Maryland appears in Richard P. Fuke, "Black Marylanders, 1864–1868" (Ph.D. diss., University of Chicago, 1973), chap. 14.

5. Constitution of Maryland, 1867, art. 3, sec. 53; Opinion of Judge Richard J. Bowie, Chief Justice, Maryland Court of Appeals, 2 July 1866, enclosed in Bvt. Maj. Wm. L. VanDerlip to Bvt. Lt. Col. W. W. Rogers, 11 July 1866, Letters Received, ser. 456, D.C. Asst. Comr.; Report of Bvt. Maj. E. M. Gregory to Bvt. Lt. Col. A. P. Ketchum, 11 April 1867, Assistant Commissioner's Quarterly Reports, ser. 1969, Md. Asst. Comr.; and Report of Bvt. Maj. Wm. L. VanDerlip to Bvt. Lt. Col. W. W. Rogers, 19 July 1867, Annual, Monthly, and Quarterly Narrative Reports, ser. 462, D.C. Asst. Comr.; RG 105, Records of the Bureau of Refugees, Freedmen, and Abandoned Lands (Freedmen's Bureau), National Archives; Wagandt, "Redemption," pp. 170, 173, 180–81.

6. Constitution of Maryland, 1864, art. 3, secs. 3, 4; Statement of Candidates Nominated by Union Convention to Represent Anne Arundel County in the Constitutional Convention, 30 March 1864, newspaper clipping, undated, in Alexander Randall Diaries, MS 652, Maryland Historical Society. The deliberations of the constitutional convention produced an arresting reversal of the argument of the Annapolis candidates. Isaac George, a delegate from Baltimore, warned that "if negro suffrage should ever prevail, it certainly would be to the interest of the smaller counties to have as large a delegation as possible from the city of Baltimore, which would present a united front on this subject." Philip B. Perlman, comp., *Debates of the Maryland Constitutional Convention of 1867* (Baltimore, 1923), p. 299.

7. *Laws of Maryland,* 1867, chap. 327, sec. 2; Constitution of Maryland, 1867, art. 3, secs. 2, 3, 4; "The New Constitution. Read before You Vote," broadside, undated, enclosed in Bvt. Maj. Wm. L. VanDerlip to Bvt. Lt. Col. W. W. Rogers, 17 September 1867, Letters Received, ser. 456, D.C. Asst. Comr., RG 105, Records of the Freedmen's Bureau.

8. Constitution of Maryland, 1867, art. 8; *Laws of Maryland,* 1868, chap. 407; Cecil *Whig,* 4 April 1868.

9. Cecil *Whig,* 5 January, 9 February, 21 September 1867; 1 February 1868; Wagandt, "Redemption," pp. 161–76; Baker, *Politics of Continuity,* chap. 6.

10. Cecil *Whig,* 2 September, 28 October 1865, 19 May, 17 November 1866; 12, 26 January, 2, 9, 16 February 1867; *Laws of Maryland,* chaps. 11, 17; Wagandt, "Redemption," pp. 165–71.

11. Cecil *Whig,* 19 May, 30 June, 17 November 1866, 2, 9, 16, 23 March 1867, 25 January, 1, 22, February, 14 March, 20 June 1868; Wagandt, "Redemption," p. 171, 180.

12. Art. 24 of the Declaration of Rights held that slavery "shall not be re-established," but also insisted that former slaveowners in Maryland were entitled to compensation from the federal government, under whose "policy and authority" emancipation had taken place. Also see *Laws of Maryland,* 1867, chap. 189, which provided for a "commissioner of slave statistics" to record information supporting the claims of former owners for compensation. Sec. 4 of the fourteenth amendment to the United States Constitution finally ended these lingering hopes.

13. Dr. Samuel A. Harrison Journal, MS 432.1, Maryland Historical Society, 2 October 1863, 4, 6, 11 November 1864; Kelita Suit to Gen. [Lew] Wallace, 21 December 1864, S-574 1864, Letters Received, ser. 2343, Middle Dept. & 8th Army Corps, RG 393 Pt. 1, Records of the U.S. Army Continental Commands, National Archives [C-4144].

14. *Laws of Maryland,* 1865, chap. 166; *Maryland Code of Public General Laws,* 1860, art. 66, sec. 83; Cecil *Whig,* 15 April 1865. Also see Bvt. Brig. Gen. C. H. Howard to Maj. Gen. O. O. Howard, 27 March 1866, C-124 1866, Letters Received, ser. 15, Washington Hdqrs., RG 105, Records of the Freedmen's Bureau [A-9706].

15. Andrew Stafford to Gen. Henry H. Lockwood, 2 November 1864, Stafford to Lockwood, 4 November 1864, and John E. Graham to Maj. Gen. Lew Wallace, 15 November 1864, filed with M-1932 1864, Letters Received, ser. 12, RG 94, Records of the Adjutant General's Office, National Archives [K-4]; Bartus Trew to Maj. Wm. M. Este, 15 November 1864, T-320 1864 [C-4146] and Brig. Gen. Henry H. Lockwood to Lt. Col. S. B. Lawrence, 15 December 1864, L-414 1864 [C-4139], Letters Received, ser. 2343, Middle Dept. & 8th Army Corps, RG 393 Pt. 1, Records of the U.S. Army Continental Commands; W. B. to Maj. Este, 15 November 1864 and Capt. Geo. W. Curry to Col. John Woolley, 15 November 1864, in "Communication from Maj. Gen'l Lew. Wallace in Relation to the Freedman's Bureau, to the General Assembly of Maryland," 31 January 1865, *Maryland House Journal and Documents,* 1865, doc. J; Joseph Hall to Maj. Gen. O. O. Howard, 12 August 1865 and Hall to Howard, 30 August 1865 [A-9853] and Lt. S. N. Clark to Col. John Eaton, Jr., 21 August 1865 [A-9860], Unregistered Letters Received, ser. 457, D.C. Asst. Comr.; Samuel Sawyer to Maj. Gen. O. O. Howard, 28 October 1865, Letters Received by Acting Assistant Commissioner, ser. 1964, Md. Asst. Comr. [A-9647]; Bvt. Brig. Gen. C. H. Howard to Maj. Gen. O. O. Howard, 27 March 1866, C-124 1866 [A-9706] and R. T. Turner to Maj. Gen. O. O. Howard, 30 April 1866, T-168 1866 [A-9661], Letters Received, ser. 15, Washington Hdqrs.; Bvt. Maj. Wm. L. VanDerlip to Bvt. Lt. Col. W. W. Rogers, 11 July 1866, #1809, Letters Received, ser. 456, D.C. Asst. Comr.

[A-9772]; Ann Maria Nicholaus to Maj. Gen. [O. O.] Howard, 11 October 1866, filed with Lt. Jas. M. Johnston to Capt. J. F. Chur, 20 July 1866, Letters Received, ser. 2009, Md. Complaint Division [A-9680]; Lt. Jas. M. Johnston to Capt. Jacob F. Chur, 25 July 1866, J-8 1866, Letters Received, ser. 1962, Md. Asst. Comr. [A-9619]; and Report of Bvt. Maj. E. M. Gregory to Maj. Gen. O. O. Howard, 3 November 1866, Assistant Commissioner's Quarterly Reports, ser. 1969, Md. Asst. Comr.; RG 105, Records of the Freedmen's Bureau; Harrison Journal, 2, 11 November 1864; *Laws of Maryland,* 1839, chap. 35; Cecil *Whig,* 3 December 1864; Petition of Wm. Boyd, M.D. to Hon. S. Colfax, 1 January 1867, 39A-H14.10, Petitions and Memorials, ser. 493, 39th Congress, RG 233, Records of the U.S. House of Representatives [D-6]; James M. Wright, *The Free Negro in Maryland, 1634–1860* (New York, 1921), pp. 130–48; Jeffrey R. Brackett, *The Negro in Maryland: A Study of the Institution of Slavery* (Baltimore, 1889), pp. 219–20; Wagandt, "Redemption," pp. 154–56; Fuke, "Black Marylanders," chaps. 9, 10.

16. John Dennis to Hon. Sir, undated, and John Dennis to Gen. [Lew] Wallace, 6 December 1864, in "Communication from Gen. Wallace"; Harrison Journal, 2, 11, 13 November 1864; R. T. Turner to Maj. Gen. O. O. Howard, 30 April 1866, T-168 1866, Letters Received, ser. 15, Washington Hdqrs. [A-9661]; Report of Bvt. Capt. S. N. Clark to Bvt. Brig. Gen. C. H. Howard, 16 June 1866, Annual, Monthly, and Quarterly Narrative Reports, ser. 462, D.C. Asst. Comr.; Bvt. Maj. Wm. L. VanDerlip to Bvt. Lt. Col. W. W. Rogers, 11 July 1866, #1809, Letters Received, ser. 456, D.C. Asst. Comr. [A-9772]; Register of Complaints, ser. 2021, Rockville, Md. Supt.; Registers of Complaints, ser. 2008, Md. Complaint Division; and Register of Complaints of Illegal Apprenticeships, ser. 1979, Md. Asst. Comr.; RG 105, Records of the Freedmen's Bureau; Chestertown *Transcript,* 28 January, 12 August 1865.

17. Statement of Hester Anthony, undated, in "Communication from Gen. Wallace"; John H. Butler to Bvt. Maj. Wm. L. VanDerlip, 16 November 1867, Letters Received, ser. 2013, Annapolis, Md. Agt.; Complaint of Mary Hawkins, 19 October, 1 December 1866, Register of Complaints, ser. 2021, Rockville, Md. Supt.; RG 105, Records of the Freedmen's Bureau.

18. Complaints of Henrietta Kelly and Susan Ringle, 23 April 1868, Register of Complaints, ser. 2021, Rockville, Md. Supt.; Bvt. Brig. Gen. C. H. Howard to Maj. Gen. O. O. Howard, 27 March 1866, C-124 1866 [A-9706] and R. T. Turner to Maj. Gen. O. O. Howard, 30 April 1866, T-168 1866 [A-9661], Letters Received, ser. 15, Washington Hdqrs.; Joseph Hall to Maj. Gen. O. O. Howard, 12 August 1865, Unregistered Letters Received, ser. 457, D.C. Asst. Comr. [A-9853]; Report of Bvt. Capt. S. N. Clark to Bvt. Brig. Gen. C. H. Howard, 16 June 1866, Annual, Monthly, and Quarterly Narrative Reports, ser. 462, D.C. Asst. Comr.; and Bvt. Maj. Wm. L. VanDerlip to Bvt. Lt. Col. W. W. Rogers, 11 July 1866, #1809 [A-9772] and VanDerlip to Rogers, 2 August 1866, Letters Received, ser. 456, D.C. Asst. Comr.; RG 105, Records of the Freedmen's Bureau.

19. Complaint of Peggie Tie, Register of Complaints, ser. 2021, Rockville, Md. Supt.; and Lt. Edward F. O'Brien to Lt. S. N. Clark, 27 July 1865, Unregistered Letters Received, ser. 457, D.C. Asst. Comr. [A-9849]; RG 105, Records of the Freedmen's Bureau.

20. Charles L. Wagandt, ed., "The Civil War Diary of Samuel A. Harrison," *Civil War History* 13 (June 1967): 136; W. B. to Maj. Este, 15 November 1864, in "Communication from Gen. Wallace"; James Murray to Maj. Gen. [Lew] Wallace, 14 November 1864, forwarded by Maj. Gen. Lew Wallace to the Adjutant General of the Army, filed with M-1932 1864, Letters Received, ser. 12, RG 94, Records of the Adjutant General's Office [K-4]; Kelita Suit to Gen. [Lew] Wallace, 21 December 1864, S-574 1864, Letters Received, ser. 2343, Middle Dept. & 8th Army Corps, RG 393 Pt. 1, Records of the U.S. Army Continental Commands [C-4144]; Lt. S. N. Clark to Col. John Eaton, Jr., 21 August 1865 [A-9860], and Joseph Hall to Lt. S. N. Clark, 25 April 1866, Unregistered Letters Received, ser. 457, D.C. Asst. Comr.; and Bvt. Maj. Gen. E. M. Gregory to Maj. Gen. O. O. Howard, 13 October 1866, with accompanying statements and affidavits, M-460 1866, Letters Received, ser. 15, Washington Hdqrs. [A-9642]; RG 105, Records of the Freedmen's Bureau; Cecil *Whig,* 8 September 1866.

21. Narrative of Tom Randall, in George P. Rawick, ed., *The American Slave: A Composite Autobiography* (Westport, Conn., 1972), 16: 57–59; Statement of Essex Barbour, 7 February 1866, and Charles A. Watkins to Gen. [O. O.] Howard, 13 March 1866, in *Freedom: A Documentary History of Emancipation, 1861–1867,* ser. 2: *The Black Military Experience,* ed. Ira Berlin, Joseph P. Reidy, and Leslie S. Rowland (New York, 1982), docs. 355, 357; Statement of James Spencer and Matthew Turner, 9 August 1865, filed with Wm. Daniel to Maj. Gen. O. O. Howard, 10 August 1865, D-6 1865 [A-9662] and Bvt. Brig. Gen. C. H. Howard, 27 March 1866, C-124 1866 [A-9706], Letters Received, ser. 15, Washington Hdqrs.; Lt. S. N. Clark to Col. John Eaton, Jr., 21 August 1865, Unregistered Letters Received, ser. 457, D.C. Asst. Comr. [A-9860]; and Bvt. Maj. Fred. C. von Schirach to Capt. Jacob F. Chur, 16 June 1866, Unregistered Letters Received, ser. 1963, Md. Asst. Comr. [A-9635]; RG 105, Records of the Freedmen's Bureau.

22. A. W. Wayman et al. to Sec. of War Edwin Stanton, 1 June 1864, W-191 1864, Letters Received, RG 107, Records of the Office of the Secretary of War [L-53]; Adam Wallace to Brig. Gen. [John R.] Kenly, 5 July 1865, K-11 1865, Letters Received, ser. 2343, Middle Dept. & 8th Army Corps, RG 393 Pt. 1, Records of the U.S. Army Continental Commands [C-4149]; Wm. Daniel to Maj. Gen. [O. O.] Howard, 29 July 1865, Daniel to Howard, 3 August 1865, and Statement of James Spencer and Matthew Turner, 9 August 1865, filed with Daniel to Howard, 10 August 1865, D-6 1865 [A-9662], Bvt. Brig. Gen. C. H. Howard to Maj. Gen. O. O. Howard, 27 March 1866, C-124 1866 [A-9706], and Bvt. Brig. Gen. C. H. Howard to Lt. J. A. Sladen, 18 May 1866, C-173 1866 [A-9713], Letters Received, ser. 15, Washington Hdqrs.; Capt. A. W. Bolenius to Capt. Jacob F. Chur, 31 May 1866, Unregistered Letters Received, ser. 1963, Md. Asst. Comr. [A-9635]; Thos. Timmons to Maj. Gen. [E. M.] Gregory, 6 December 1866, T-9 1866, Letters Received, ser. 1962, Md. Asst. Comr. [A-9622]; Joseph Hall to E. B. Gates, 4 July 1866, Letters Received, ser. 456, D. C. Asst. Comr.; and Report of Bvt. Lt. Col. R. G. Rutherford to Bvt. Brig. Gen. C. H. Howard, 27 October 1866, Annual, Monthly, and Quarterly Narrative Reports, ser. 462, D.C. Asst. Comr.; RG 105, Records of the Freedmen's Bureau; Charles A. Watkins

to Gen. [O. O.] Howard, 13 March 1866, in Berlin et al., eds., *Black Military Experience,* doc. 357; Cecil *Whig,* 16 November 1867.

23. John Diggs to Lt. Col. W. E. W. Ross, 20 December 1864, D-320 1864, Letters Received, ser. 2343, Middle Dept. & 8th Army Corps, RG 393 Pt. 1, Records of the U.S. Army Continental Commands [C-4134]; Affidavit of Robert Rylum, 13 September 1865, and Danl. J. Thomas et al. to Col. Jno. Eaton, Jr., 17 August 1865, enclosed in John Eaton, Jr. to Maj. Gen. O. O. Howard, 18 September 1865, Unregistered Letters Received, ser. 16, Washington Hdqrs. [A-9674]; Lt. S. N. Clark to Col. John Eaton, Jr., 21 August 1865 [A-9860] and Capt. R. G. Rutherford to James C. Carlisle, Esq., 12 June 1866 [A-9685], Unregistered Letters Received, ser. 457, D.C. Asst. Comr., RG 105, Records of the Freedmen's Bureau; Ellicott's Mills *Record,* reprinted in *Prince Georgian,* 8 September 1865.

24. Gov. Thomas Swann to Maj. Gen. O. O. Howard, 22 August 1866, Letters Received, ser. 456, D.C. Asst. Comr.; and William Brooke to Gen. [O. O.] Howard, 6 July 1866, B-189 1866, Letters Received, ser. 15, Washington Hdqrs.; RG 105, Records of the Freedmen's Bureau; Message of Gov. Thomas Swann to the General Assembly, *Maryland Senate Journal and Documents,* 1867; Harrison Journal, 25 September 1863.

25. Report of Bvt. Capt. J. C. Brubaker to Bvt. Lt. Col. W. W. Rogers, 29 October 1866 and Report of Agt. John H. Butler to the Assistant Commissioner, 19 August 1867, Annual, Monthly, and Quarterly Narrative Reports, ser. 462, D.C. Asst. Comr.; and John H. Butler to Bvt. Maj. W. L. VanDerlip, 9 September 1867, and Joseph Hall to Bvt. Maj. W. L. VanDerlip, 20 May 1867, Letters Received, ser. 2013, Annapolis, Md. Agt.; RG 105, Records of the Freedmen's Bureau.

26. Wagandt, ed., "Diary of Samuel A. Harrison," pp. 136, 138; Lt. S. N. Clark to Col. John Eaton, Jr., 21 August 1865, Unregistered Letters Received, ser. 457, D.C. Asst. Comr., RG 105, Records of the Freedmen's Bureau [A-9860].

27. See Frederick Douglass, *My Bondage and My Freedom* (1855; repr. New York, 1969), p. 95, for a discussion of the risks and benefits of resistance.

28. Joshua S. Clarke to Col. John Eaton, [September ? 1865], Miscellaneous Records, ser. 499, D.C. Asst. Comr. [A-9915]; Bvt. Brig. Gen. C. H. Howard to Maj. Gen. O. O. Howard, 27 March 1866, C-124 1866, Letters Received, ser. 15, Washington Hdqrs. [A-9706]; Capt. R. G. Rutherford to James C. Carlisle, Esq., 12 June 1866, Unregistered Letters Received, ser. 457, D.C. Asst. Comr. [A-9684]; and Report of Bvt. Maj. Gen. E. M. Gregory to Maj. Gen. O. O. Howard, 3 November 1866, Assistant Commissioner's Quarterly Reports, ser. 1969, Md. Asst. Comr., RG 105, Records of the Freedmen's Bureau.

29. Lt. Col. A. M. York to Brig. Gen. C. B. Fisk, 2 October 1865, Y-7 1865, Registered Letters Received, ser. 3379, Tenn. Asst. Comr., RG 105, Records of the Freedmen's Bureau [A-6129]. Leslie S. Rowland, in her work in progress on the war and emancipation in Kentucky, has been first and most systematic in drawing attention to the enormous influence that the order of recruitment and the pattern of assignment and discharge of black soldiers exerted upon the after-

math of emancipation. Also see Berlin et al., eds., *Black Military Experience,* pp. 733–34.

30. General Orders No. 112, Hdqrs., Middle Dept. & 8th Army Corps, 9 November 1864, in "Communication from Gen. Wallace"; Wagandt, "Redemption," p. 156. The most comprehensive treatment of the Freedmen's Bureau's activities in Maryland appears in Fuke, "Black Marylanders." Also see W. A. Lowe, "The Freedmen's Bureau and Education in Maryland," *Maryland Historical Magazine* 47 (March 1952): 29–40, and "The Freedmen's Bureau and Civil Rights in Maryland," *Journal of Negro History* 37 (July 1952): 221–76.

31. Samuel B. Lawrence to Brig. Gen. H. H. Lockwood, 8 December 1864, M-841 1864, Letters Received, ser. 4921, 8th Army Corps & District of the Eastern Shore, Md., RG 393 Pt. 2 No. 319 [C-4118]; and Circular, 6 December 1864, enclosed in Brig. Gen. Henry H. Lockwood to Lt. Col. S. B. Lawrence, 15 December 1864, L-414 1864, Letters Received, ser. 2343, Middle Dept. & 8th Army Corps, RG 393 Pt. 1 [C-4139]; Records of the U.S. Army Continental Commands; Lt. Jas. M. Johnston to Capt. Jacob F. Chur, 25 July 1866, J-8 1866 Letters Received, ser. 1962, Md. Asst. Comr. [A-9619]; Report of Bvt. Maj. Gen. E. M. Gregory to Bvt. Lt. Col. A. P. Ketchum, 11 April 1867, Assistant Commissioner's Quarterly Reports, ser. 1969, Md. Asst. Comr.; and Report of J. C. Brubaker to Maj. D. G. Swaim, 25 September 1868, Annual, Monthly, and Quarterly Narrative Reports, ser. 462, D.C. Asst. Comr.; RG 105, Records of the Freedmen's Bureau; Chestertown *Transcript,* 26 November, 17 December 1864. The legal and political maneuverings incident to the rise and fall of apprenticeship in Maryland receive detailed treatment in Fuke, "Black Marylanders," chap. 9 and esp. chap. 10. For a very different apprenticeship story, see Rebecca Scott, "The Battle over the Child: Child Apprenticeship and the Freedmen's Bureau in North Carolina," *Prologue* 10 (Summer 1978): 101–13. Unlike Freedmen's Bureau officers in Maryland, who took the offensive against apprenticeship, those in North Carolina were actually—through their supervision of indenture contracts—parties to it.

32. Lucy Lee to Sir, 2 December 1864, in "Communication from Gen. Wallace."

33. Lt. Edward F. O'Brien to Lt. S. N. Clark, 27 July 1865, Unregistered Letters Received, ser. 457, D.C. Asst. Comr., RG 105, Records of the Freedmen's Bureau [A-9849]; Edward F. O'Brien to Lt. S. N. Clark, 7 February 1866, in Berlin et al., eds., *Black Military Experience,* doc. 355.

34. Gov. A. W. Bradford to Maj. Gen. O. O. Howard, 4 October 1865, M-28 1865, Letters Received, ser. 15, Washington Hdqrs. [A-9675]; Report of Bvt. Capt. S. N. Clark to Bvt. Brig. Gen. C. H. Howard, 16 June 1866, Report of Bvt. Maj. Wm. L. VanDerlip to Bvt. Lt. Col. W. W. Rogers, 17 July 1867, and Report of Bvt. Maj. Wm. L. VanDerlip to Bvt. Lt. Col. W. W. Rogers, 8 October 1867, Annual, Monthly, and Quarterly Narrative Reports, ser. 462, D.C. Asst. Comr.; and Report of Bvt. Maj. Gen. E. M. Gregory to Bvt. Brig. Gen. F. D. Sewall, 11 July 1867, Assistant Commissioner's Quarterly Reports, ser. 1969, Md. Asst. Comr.; RG 105, Records of the Freedmen's Bureau; *Laws of Maryland,* chap. 144.

35. Gov. A. W. Bradford to Maj. Gen. O. O. Howard, 4 October 1865, M-28 1865, Letters Received, ser. 15, Washington Hdqrs. [A-9675]; Gov. Thos.

Swann to Maj. Gen. O. O. Howard, 22 August 1866, Letters Received, ser. 2013, Annapolis, Md. Agt.; and Report of Bvt. Maj. Wm. L. VanDerlip to Bvt. Lt. Col. W. W. Rogers, 20 July 1866, Annual, Monthly, and Quarterly Narrative Reports, ser. 462, D.C. Asst. Comr.; RG 105, Records of the Freedmen's Bureau.

36. Report of Bvt. Capt. S. N. Clark to Bvt. Brig. Gen. C. H. Howard, 16 June 1866, Report of Bvt. Maj. Wm. L. VanDerlip to Bvt. Lt. Col. W. W. Rogers, 29 October 1866, and Report of VanDerlip to Rogers, 19 July 1867, Annual, Monthly, and Quarterly Narrative Reports, ser. 462, D.C. Asst. Comr.; Bvt. Maj. Wm. L. VanDerlip to Bvt. Lt. Col. W. W. Rogers, 18 December 1866, #419, Letters Received, ser. 456, D.C. Asst. Comr. [A-9697]; and Bvt. Brig. Gen. Charles H. Howard to Bvt. Maj. W. L. VanDerlip, 18 December 1866, Isaac Brooks, Jr. to Bvt. Maj. W. L. VanDerlip, 19 December 1866, Bvt. Lt. Col. W. W. Rogers to Bvt. Maj. W. L. VanDerlip, 20 December 1866, and Rogers to VanDerlip, 21 December 1866, Letters Received, ser. 2013, Annapolis, Md. Agt.; RG 105, Records of the Freedmen's Bureau; Affidavit of Charles Harris and William Stepney, enclosed in Petition of Wm. Boyd, M.D. to Hon. S. Colfax, 1 January 1867, 39A-H14.10, Petitions and Memorials, ser. 493, 39th Congress, RG 233, Records of the U.S. House of Representatives [D-6].

37. Bvt. Brig. Gen. C. H. Howard to Maj. Gen. O. O. Howard, 27 March 1866, C-124 1866, Letters Received, ser. 15, Washington Hdqrs., RG 105, Records of the Freedmen's Bureau [A-9706]; *Laws of Maryland,* 1867, chap. 64; Cecil *Whig,* 26 January 1867.

38. Report of Bvt. Maj. Gen. E. M. Gregory to Bvt. Lt. Col. A. P. Ketchum, 11 April 1867, Assistant Commissioner's Quarterly Reports, ser. 1969, Md. Asst. Comr., RG 105, Records of the Freedmen's Bureau. The relative numbers involved counsel skepticism toward Fuke's assertion that apprenticeship caused the freedmen to miss the "economic opportunities of emancipation" and thus to be more easily "suppress[ed] into second-class citizenship." Fuke, "Black Marylanders," p. 216.

39. H. Stockbridge to Bvt. Maj. W. L. VanDerlip, 16 October 1867, Stockbridge to VanDerlip, 18 October 1867, and J. H. Butler to Bvt. Maj. W. L. VanDerlip, 15 November 1867, Letters Received, ser. 2013, Annapolis, Md. Agt.; Report of Bvt. Maj. Wm. L. VanDerlip to Bvt. Lt. Col. W. W. Rogers, 28 September 1868, Annual, Monthly, and Quarterly Narrative Reports, ser. 462, D.C. Asst. Comr.; and Registers of Complaints, ser. 2008, Md. Complaint Division; RG 105, Records of the Freedmen's Bureau; Wagandt, "Redemption," p. 156; Fuke, "Black Marylanders," chap. 10.

40. Bvt. Maj. Wm. L. VanDerlip to Bvt. Lt. Col. W. W. Rogers, 17 October 1866, Letters Received, ser. 456, D.C. Asst. Comr.; Complaint of Simon Ross, 16 February 1868, Registers of Complaints, ser. 2008, Md. Complaint Division; RG 105, Records of the Freedmen's Bureau.

41. Complaint of John Maynard, 4 May 1869, Registers of Complaints, ser. 2008, Md. Complaint Division, RG 105, Records of the Freedmen's Bureau.

42. Henry Stockbridge to Bvt. Maj. W. L. VanDerlip, 5 December 1867, Letters Received, ser. 2013, Annapolis, Md. Agt.; Complaint of Araminta Hazard, 27 June 1868, Registers of Complaints, ser. 2008, Md. Complaint Division, RG

105, Records of the Freedmen's Bureau; Christopher Lasch, *Haven in a Heartless World: The Family Besieged* (New York, 1977).

43. Complaint of Ellen Lea and Complaint of Henry Offutt, Register of Complaints, ser. 2021, Rockville, Md. Supt.; and Complaint of Joanna Brown, 17 February 1868 and Complaint of Martha Brown, 12 February 1868, Registers of Complaints, ser. 2008, Md. Complaint Division; RG 105, Records of the Freedmen's Bureau.

44. Complaint of Henry Smith, 12 June 1868, Complaint of Elizabeth Barney, 22 May 1868, and Complaint of Annie Cornish, 29 August 1868, Registers of Complaints, ser. 2008, Md. Complaint Division, RG 105, Records of the Freedmen's Bureau. Through careful and imaginative use of the records concerning apprenticeship, a scholar desiring to do so could develop interesting elaborations of Herbert G. Gutman's trail-blazing discussion of "adaptive kin networks" among slaves. See *The Black Family in Slavery and Freedom, 1750–1925* (New York, 1976), esp. chaps. 2 and 5.

45. See Lawrence N. Powell, *New Masters: Northern Planters during the Civil War and Reconstruction* (New Haven, Conn., 1980).

46. Lt. S. N. Clark to Bvt. Brig. Gen. C. H. Howard, 8 March 1866, Unregistered Letters Received, ser. 457, D.C. Asst. Comr. [A-9886] and Capt. C. B. Wilder to Maj. Gen. O. O. Howard, 27 June 1865, W-13 1865, Letters Received, ser. 15, Washington Hdqrs. [A-9655]; RG 105, Records of the Freedmen's Bureau. Faith in the principles of political economy as a universal and automatic imperative of human behavior, operating upon individuals regardless of social institutions, survives in studies of the post–Civil War South founded on neoclassical econometric models. For criticisms of that approach, see Harold D. Woodman, "Sequel to Slavery: The New History Views the Postbellum South," *Journal of Southern History* 43 (November 1970): 523–54, and Barbara Jeanne Fields, "The Nineteenth-Century American South: History and Theory," *Plantation Society in the Americas* 2 (April 1983): 7–27.

47. Though the efforts of Eugene D. Genovese (esp. *The Political Economy of Slavery: Studies in the Economy and Society of the Slave South* [New York, 1965], chap. 1, and *Roll, Jordan, Roll: The World the Slaves Made* [New York, 1974], pp. 44–45) ought to have cleared the matter up, confusion still prevails over what constitutes capitalist social relations. Errors generally fall into two classes. The first embraces the misconception that all production for the market, or with a view toward profit, is capitalist production (but hunters and gatherers may produce baubles that end up in the market and the Barbary pirates did their work with a view toward profit). The second equates markets for laborers (that is, slave markets)—to which the laborers themselves are not a party—with markets for labor time or capacity for labor—in which the laborers have full and formally equal standing. Those subscribing to this view end by concluding that slavery is only a version of capitalist relations, since in both cases "labor" is a commodity. Typical of the first category is Robert W. Fogel and Stanley L. Engerman, *Time on the Cross: The Economics of American Negro Slavery,* 2 vols. (Boston, 1974). Exemplary of the second is the entire neoclassical school of studies of the postbellum South, which treats emancipation as little more than an adjustment in the "labor market."

A particularly clear instance is Ralph Shlomowitz, " 'Bound' or 'Free'? Black Labor in Cotton and Sugarcane Farming, 1865–1880," *Journal of Southern History* 50 (November 1984): 569–96. Straddling the two categories is Gavin Wright, *The Political Economy of the Cotton South: Households, Markets, and Wealth in the Nineteenth Century* (New York, 1978).

48. Chestertown *Transcript,* 28 January 1865; Complaint of Dr. Washington Duvall, Register of Complaints, ser. 2021, Rockville, Md. Supt.; and Lt. S. N. Clark to Col. John Eaton, Jr., 21 August 1865, Unregistered Letters Received, ser. 457, D.C. Asst. Comr. [A-9860]; RG 105, Records of the Freedmen's Bureau; "Memorial of the Grand Jury of Baltimore City Praying that a Place of Punishment May Be Provided for Minor Colored Children," *Maryland House Journal and Documents,* 1867, doc. X; *Report on the Public Charities, Reformatories, Prisons, and Almshouses of the State of Maryland* (Frederick, Md., 1877); Susanna Warfield Diaries, MS 760, Maryland Historical Society, May 1878. See Chestertown *Transcript,* 24 November 1864, for an account of a meeting of former slaveholders in Charles County which recommended that "to the best of their means" all former owners should look after the old and infirm until the law made provision for them. Genovese, in *Roll, Jordan, Roll,* offers many elegant demonstrations of the very different meanings ascribed by masters and slaves to the paternalist relationship that bound them together. See especially his perceptive comment (p. 128) on what might easily be mistaken for nostalgia for slavery on the part of the freedmen: "The slaves wanted a freedom that gave them more, not less, than they had had in slavery. [I]t was not slavery but a healthier version of its doctrine of reciprocal obligations that remained attractive to them."

49. *Laws of Maryland,* 1867, chap. 290; Maj. S. N. Clark to Bvt. Maj. W. L. VanDerlip, 9 December 1867 and John W. Masquess to [Bvt. Maj. W. L.] VanDerlip, 28 August 1868, Letters Received, ser. 2013, Annapolis, Md. Agt.; Bvt. Maj. Wm. L. VanDerlip to Maj. S. N. Clark, 10 December 1867, V-2 1867, Letters Received, ser. 523, Assistant Inspector General, D.C. Asst. Comr. [A-9930]; and Report of W. R. Wilmer to Maj. D. G. Swaim, 22 December 1868, Annual, Monthly, and Quarterly Narrative Reports, ser. 462, D.C. Asst. Comr.; RG 105, Records of the Freedmen's Bureau.

50. Capt. Wm. F. Spurgin to Col. John Eaton, Jr., 16 August 1865 [A-9856], Capt. Wm. F. Spurgin to Lt. S. N. Clark, 22 August 1865 [A-9855], Deposition of Lewis W. Bruning, 25 September 1865 [A-9880], and Lt. S. N. Clark to Bvt. Brig. Gen. C. H. Howard, 8 March 1866 [A-9866], Unregistered Letters Received, ser. 457, D.C. Asst. Comr., RG 105, Records of the Freedmen's Bureau. Spurgin considered it entirely proper, however, for the Bureau itself to serve as an employment office to which those seeking hired help might have recourse.

51. Oliver Wood to [Maj. Gen. O. O. Howard], 22 August 1865 [A-9861], Wood to Howard, 4 September 1865 [A-9861], Wood to Howard, 15 September 1865 [A-9879], Hugh L. Bond to Capt. Wm. F. Spurgin, 14 August 1865 [A-9880], and Deposition of Lewis W. Bruning, 25 September 1865 [A-9880], Unregistered Letters Received, ser. 457, D.C. Asst. Comr.; and Oliver Wood to A. J. Vandergrift, 27 November 1865, enclosed in Oliver Wood to Brig. Gen. C. H. Howard, 26 March 1866 [A-9788], Affidavit of Wm. Washington Banks, 11 May

1866, enclosed in Wm. F. Spurgin to Lt. Col. W. W. Rogers, 11 May 1866, #1447 [A-9758], and Oliver Wood to Gen. [George J.] Stannard, 22 May 1866, filed with Spurgin to Rogers, 11 May 1866, Letters Received, ser. 456, D.C. Asst. Comr.; RG 105, Records of the Freedmen's Bureau; *Laws of Maryland,* 1866, chap. 89; Fuke, "Black Marylanders," chap. 3.

52. S. Bentz to Capt. Wm. F. Spurgin, 16 August 1865, and Bentz to Spurgin, 21 August 1865, enclosed in Capt. Wm. F. Spurgin to Lt. S. N. Clark, 22 August 1865, Unregistered Letters Received, ser. 457, D.C. Asst. Comr., RG 105, Records of the Freedmen's Bureau [A-9855].

53. Lt. S. N. Clark to Col. John Eaton, Jr., 21 August 1865 [A-9860] and Lt. S. N. Clark to Bvt. Brig. Gen. C. H. Howard, 8 March 1866 [A-9886], Unregistered Letters Received, ser. 457, D.C. Asst. Comr.; Report of Bvt. Maj. George E. Henry to Bvt. Lt. Col. W. W. Rogers, 22 October 1866, Report of Bvt. Lt. Col. R. G. Rutherford to Bvt. Brig. Gen. C. H. Howard, 27 October 1866, Report of Bvt. Maj. George E. Henry to Bvt. Lt. Col. W. W. Rogers, 19 July 1867, Report of Bvt. Maj. Wm. L. VanDerlip to Bvt. Lt. Col. W. W. Rogers, 19 July 1867, Report of Bvt. Maj. George E. Henry to Bvt. Lt. Col. W. W. Rogers, 2 October 1867, Report of Bvt. Maj. Wm. L. VanDerlip to Bvt. Lt. Col. W. W. Rogers, 8 October 1867, and Report of W. R. Wilmer to Bvt. Maj. S. N. Clark, 30 October 1867, Annual, Monthly, and Quarterly Narrative Reports, ser. 462, D.C. Asst. Comr.; RG 105, Records of the Freedmen's Bureau.

54. Register of Complaints, ser. 2016, Bladensburg, Md. Supt., RG 105, Records of the Freedmen's Bureau. The figure must be treated with due caution. On the one hand, not all complaints found their way to the files: some freedmen feared retaliation if they lodged complaints against white persons. On the other hand, not all complaints were necessarily well-founded: some doubtless arose from legitimate confusion and error, some perhaps from cupidity or malice.

55. Report of Capt. A. A. Lawrence to Bvt. Brig. Gen. [D. G.] Swaim, 10 October 1868, Annual, Monthly, and Quarterly Narrative Reports, ser. 462, D.C. Asst. Comr.; Statement of Harry H. D. Byron, 13 October 1865, enclosed in Lt. Edward F. O'Brien to Lt. S. N. Clark, 13 October 1865, #134, Letters Received, ser. 456, D.C. Asst. Comr. [A-9727]; and Lt. S. N. Clark to Bvt. Brig. Gen. C. H. Howard, 8 March 1866, Unregistered Letters Received, ser. 457, D.C. Asst. Comr. [A-9886]; RG 105, Records of the Freedmen's Bureau.

56. Report of Bvt. Maj. George E. Henry to Bvt. Lt. Col. W. W. Rogers, 22 October 1866, Annual, Monthly, and Quarterly Narrative Reports, ser. 462, D.C. Asst. Comr., RG 105, Records of the Freedmen's Bureau; James Higgins, "A Succinct Exposition of the Industrial Resources and Agricultural Advantages of the State of Maryland," *Maryland House Journal and Documents,* 1867, doc. DD.

57. Report of Bvt. Lt. Col. R. G. Rutherford to Bvt. Brig. Gen. C. H. Howard, 27 October 1866 and Report of Bvt. Maj. Wm. L. VanDerlip to Bvt. Lt. Col. W. W. Rogers, 19 July 1867, Annual, Monthly, and Quarterly Narrative Reports, ser. 462, D.C. Asst. Comr.; and Lt. Edward F. O'Brien to Lt. S. N. Clark, 13 October 1865, Letters Received, ser. 456, D.C. Asst. Comr. [A-9727]; RG 105, Records of the Freedmen's Bureau.

58. Warfield Diaries, 6 January 1865 and undated, 1865; Lt. Jas. M. Johnston

to Capt. Jacob F. Chur, 19 July 1866, J-5 1866, Letters Received, ser. 1962, Md. Asst. Comr., RG 105, Records of the Freedmen's Bureau [A-9617]. Also see the sensitive discussion of freedmen's decisions to leave old homes in Leon F. Litwack, *Been in the Storm So Long: The Aftermath of Slavery* (New York, 1979), chap. 6.

59. Lt. Jas. M. Johnston to Capt. Jacob F. Chur, 19 July 1866, J-5 1866 [A-9617] and Johnston to Chur, 25 July 1866, J-8 1866 [A-9619], Letters Received, ser. 1962, Md. Asst. Comr.; Bvt. Maj. George E. Henry to Lt. Col. W. W. Rogers, 14 July 1866, #1842 [A-9776] and Bvt. Maj. Wm. L. VanDerlip to Bvt. Lt. Col. W. W. Rogers, 11 July 1866, #1809 [A-9772], Letters Received, ser. 456, D.C. Asst. Comr.; Report of Bvt. Maj. George E. Henry to Bvt. Lt. Col. W. W. Rogers, 22 October 1866, Annual, Monthly, and Quarterly Narrative Reports, ser. 462, D.C. Asst. Comr.; J. L. Belt to T. J. Jackson, 27 April 1867, Unregistered Letters Received, ser. 1963, Md. Asst. Comr. [A-9638]; and Oliver Wood to Maj. Gen. O. O. Howard, 15 September 1865, Unregistered Letters Received, ser. 457, D.C. Asst. Comr. [A-9879]; RG 105, Records of the Freedmen's Bureau.

60. Chestertown *Transcript,* 26 November, 3 December 1864, 8 July 1865; Karl Marx, *Capital* (Middlesex, Eng., 1976; orig. ed. 1867), 1: 385. Portions of the *Transcript* editorials are quoted in Fuke, "Black Marylanders," p. 26.

61. Fuke, "Black Marylanders," argues that "racist" planters and "conservative" Freedmen's Bureau agents failed to appreciate the fact that "Negro movement stemmed essentially from blacks' effort to improve their economic status" (pp. 87–90). This argument parallels that of Fogel and Engerman, *Time on the Cross,* which attributes to racism arguments that slaves were not efficient workers seeking "mobility" within the slave system. An especially gross example of the effort to squeeze the freedmen into the categories of neoclassical econometric analysis is Robert Higgs, *Competition and Coercion: Blacks in the American Economy, 1865–1914* (Cambridge, Eng., 1977). See especially chapter 1, which reduces the freedmen's actions to "investment decisions."

62. I have tried to explain why racial ideology assumed this role in my "Ideology and Race in American History," in J. Morgan Kousser and James M. McPherson, eds., *Region, Race, and Reconstruction: Essays in Honor of C. Vann Woodward* (New York, 1982).

CHAPTER 7

1. C. Vann Woodward, *Origins of the New South, 1877–1913* (Baton Rouge, La., 1971; orig. ed. 1951); Robert L. Brandfon, *Cotton Kingdom of the New South: A History of the Yazoo Mississippi Delta From Reconstruction to the Twentieth Century* (Cambridge, Mass., 1967); Harold D. Woodman, *King Cotton and His Retainers: Financing and Marketing the Cotton Crop of the South, 1800–1925* (Lexington, Ky., 1968); idem, "Sequel to Slavery: The New History Views the Postbellum South *Journal of Southern History* 43 (November 1977): 523–54; idem, "The Revolutionary Transformation of the South after the Civil War" (paper presented at the University of Missouri–St. Louis Conference on the First and Second Reconstructions, February 1978); idem, "Post-Civil War Southern Agriculture and the Law,"

Agricultural History 53 (January 1979): 319–37; idem, "Comment" upon Jonathan M. Wiener, "Class Structure and Economic Development in the American South, 1865–1955," *American Historical Review* 84 (October 1979): 970–1006; idem, "Agriculture and Business in the Postbellum South: The Transformation of a Slave Society," in Fred Bateman, ed., *Business in the New South: A Historical Perspective* (Sewanee, Tenn., 1981); idem, "Postbellum Social Change and Its Effects on Marketing the South's Cotton Crop," *Agricultural History* 56 (January 1982): 215–30; and idem, "The Reconstruction of the Cotton Plantation in the New South" (Walter Prescott Webb Lecture, University of Texas, Arlington, March 1983); Lawrence N. Powell, *New Masters: Northern Planters during the Civil War and Reconstruction* (New Haven, Conn., 1980); Steven Hahn, *The Roots of Southern Populism: Yeoman Farmers and the Transformation of the Georgia Upcountry, 1850–1890* (New York, 1983), and "Landed Elites and National Unification in Post-Emancipation Societies: Southern Planters in Comparative Perspective" (John Lax Lecture, Mount Holyoke College, October 1983); Michael Wayne, *The Reshaping of Plantation Society: The Natchez District, 1860–1880* (Baton Rouge, La., 1983); and Barbara J. Fields, "The Nineteenth-Century American South: History and Theory," *Plantation Society in the Americas* 2 (April 1983): 7–27, and "The Advent of Capitalist Agriculture: The New South in a Bourgeois World" (Walter Prescott Webb Lecture, University of Texas, Arlington, March 1983).

2. Eleanor Bruchey, "The Industrialization of Maryland, 1860–1914," in Richard Walsh and William Lloyd Fox, eds., *Maryland: A History, 1632–1974* (Baltimore, 1974); John A. James, "Financial Underdevelopment in the Postbellum South," *Journal of Interdisciplinary History* 11 (Winter 1981): 443–54; Donald McCauley, "The Urban Impact on Agricultural Land Use: Farm Patterns in Prince George's County, Maryland, 1860–1880," in Aubrey C. Land, Lois Green Carr, and Edward C. Papenfuse, eds., *Law, Society, and Politics in Early Maryland* (Baltimore, 1977), p. 233.

3. J. R. Dodge, "Statistics of Manufacturers of Tobacco and of its Commercial Distribution, Exportation, and Prices," in U.S. 10th Census, 1880, *Agriculture* (Washington, D.C., 1883), p. 888; Fred A. Shannon, *The Farmer's Last Frontier: Agriculture, 1860–1897* (1945; repr. White Plains, N.Y., 1977), pp. 177–20; Joseph T. Singewald, *The Iron Ores of Maryland* (Baltimore, 1911), p. 135; *Maryland Farmer* 5 (May 1868): 133; Baltimore *Sun,* 4 July 1873; Bruchey, "Industrialization," p. 432; Ernest Ingersoll, *The History and Present Condition of the Fishery Industries: The Oyster Industry* (Washington, D.C., 1881), pp. 157–62, 168.

4. Bruchey, "Industrialization," pp. 424–25.

5. William H. Brewer, "Report on the Cereal Production of the United States," in U.S. 10th Census, *Agriculture,* pp. 440, 471; Message of the Executive to the General Assembly, January 1874, *Maryland Senate Documents,* 1872–73. Percentages calculated from U.S. 10th Census, *Population* (Washington, D.C., 1883), pp. 760–74.

6. Message of Gov. Swann to the General Assembly, January 1867, doc. A, and Report of the Committee on Labor and Immigration, doc. Y, *Maryland Senate Journal and Documents,* 1867.

7. *Maryland Farmer* 5 (February 1868): 53; Montgomery *Sentinel,* 17 January 1873.

8. Message of Gov. Swann to the General Assembly, January 1867; Report of the Commissioner of Immigration, *Maryland House Journal and Documents,* 1867, doc. N; *Maryland Farmer* 5 (March 1868): 66–67; Richard P. Fuke, "Black Marylanders, 1864–1868" (Ph.D. diss., University of Chicago, 1973), p. 81. The notion of a "taste for discrimination"—which white people indulged after calculating its economic cost—appears in Gary S. Becker, *The Economics of Discrimination,* 2d ed. (Chicago, 1971), where it constitutes an unintentional reductio ad absurdum of the effort to impose the categories of neoclassical microeconomic analysis upon refractory evidence by main force. Robert Higgs, *Competition and Coercion: Blacks in the American Economy, 1865–1914* (Cambridge, Eng., 1977), pp. 6–11, expresses some uneasiness about the fact that this "model" of discrimination applies only to the private market sector; but he accepts the underlying theoretical premise.

9. Report of the Commissioner of Immigration, 1867; Message of Gov. Swann, 1867; Report of the Commissioner of Immigration, *Maryland House Documents,* 1868, doc. R; *Maryland Farmer* 5 (August 1868); 225–26; Message of the Executive to the General Assembly, 1874.

10. Port Tobacco *Times and Charles County Advertiser,* 17 August 1877; Montgomery *Sentinel,* 21 February 1879.

11. Eric J. Hobsbawm, *The Age of Capital, 1848–1875* (London, 1975), chap. 10; Petition of Howard County Farmers, 29 July 1878, doc. 1104, 1878, City Records Office, Baltimore.

12. Hobsbawm, *Age of Capital,* pp. 178–79; Bruchey, "Industrialization," pp. 397–401; *Maryland Farmer* 5 (May 1868): 133; Charles C. Hopper Papers, MS 461, typescript at Maryland Historical Society, Baltimore; McCauley, "Agricultural Land Use." Figures calculated from U.S 8th Census, 1860, *Agriculture* (Washington, D.C., 1864), pp. 72–73; U.S. 10th Census, *Agriculture,* pp. 156–57, 282–85; and U.S. Census, *Historical Statistics of the United States: Colonial Times to 1970,* part 1 (Washington, D.C., 1975), p. 201.

13. Figures calculated from U.S. 7th Census, 1850, *Population* (Washington, D.C., 1853), pp. 226–27; U.S. 10th Census, *Agriculture,* pp. 25, 119. Also see Bruchey, "Industrialization," pp. 398–99.

14. Figures calculated from U.S. 10th Census, 1880, *Population* (Washington, 1883), pp. 394–95.

15. Fuke, "Black Marylanders," pp. 76–83. Percentages and averages calculated from data provided in ibid., table 6, p. 77.

16. The discussion in this and following paragraphs is based on analysis of all the black farmers I could identify in the manuscript census schedules for the three counties. Because the manuscript agricultural schedules do not indicate the farmers' race, I was obliged to locate black farmers in the population schedules and then cross-match with the agricultural schedules. The success of this operation varied. In Kent County, I succeeded in finding in the agricultural schedules 85 percent of black people listed as farmers in the population schedules; in Frederick, 84 percent;

and in Charles, 63 percent. The appendix discusses in more detail the problems and anomalies of this source.

17. Figures for white tenants are approximations, arrived at by subtracting the black totals as tabulated from the manuscript schedules from county totals in U.S. 10th Census, *Agriculture,* pp. 60–61. The results are, in consequence, only as reliable as the black totals; see note 16 and Appendix. On the distinction between sharecroppers and share tenants, see Shannon, *Farmer's Last Frontier,* pp. 88–89; Thavolia Glymph, "Wages, Share Wages, Sharecropping: The Transition from Slavery to Freedom in the Rural South, 1860–1880" (paper presented at Association for the Study of Afro-American Life and History Annual Meeting, October 1976); and Woodman, "Southern Agriculture and the Law." McCauley, "Agricultural Land Use," pp. 231–33, and Bruchey, "Industrialization," pp. 398–99, both assume—unwarrantably—that all those classed as share tenants in the published census of 1880 were in fact sharecroppers.

18. Bvt. Maj. George E. Henry to Lt. Col. W. W. Rogers, 14 July 1866 [A-9776] and J. C. Brubaker to Lt. Col. W. W. Rogers, 26 August 1866, #2132 [A-9784], Letters Received, ser. 456, D.C. Asst. Comr.; and Report of Bvt. Maj. George E. Henry to Bvt. Lt. Col. W. W. Rogers, 22 October 1866, Report of Bvt. Lt. Col. R. G. Rutherford to Bvt. Brig. Gen. C. H. Howard, 27 October 1866, Report of Lt. R. G. Rutherford to Bvt. Lt. Col. W. W. Rogers, 19 July 1867, Report of Bvt. Maj. George E. Henry to Bvt. Lt. Col. W. W. Rogers, 19 July 1867, Report of W. R. Wilmer to Bvt. Maj. S. N. Clark, 30 October 1867, and Report of Capt. A. A. Lawrence to Bvt. Brig. Gen. D. G. Swaim, 10 October 1868, Annual, Monthly, and Quarterly Narrative Reports, ser. 462, D.C. Asst. Comr.; RG 105, Records of the Bureau of Refugees, Freedmen, and Abandoned Lands (Freedmen's Bureau), National Archives. The "share wage" system receives attention in Thavolia Glymph, "Freed People and Ex-Masters: Shaping a New Order" (Walter Prescott Webb Lecture, University of Texas, Arlington, March 1983) and "Wages, Share Wages, Sharecropping."

19. Manuscript Census, 1880, Schedule 2 (Agriculture), Charles, Kent, and Frederick counties.

20. Higgs, *Competition and Coercion,* p. 69, makes this argument on slender evidence. It is at least as likely that the community at large would have preferred a dependable and efficient sharecropper who, besides being a good credit risk and a source of profit for the landowner, also occupied a properly subordinate and dependent status.

21. Mortgage, John T. Norris to John L. Lancaster, 4 May 1871, item 1688, Blackistone Collection of Dent Family Papers, MdHR M2680, Maryland Hall of Records, Annapolis. The record does not indicate Norris's color.

22. Rent Agreement for 1882 between John F. Dent and J. F. Dines for Pavilion Farm, 13 August 1881, item 1700, Blackistone Collection of Dent Family Papers.

23. Calculated from Manuscript Census, 1880, Schedule 2, Charles, Kent, and Frederick counties, and Schedule 1 (Population), Charles County. Some of the agricultural laborers may, of course, have been sons or daughters—that is, probable heirs—of landowning farmers. Their presence in significant numbers would tend

to exaggerate the age difference between black farmers as a class and black farm laborers as a class. However, few census enumerators failed to distinguish young people working on the family farm from those hired out for wages, and the enumerator of Charles County's first election district appears to have been scrupulous in this particular. At all events, given how few landowning black farmers there were, the expectations of their sons and daughters cannot have affected the overall situation very noticeably.

24. The following discussion is based on an analysis of Manuscript Census, 1870, Schedule 1 (Population), Anne Arundel County (excluding Annapolis). County population totals are calculated from U.S. 9th Census, 1870, *Population* (Washington, D.C., 1872), p. 163.

25. Tabulated from Manuscript Census, 1880, Schedule 1, Anne Arundel County (excluding Annapolis). County population figures are calculated from U.S. 10th Census, 1880, *Compendium* (Washington, D.C., 1883), pp. 354, 388–89.

26. The larger number of skilled workers in the county in 1880 is not necessarily a favorable sign. In June, when the census was taken, summer farm work might have attracted to the country people unable to work at their trades elsewhere. On unemployment among skilled black workers in Anne Arundel County, see p. 189 above.

27. Ingersoll, *Oyster Industry,* p. 170; *Report on the Fisheries and Water-Fowl of Maryland,* 1 January 1872 (Annapolis, 1872), p. 31.

28. *Report on the Oyster Fisheries,* pp. 13–18.

29. Frederick Douglass, *My Bondage and My Freedom* (New York, 1969; orig. ed. 1855), pp. 185–86; *Report on the Oyster Fisheries,* p. 15; Ingersoll, *Oyster Industry,* pp. 157, 162.

30. *Laws of Maryland,* 1876, chaps. 95, 277, 380, 381, 396, and 405; 1878, chaps. 36, 198.

31. Bureau of Industrial Statistics and Information of Maryland, *Fourth Biennial Report,* 1890–91 (Annapolis, 1892), p. 16.

32. Gilbert Byron, *The Lord's Oysters* (Baltimore, 1971), pp. 17, 37–38, 310–11.

33. Andrew Johnson, Veto Message, 19 February 1866, in LaWanda Cox and John H. Cox, eds., *Reconstruction, the Negro, and the New South* (Columbia, S.C., 1973), pp. 39–40.

34. The most vigorous modern proponent of Johnson's approach to this matter is Higgs, *Competition and Coercion.* Other examples include: Stephen J. DeCanio, *Agriculture in the Postbellum South: The Economics of Production and Supply* (Cambridge, Mass., 1974); Joseph D. Reid, Jr., "Sharecropping as an Understandable Market Response: The Post-Bellum South," *Journal of Economic History* 33 (March 1973): 106–30; and Ralph Shlomowitz, " 'Bound' or 'Free'? Black Labor in Cotton and Sugarcane Farming, 1865–1880," *Journal of Southern History,* 50 (November 1984): 569–96. Roger L. Ransom and Richard Sutch, *One Kind of Freedom: The Economic Consequences of Emancipation* (Cambridge, Eng., 1977), sketches a more realistic picture but does not frontally challenge the proposition that a freely competitive market could work the marvels claimed for it—only the assumption that

such a market prevailed in the postbellum South. Woodman, "Sequel to Slavery," discusses the limitations of the neoclassical market approach.

35. Lt. Jas. M. Johnston to Capt. Jacob F. Chur, 19 July 1866, J-5 1866 [A-9617], and Johnston to Chur, 25 July 1866, J-8 1866 [A-9619], Letters Received, ser. 1962, Md. Asst. Comr.; Bvt. Maj. George E. Henry to Lt. Col. W. W. Rogers, 14 July 1866, #1842 [A-9776], and Bvt. Capt. J. C. Brubaker to Lt. Col. W. W. Rogers, 26 August 1866, #2132 [A-9784], Letters Received, ser. 456, D.C. Asst. Comr.; and Report of Bvt. Lt. Col. R. G. Rutherford to Bvt. Brig. Gen. C. H. Howard, 27 October 1866, Report of Bvt. Capt. J. C. Brubaker to Bvt. Lt. Col. W. W. Rogers, 29 October 1866, Report of Bvt. Maj. George E. Henry to Bvt. Lt. Col. W. W. Rogers, 19 July 1867, and Report of W. R. Wilmer to Bvt. Maj. S. N. Clark, 30 October 1867, Annual, Monthly, and Quarterly Narrative Reports, ser. 462; RG 105, Records of the Freedmen's Bureau; *Maryland Farmer* 5 (March 1868), pp. 66–67; Susanna Warfield Diaries, MS 760, Maryland Historical Society, 1 December 1882; Fuke, "Black Marylanders," p. 81.

36. Report of Bvt. Lt. Col. R. G. Rutherford to Bvt. Brig. Gen. C. H. Howard, 27 October 1866, Annual, Monthly, and Quarterly Narrative Reports, ser. 462, D.C. Asst. Comr.; also see Report of Bvt. Maj. E. M. Gregory to Bvt. Lt. Col. A. P. Ketchum, 11 April 1867, Assistant Commissioner's Quarterly Reports of Operations, ser. 1969, Md. Asst. Comr.; RG 105, Records of the Freedmen's Bureau.

37. Tabulated from Manuscript Census, 1880, Schedule 1, Charles County.

38. Manuscript Census, 1880, Schedule 1, Anne Arundel County; Singewald, *Iron Ores of Maryland,* pp. 258–59.

39. Manuscript Census, 1880, Schedule 1, Anne Arundel County.

40. Percentages calculated from U.S. 10th Census, *Compendium,* p. 478. Starting from ostensibly opposed theoretical assumptions, Higgs, *Competition and Coercion,* pp. 26–27, and Jay R. Mandle, *The Roots of Black Poverty: The Southern Plantation Economy after the Civil War* (Durham, N.C., 1978), p. 37, agree in treating migration as a market decision.

41. Theodore Rosengarten, ed., *All God's Dangers: The Life of Nate Shaw* (New York, 1974), p. 500. Between 1860 and 1880, Baltimore's percentage of the state's black population rose from 16 percent to 20 percent. Calculated from U.S. 10th Census, *Population,* p. 394.

42. Warfield Diaries, April 1875, April, October 1876, 10 January, 23 March, 27 October 1877, 29 January 1878; *Report on the Public Charities, Reformatories, Prisons, and Almshouses of the State of Maryland* (Frederick, Md., 1877), p. 29.

43. *Report on Public Charities,* p. 29; Warfield Diaries, 12 March 1877, December 1878, 23 March 1881.

44. Higgs, *Competition and Coercion,* p. 64.

EPILOGUE

1. Message of Gov. John Lee Carroll to the General Assembly, January 1878, *Maryland Documents,* 1876–77; Baltimore *Sun,* 20 July 1877; Robert V. Bruce, *1877: Year of Violence* (Chicago, 1970; orig. ed. 1959), pp. 90–91.

2. Cumberland *Alleganian and Times,* 20 February, 6, 22 March 1877.

3. Reprinted in Cumberland *Alleganian,* 19 February 1877.

4. Cumberland *Alleganian,* 24 February, 6 March 1877; Message of Gov. Carroll, January 1878. The B & O maintained a special relationship with the state Democratic machine and with the General Assembly. John Garrett, its president, could usually expect to get what he and the B & O wanted. But the special relationship started to come unstuck as the machine began consolidating its own power at the expense of its ally. The challenge to the B & O's tax exemption figured in this process. The breach between the railroad and the Democratic machine did not become absolute until 1884, when the railroad discovered an urgent need for political reform and went over to the opposition. See James B. Crooks, "Maryland Progressivism," in Richard Walsh and William Lloyd Fox, eds., *Maryland: A History, 1632–1974* (Baltimore, 1974), pp. 596–97.

5. Cumberland *Alleganian,* 6 March 1877; Second Annual Report of Owen Riordan, Inspector of Mines for Allegany and Garrett Counties, 31 December 1879, *Maryland Documents,* 1878–79.

6. Message of Gov. Carroll, January 1878. Canal boatmen faced, not a wage reduction, but a squeeze between the freight charges they could levy upon the public (dictated by competing railroad rates) and the tolls they had to pay to the canal company. Bruce, *Year of Violence,* pp. 95–96, 100–01.

7. Bruce, *Year of Violence,* presents a thorough and most elegantly crafted account of the railroad strike of 1877. The riot in Baltimore is the subject of chapter 6, from which most of the account in the foregoing paragraph has been distilled. The governor's account of his actions appears in Message of Gov. Carroll, January 1878.

8. Baltimore *Sun,* 21 July 1877; Bruce, *Year of Violence,* p. 114.

9. Baltimore *Sun,* 23 July 1877.

10. Ibid., 25 July 1877.

11. Ibid., 23, 24 July, 4 September 1877; Port Tobacco *Times and Charles County Advertiser,* 14 September 1877.

12. Baltimore *Sun,* 4 September 1877.

13. Port Tobacco *Times,* 14 September 1877; Bruce, *Year of Violence,* pp. 316–17.

14. Susanna Warfield Diaries, MS 760, Maryland Historical Society, Baltimore, 18 July, 29 August 1875; 20 July 1877.

15. In the New England and Middle Atlantic states, manufacturing, mechanical, and mining industry accounted for 38 percent of the gainfully employed population. Calculated from U.S. 10th Census, 1880, *Population* (Washington, D.C., 1883), pp. 760–74. Also see Eleanor Bruchey, "The Industrialization of Maryland, 1860–1914," in Walsh and Fox, eds., *Maryland: A History,* pp. 402–03; Charles Hirschfeld, *Baltimore 1870–1900: Studies in Social History* (Baltimore, 1941), pp. 37–38.

16. Cumberland, a distant second to Baltimore, had a population of 10,693 in 1880. The capital city, Annapolis, was by then a quaint, rather charming little colonial relic dozing by the Severn River, as it remains today, despite the presence

of the state government and the United States Naval Academy. U.S. 10th Census, *Compendium* (Washington, D.C., 1883), p. 388.

17. U.S. 10th Census, *Compendium,* p. 977; Bruchey, "Industrialization," p. 408. Figures concerning manufacturing industry in Baltimore do not include then unannexed outskirts of the city in Baltimore County.

18. Bureau of Industrial Statistics and Information of Maryland (BISI), *Biennial Report,* 1888–89, p. 10; 1884–85, pp. 36–37, 54, 67–68.

19. BISI, *Biennial Report,* 1884–85, pp. 36–37, 59; Ernest Ingersoll, *The History and Present Condition of the Fishery Industries: The Oyster Industry* (Washington, D.C., 1881), p. 169; Baltimore *Sun,* 20 July 1877; Bruchey, "Industrialization," pp. 487–88.

20. BISI, *Biennial Report,* 1884–85, pp. 36–37, 59–60, 66; 1888–89, p. 6; Ingersoll, *Oyster Industry,* p. 169.

21. Ingersoll, *Oyster Industry,* p. 160; BISI, *Biennial Report,* 1884–85, p. 68; Grace Hill Jacobs, "The Negro in Baltimore" (M.A. thesis, Howard University, 1945), p. 57.

22. Joseph F. Dudley to the Mayor and City Council, 5 January 1877, doc. 949, 1877, City Records Office.

23. Petition of Workingmen, 1 April 1878, doc. 1078, 1878; Report of the Joint Standing Committee on City Property, doc. 1459, 1878; Opinion of the Law Officers in Relation to the Regulating of Pay for Laborers, 21 May 1879, doc. 846, 1879; and Veto Message of Mayor F. C. Latrobe, 24 February 1880, doc. 433, 1880; City Records Office.

24. Message of Mayor F. C. Latrobe to City Council, doc. 851, 1879; and Report of the Joint Special Committee and Ordinance Appropriating Money for Celebration of City's 150th Anniversary, doc. 1159, 1880; U.S. Census, *Report on the Statistics of Wages in Manufacturing Industries* (Washington, D.C., 1886), pp. 128, 345–46; BISI, *Biennial Report,* 1884–85, pp. 12–13; Bruchey, "Industrialization," p. 450.

25. Isaac Myers to Maj. Gen. O. O. Howard, 23 May 1866, Letters Received by President Andrew Johnson Relating to Bureau Affairs, ser. 17, Washington Hdqrs., RG 105, Records of the Bureau of Refugees, Freedmen, and Abandoned Lands, National Archives [A-27]; BISI, *Annual Report,* 1899, p. 14; Jacobs, "Negro in Baltimore," pp. 96–97; Richard P. Fuke, "Black Marylanders, 1864–1868" (Ph.D. diss., University of Chicago, 1973), pp. 113–19.

Index

Agricultural reform: antebellum, 18–19; postbellum, 170–71, 174–75, 187, 192

Allegany County, 6, 96, 173, 195. *See also* Cumberland, Maryland; Northern Maryland

American party. *See* Know-Nothing party

American Revolution: and manumission, 4; and tobacco economy, 5; and growth of Baltimore, 7, 40, 42

Amos (slave in Carroll County), 84

Andrew, John A., 103–04

Annapolis, Maryland, 14, 42, 43, 96; and agriculture in Southern Maryland, 17; free blacks in, 35, 79; Know-Nothing party in, 58; during Civil War, 98, 124; freedmen in, 148, 152, 153

Annapolis and Elk Ridge Railroad, 95

Annapolis *Gazette,* 81

Anne Arundel County, 6, 22, 102, 134; population, 14; agriculture in, 17, 18, 175–77; and slave trade, 24; during Civil War, 126, 130; apprenticeship in, 142; violence in, 143, 144; freedmen in, 144, 175–77, 181–82, 189; unemployment in, 189. *See also* Annapolis, Maryland; Southern Maryland

Anthony, Hester, 141

Antietam, battle of, 117

Antislavery ideas and agitation: and manumission, 4, 5–6; and fugitive slaves, 16; and slave discipline, 53; and proslavery violence, 63–65

Apportionment, legislative. *See* General Assembly

Apprenticeship: and free blacks, 35, 79, 154; and emancipation, 139–42; and federal army, 148–49; and Freedmen's Bureau, 149, 153–56; and state government, 151, 154; and freedmen's family life, 155–56

Article of War (*1862*), 110–11, 117

Artisans, black, 181–82, 189

Baker, Samuel, 65

Baltimore, Cecilius Calvert, Second Lord, 19

Baltimore, Maryland: and slavery, 7–8, 16, 20–22, 40–62 passim, 69; commerce of, 7–8, 41–43, 44, 200–01; industry in, 7, 17, 43, 54–55, 169, 200–02, 225*n;* population, 8, 44, 256*n;* foreign immigrants in, 12–14, 172–73, 201–02; as agricultural market, 17–19, 170, 174; and legislative apportionment, 21, 134; free blacks in, 31, 33–35, 37–38, 48, 79, 129; descriptions of, 40–41; riots in, 45–47, 93–94, 196–97; political clubs in, 47; slaves in, 47, 52, 54–55; and Know-Nothing party, 58–62; depression in, 61, 204; during Civil War, 93–94, 97–98, 107, 121, 230*n;* freedmen in, 133, 191; and *1877* railroad strike, 196–97; and Workingmen's party, 198–99

Baltimore *American,* 72–73, 93, 112, 129

Baltimore and Cumberland Road, 43

Baltimore and Ohio Railroad, 44, 195, 196–97, 200, 257*n*

Baltimore and Reisterstown Canal, 22

Baltimore City Council, 202–04

Baltimore County, 6, 21, 121; agriculture in, 4, 17; industry in, 7, 17; population, 14; slave trade, 24; foreign immigrants in, 173. *See also* Northern Maryland

Baltimore Criminal Court, 61, 151

Baltimore Police Department, 46, 62

Baltimore *Sun,* 46, 61, 169, 194, 197–98
Banking system, 45, 168
Bank of Maryland, 45
Banks, Nathaniel P., 94, 99, 104
Barbour, Essex, 144
Barker, John, 145
Barney, Elizabeth, 156
Barnum's Hotel, 45
Bates, Edward, 113
Bayne, John H., 112
Bentz, Samuel, 160
Berry, J. H., 127
Betty (domestic servant in Carroll
    County), 162
Birney, William, 123, 124–25
Blair, Francis P., 18
Blair, Montgomery, 125, 135
Blood Tubs, 60
Bond, Hugh Lennox: on nonslaveholders,
    82; and emancipation, 122, 128; and
    recruitment of black men, 123, 128;
    and apprenticeship, 151; and labor
    agents, 160
Border states: free blacks in, 2, 4; slavery
    in, 23; and outbreak of Civil War, 90–
    92. *See also* Delaware; Kentucky;
    Missouri
Boston, John, 105–06, 118
Bowers, James L., 63–64, 65, 66, 72
Bradford, Augustus W., 194; and fugitive
    slaves, 106, 113, 120; and recruitment
    of black men, 125, 126; and freedmen,
    150–52
Bragg, Braxton, 116
Brandywine, Maryland, 26
Briggs, Henry S., 103
Brown, Frisby, 64–65
Brown, Joanna, 155
Brown, John, 61, 76
Brown, Philip, 144
Buell, Don Carlos, 116
Buena Vista Post Office, Maryland, 26
Bull Run, first battle of, 99; second battle
    of, 116
Butler, Benjamin F., 90, 95–96, 97–98,
    99
Butler (free black man in Kent County),
    63

Cadwalader, George, 99
Calvert, Charles B., 18, 101, 113
Calvert County, 6; slaves in, 25, 26, 30;
    freedmen in, 141, 145, 147, 151, 154,
    159; violence in, 142, 145, 151. *See also*
    Southern Maryland

Cambridge, Maryland, 67, 68
Cameron, Simon: and secession crisis in
    Maryland, 94, 97; and fugitive slaves,
    104, 107; and recruitment of slaves,
    109, 114; and proposal to sever Eastern
    Shore from Maryland, 215*n*. *See also*
    War Department
Capitalist social relations: resistance to, by
    former slaveholders, 157–58, 160–61;
    resistance to, by freedmen, 157–58,
    161–63; and slavery, 157–58, 163–64,
    167, 248–49*n;* and emancipation, 158–
    65
Capron, Horace, 18
Caribbean, 2–3, 7, 42
Caroline County, 6. *See also* Eastern Shore
Carroll, John Lee, 194, 195–97, 206
Carroll, Robert, 145
Carroll County, 6, 57; slaves in, 24, 32;
    free blacks in, 31, 32; and emancipation,
    130; freedmen in, 160; foreign immi-
    grants in, 173; tramps in, 191–92. *See
    also* Northern Maryland
Cecil County, 6, 76; free blacks in, 30, 37,
    64, 73; slaves in, 30, 73; freedmen in,
    133, 155; lumber industry in, 169. *See
    also* Eastern Shore
Cecil *Democrat,* 72
Cecil *Whig,* 96; on legislative apportion-
    ment, 21; on taxation, 21; on slavehold-
    ers' conventions, 73, 74–75; on free
    black legislation, 81, 138–39, 153; on
    secessionists, 93; on emancipation, 118,
    128–29; on recruitment of black men,
    122–23; on fugitive slaves, 126; on
    black suffrage, 132; on public school
    law, 134–35; on Thomas Swann, 136;
    on Andrew Johnson's supporters, 136–
    37; on plan to sever Eastern Shore from
    Maryland, 215*n;* on woman suffrage,
    241*n*
Centreville, Maryland, 141, 144, 156
Centreville *State-Rights Advocate,* 74
Cereals: and spread of free labor, 5, 19;
    and Eastern Shore, 6; trade in, 7, 42,
    44, 170, 173; and Northern Maryland,
    19; and Western competition, 170, 173.
    See also Wheat
Chambers, E. F., 65–66
Chaptico, Maryland, 144
Charles (slave in Carroll County), 31, 85
Charles County, 6, 99; Union soldiers in,
    102; fugitive slaves in, 102, 119; vio-
    lence in, 142, 145; freedmen in, 145,
    164, 175–77, 178, 181, 188–89; farm

tenancy in, 177, 178, 181; unemployment in, 188–89. *See also* Southern Maryland
Chase, Salmon P., 153, 155
Chesapeake and Ohio Canal, 43–44, 196, 197, 220n
Chesapeake Bay, 7, 43, 182, 184
Chester County, Pennsylvania, 16
Chester Parish, 158
Chestertown, Maryland, 64–65, 144
Chestertown *Transcript,* 129, 164–65
Chew, Mr. (railroad conductor), 191
Childs, Joseph, 154
Cholera, 45
Churches, black, 78, 84–85, 144–45
Cigar-making industry, 7, 43
Civil Rights Act (*1866*), 134
Clarksburg, Maryland, 144
Clary (former slave in Carroll County), 159
Clothing industry, 43, 201, 225n
Coal industry, 168, 194–95, 195–96
Cobb, Ned (Nate Shaw), 191
Cohn, R. S., 169
Colonization, 10
Columbia Fire Company, 47
Comas, W., 162
Committee on Colored Population (House of Delegates), 61, 76–78, 81–82, 123–24
Committee on Military Affairs (House of Representatives), 109
Comparative advantage, 56
Confederate army, 94, 97, 116–17, 123, 142
Confiscation act, first, 106–07; second, 115–16, 117
Congress, 121, 152; and compensated emancipation, 110; and new article of war, 110; and abolition of slavery in the District of Columbia, 111; and militia act, 114–15; and second confiscation act, 115; refusal to intervene in Maryland, 135. *See also* House of Representatives; Senate, U.S.
Consolidation Railroad, 195
Constitutional convention: of *1850–51,* 79–80; of *1864,* 129; of *1867,* 134, 241n
Constitution of Maryland: *1776,* 131; *1851,* 20–21, 131, 215n; *1864,* 131–32, 134, 135, 142; *1867,* 131, 134, 137
Contraband camps, 112
Convention, radical border state, 133
Conventions, black, 133

Convicts, sale of, 35, 61, 79
Copper industry, 168
Corn. *See* Cereals
Cornish, Annie, 156
Cotton textile industry, 7, 43
Craig, Isaac, 145
Credit, agricultural, 168, 179–80
Cresswell, John A. J., 155
Crisfield, John, 85
Crop lien, 168
Cumberland, Maryland, 58, 196
Cumberland *Alleganian and Times,* 195
Cumberland *Democratic Alleganian,* 81

Dairy farming, 17–18, 174–75
Dames Quarter, Somerset County, 169
Davis, Henry Winter, 122, 128, 132
Davis, William H., 60
DeBow, J. D. B., 41–42
Delaware, 1–2, 36, 37, 119, 209n
Democratic party, 60, 61–62, 76, 134, 135–37
Dennis, John Q. A., 28
Dent, John F., 94, 180
Depression, 61, 189, 191–92, 194, 202–04
Diggs, John, 26, 145
Dines, J. F., 180
District of Columbia, 93, 98; and agriculture in southern Maryland, 17; and fugitive slaves, 108, 111–12, 119, 126; abolition of slavery in, 108–09, 111, 112; freedmen in, 159, 188, 190, 191; migration to, 190, 191
Dix, John A., 101, 107
Domestic service, 47, 162–63, 201, 202
Dorchester County, 6, 68, 69; slaves in, 67; violence in, 145; freedmen in, 157, 175–77. *See also* Eastern Shore
Doubleday, Abner, 110
Douglass, Frederick, 45, 62, 193; on slavery, 23, 33, 39; separation from mother, 27–28; and free blacks, 31, 39; and runaway plot, 33; on Baltimore, 33–34, 40; on race, 39; as hired slave, 47, 49; as disciplinary problem, 52, 53–54; on border states during Civil War, 90; on oystermen, 183–84
Dred Scott decision, 151
Duckett, Benjamin, 26
Du Val, Marcus, 26
Duvall, Edmund B., 26
Duvall, Washington, 158

Easter (freed slave from Carroll County), 31

Eastern Neck Island, Maryland, 65
Eastern Shore, 40, 77, 85, 125, 127, 191;
    agriculture on, 4–5, 17–19, 162, 169,
    170, 174; social character of, 6–7; popu-
    lation, 8, 10, 11–12, 14, 15, 69–70,
    175; free blacks on, 11–12, 29–30, 69–
    71, 124; foreign immigrants on, 14; and
    intrastate migration, 14; and slave trade,
    17, 24; separatism, 19–20, 215*n;* and
    legislative apportionment, 20–21, 83;
    slaves on, 23–24, 28, 29–30, 63–64,
    68; slaveholdings, 25, 83; and fugitive
    slaves, 35, 65, 67; slaveholders' conven-
    tions, 65–66, 67–69; and labor short-
    age, 70–71; and recruitment of free
    black men, 124; and apprenticeship,
    139–40, 141, 148–49, 155, 156; and
    violence, 139–40, 144, 145; and land-
    ownership by black people, 175–77. *See
    also* Cecil County; Dorchester County;
    Kent County; Queen Anne's County;
    Somerset County; Wicomico County;
    Worcester County
Eastern Shore convention (*1858*), 20
Eastern Shore law, 20, 136
Easton *Star,* 81, 86
Economies of scale, 56–57
Elections: of *1859,* 76; of *1861,* 100; of
    1866, 133
Eliza Ann (fugitive slave), 26
Elkton, Maryland, 169
Ellen (domestic servant in Carroll
    County), 162
Ellicott's Mills, Maryland, 44, 143–44,
    145–46
Ellicott's Mills *Record,* 145–46
Emancipation Proclamation: preliminary,
    117–18; final, 117–18, 121
Embargo act (*1807*), 7, 42
Enlistment. *See* Recruitment
Enrollment act (*1863*), 121–22
Ewing, Edwin E., 96

Factories, 7, 225*n*
Farmer, John H., 151
Farmers: white, efforts to encourage immi-
    gration of, 171–73; black, and land ten-
    ure, 177–78, 180–81, 184, 254–55*n.*
    See also Sharecropping; Tenancy
Fifteenth amendment, 134
Fire companies, 46–47
Flour-milling industry, 42, 168
Folly, John T., 202
Food processing industry, 48, 174, 201
Forbes, Philip, 151
Fortress Monroe, Virginia, 99

Fourteenth amendment, 133–34
Frederic (freed slave from Carroll County),
    31
Frederick, Maryland, 96, 116, 117, 124,
    133
Frederick County, 6; agriculture in, 4, 19,
    177, 178, 181; and fugitive slaves, 36;
    and Civil War, 96, 116, 117; and re-
    cruitment, 124; freedmen in, 133, 177,
    178, 181. *See also* Northern Maryland
Frederick County Almshouse, 192
Free blacks: population, 1–2, 8, 9, 10–12,
    29, 44; social role of, 3–4; efforts to ex-
    pel, 10, 28; emigration of, 16–17; ties
    with slaves, 28–32, 53, 67; and agricul-
    tural labor, 31, 70–71; and limitations
    imposed by slavery, 32–33, 39, 53, 87–
    88; and intrastate migration, 33–35; in
    cities and towns, 33–35, 37–38, 48, 79;
    legal restrictions upon, 35–37, 64, 79,
    80, 81–82, 84–87, 154; and reenslave-
    ment, 36, 68–69, 71–76, 77–82, 84–
    86; occupations of, 37–38, 83; competi-
    tion with white workers, 38; literacy
    among, 39; and fugitive slaves, 67, 111,
    119; efforts to control, 68–69, 71–82,
    84–86; recruitment of, by federal army,
    123–26; and constitutional convention,
    1864, 129
Freedman's Bureau (of Lew Wallace), 148
Freedmen: and civil and political rights,
    133–34, 138–39, 150–51; and former
    owners, 138, 139–42, 149, 153–55; vi-
    olence against, 139–40, 143–47, 150–
    51; and apprenticeship, 139–42, 149,
    151, 153–56; and state and local offi-
    cials, 147–48; and federal officials, 149–
    50; and sale into slavery, 152–53; family
    relations of, 155–56; and resistance to
    capitalist social relations, 157–58, 161–
    63; work habits of, 161–64; and land-
    ownership, 175–77, 178–79; and farm
    tenancy, 177–78; and sharecropping,
    177–78; and migration, 189–91
Freedmen's Bureau (Bureau of Refugees,
    Freedmen, and Abandoned Lands), 148,
    158, 177–78, 188; agents of, 149–50;
    and apprenticeship, 149, 153–56; and
    Maryland officials, 150; ar   sale of
    freedmen into slavery, 152–53; and free
    labor system, 157, 159–60, 161
Freedmen's Bureau bill (*1866*), 186
Freedmen's schools, 144–45, 147
Frémont, John C., 90, 107, 113, 225*n*
Frentz (resident of Baltimore), 47
Frostburg *Journal,* 195

Fruit, cultivation of, 18, 169, 174
Fugitive slave act (*1850*), 67, 83, 115
Fugitive slaves: during antebellum period, 16–17, 26, 34–35, 67; and outbreak of Civil War, 100–01; and Union soldiers, 101–05; and slave discipline, 105–06; and Union army's fugitive policy, 107–08, 120–21; and abolition of slavery in the District of Columbia, 111; and second confiscation act, 115–16; and Confederate invasion, 117; and Emancipation Proclamation, 118; and risks of attempted escape, 118–19; and slaveholders, 127

Gailes, Jimmy, 141
Galloway, Robert, 145
Garner, W. H., 127
Garrett, Ashton, 141
Garrett, John, 257*n*
General Assembly, 87, 171; and slavery, 20, 67, 109; and elections to U.S. Senate, 20, 136, 137; apportionment of, 20–21, 83; and free blacks, 29, 31, 81–82, 84, 88; and Know-Nothing party, 58, 221*n;* and Democratic party, 76, 134; and secession crisis, 93, 95–97, 99–100; and abolition of slavery in the District of Columbia, 111; and fourteenth amendment, 133–34; and freedmen, 133–34, 138, 154, 159; and public schools, 134–35; and immigration, 172; and oyster legislation, 184–85; and trade unions, 205; and enlistment of slaves, 239*n;* and the B & O Railroad, 257*n*. *See also* House of Delegates; Senate, Maryland
General Order *329,* 125–26
George, Isaac, 241*n*
Gettysburg, battle of, 123
Gilmor, Robert, 40
Good, Joseph, 202
Gordon, John Montgomery, 28
Graham, Mr. (delegate at Workingmen's meeting), 198–99
Groome, James B., 154

Hagerstown, Maryland, 58
Hall, Joseph, 147
Hambleton, Samuel, 68
Harford County, 4, 6; population, 14; slave trade, 24; and constitution of *1864,* 130; violence in, 145; foreign immigrants in, 173. *See also* Havre de Grace, Maryland; Northern Maryland
Harper's Ferry, [West] Virginia, 76, 97, 191

Harris, Benjamin G., 127
Harris, Martha E., 127
Harris, Richard, 153
Harrison, Morrison, 96
Harrison, Samuel A.: on fugitive slaves, 127, 128; on nonslaveholders, 128; on freedmen's desertion of former owners, 138; on violence against blacks and unionists, 142, 147
Havre de Grace, Maryland, 116, 145
Hawkins, Mary, 141
Hayes, Rutherford B., 197
Hazard, Araminta, 155
Hendrickson, Peregrine, 155
Hetty (free black woman in Carroll County), 32
Hicks, Thomas Holliday, 194; and Eastern Shore separatism, 20; and foreign immigrants, 61; and free blacks, 61, 87; on the Union, 92; and secession crisis, 93, 94–96, 99–100; conflict with Benjamin Butler, 95–96; and fugitive slaves, 106; and emancipation, 129
Ho̠an, John, 47
Hood's Mills, Maryland, 160
Hopper, Charles C., 174
Horse Head Post Office, Maryland, 83
House of Delegates: officers of, 20; and free blacks, 76, 77–79; and *1861* elections, 100; apportionment of, 134. *See also* General Assembly
House of Representatives: and fugitive slaves, 106, 108, 109, 115; and District of Columbia jail, 108; proposal for new article of war, 109; and enlistment of slaves, 114; and apprenticeship in Maryland, 140. *See also* Congress
Howard, Oliver O., 150, 151–52
Howard County, 24, 143–44, 145–46, 174
Hunter, David, 113, 114

Immigrants, foreign: and slavery, 5; population, 12–14; in Northern Maryland, 42, 44; in Southern cities, 55; efforts to attract, 172–73; in industry, 201–02
Indian Queen Hotel, 47
Industry, 17, 54–57, 168, 200–01. *See also* Cigar-making industry; Clothing industry; Coal industry; Copper industry; Cotton textile industry; Flour-milling industry; Food processing industry; Iron industry; Lumber industry; Oyster industry; Shipbuilding industry
Iron industry, 168, 169, 189

Jackson, Andrew, 194

Jackson, T. J. ("Stonewall"), 116
Jacobs, C. W., 82, 83; and free black legislation, 69, 71, 75–79, 87; and Committee on Colored Population, 76–77; at constitutional convention, *1850–51,* 79
Jacobs Committee. *See* Committee on Colored Population
Jefferson, Thomas, 7, 42
Jessup's Cut, Maryland, 143
Johnson, Andrew, 135, 186–87
Johnson, Bradley T., 93
Johnson, Reverdy, 109, 125, 129, 135
Johnson, Samuel, 26
Judiciary Committee (House of Representatives), 109

Kean, James B., 236n
Kelly, Henrietta, 141
Kennard, Sarah Ann, 156
Kennedy, John Pendleton, 96, 129
Kent County, 6; agriculture in, 19; slave trade, 24; free blacks in, 37; violence in, 63–65, 66, 144; slaveholders in, 65–66; apprenticeship, 139–40, 141; freedmen in, 139–40, 158, 175–77, 178, 181. *See also* Eastern Shore
Kentucky, 2, 105, 116, 125. *See also* Border states
Kitty (domestic servant in Carroll County), 162
Know-Nothing party: and slaveholders, 58–59; in Baltimore, 58–62; leadership of, 59; and slaveholders' convention, 72–73; and free blacks, 81; and nativist societies, 221n

Labor agents, 159–60
Laborers: agricultural, 89, 187–89, 254–55n; urban, 89, 202–04. *See also* Free blacks; Freedmen; Sharecropping
Lafayette Fire Company, 47
Lancaster, John L., 180
Lane, James H., 107
Latin America, 2–3
Latrobe, Ferdinand, 204
Laurel, Maryland, 18
Lea, Ellen, 155
Leary, Cornelius L. L., 121
Lee, George, 26
Lee, Lucy, 149
Lee, Robert E., 116–17
Liberia, 10
Ligon, Thomas Watkins, 221n
Lincoln, Abraham, 127–28; border-state policy of, 91; and secession crisis in Maryland, 94, 95, 98–99; and fugitive

slaves, 101, 106, 107, 112–13; and John C. Frémont, 107; and recruitment of black men, 109, 122, 125, 239n; and compensated emancipation, 110, 113–14; and David Hunter, 113; and second confiscation act, 115; and Emancipation Proclamation, 117–18; and Maryland emancipationists, 121, 128
Lister, James, 29
Livestock, 17–18, 174–75
Lloyd, Edward, 23, 128, 146
Lockwood, Henry H., 120–21, 148–49
Lonaconing, Maryland, 96, 195
Louisa (domestic servant in Carroll County), 162
Louisville, Kentucky, 54–55. *See also* Kentucky
Loveridge, Henry, 195
Lowe, Enoch L., 93
Lumber industry, 169

McClellan, George B., 103–04, 108, 112, 116, 117
McCook, Alexander McD., 105
MacDaniel, William, 141
McKinney, Mrs. Philip, 154–55
McKinney, Philip, 154
McQuay, John R., 141
Magothy Methodist Episcopal Church, 144
Magruder, D. R., 152, 159
Manufacturers' Record, 168
Manumission: efforts to restrict, 10, 32, 81; and slave population, 15–16, 32; and family ties between slaves and free blacks, 30–31; and friendships between slaves and free blacks, 31; and financial position of owner, 36; conditional, 78; and prohibition of *1860,* 81, 84
Market gardening, 17, 174
Martin, William A., 37
Martinsburg, West Virginia, 200
Marx, Karl, 90, 165
Maryland. *See* Eastern Shore; Northern Maryland; Southern Maryland
Maryland Agricultural College, 18, 173
Maryland Board of Immigration, 173
Maryland Bureau of Industrial Statistics and Information, 201, 202
Maryland Bureau of Labor and Immigration, 172
Maryland Club House, 148
Maryland Coal Company, 195
Maryland Commissioner of Labor and Immigration, 172
Maryland Farmer, 171, 174, 187

Maryland Fisheries Commissioner, 184
Maryland Historical Society, 40, 45
Maryland in Africa, 10
Maryland National Guard, 196–97
Maryland Senate. *See* Senate, Maryland
Maryland State Penitentiary, 7, 14
Maryland Superintendent of Labor and
  Agriculture, 171
Massachusetts, 103–04
Master Hugh [Auld], 49
Maynard, John, 154–55
Meat, production of, 174
Methodists, 142–43, 144
Middle Department, 105, 120, 122, 148
Migrants: interstate, 14; intrastate, 14,
  33–35
Militia act (*1862*), 114–15
Minimum wage legislation, 203–04
Missouri, 2. *See also* Border states
Mitchell, W. H., 111
Montgomery County, 6; agriculture in, 17,
  18; and fugitive slaves, 101; violence in,
  144, 145; freedmen in, 144, 145, 158,
  175–77, 188. *See also* Southern
  Maryland
Montgomery *Sentinel,* 171, 173–74
Moses (street vendor in Baltimore), 45
Myers, Emanuel, 36

Nanjemoy District, Charles County, 67,
  111
Napoleonic Wars, 7, 42
Nativism, 47, 58, 60
Nelson, Richard F., 102
New Orleans, Louisiana, 54–55
New York, 104
New York, New York, 41
Nick, Joe, 143–44
Nonslaveholders, 16, 31, 82–83, 84, 123–
  24, 128
Norris, John T., 180
Northern Central Railroad, 93
Northern Maryland, 77; agriculture in, 4,
  5, 17–19, 174; and slavery, 4, 6, 7–8,
  24, 25, 35, 83; social character of, 6,
  7–8, 42; industry in, 7, 17, 43, 54–55,
  169, 200–02, 225*n;* population, 8–9,
  10–11, 14, 15, 29–30, 33, 69, 175; and
  intrastate migration, 14; foreign immigrants in, 14, 172–73; and legislative
  apportionment, 20–21, 83, 134; free
  blacks in, 29–30, 33, 35, 37–38; and
  Civil War, 96, 117; freedmen in, 133,
  149, 177, 178, 181, 191. *See also* Allegany County; Baltimore, Maryland; Baltimore County; Frederick, Maryland;

Frederick County; Harford County;
  Washington County
Nottingham, Maryland, 26

O'Brien, Edward F., 149–50
Offutt, Henry, 155
Ohio, 8, 104, 105
Orphans' Courts, 35, 36–37, 79, 139, 154
Oyster industry, 169, 182–86, 201, 202
Oyster legislation, 184–85

Page's Chapel, Maryland, 26
Panic of *1857,* 61
Patapsco River, 41
Pearce, James A., 65–66
Pennsylvania, 8, 41; migrants from, 5, 14,
  42; and arrest of Maryland slave-catcher,
  36; soldiers from, and fugitive slaves,
  102, 104; Maryland natives in, 190
Pennsylvania Central Railroad, 94
Perkins, Isaac, 65
Peterson, Fred, 202
Phelps, John W., 114
Philadelphia, Pennsylvania, 41
Philadelphia, Wilmington and Baltimore
  Railroad, 93
Phillips, Wendell, 90, 103, 106, 118, 128
Pinkney, Margaret, 26
Piscataway, Maryland, 26, 119
Planters' Advocate: on Know-Nothing
  party, 58; on slaveholders' convention,
  72, 73–74, 75; on Baltimore *American,*
  72–73; on free black legislation, 77, 88;
  on C & O Canal, 220*n.*
Plug-Uglies, 60, 136
Point Lookout, Maryland, 115–16, 120,
  127
Point of Rocks, Maryland, 97
Poolesville, Maryland, 101
Port Deposit, Maryland, 133
Port Tobacco, Maryland, 164, 189
Port Tobacco *Times and Charles County
  Advertiser,* 173–74, 199
Potomac River, 185
Powell, Hilliary, 145
Pratt, Thomas G., 93
Price, William, 96
Prince Frederick District, Calvert County,
  159
Prince George's County, 6; agriculture in,
  17, 18; slave trade, 24; and fugitive
  slaves, 26, 119, 121; free blacks in, 83;
  and recruitment of slaves, 126; freedmen
  in, 138, 145, 162, 175–77; violence in,
  142, 145. *See also* Southern Maryland
Princess Anne, Maryland, 169

Priscilla (free black woman), 29
Public schools, 134–35

Queen Anne's County, 6; free blacks in, 37, 123; freedmen in, 141, 144, 156, 175–77; apprenticeship in, 141, 156; violence in, 144, 145; agriculture in, 174. *See also* Eastern Shore

Racial ideology, 87, 88, 164–66
Radical Republicans, 135
Railroad strike, *1877,* 196–97, 198
Randall, Alexander, 96–97
Recruitment, 122–27, 128, 239–40n
Religious ideology, 4, 84–85, 86
Removal Law (*1832*), 28, 85–86
Republican party, 133, 241n. *See also* Radical Republicans; Unconditional Unionists; Union party
Ricaud, James B., 65–66
Richardson, Maria, 25
Richmond, Virginia, 54–55
Ringle, Susan, 141
Rockville, Maryland, 145
Ross, Joseph, 105

St. Louis, Missouri, 54–55
St. Mary's County, 6; fugitive slaves in, 115–16, 120, 127; violence in, 125, 142, 144, 145, 150; apprenticeship in, 142; freedmen in, 142, 144, 145, 150, 152, 157, 162, 175–77; agriculture in, 180. *See also* Southern Maryland
Salisbury, Maryland, 126, 169
Sam (slave in Carroll County), 85
Sarah (free black woman in Baltimore), 28
Schenck, Robert C., 105, 120, 122, 123, 124, 128
Schools. *See* Freedmen's schools; Public schools
Scott, Winfield, 94, 95, 96, 97–98, 99
Scroggins, Jack, 119
Secessionists, 92, 93, 99–100, 117
Sectionalism, intrastate, 20–21, 22
Sembley, Charles, 26
Senate, Maryland, 79. *See also* General Assembly
Senate, U.S., 20, 136, 236n. *See also* Congress
Seward, William H., 107, 108
Sewell, Milly, 145
Sharecropping, 177–78
Shipbuilding industry, 42, 168
Ship-caulkers, 37, 38, 205
Sickles, Daniel E., 226n
Singer, John, 124

Skinner, Isaac, 153
Skinner, Jeremiah P., 38
Slaveholders: and fugitive slaves, 11–13, 16, 26, 127; and General Assembly, 20–21, 61–62, 83; interstate migra' ɔn of, 24; and free blacks, 31–32, 8˚ ɔ6; and city of Baltimore, 49, 61–62; and religious ideology, 84–85, 86; and white laboring class, 88–89; and Civil War, 92, 101–03, 105, 117; and Union soldiers, 101–03, 104–05, 125, 126; and recruitment of black men, 123–24; and emancipation, 128; and freedmen, 138, 157–58; resistance to capitalist social relations, 157–58, 160–61
Slaveholders' conventions, 65–66, 67–69, 71–76, 79
Slaveholdings, 24–25, 83, 227n
Slaves: population, 1, 9, 15, 29–30, 47, 48; and manumission, 15–16, 30–31, 32, 36, 78, 84; and forced migration, 17, 24; and slave trade, 17, 24–25, 28, 32–33; and legislative apportionment, 21; and taxation, 21; family life of, 24–28, 30–31; and small slaveholders, 25–27; hiring of, 27–28, 47, 48–49, 84; and free blacks, 28–32, 35, 39, 111; in cities and towns, 47, 48–49, 50, 52–54, 222n; in industry, 54–55; and outbreak of Civil War, 92; recruitment of, by federal army, 124–26, 239–40n; and owners' loss of authority, 127–28. *See also* Fugitive slaves
Slave trade: interstate, 17, 24–25, 27, 28, 30, 32–33; intrastate, 24, 25
Smith, B. Everett, 94
Smith, E. Kirby, 116
Smith, Henry, 156
Smoot, A. J., 102
Snow, Risdon, 29
Soldiers: Union, 101–05, 112, 124–25, 126; black, 124–25, 126, 143–44, 148, 150; Confederate, 143, 144, 150
Somerset County, 6, 126, 144, 169. *See also* Eastern Shore
Sommers, A. H., 145
Sothoron, John H., 125
Southern Maryland, 77; agriculture in, 5, 17–19, 162, 170, 174; social character of, 6–7; population, 8, 9, 10, 14, 15, 29–30, 69–70, 175; foreign immigrants in, 14; and intrastate migration, 14; and slave trade, 17, 24, 30; and legislative apportionment, 21, 83; slaveholdings in, 25, 83; free blacks in, 29–30, 69–70, 83; slaves in, 29–30, 70; apprenticeship

in, 149; freedmen in, 149, 175–77. *See also* Annapolis, Maryland; Anne Arundel County; Calvert County; Charles County; Howard County; Montgomery County; Prince George's County; St. Mary's County
Spear, J. Z., 116
Spence, Irving, 140
Spurgin, William F., 159
Standard Oil, 169
Stanton, Edwin M., 112, 114, 123. *See also* War Department
Stepney, William, 153
Steuart, R. S., 8
Stirling, Archibald, 122
Stockbridge, Henry, 41, 122, 153–54
Stone, Charles P., 104
Stuart, J. E. B., 124
Suffrage, 133
Sunderlandville, Maryland, 154
Susquehanna Valley, 42
Swann, Thomas, 137, 194; as mayor of Baltimore, 46–47; and emancipation, 129, 136; break with Union party, 135, 136; and *1867* senatorial election, 136; conflict with Freedmen's Bureau, 152; on sale of freedmen into slavery, 152–53

Talbot County, 6, 23, 40; agriculture in, 18; and Eastern Shore separatism, 20; slave trade, 24; and Eastern Shore slaveholders' convention, 68; violence in, 142. *See also* Eastern Shore
Taylor, Susan, 153–54
Temperance, 58
Tenancy, 175, 177–80
Ten-hour legislation, 203–04
Thirteenth amendment, 133
Thomas, Francis, 121
Thomas, Philip F., 136
Tilden, Charles, 139–40
Tillison (free black woman in Kent County), 63
Tobacco, 4–5, 6, 7, 19, 42, 43, 169, 170
Toogood, Hannah, 29
Townsend, Teagle, 94
Townshend, John, 26
Trade unionism, 204–05
Tramps, 191–92
Tredegar Iron Works, 56
Trimble, Isaac R., 94
Truck farming, 17, 174
Tuck, W. H., 152
Tucker (slaveholder in Anne Arundel County), 102, 106
Turner, R. T., 148

Turney, Joseph, 154
Turton, Thomas G., 26
Twenty-fifth Army Corps, 148

Uncle Ned (free black man), 89
Unconditional Unionists, 121–22, 123, 129, 136. *See also* Radical Republicans; Republican party; Union party
Underground railroad, 67
Unemployment, 188–89
Unionists, 114, 142–43. *See also* Radical Republicans; Republican party; Unconditional Unionists, Union League; Union party
Union League, 96, 121
Union Manufacturing Company, 43
Union party, 122, 132–33, 135–36. *See also* Radical Republicans; Republican party; Unconditional Unionists; Union League
United Fire Department, 46
Upper Marlboro, Maryland, 119, 126, 145

Vickers, George, 136
Vienna, Maryland, 145
Violence: proslavery, 63–65, 66; against black people, 63, 143–47; against unionists, 142–43; against freedmen's schools, 144–45; and role of laboring classes, 146–47; and role of "respectable classes," 146–47
Virginia, 1, 6, 115–16, 145, 159, 190

Wade, Richard, 49–50, 51, 54
Wallace, Lew, 148
Ward, J. J., 198
War Department, 99, 113, 114, 123, 125–26. *See also* Cameron, Simon; Stanton, Edwin M.
Warfield, Susanna: on city of Baltimore, 57; and slave hiring, 84; slaves of, 85, 159; and domestic servants, 162; on tramps, 191–92; on *1877* railroad strike, 200; on emancipation, 200
War of *1812*. *See* Napoleonic Wars
Warwick, Maryland, 155
Washington, D.C. *See* District of Columbia
Washington County, 6, 19, 109, 173. *See also* Hagerstown, Maryland; Northern Maryland; Williamsport, Maryland
Watkins, Charles A., 144
Wayson, Dr. (delegate at Workingmen's party meeting), 198

Weeks, Thomas, 201–02
Western grange, 173
Wheat, 4–5, 6, 19, 42, 170. *See also*
    Cereals
Whistling Bob (street vendor in Balti-
    more), 45
Whyte, William Pinkney, 170, 173
Wickliffe, Charles A., 114
Wicomico County, 169. *See also* Eastern
    Shore
Wilkins, Mrs. (Baltimore resident), 44–45
Williams, Barbary, 26
Williamsport, Maryland, 58
Winans, Ross, 98–99
Witnesses, black, 64, 132, 134, 150–51

Women: in free black population, 29; in
    slave population, 29–30; as factory
    workers, 61, 225*n;* freed, and former
    owners, 138; in food processing indus-
    try, 201–02; as oyster shuckers, 202;
    and domestic service, 162–63, 187, 202
Wood, Jane, 145
Wood, Oliver, 160
Worcester County, 6; slaves in, 28; and
    slaveholders' conventions, 67–68, 69,
    71; slaveholdings in, 83; apprenticeship
    in, 140. *See also* Eastern Shore
Workingmen's party, 198–99
Wright, Julian, 198
Wright, Maria, 156